The Care and Feeding of Sailing Crew

By the same authors

Cruising in Seraffyn
Seraffyn's Mediterranean Adventure
Seraffyn's European Adventure
Seraffyn's Oriental Adventure
The Self-Sufficient Sailor
The Capable Cruiser
Storm Tactics Handbook
The Cost-Conscious Cruiser

By Larry Pardey

Details of Classic Boat Construction: The Hull

DVDs

Storm Tactics
Get Ready to Cruise—Offshore Sailing, Part One
Get Ready to Cross Oceans—Offshore Sailing, Part Two

Lin and Larry's Newsletter and Cruising Tips: *www.landlpardey.com*

The Care and Feeding of Sailing Crew

Third edition—revised and expanded

LIN PARDEY
with Larry Pardey

Pardey Books
Arcata, California

Third edition.

© 1980, 1995, 2006 by Mary Lin Pardey and Lawerence F. Pardey

PRINTING HISTORY:

First edition: W. W. Norton, 1980 (four printings)

Second completely revised and updated edition: W. W. Norton, 1995

Reissued second edition: L and L Pardey Books, 1996 (three printings)

Pardey Books
P.O. Box 29, Arcata, California 95518 USA
Phone: (707) 822-9063
Fax: (707) 822-9163
E-mail: info@paracay.com

Cartoon illustrations:	**Tadami Takahashi**
Cover design:	**Rob Johnson**
Book design:	**Moira Durham, Artlinx Ltd.**
Copyediting:	**Kathleen Brandes**
Index:	**Sandra Farrell**
USA distribution:	**Paradise Cay Publications,** P.O. Box 29, Arcata, California 95518. E-mail: info@paracay.com
Trade distribution:	**Midpoint Trade Books,** 27 West 20th Street, Suite 1102, New York, NY 10011. E-mail: midpointny1@aol.com
New Zealand distribution:	**Boat Books,** 22 Westhaven Drive, Auckland, New Zealand. E-mail: crew@boatbooks.co.nz
UK distribution:	**Kelvin Hughes Ltd.,** New North Road, Hainault, Ilford, Essex 1G6 2UR England. E-mail: marketing@kelvinhughes.co.uk

Printed in USA

1 2 3 4 5 6 7 8 9 0

ISBN-13: 978-1-92921-407-5

ISBN-10: 1-92921-407-3

Publisher's Cataloging-in-Publication
(Provided by Quality Books, Inc.)
Pardey, Lin.
The care and feeding of sailing crew / Lin Pardey with Larry Pardey. -- 3rd ed., rev. and expanded.
p. cm.
Includes index.
ISBN-13: 978-1-92921-407-5
ISBN-10: 1-92921-407-3
1. Cookery, Marine. 2. Sailboat living.
I. Pardey, Larry. II. Title.
TX840.M7P35 2006 641.5'753
QBI05-200199

To Larry—editor, encourager, test pilot, and survivor
of all the recipes in this book

Contents

Acknowledgments

Over the past 25 years, *The Care and Feeding of Sailing Crew* has come to be my personal favorite among the books Larry and I have written. I feel a glow of satisfaction as I recall the sailors—in anchorages around the world, at boat shows and seminars, in letters and e-mails—who have told me that this book influenced and encouraged them to enjoy venturing away from shore. It is because of them that I feel encouraged to create this newest edition, and I thank each of them. In order to thank those who contributed to the creation of the original book and each of its subsequent editions, I would like to share a bit of its history.

It was 1974, and Larry and I had been wandering the oceans on board 24-foot, 4-inch *Seraffyn* for almost six years. We had been writing sailing stories for two years when we settled in at Gibraltar to hide from the stormy weather of the wintry Mediterranean and to earn more cruising funds. About 20 cruising boats, plus another 15 charter boats, were moored around us, their crews busily preparing for upcoming voyages. Larry quickly had his winter work quota filled with repair jobs for cruising boats and upgrades to boats used by local sailors. I settled in to write some articles in the morning and help Larry by painting or varnishing the woodwork he did all day long. Then local politics forced its way into our lives. Spain, in an attempt to regain control of this small, British-controlled peninsula, had closed the border to all goods. Any ship whose manifest held provisions for Gibraltar was forbidden entry to Spanish ports. Then the British supply ship was confined to port due to a labor dispute. To add to the confusion, the local bakers went on strike. Within a week, there was an acute shortage of bread, and then flour; by the end of another week, yeast, sugar, fruit, and vegetables were unobtainable. Next to go were propane and butane. This led to our first and only foray into smuggling for gain.

With the acquiescence of a local customs official (whose wife definitely wanted to share in the venture), we set sail for the North African port of Ceuta, 16 miles across the strait. In *Seraffyn's Mediterranean Adventure,* we wrote at length about what turned into a bigger adventure than expected, but it is the end results that matter here. When cooks from the various boats came to buy flour and yeast from us, we found out that many did not know how to bake their own bread. So I wrote out the first version of the chapter on bread baking that appears in this book. A few days later, Cathy Everett, the cook from one of the bigger charter boats, came by and asked if I had any more ideas about cooking on boats, as all of her experience had been in cafés ashore. Two weeks later, when Cathy invited us for a farewell dinner on board, she stated, "Lin, you really should write a book for folks like me."

A week later, I sent a book proposal to Steve Doherty at Seven Seas Press. His reply was quick and unexpected: "My wife just wrote a sailors' cookbook. How about writing about your adventures on *Seraffyn* instead? I'd love to publish that." And that is what we did. But from the day Cathy suggested it, the ideas for this book rattled around in the corners of my mind.

It was almost five years before the first edition of this book actually came to be written. "Lin, you'll go crazy being at sea for at least 40 or 50 days," Larry said as we prepared to sail from Japan to Canada. "You need something to keep your mind busy. How about writing the book Cathy suggested?" Even then, Eric Swenson, our editor at W. W. Norton, was not particularly interested in publishing it. He asked for another cruising narrative, because there was "not much market for a book about caring for people on boats. Boats are for men, men aren't interested in comfort, just adventure." My champion, Larry, was at my side in Eric's office and shocked me by stating, "If you want the cruising story Lin just finished, you have to publish this one first." Eric was a real gentleman when he called to tell us that the book he called, "The Gales and Garlic Special" was selling so nicely that he wanted an updated edition. That edition was written while we were exploring South Africa.

This latest edition includes ideas contributed over the years by other sailors, and folks ashore, plus those added as we continued voyaging for the second time through European waters, to many ports on the eastern seaboard of the United States, then to Brazil, Argentina, Chile, around Cape Horn, and on through the Pacific to British Columbia. Our thanks go to all of the following (in alphabetical order) for their assistance with content: Mark Adcock, Shirley Adcock, Jeanne Bach, Michael Bates, Maureen Bernard, Chris Bonnett, Libby Bonnett, Katie Braun, Kurt Braun, Diana Burke, Pam Clay, Anouk Edwards, Aorea Edwards, Chris Edwards, Eric Goetz, Heather Hurenkamp, Dudley Kendall, Beth Leonard, Harriett Linskey, Tom Linskey, Rodger Martin, Mal Mostert, Doug Schmuck, Helen Schmuck, Dorothy Skeates, Evans Starzinger, and Cris Todd.

Several people in the publishing industry deserve special thanks. For the previous editions of this book, these include Eric Swenson of W. W. Norton; Matt and Jim Morehouse of Paradise Cay Publications; Oscar, Stacia, Robert, and all the folks at Robert Hale Co.; plus Gail Kump and the crew at Midpoint Trade Books. Then there are those who have helped with this newest edition:

Moira Durham, text design; Rob Johnson, cover design; Kathleen Brandes, editor. Here at our island home base in New Zealand, Helen Jeffery has digitized every word of the original book so we could update all of the information in the first two editions. Thanks! Every one of you has helped make this fun instead of work.

A final word of thanks may sound a bit corny, but thanks, Mom (Marion Dryer)—you made cooking and caring for people more like a hobby than a chore.

Throughout the text, I try to share the credit for any ideas other sailors have contributed. There may be people who will read something here and say, "I told Lin about that." If I have not included your name here, I apologize, and I hope I have passed on your ideas as intended.

Many of the articles in this book have appeared previously in magazines, including *Cruising Helmsman* (Australia), *Cruising World* (USA), *Sail* (USA), *Good Old Boat* (USA), *Practical Boat Owner* (UK), *South African Yachting* (South Africa), *Yachting Monthly* (UK), *Yachting* (Germany).

. . . .

The Care and Feeding of Sailing Crew

Introduction to the Third Edition

The days grow shorter, the nights cooler. A trickle of northbound cruising yachts comes in to anchor near our New Zealand home base on an island between Auckland and the Bay of Islands. Like the arctic terns, these sailors are fleeing from the first blast of winter toward the balmy weather of the tropical islands a thousand miles beyond our bay. Many of them row ashore for a farewell drink, and their excited anticipation whets our appetite for further sailing adventures. Gina and Christian Salares stop in to share one last evening before her first foray offshore. When the men wander down to the boatshop to search for a perfect bolt for a repair job, Gina asks, "How many cabbages do you think I should buy? Do you think I have enough fresh food for the crossing? What should I prepare for Christian to eat if I get seasick?" I remind her, "You're good at organization. You'll do just fine. I promise once you've made two or three passages you'll learn that any well-prepared cook really has little to worry about."

A few evenings later, two couples, who have each crossed the Pacific to spend a season exploring New Zealand, come by and invite us out to their boat for a meal. "What watch system do you guys use? I never got enough sleep when we were sailing down here," someone says. "While we're talking about night watches, what do you do to keep warm until you get farther north?"

These conversations reminded me that, when it comes to taking care of crew on a cruising boat, little has changed in the years since the publication of the first edition of *The Care and Feeding of Sailing Crew*. Though a look at yachting magazines and marine-store catalogs might make you think otherwise, for the person in charge of crew comfort and security, all of the same concerns and challenges still exist.

Today, just as when I wrote the first edition, I cannot find one other volume that deals with the problems of cooking in a small galley. Several suggest good ways of using native foods, of catching and preparing seafood. A dozen books show how to combine two, three, or five cans of food and spice up the mixture. Some books give recommended stores lists for cruising sailors on their first voyage away from home. But all of these books have some basic omissions as far as people like Gina and most sailors are concerned. All assume that the voyage will be from home to somewhere else. The stores recommended are easy to find in the United States or England, not so easy in Tonga, Grenada, or the Cape Verde Islands. Each of these books is devoted mostly to recipes and tips for galleys, but not one tells what it is really like when you need to contend with motion, fatigue, and sometimes seasickness. It is hard to find a useful account of what people eat and how they prepare food underway, where the weather, sea conditions, and the cook's mood often decide each day's menu.

The idea for the first edition of this book came about as we were sailing north from Manila toward Japan. Larry suggested, "Why not write a log of all your thoughts and activities as we cross the Pacific from Yokohama to Victoria? That will be a good, long voyage. You'll be buying stores in a strange land and the weather conditions are bound to be changeable. You'll have at least 40 to 45 days to think of all the problems you've faced, all the solutions you've found over the years."

I agreed. Keeping a log would serve a twofold purpose. I'd be able to share the experience we'd gained in a round-the-world voyage—delivering yachts, racing, and of course chatting with other voyagers. I'd have something to occupy my thoughts during what finally turned out to be a rough, storm-filled, 4,500-mile, 49-day passage.

After writing that first edition, we built ourselves a larger (29 feet, 9 inches) cruising boat and set off for another 20 years of voyaging, including forays as far north as Oslofjord and as far south as Cape Horn, meandering around the world and putting another 100,000 sea miles under our stern. Along the way, we have met hundreds of sailors who told us this book helped them feel more confident about the adventures ahead or provided information as they voyaged. Many offered tips that are included here. We've also tested many new ideas and looked out for new and improved gear to use afloat. We have updated this edition to include information on as much of this gear as possible, including thoughts on watermakers, instant packaged foods, refrigeration upgrades, and modern sailing clothing. Almost every chapter has been expanded, and there are several new sections, including discussions on entertaining afloat, dealing with officials, and handling finances in foreign ports.

Although much has changed in this third edition, we have decided to include the account of our 1978 voyage across the North Pacific on *Seraffyn* exactly as it first appeared, as there is no better way to show what it is like to buy stores for a voyage to or from a foreign land, to cook in a seaway, to have one's moods affected by wind strength, to deal with health problems at sea, and to explain what the cook does besides preparing the meals. Each day's menu for the 49-day passage—one that was far rougher than

I had anticipated—is included, along with recipes for those dishes whose preparations are not obvious. Many readers have told us the cook's log of the passage described in this book helped them over some rough times at sea. As one said, "I figured if you could cope in that small galley in those conditions, I could definitely handle crew care on my boat."

The food we ate during that passage may be quite different from what you'd choose. Our stores buying at that time was governed by a tightly limited cruising budget—one that was offset only partially by our willingness to spend more money for food during ocean passages because good eating is our main form of entertainment when we are a thousand miles from the nearest land. Since the passage described here, our tastes have changed, as has our budget. The ability to keep meat and produce fresh for longer periods and our faster passage times mean that I rarely have to stretch my imagination as much as I did on that Pacific voyage. I use a wider variety of spices afloat (probably because I have a bigger spice rack). Chutneys, pickled onions, and other condiments enhance our at-sea fare. New cheese preservation methods have increased our use of this versatile ingredient, and we tend to eat less red meat than we did on board *Seraffyn*. On the other hand, two years ago, on our passage from Chile to the Marquesas, I pulled out my original copy of *The Care and Feeding of Sailing Crew* looking for ideas to enliven our meals after 25 days at sea. The bread pudding I served that evening drew rave reviews.

I have heard from men who had never cooked before that the recipes given for each day's menu were simple enough to introduce them to cooking afloat. But, even though this volume includes several dozen recipes, it is not intended to be a cookbook. My goal with each new edition has been to help demystify all aspects of keeping crew happy and healthy afloat—from the initial layout of galleys to the issues surrounding keeping the crew well rested and healthy. It is a different world out there. Not only are you far from easy shopping facilities, but you are in ever-changing climates, limited space, and limited facilities; the constant demands of keeping a boat moving and secure only add to the pressure on the person in charge of crew care. It is a challenge I relish, one I hope this third edition of *The Care and Feeding of Sailing Crew* encourages you to try. I still love seeing, tasting, trying to adapt, and then adopting the new foods we find in each country we visit. And after 40 years of exploring the oceans of the world under sail, serving as CME (crew maintenance engineer) on more than 20 different yachts and fishing boats, I've learned that by carrying a good supply of basic provisions, no one ever needs to go hungry. Yet it is a never-ending challenge to try to make eating for both the crew and me as pleasurable afloat as it is onshore. To this day, just before any passage, I do a last-minute rush-around—looking for one more treat to stash on board, checking for one more item I might have forgotten. And each time we reach our destination, I find that my concerns were of little import, my lockers still have supplies in them, and my crew remembers the interesting meals and has forgotten the forgettable ones.

Now, as I put the last touches on this new edition, I enjoy reading the latest adventure-filled letters from Gina, describing new landfalls, new destinations. As I savor her enthusiasm, it becomes apparent that she now believes my parting words: "Any well-prepared cook really has little to worry about."

Lin Pardey
Kawau Island, New Zealand
April 2006

· · · · · · ·

Figures quoted are in $US throughout, unless stated otherwise.

All the recipes in this book use U.S. measurements. To help readers who normally use metric measurements, the following tables show liquid and dry measure volume and weight equivalents.

LIQUID MEASURE VOLUME EQUIVALENTS

1 U.S. teaspoon	= 5 milliliters
1 U.S. tablespoon	= 15 milliliters
1 U.S. cup	= 0.25 liter (approx.)
1 U.S. gill	= 0.118 liter
1 U.S. pint	= 0.4732 liter
1 U.S. quart	= 0.9463
1 U.S. gallon	= 3.785 liters

METRIC DRY MEASURE VOLUME EQUIVALENTS

1 U.S. pint	= 0.551 liter
1 U.S. quart	= 1.101 liters
1 U.S. peck	= 8.81 liters
1 U.S. bushel	= 35.24 liters

WEIGHT EQUIVALENT IN GRAMS

1 U.S. ounce	= approximately 30 grams
1 U.S. pound	= approximately 454 grams
1 teaspoon cornstarch	= 3 grams
½ cup less 1 tablespoon butter (7 tablespoons)	= approximately 100 grams
¾ cup flour less 1 tablespoon of all-purpose flour (11 tablespoons)	= approximately 100 grams
½ cup less 1 tablespoon (7 tablespoons or 21 teaspoons)	= approximately 100 grams
2 oz. egg	= approximately 60 grams
1 microgram	= 0.001 milligram
1 milligram	= 1,000 micrograms
1 gram	= 1,000 milligrams

LINEAR MEASURES

1 inch	= 2.54 centimeters
1 centimeter	= 0.394 inch
1 meter	= 39.37 inches

Many readers have grown up with older British measurements. These often have the same name as U.S. measurements, but though weights are equivalent, volumes are not. The British gallon has five quarts; the U.S. gallon, four. Therefore, cooks will find their recipes could be failing due to the 25 percent difference. The following chart will help you compensate and let you use older cookbooks from England, a source of fine farmers' recipes, ones that often can be used for ideas afloat.

LIQUID MEASURE VOLUME EQUIVALENTS

1¼ U.S. teaspoons	= 1 English teaspoon
1¼ U.S. tablespoons	= 1 English tablespoon
1 U.S. gill	= ⅚ English teacup
2 U.S. gills	= ⅚ English breakfast cup
1 U.S. cup	= ⅚ English breakfast cup
1 U.S. gill	= ⅚ English imperial gill
1 U.S. pint	= ⅚ English imperial pint
1 U.S. quart	= ⅚ English imperial quart
1 U.S. gallon	= ⅚ English imperial gallon

DRY MEASURE VOLUME EQUIVALENTS

1 U.S. pint	= 1 English pint
1 U.S. quart	= 1 English quart
1 U.S. peck	= 1 English peck
1 U.S. bushel	= 1 English bushel

WEIGHT EQUIVALENTS

1 U.S. ounce	= 1 English ounce
1 U.S. pound	= 1 English pound

COMPARATIVE U.S. AND BRITISH MEASUREMENTS

8 U.S. ounces = 16 U.S. tablespoons = 48 U.S. teaspoons

1 Standard Measuring Cup or 2 U.S. Gills for Both Solids and Liquids

10 English Imperial ounces = 20.8 U.S. tablespoons = 62½ U.S. teaspoons

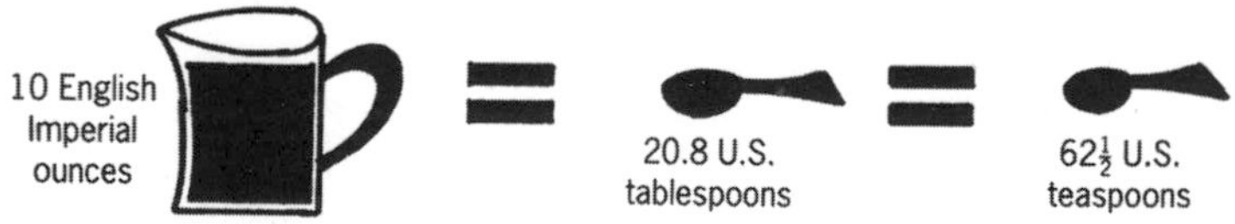

1 English Breakfast Cup or 2 Imperial Gills for Both Solids and Liquids

The Care and Feeding of Sailing Crew

The Day Before

Tied up at Yokohama Shimin Yacht Haven
Sunny, warm weather

Except for the unusually delightful farewell party that ended it all, today was a normal last day in port. I started out worrying. Had I forgotten to order something? Would the chandlers remember to bring things today? Would they bring the right things? Had I bought enough canned goods in Singapore and Manila or should I try to find more?

Larry stayed at the yacht club to finish putting water on board, receive stores, and generally get *Seraffyn* ready for sea. I took the bus into Yokohama city to get our port-clearance papers and pick up some more yen. Unfortunately for us, during our 4-week stay in Japan, the American dollar had dropped drastically, so instead of needing to change $280 to pay for the stores we'd ordered, we had to change $350. This was an unusual situation; rarely did the value of the dollar fluctuate more than 3 or 4 percent during our stay in any country. But we've found it's wise to set aside extra money for stores whenever we are preparing for an offshore voyage. Something always seems to foul up the budget.

By the time I got back to *Seraffyn*, the first of our stores had arrived from the chandler who carried duty-free wine and liquor. Usually duty-free stores have to be delivered in the presence of a customs officer. They are then put on board into a locker, which the customs officer plasters with paper seals you aren't supposed to break until you are at sea. But the Japanese officials waived the sealed-locker requirement because of our small order (only two cases of wine, one of rum, and one of Coca-Cola). So the dock in front of *Seraffyn* was loaded with those four crates plus two more of vegetables.

Before we could eat a quick lunch, the second chandler arrived with 12 steaming kilos of dry ice, 20 kilos of regular ice, two kilos of frozen shrimp, five kilos of cheddar cheese, and three cases of special canned goods (mostly peanut butter and jam). Because there is at least a 100 percent duty on all food imports in Japan, we saved a tremendous amount by buying what we could through the chandlers. A pound of Australian cheese in the local stores was $6; we paid $2. Shrimp ran $9 to $12; we paid $1.80. The only problem with buying through chandlers is that they are set up to deal with big ships, so most items are in tins or sizes too large for us to handle. If we had had storage space for a 25-pound piece of beef (the minimum order), we could have bought Australian first-grade sirloin for $1.50 a pound duty-free. In the local stores, any beef started at $17.

I left Larry to finish his preparations and walked the mile to the local public market. Three days earlier, I had inspected each stall until I found that Stall 196 carried most of the vegetables I needed. No one there spoke English, but as soon as they saw I was trying to ask something important, one of the men ran off and returned minutes later with a tall, carefully dressed young man in tow. After apologizing for his poor English, he explained that he had a photographic shop deeper in the market and that he'd like to know what my problem was.

"My husband and I are setting sail for Canada on board a small sailing boat this Saturday, and we need lots of produce specially chosen so that it will last at least a month." His astonishment was matched by that of all four people in the vegetable stall. I was glad I'd carried some wallet photographs of *Seraffyn*, Larry, and the two of us out sailing. "Ah so, ah so," murmured each of my new acquaintances, bowing and looking at each other. The "ah so's" traveled from stall to stall along with the photos, and 15 minutes and as many questions later, our translator started making a meticulous list of what I needed—first in English and then in Japanese characters. When I left, polite bows followed me all the way through the market.

Now, when I returned to the covered market area, I realized that the news had spread, and the photographer-*cum*-translator walked out to meet me. "Everything you ordered has arrived; a man is waiting to deliver it."

I was delighted with the beautiful produce that Stall 196 had found. But, as usual, Japanese prices shocked me, and I was caught short of yen. The two of us went through my order, but there was nothing I was willing to delete. I had U.S. cash with me, but no bank except the central ones eight miles away would change foreign currency. "No problem," the photographer said. "I'll drive you to the bank." As we rode to the bank and back, the photographer fired question after question. Everywhere we've cruised we've had the same results. With patience, lots of smiles, and some photos in our wallet, we've always found someone with enough knowledge of English or Spanish who has been willing to help out. I've tried reciprocating by offering a cup of coffee, lunch, or a glass of wine, but a gift photograph of the boat always seems to be the best thank-you of all.

28

Our produce was loaded onto a specially designed Japanese motorcycle:

100 farm-fresh eggs
25 tomatoes
2 large heads of lettuce
25 carrots
30 small green peppers
15 pieces of ginger
2 large pumpkin squashes
30 heads of garlic
10 cucumbers
6 giant apples
3 bunches of bananas
3 cantaloupe-type melons

The chandler had already brought us:

9 kilos of cabbage with outer leaves left intact
9 kilos of onions
4 kilos of potatoes

I used up the last of our yen buying fresh meat. The extremely high price of non-duty-free meat in Japan affected what we took for that one passage. Normally, I'd have bought three times as much fresh meat to put in the ice chest. For $30, I only bought:

½ pound beef steak
¼ pound sliced ham
1½ pounds ground beef
½ pound chipped pork
¾ pound boneless chicken breasts

This time, when I got back to *Seraffyn*, utter chaos reigned. The dock in front of our boat was full of crates and boxes; Larry was upside down in the cockpit locker rearranging boat gear so he could store away a few more spare water jugs; the inside of the cabin was littered with fruit and vegetables. One look at the clock gave me the jitters—our Japanese friends would be down in an hour and a half for last farewells.

As usual, Larry's calm logic saved my day. "Forget about storing anything away today. We'll set it on the side deck, cover it with a canvas for tonight, then set it all on the cabin sole tomorrow before we sail. We can store it once we're underway. Right now, let's have a drink, then one last hot shower."

Larry helped me spruce up *Seraffyn* for our guests; we showered and shared a drink, then our guests began to arrive.

Eleven Japanese sailors, including both the female and male Laser dinghy champions, showed up accompanied by two translators. Each new friend presented us with a beautiful souvenir of our 3-week stay in Yokohama. We set up a display of the lovely gifts in our quarter berth: a hand-painted porcelain ceremonial tea set, a pair of happi coats, bottles of Suntory whiskey, sake, a lacquered musical jewelry box, a hand-painted umbrella, and half a dozen beautiful ears of fresh corn.

I was glad I'd prepared an American dish to serve, because our friends had brought their guitars, a violin, and a banjo. Our open-house cocktail party turned into an evening of song and laughter. Bluegrass music rang across the Yokohama Shimin Yacht Haven until 10 minutes before midnight. We danced on the dock, sang, laughed, and promised we'd return some day. By the time the final farewell bows had been exchanged, our friends had to run to catch the last train to Tokyo and central Yokohama.

We climbed into our bunk still humming, completely undaunted by the pile of stores waiting to be put away when we set off to sea.

. . . .

SLOPPY JOES FOR A FAREWELL PARTY

Sauté until browned
- 1 large onion, chopped
- 1 lb. ground beef
- 1 tbs. cooking oil

Add
- 1 can peeled whole tomatoes
- 1 can tomato paste
- 1 can tomato sauce
- ¼ cup sugar
- 1 tsp. oregano
- 2 tsp. chili powder
- 1 tsp. garlic powder
- 1 green pepper, cut into small chunks

Simmer 40 minutes, stirring occasionally, until the sauce thickens. Pour a big portion of sauce into a hamburger bun, top with a slice of cheese, and serve with lots of napkins.

. . . .

Day 1

Heavy rain, clear toward evening
Eight-knot breeze, fog

>*Breakfast for us and farewell-wishers*
>>banana nut cake
>>coffee and tea
>
>*Lunch for us and two guests*
>>egg salad sandwiches
>>fresh whole tomatoes
>>tossed salad with mayonnaise-and-lemon dressing
>>gift cake
>
>*Snack*
>>hot buttered rum and apple slices
>
>*Dinner at anchor*
>>fried beefsteak with wine sauce
>>fresh corn on the cob
>>broiled tomatoes (grilled)
>>Camembert cheese (Dufo brand Danish canned Camembert
>>   —best we've ever tasted)
>>biscuits
>>red Bulgarian wine

. . . .

HOT BUTTERED RUM

Mix
>1 in. dark or gold rum in a coffee mug
>2 level tsp. sugar
>1 tsp. lemon juice
>dash of cinnamon

Fill mug with hot water; put a dab of butter on top and stir lightly.

. . . .

Storing Fresh Food

When the rain started hitting our faces about 0400 hours, we woke up, and Larry closed the forehatch over our double bunk. I was almost asleep again when I remembered the pile of stores sitting on deck. Both of us scrambled out of the bunk and tossed the crates, boxes, and baskets onto the cabin sole, onto the quarter berth, and on top of the stove. Then we climbed back into the bunk.

The 0730 alarm came much too early. In the gray, damp daylight, the mess in the main cabin looked formidable. I cleared a path, set coffee to perk, and got out the baskets we use for storing fruit and vegetables. Since we almost never use the double bunk forward for sleeping when we are at sea, it becomes the extra storage area we need for long passages. We cover the cushion with old charts and then line the bunk with the baskets.

Although hand-woven natural baskets are more handsome and allow a better flow of air around your produce, we've found that they create a storage problem between passages. Cardboard boxes harbor insects and their eggs and don't allow enough air circulation; wooden crates scratch the boat; hammock nets require too much room, since they must be free to swing without hitting anything. So for long-distance voyages when we need food to last more than a week, we've finally settled for the nesting plastic baskets that are rather like the handled shopping baskets some small markets use. These are lightweight, easy to wash, and inexpensive (in Singapore, we paid a dollar each). And since they stack, we can stash them in a stern locker between voyages.

Potatoes and onions went together into one large basket. Cabbages and carrots filled two others. Softer fruits went into individual baskets—melons in the chain locker with rags under them to keep them from moving. We've found that the chain locker is a good place for watermelons as well as cantaloupes—the ventilator scoop keeps them well aired. Soon the forepeak and bunk looked almost like Stall 196. I put up the lee cloth and wedged some books between the mast and the baskets so they couldn't shift. Our guitar and gifts from the previous night filled the rest of the bunk.

Before we could drink our coffee and tea, the commodore of the New Yokohama Yacht Club came to present us with a parting gift of a crate of fresh tomatoes. There were 20 $3/4$-pound tomatoes in the cardboard crate, each the same shape and the same glossy red. The tomatoes looked too ripe to last, and I already had a basketful. But thanks to the extremely careful handling given Japanese produce, we found that with careful storage and cool weather, they lasted 23 days.

As we were bowing our gratitude to the commodore, Jim Parker arrived with a banana nut cake sent by his Japanese wife, Sanae. Jim, an English-language instructor who has lived in Japan 14 years, loves sailing. We'd met on the dock at the yacht club, and he and his wife had spent most of their spare time introducing us to Japan. We had invited them to join us for the sail to the mouth of Tokyo Bay. Sanae had to work, but, in spite of the rain, Jim was eager to go with us.

By 0900, the dock was full of umbrella-covered Japanese friends. Jim was busy helping pile cases of duty-free liquor and cola between the forward bunk and the linen locker. A box of unstored cans nestled next to the stove. It was next to impossible to get into the forepeak. "We'll put it all away when we get out to sea," Larry reminded me. "Right now, forget about it and enjoy saying good-bye. These people want to get out of the rain." So we finished lashing the six 5-gallon spare water jugs in place, topped up our gravity-feed deck tank, and unbagged our sails.

Just about this time, we spotted the only other American we'd come to know during our 3-week stay in Yokohama. Don Harrington, professor of English, dreamed of cruising off some day. When we said, "Join us for the reach down the bay," he hesitated only momentarily, jumped on board, and helped Larry set our sweep in place to row 200 yards from the dock to where a breeze was blowing. Eager hands helped us cast off. "Sayonara" rang across the water. Our two guests helped set the main and the jib. *Seraffyn* heeled lightly and slowly gained speed as if she were half-reluctant, half-eager to challenge the Pacific. *Rinky Dink* trailed docilely behind.

I shed my wet gear and climbed below to hide from the rain and try to make some order out of the chaos. By the time I was ready to make lunch, most of the canned goods were in their proper lockers. That's when I discovered that I needed a new jar of mayonnaise. Of course, the spare mayonnaise is stored under the forward bunk, which is now covered with all the fresh stores. I could have dreamed up something else to serve for lunch, but my stubborn streak made me climb over all the boxes and stores and move the guitar, six boxes of gifts, and the cushion to retrieve one of the six mayonnaise jars from its locker.

The three men seemed to love the rain and wolfed down lunch as we approached the narrow mouth of Tokyo Bay. We planned to row Jim and Don ashore near the entrance to the bay, but the closer we got to the congested area at the narrows, the foggier the air became. After talking it over, we decided against sailing into the heavy shipping lanes until the fog cleared. So we reached into a small fishing port 11 miles from where we'd started, set our anchor, and warmed our damp crew with hot buttered rum.

After we'd rowed Jim and Don ashore, we spent the afternoon putting away our duty-free stores. We used the area under the floors for the two cases of wine and the case of cola. This area sometimes gets wet, but that doesn't bother bottles. Moreover, wine and cola stay cooler in the bilges. Also, the weight is centered and low, where it should be, and the chance of breakage is nil. We have no engine, and thus no oil, so every bit of the bulge can be used for clean storage.

This was not the first time we'd set sail on a voyage only to anchor in a harbor just down the line, to sort ourselves out. What with farewell parties, last-minute showers, and the dozen distractions of sailing day, it's usually impossible to get everything stowed away properly. I recommend that everyone setting out on a first voyage have their farewell parties, sail away from their home dock, and find a quiet anchorage for the night—even if it is only on the other side of the bay. Then you can set the boat to rights, have a quiet evening, get a good night's sleep, and set off on your voyage in a refreshed frame of mind.

We did it. By the time we went to bed together in our double bunk for the last time in 49 days, every bottle, can, and jar, every gift, and each vegetable had its place. The rain stopped, and we'd taken one last row around *Seraffyn* to see if she was sitting level in the water. We had hoisted the dinghy on board and lashed it down; rigged the spare water jugs more securely; put up our offshore, shoulder-height lifelines; and turned in for the night.

. . . .

Day 2

*Beating in light winds through heavy shipping
Sunny and clear*

Breakfast
whole fresh tomatoes with salt
bread and jam
coffee, tea

Lunch
mackerel salad sandwiches with sliced sweet pickles and tomatoes

Dinner
broiled pork chops
steamed carrots
tossed salad: lettuce, tomatoes, onions, Thousand Island dressing

....

MACKEREL SALAD

Drain
1 small can mackerel in brine

Chop
1 small green pepper
1 small onion

Mix with
3 tbs. mayonnaise
½ tbs. sugar
1 tsp. lemon juice

> Let stand 1 hour in a
> cool place before using.

....

. . . .

THOUSAND ISLAND DRESSING

Combine

2 parts mayonnaise

1 part ketchup

1 tsp. lemon juice

pinch of salt

pinch of garlic

1 part pickle relish (optional)

. . . .

I must say that it is nice to start out fresh. We both feel relaxed and ready to go. Now that all the stores are organized, I can see that we have enough. But I do know that *Seraffyn* is too small to carry the stores I'd like to have if three people were making the passage instead of only two.

We figure on making an average speed of 100 nautical miles a day for ocean passages. We have 4,500 miles to go. As a safeguard, I usually plan to have stores to last the number of days we expect to be at sea plus 50 percent extra to cover the possibility of a slow passage. Then we carry survival rations for 20 more days. The survival rations consist of rice, grain, pasta or cereals ($3/4$ cup of dried ingredients per person per day), plus one can of fruit or fruit juice per day, and vitamin pills.

This is the longest single passage we've ever planned on board *Seraffyn*. In addition to our worldly possessions, she is carrying canned and packaged stores for 60 to 70 days, the survival rations, and:

70 gallons of water

100 eggs

120 pounds of fresh vegetables

60 pounds of ice

2   cases of wine

2   cases of rum

1   case of whiskey

1   case of Coca-Cola

2   shopping bags full of paperback books

gifts for our families

gifts from our Japanese friends

That totals almost 1,000 pounds more than we normally carry, and, to prove it, *Seraffyn* is two inches below her load waterline.

Cargo Capacity for Cruising

When we were rowing around *Seraffyn* for our one last look yesterday, we got into quite a discussion about light-displacement versus heavy-displacement boats for cruising. Larry commented, "Almost everyone we know averages 100 to 120 miles a day, year in and year out, if they have a boat from 24 to 45 feet on deck. So they have to carry just as many stores as we do when they are making an ocean passage, and if their boat is bigger, they'll have heavier boat gear to carry besides. If you load 1,100 pounds of extra stores into a 24-footer that is designed to sail her best at 5,000 pounds of displacement, she's going to be affected a lot more than if you loaded the 1,100 pounds on a 24-footer that is designed to sail well at 11,000 pounds displacement.

If you are looking at offshore cruising boats, consider the ones that float three or four inches high when they are launched. Then look at their displacement in proportion to the 1,000 pounds of stores minimum that each person requires for passagemaking and cruising. It will be easy to fill any boat with enough cargo to get it down to its waterline marks. But it is almost impossible to put an overweight boat on a diet, and boats that are down on their lines just don't perform as well.

DAY 2. *That final pause before setting sail keeps the cook from feeling buried under an avalanche of stores.*

Someone asked Larry why he chose *Seraffyn* for cruising. He answered, "She is the only 24-footer I know that can carry 3,000 pounds of cargo and still sail well." *Seraffyn* is 24 feet on deck and stripped weighs about 8,000 pounds. With all her cruising gear, our possessions, and basic local cruising stores on board, she is right on her waterline and displaces 10,800 pounds. So the extra pounds we've put on for this voyage will make her a bit slower in light winds.

When I look at the provisions we bought for 29-foot, 9-inch Taleisin's *voyage from the Madeira Islands to Bermuda, I wonder how we ever carried enough to cross the North Pacific on board 24-foot, 4-inch* Seraffyn.

Planning a Stores List

Buying sufficient stores for any voyage takes planning and can make the difference between pleasant living on board or just getting there. I refrain from saying "pleasant eating" because "stores" includes much more than just food. Toilet paper, flashlight batteries, bicarbonate of soda, Band-Aids, dish soap are all stores, and on most voyages I've been on, they've been the responsibility of the cook or whoever is assigned the job of buying food.

When it became clear that we were really going to get off on our first long voyage, I went to the library, borrowed all the cruising books I could find, and read their stores lists. Not one seemed fully suited to our plans. They had different tastes, more or less money to spend, more or less galley space, and so on.

So, for the six months before we actually bought stores for our first long voyage, I kept a list of everything we bought for our house that wasn't main-course food. I kept track of the amount of salt, Worcestershire sauce, flour, and even dish soap we used. I found items on my list such as toothbrushes, Scotch tape, toothpicks, black mending thread, erasers, and flashlight bulbs. This 6-month survey revealed the shocking amount of peanut butter we consumed.

At the same time, we started a custom we call "Can Night." At least one night a week, we ate a meal prepared from canned or packaged goods such as we might have had left after a week or two at sea. This gave us a chance to see which canned goods we liked and which we didn't. It helped us avoid the problem of buying a case of canned stew that we hated but couldn't afford to throw away. "Can Night" also gave me a chance to come up with some good at-sea meals before we were actually at sea. We've continued this practice as we've cruised. Soon after we arrive in each new country, I buy some of the local canned or packaged products and try them out. If the goods aren't labeled in English, I open them for snacks or lunch so that I don't ruin a main meal if the contents aren't to our liking. I'd say our success rate on foreign canned goods has been 50-50.

It is well worth taking the time to look at prices, sizes, and contents of different packages in different stores. I've found that supermarkets often have lower prices than cash-and-carry firms, especially if they package their own brand-name products. Supermarkets also tend to carry more individual-serving-size cans than cash-and-carry shops, chandlers, or wholesalers do. But try store brands before you stock up. Larry loves Safeway tomato soup, but he won't eat Sainsbury's version.

Examine and compare the ingredients and weights on different packages. On all American and English packages, ingredients are listed in the order of their volume. One beef stew might have its ingredients listed as beef, potatoes, carrots, starch; another label might list potatoes, beef, starch. The first can will have more meat in it. A whole canned chicken is usually no bargain. You are paying for bone, water, and skin. Three small tins of chicken meat cost about the same as the whole canned chicken. They contain solid meat and take up half the space and preparation time. Condensed soup gives you twice the soup for only 10 percent extra cost.

FIGURE 1. *It is worth taking time to read the ingredients list on canned or packaged goods. Ingredients are, by law, listed in order of volume. In the United States, this product can be labeled Pork and Beans, even though, as the ingredients list indicates, it really contains a lot of beans with just a bit of pork added. In New Zealand, Canada, and the European Union, it would be labeled Beans in Tomato Sauce with Pork.*

Some freeze-dried products provide excellent results, take up little space, and are lightweight. But there is a catch: They require extra water, fuel, and preparation time. Before you invest too heavily in these, try any you think you'd like. Several times in our foreign cruising, people from other boats have offered to trade leftover freeze-dried products in 5-pound cans. Their crew has simply grown tired of them.

Try some of the canned goods sold in the refrigerated section of the market. Most of them keep extremely well when stored low in the boat. Canned Brie and Camembert cheeses keep for two or three months if stored at about 70 degrees. Since the lockers below your waterline will stay at about water temperature, you can be sure that many of these items will last well except in the deep tropics or the Red Sea, where water temperatures exceed 78 degrees F. The same goes for sausages such as salami or pepperoni, and hard cheeses packed in wax. They'll keep up to four weeks in a cool place.

Economy sizes have no place on a boat with a crew of fewer than five. A small container of dish soap is easier to handle and easier to store. If it breaks open, it makes less of a mess. Noodles in meal-size packages are the only way to go; unused noodles attract weevils and mold. Leftovers are difficult to keep on board at sea. A can just large enough for one meal means you can clean up the galley without having to find a way to preserve half a can of corn. This is especially important in the tropics, where food that isn't refrigerated rarely lasts two days.

Evaluate the different types of packaging. Cans are heavy and require more space than flexible foil packages, but they protect the contents better I buy coffee that comes in well-sealed foil bags, but if I plan to keep it longer than three or four months, I purchase canned coffee instead. I buy sugar, flour, and rice in 3- or 5-pound bags; then I seal each one in two plastic bags, one inside the other. This way, if one package of rice or sugar goes bad or breaks, I haven't lost my whole supply. (See Day 15, "Tips on Baking Bread," for hints on buying and storing flour.)

There were times when it took three trips with the dinghy to carry out all the provisions we needed for a voyage. This is a heavy load, as you can see by Cheeky's *decreased freeboard.*

Avoid large, flexible plastic containers for such things as cooking oil, syrup, and mayonnaise. If you can press your finger and cause an indentation in the container, it might break under the conditions in a storage locker during a gale at sea. I speak from experience. I had to clean out a whole can locker, Larry's tool locker, and the bilge when a plastic pint container of cooking oil split and spilled. Larry had an even worse job when a quart of boiled linseed oil in a plastic container developed a leak. Glass is much safer. To date, I have never broken a glass container—either while it was stored or when I was using it on board. And glass containers are easily reusable for canning, storage, or painting. If you accumulate too many empties during a long passage, they are easy to sink.

As freight and commodity prices rise, plus the demand for single meal servings, more products are being packaged in lightweight containers. Although I like the ease of storage and the lighter weight of nonglass and nonmetal containers, I have found that longevity has been compromised.

Paper-covered foil packets used for instant soups, sauces, and pudding mixes tend to allow moisture into the products after three or four months. Therefore, I package half of my voyaging supply in heavy-duty plastic bags to ensure a longer shelf life. For this purpose, I find Ziploc-style plastic bags indispensable and preferable to having a vacuum storage-bag system on board, especially as the Ziplocs are reusable and readily available in most reprovisioning ports.

Wax-coated cardboard containers such as those used for long-life milk, casks of wine, and some sauces are prone to leaking if they are allowed to shift in the lockers. The wax gets chafed off the corners and spoilage soon follows. Furthermore, temperatures above 75 degrees F soften the wax and make it porous. These containers should be stored low in the boat and packed tightly to ensure the longest possible life.

Once the initial product-and-price research is over, how do you do your actual list planning? Few long-distance cruising or racing cooks depend on a menu plan for voyages of more than a week. It just doesn't work. After the first time, few of these people make a detailed shopping list. Instead, most seem to use a method similar to ours. I go to the shops I've found to be the best value and buy main-course items for the length of our voyage plus 50 percent. In other words, during this passage we figure an average speed of 100 miles a day for 45 days plus 22 for unforeseeable holdups. So I buy about 65 cans of dinner-meat products plus the same number of lunch items. I figure on four eggs equaling one can. I stock up more on corned beef than I do on ham because I know of more uses for corned beef. I buy at least 24 cans of stewing beef because it can be used several different ways.

Next I purchase fruit and vegetables (canned), rice, powdered potatoes, flour, pasta, peanut butter, jam, and nonfood items to cover the same number of days. I take this all back to the boat and store it. This way, I can see how much space I have left. I then go back to the shops and buy luxury items to fill the empty spaces: tins of nuts, canned pâté, Brie, candy, dried fruits—what we call "fun foods." These add variety to our menu as we cruise.

My final purchase is 12 complete, very-easy-to-prepare meals, which I store in the most accessible place possible. These include meals such as hot dogs and baked beans, chicken in cream sauce, and beef and mushroom stew—each of which can be simply opened and heated in one pan—for those times when it's too rough for anything else. When I am too seasick to cook, Larry knows exactly where to look for something to stave off his starvation. I feel a bit better about being seasick because I did my bit when I shopped for stores.

Fresh fruit, vegetables, and meat are the last things we buy. I wait until the last possible day to pick them out. Other than potatoes and onions, I consider these to be in excess of the amount of food planned for the voyage.

New potatoes last forever, so we buy 30 pounds for the two of us whenever our stocks get low, even if we're not planning a voyage. It's the same with onions. Tomatoes purchased green ripen slowly and can be good three or four weeks later. Lemons wrapped in aluminum foil and stored in a sealed container are good for two months. Other fresh produce can be a gamble but is nice to have, so we always carry some. It's rarely wasted, but there have been times when we have had apple fritters, applesauce, and apple fruit salad all in one day in order to use up apples before they turned. (See Day 7 for guidelines on buying and storing produce.)

When the boat is full to the brim and I can't think of anything I've forgotten, I take a stroll through one or two markets and drugstores, looking at each item they sell. This often jolts my memory or else reassures me that we haven't forgotten anything. If the voyage is going to be a long one, I use this chance to buy a few surprise gifts for any birthdays on board or just joke items that might perk up an otherwise depressing day. I also spend the rest of the local currency that is lying around the bottom of my change purse.

If you are stocking up in a foreign country, making a stores list is more difficult. A good cookbook that describes vegetables and foods from all parts of the world and suggests ways to use them is invaluable. But no book tells you what is inside foreign cans, so be extra careful to try canned goods before buying by a caseload. I found this out the hard way in Antigua, British West Indies, when I bought six cans of cooking butter from Australia. It turned out to have a bright orange color. It tasted great, but the crew wouldn't spread it on their toast, and cookies made with it came out yellow. In 50 percent of the world's countries, labels are in English, but where they aren't, it pays to find a local person to go shopping with you and describe the contents. Japan presented a special problem. All labels were in kanji (Japanese characters), and the pictures on the labels didn't resemble anything I knew. An English-speaking Japanese friend tried to help as much as she could, but beyond the language barrier was a culture barrier. She couldn't imagine why I was disappointed when a can of what was described as fruit cocktail contained 1/4 fruit, 3/4 unflavored-gelatin cubes. If all else fails in a foreign country, look for Chinatown. Almost all goods shipped from China have labels in English.

One thing will soon become obvious as you cruise abroad. You won't be able to afford to eat the same way you do at home. Your stores list for offshore passages will change if you are stocking up in an island economy, where all imports are expensive, or if you are in a primitive economy like Costa Rica, where canned peaches cost five times what a pound of beefsteak does.

And finally some advice that Larry often repeats: overbuy. Fill the boat to the brim. When you see stores you like, buy them. They might not be available in the next country you visit. Keep the boat full and refill it every chance you get. Full lockers in port means freedom from that endless round of shop, cook, wash the dishes and clothes, shop, cook . . . That turns many wives away from cruising. When you are making passages, having extra food on board means you are free to change your plans, extend your stay at a deserted island, and avoid civilization for just that extra bit of time that will make your cruise a joy.

. . . .

Day 3

Noon to noon: 95 miles
Calm and sunny, moving about 3 knots on a beam reach
Wind freshened in the afternoon

Breakfast
cantaloupe
canned Danish concentrate of orange juice
coffee and tea

Lunch
grilled cheese and tomato sandwiches, soft drinks

Dinner
sautéed breast of chicken, simmered with fresh tomatoes and onions
corn on the cob
red wine

. . . .

Late last night, we saw the last of Japan's shore lights. Today we are truly "at sea." We plotted our first X on the large-scale chart of the western North Pacific. We have 2,400 miles to go until we reach the chart for the eastern North Pacific, which shows Victoria and the United States, including Hawaii. But with the weather like this, lockers overflowing with cans, a forepeak full of fresh food, and 80 paperback books to read, the distance is only a myth, a 70-inch-wide white space on two big sheets of paper.

Shopping for Stores in a Foreign Country

One of the most exciting, intriguing, unexpected, and frustrating events of your first cruise to a foreign country will happen after your anchor or mooring lines are fully secured, after you've cleared customs, and after you have enjoyed that long-anticipated hot shower. You'll row ashore looking for those fresh foods for which you have been yearning. You'll locate the shopping district. And you'll find that almost all the people in the world shop

45

for food completely differently than we North Americans do. They often use a different language. They usually use metrics, counting weight in kilos, liquids in liters. They use unfamiliar currencies. And few places have corner supermarkets. Nowhere else will you be able to buy everything you need to last for the coming week in one 90-minute stop. Ninety percent of the people in the world still shop daily in public marketplaces. They buy their food from small shops or stalls that specialize in meat, vegetables, dry goods, or fruit. To most of the world's people, shopping is not a chore but an important part of daily social life. It is a time for gossip, ribald jokes, and news exchanges.

DAY 3. *One of the most frustrating aspects of any long-distance voyage involves having to shop where no one understands a word you say.*

When you arrive fresh from an ocean passage, anxious to fill the gaps in your depleted store lockers, the vastness and confusion of your first public market can be overwhelming. The shopkeepers may be shy or even frightened because you don't speak their language. They won't understand your confusion, since the marketplace is part of their way of life. Few foreign merchants will be prepared for the vast amounts of food you as a cruising person wish to buy. No shopkeeper will understand the impatience of the average North American who is used to checkout counters, bag carriers, and computerized cash registers.

If you are on a leisurely cruise and regard shopping as one of the adventures you've come for, you might learn to prefer the marketplace way. But if you are on a delivery or making a pit stop for three days to buy provisions, then pushing on because the seasons are pressing, shopping in foreign ports can make provisioning for your sailing life a drag. Either way, there are lots of steps you can take to make provisioning more pleasant.

I've learned from repeated and sometimes expensive mistakes not to buy anything on the first day in port except food for dinner and the next morning's breakfast. Even if you only have two days to buy your provisions, it pays to spend a day looking around first. By pricing food in several places, you'll get an idea of what is available and what prices are standard. I often remember an experience we had when rushing through the Kiel Canal trying to leave the Baltic before a November snowstorm caught us. As soon as we docked in Cuxhaven, we rushed into the first butcher shop we saw, pointed at three lamb chops, and almost gasped when we realized we'd spent $7 for less than a pound of meat. We walked back toward the boat along a different route and saw other, slightly less elegant shops where nice-looking pork chops could have made us a meal for only $3 a pound.

By spending the first afternoon window shopping, you'll get some idea of how to organize provisioning day, and you'll probably see some items to add to your list. You'll know what to carry with you when you are ready to shop and where the banks or money exchanges are.

If you are buying provisions for a long voyage from a foreign port, check out not only the public market and local shops but also the wholesalers and ship chandlers. It will pay to talk to any other cruising sailor who has been in the port longer than you have. If there is a yacht club nearby, try to meet some of the members and their wives. Pleasant conversations around many yacht club lounges have turned into wonderful outings after the local women have realized how little I knew about the shopping facilities of their hometown. In Port Said, Egypt, Marja, the wife of the port health officer, took me along as she did her daily shopping. Without her guidance, I never would have found the only shop in the city that sold cheese; it was tucked away on a side street in the basement of an office building four blocks from the main shopping street. Not only did I learn where to shop, but Marja told me what to bargain for. Her hints on her country and its customs couldn't have been culled from a book.

Other cruising people can be good guides, but most have one drawback: Because they don't own cars and have not lived in the area for very long, their knowledge of the shopping places beyond walking distance is definitely limited. If you are buying food to last for the next four or five days, take your new cruising friends' advice. But when you are buying for a long passage, check every possibility for yourself. Doing so will save you money and get you food of the best quality, greatest longevity, and widest variety.

The public marketplace is almost always the best place to buy fresh fruit, vegetables, and eggs. Meat bought in the market is usually fresher than that found in small shops because it is brought in daily. Prices are usually lower because of the direct competition among the stallkeepers. But canned food often stays on the shelves longer in public markets, so cans may already be rusty when you buy them. We've been in public markets in at least 50 countries—they can range from delightful to depressing. The most primitive ones—in Egypt, Sri Lanka, and Tunisia—had muddy floors, beggars, crowing chickens, and animals being slaughtered on the spot. But this is not the norm. Most governments provide clean, well-ventilated buildings where the local farmers and vendors set up their stalls.

Because of the lack of laws governing packaging and meat vending, it is normal for animals to be sold with their heads on so that the local people can tell what they are getting. Cows that have been freshly slaughtered have bright, shiny eyes, just like freshly caught fish. Rabbit heads are left on so cats can't be mistaken for rabbits. After the plastic packages of the American-style supermarket, all of this might seem strange and possibly repulsive to the cruising sailor. But it pays to get used to patronizing the public market, because that is where you will do most of your outfitting for offshore passages once you go foreign.

Local small shops and minimarkets have one distinct advantage over the public market: Here you are most likely to find people who speak a little English. They also appear to be more organized, and their canned goods are usually fresher. Be sure to ask for anything you don't see on the shelves—a small shop often has a back room full of treasures. If the shopkeeper doesn't have what you want, he'll probably direct you to the shop that has it. If you buy more than $50 worth of goods in most shops in southern Europe, Africa, or the Far East, you'll probably be entitled to a 10 percent discount. Such a quantity is considered a wholesale lot when you are shopping where the average income is less than $60 a week.

Throughout the Pacific and the Far East, you'll find Indian and Chinese shops in competition with each other. Though the Chinese shops will often appear cleaner and more tasteful to the Western eye, I've found that Indian shops tend to have lower prices. On the other hand, the Chinese shops usually carry a larger variety of packaged goods, so it pays to check out both.

Wholesalers can offer you savings of up to 35 percent on some brands of canned and packaged goods. I try to find those who supply the goods for the corner stores, as they will have the largest variety available. Supermarket chains in some large ports (such as Singapore and Yokohama) have wholesale outlets that supply big ships. Their prices tend to be lower than those of general wholesalers. Look for the office numbers of these suppliers in the telephone directory for the port, or ask the local shopkeepers.

Ship chandlers will supply yachtsmen who are going foreign. Often they are the only good source of those imported (American, English) brands you miss so much, even though you want to use local foods. The chandler is also the source of the cruising man's delight—duty-free liquor—and, for the smoker, duty-free cigarettes. If not, ask the port captain, customs officer, or any ship agent. Before you start any large shopping expedition, ask several chandlers for a printed price list. If you don't see an item you need, ask the chandler to find a price for you. All chandlers have someone in their office who speaks English; all their lists are available in English. Check the different price lists and use them as a guide to your survey of the local markets and wholesalers. When it is time to order from the chandler, don't be shy about placing orders with two or three different ones. One chandler in Yokohama listed only hard liquor, with Black & White whiskey costing $2.25 a fifth. He also had Skippy peanut butter at wholesale American prices. The other chandler had both wine and hard liquor plus a wonderful selection of canned and processed cheeses at rock-bottom prices, but his Black & White whiskey cost $2.85 a fifth, and he had no peanut butter at all.

But all is not roses with chandlers. They are only found in big ports that have extensive international shipping traffic. They can only put duty-free stores on board vessels that are bound overseas, and a customs officer has to come and seal these stores, so you can't get them put on board until the day you are leaving. The stores most chandlers carry are planned for large ships; usually only case lots or huge containers are available. Some chandlers will split cases if you ask, but they can't give you five pounds of instant mashed potatoes out of a 25-pound can. And, finally, the prices chandlers charge for canned goods may not be as low as those you'll find in the local shops or wholesalers.

Once you've looked around but before you're ready for the first major assault on the marketplace, consider several ways to make the experience more pleasant.

Before you go cruising, start learning about metric weights and measures. Many of today's cans and packages list their metric equivalents. If you start noticing the difference between metric measurements and pounds now, it will be one less problem to overcome. Since a kilo equals 1,000 grams, you'll find it easier to figure prices using metrics. Meat that costs 30 cents for 100 grams costs $3 for a kilo, $1.20 for 400 grams. Try figuring that for something that costs 30 cents an ounce. Since I was brought up with pounds, I convert by thinking, "400 grams equals nearly a pound, 100 grams a quarter of a pound." It's close enough.

Before you go shopping, figure out the conversion rate for the local currency. Make a small chart and choose one of the local coins or bills that has a similar value to a coin from your own country. Then use that coin as your rough standard for figuring prices. In the United Kingdom, 50 pence was equal to 93 U.S. cents, so I equated a 50-pence coin to a dollar. Something that cost me £5 would therefore be 10 times a dollar.

Once you are familiar with the local currency, glance through your translation dictionary. If you need specific items, make a list in both English and the local language. Print this list clearly and in big letters, so that when all else fails—after you've tried pronouncing the words with your finest Spanish accent and still can't make your request understood—you can pull out the piece of paper and find someone who can read it. In developing countries, don't be surprised if you need to stop five or six people before you can find someone who reads. Language is a problem, but you'll find that most of your shopping can be done by the point-and-picture method, plus a bit of dictionary writeout. If you keep your sense of humor and are patient, this language barrier can add a lot of fun to your day. I remember my very first encounter with a big Mexican public market. It took five or 10 minutes of strolling around before I was brave enough to approach an uncrowded produce stall. I pointed to the oranges, held up two fingers, and said, "Dos, por favor."

The woman behind the stall laughed and said, "Na-ran-ha."

I obviously didn't understand her, so she picked up an orange, pointed at it, and repeated, "Na-ran-ha."

I then realized she was telling me the word for orange. I repeated, "Na-ran-ha."

She applauded, picked up a lettuce, and carefully said, "Lechuga." By the time my basket was full, several other Mexicans had gathered around to encourage and assist me. I left with a basket of lovely produce, my head swimming with new Spanish words, and my fears of shopping in a public market where I didn't understand the language laid to rest.

You do need special equipment to shop overseas, even if you aren't provisioning for a voyage. Few shops in foreign countries provide any kind of bags, so it is usually a good idea to buy stretchy woven nylon bags, such as the kind sold in import shops at home or in marketplaces abroad. These bags are easy to carry in your purse or daypack. They expand to carry more than you'll be able to lift, and they are incredibly strong. On the boat, they'll store in any corner; six of them won't even fill half a shoebox. They can be washed with the laundry and dried just by shaking. We use them for dozen of things besides shopping.

Woven baskets may look prettier than nylon mesh bags, but they are bulky to store and unsafe to use because they can harbor insects or their eggs. In Sri Lanka, a friend lent us a rattan shopping bag to carry some eggs, tomatoes, and fruit back to the boat. Back on board *Seraffyn*, I grabbed for a tomato and a 3-inch-wide tarantula ran out of the bag, over my arm, across the bunk, and down between the frames. Hearing my screams, Larry came running. He tore out the cushions and bunk boards, found the hairy monster, and killed it with a wooden mixing spoon. It's not common to find tarantulas in woven shopping baskets; usually, cockroach eggs or ants make their homes between the rattan pieces. Washing destroys the shape and beauty of a natural basket, so any leaky packages, squashed fruit, or dirt will create a smell that is difficult to remove.

Farmers' market day in Hilo, Hawaii. All four voyaging crews who were planning to depart toward Canada and the U.S. mainland shared a taxi to get into town for the freshest vegetable choices.

We cruised quite happily for six years using only nylon shopping bags. Then we delivered a 54-foot ketch from Spain to the United States; on board was a wheeling, folding shopping cart. You've probably seen the type—we used to call them granny baskets. You can find them in most luggage stores or make your own from a collapsible luggage carrier. Get one that has the largest possible rubber wheels that swivel independently like casters. Other good features: a removable bag that you can wash and a top that you can snap shut. These carts are great, and they take the shopping loads off your shoulders. The cart stands on its own while you select your next vegetables. It's easy to lift on board, and if it has good wheels, even a lightweight like me can easily pull a 50-pound load down the street. That's why Larry likes it so much. He says that since I have one for myself, I don't ask him to go along as a pack mule nearly so often. One warning, though: Watch out for the toes of passersby.

Each time you are on your way to the market, toss a few plastic bags into your cart. Most public-market vendors sell fish and meat wrapped only in paper. Without a plastic bag, leakage could spoil anything under or near your fish. Take along some egg cartons, since eggs are often sold individually, and, if you intend to buy ice, a canvas ice carrier. Many taxi drivers will refuse to carry ice loose in their trunks because of the leakage. Though you can usually talk them into it, it is easier to be prepared. Besides, it simplifies the process of transferring ice to the boat.

In a delightful small village in Mexico, the chief of police heard that we had gotten $600 in cash at the local bank. He took us aside and gave us some excellent advice: "Don't come ashore with more money in your purse than you can afford to lose. To our people, you look very rich. If they see you opening a wallet with more money in it than they can earn in two weeks, they are only human; they could become tempted and even steal." His counsel is worth heeding. Carry small bills and lots of coins in a separate change purse so that you don't appear to have a lot of money when you are in a public market.

On shopping days, most cruising people have found that it pays to arrive at the public market early, dressed quite conservatively. *Dress does matter*—not only because you might be the only foreigner but also because you'll get better service. Most of the housewives who are out shopping dress very conservatively. I've seen merchants who obviously resent customers who are too casually dressed shopping at their stall. In Italian, Spanish, and Portuguese markets, tight trousers, shorts, and backless dresses are invitations to some painful and embarrassing pinches.

If you are planning to buy more than one basketful of food, find a café located in or adjacent to the market area. Order a coffee or tea, then ask permission to use the café as a depot for your shopping. Don't be embarrassed; if you look around, you'll find that many of the local people do the same. Then go out and shop, bring back a load of provisions, and store it in an out-of-the-way corner of the café. It there are more than two of you, the café makes a good meeting place where you can compare notes, rest over a cool drink, then plan your next move. If there are no cafés close by, ask a stallkeeper if you can leave your purchase with him or her. They'll rarely say no.

Gayle Summers carries this folding cart on board
Dragon's Lair. *It definitely came in handy at Nuku Hiva.*

When I am buying for an extended voyage, I plan my shopping so that I get my fresh fruit and tomatoes first, then my meat. These items disappear first from the stands. I buy soft vegetables like lettuce and spinach next, and finally I look for cheeses, sausages, and hard vegetables such as onions and potatoes. These don't bruise easily and aren't wilted or damaged by the handling other shoppers give them.

When the shopping is done, our corner of the café usually looks like a small army stores depot. After one last cool drink, we call a taxi, load it up with our stores, and head for the ice plant before we return to the harbor. The taxi may sound like an extravagance when local buses only cost pennies a ride. But I've found that when I'm finished shopping for a week's provisions, I'm too tired and overloaded to handle the struggle of a bus.

Larry has a problem with taxi drivers. He is convinced they sense that he hates to bargain. But he has learned. Ask the driver the fare. If it is too high, just walk away and ask another driver. If there is a meter in the taxi, ask the driver to turn it on as soon as you get into the taxi. If at all possible, carry a small map of the town with you and show the taxi driver exactly where your boat is located. That way, he will know you have an idea of how far you are going to ride. Don't let unscrupulous taxi drivers ruin your day, and don't think that unscrupulous taxi drivers are found only in foreign countries.

I've had different experiences with taxi drivers. Since many of them pick up foreign passengers, they often speak a smattering of English when no one else does. They know an area well and can guide you to the one item you can't find in the marketplace.

Rickshaw and trickshaw (the latter a 3-wheeled, bicycle-powered rickshaw) drivers are the same. In the Far East, we found some who actually helped with the shopping. In Penang, Malaysia, the slight-looking trickshaw driver I'd hired for a dollar an hour came into a shop where I was buying $75 worth of groceries and said to the owner, "You have given my friend her proper 10 percent discount, I trust." The shopkeeper handed me back the equivalent of $7.50. The only problem with trick- and rickshaws is that I feel guilty asking a man not much bigger than I am to pull me and all my groceries through steamy, hot streets while I lounge back in the shade of the canopied cart. I asked my favorite driver in Penang about this. His comment was, "This is a good profession. I need a license to do it and I earn a good wage for my family when many people have no jobs at all. I'll tell you if I can't carry any more. But don't worry too much. You should see some of the loads the local people expect me to carry—mother, father, three children, and groceries too. That's a real load."

We originally wanted bicycles on board *Taleisin*, our second long-term cruising home, so we could explore farther from the foreshores we visited and we could get much-needed leg exercise. The bicycles definitely served these purposes, but they proved even more valuable as tools to make shopping enjoyable. Our first pair were folding Peugeots with 22-inch wheels. They were built with luggage racks over both wheels. We added cloth saddlebags aft and found we could carry a week's worth of groceries using the two bikes. A load of 50 to 60 pounds, with most of the weight on the rear rack, was manageable if hills were not too steep. I carried 5-gallon cans of kerosene along the waterfront of Papeete using the back rack of my bike. Larry won the load-carrying contest with 50 pounds of ice and four gallon-size boxes of wine distributed fore and aft on his bike in hilly San Diego. When we wore out those two bikes (after 15 years of hard use), we purchased two bikes made by Dahon and fitted them out with the same accessories.

With the faster access provided by "wheels," I am willing to explore farther afield for fresher produce or better prices and to make two trips a day if necessary, rather than trying to find a cool place to wait out the siesta hour that's held sacred in a majority of countries. Since I do not have to carry things while I shop (the bike does the carrying), I am less tired at the end of the day. Parking is far easier with a bike than with a car, and direct access is easier in towns with one-way roads. So I have found myself turning down offers of car usage, since I have my own transport. We do have a combination lock on a chain for each bicycle, and in crowded market areas we usually ask a shopkeeper to keep an eye on the laden bikes, even if they are locked to a gate or lamppost. If you have purchased some provisions from the shopkeeper, he or she will often let you bring your bike right into the foyer of the shop for safety and convenience.

We would always choose folding bikes over solid-frame ones, as they'll fit into a taxi. This gives me the freedom to shop for small items along the way to the supermarket where I'll buy a week's worth of provisions. Then I simply call for a taxi to take me, my pile of groceries, and the bike back to the marina or anchorage.

Net bags do not work as well for bicycle shopping, so we now carry large, strong canvas tote bags like the ones sold in many marine stores for carrying ice. These bags are used for dozens of nonshopping purposes, as they are spray-resistant and very strong. Their main drawback is that they are bulky to store (we carry six of them on board) and harder to wash if meat or fish leak through the packaging. So for shopping in less-developed areas, I still carry a string bag or two, as they can be stuffed into my handbag for emergencies and washed out in seconds.

Plastic shopping bags have become the norm, even in the least-developed countries. But a word of warning: Don't trust these bags to hold more than a few pounds of groceries. They are cheaply made and often split just as you are lifting them into the dinghy. So use your own string or tote bag as reinforcement for any heavy load.

The towpaths alongside the canals in France provided perfect bicycle access to the patisseries of Chatelaine.

More and more countries along the trade-wind routes now have supermarkets. But two differences may take North American sailors by surprise. In most countries, shoppers are not allowed to carry any packages or bags into the market. Instead, right at the entrance is an attended parcel depot where you receive a ticket or identity badge in exchange for your parcels. I find this handy—as long as I don't misplace the ticket. I have never had any items damaged or stolen from one of these depots. The second difference still catches me out at times. Instead of weighing your produce as you check out, supermarkets in countries as diverse as New Zealand, Mauritius, and South Africa have an attendant in the produce section who weighs, seals, and tags each purchase. If you reach the checkout counter with untagged produce, you slow up the whole line, as someone will have to run back to the produce department for weighing and pricing. Furthermore, supermarket produce will not match what you'll find in public marketplaces, and you will still have to visit a dozen different shops to reprovision.

For shopping, do wear good walking shoes—ones with nonslip soles that can be washed easily. You'll find that market floors often are wet, as they are hosed down during the night for hygienic reasons. They can be quite slippery.

Finally, never refuse a local person's offer to take you shopping. If possible, however, ask that they do it a few days before it is time to reprovision, take note of the special places they recommend, then go back on your own for the big purchases. In Puerto Montt, Chile, as we prepared for the 7,000-mile voyage north to Hawaii, Paola, wife of one of the local yacht skippers, spent two separate mornings showing me her favorite shopping spots. Without her help, I would never have known about the excellent produce stand half a mile outside of town behind a movie theater, nor would I have found the butcher who was willing to vacuum-pack meat in meal-size portions at no extra charge. But I also found, when she was standing right with me, that I was reluctant to choose items that she regarded as extravagant or overpriced—even though, to me, they were well worth the cost. I also felt I could not slow down and take my time looking at each potato, each onion while she was with me. So instead, I purchased some of the specialty items she recommended, marked on my map the locations of the places I wanted to revisit, and had two grand lunches with a lovely lady. When I returned later that week, I found that her personal introduction had worked wonders with the shopkeepers, and they extended the same discounts to me as they had to her—discounts I might not have been offered as a one-time visitor.

When you first set off on a long cruise, you'll be shocked at how much time you spend shopping. The average North American takes two or three hours a week to buy food and provisions at home. If you have been living in the same neighborhood for ages, it can take even less time. I figure on spending six or seven hours a week buying food in foreign countries—and double that when it comes to provisioning for a long voyage. If you are moving from port to port quickly, provisioning will take longer because you won't have time to get to know the local shopping areas and markets. I've heard women list foreign shopping as one of the main reasons they hated cruising. "My life is one round of shopping, carting food back to the boat, making meals, washing clothes, shopping." I can appreciate the feeling. However, if you can split up the shopping chores and laundry among the crew, arrive with the proper equipment, and learn to shop the way the locals do—using a café as a welcome rest point—shopping may become one of your favorite cruising activities.

Cash and Cruising

Three weeks slip past as we lay at anchor in Cocos-Keeling Lagoon. Skin diving, beachcombing, finding new ways to cook our latest finds—each day is full to the brim. Sharing meals with a kaleidoscope of international voyagers bound for Chagos Archipelago or Africa accelerates consumption of the provisions we've laid on to feed us from Fremantle, Australia, to Durban, South Africa. We take the biweekly ferry to West Island, where the market manager shakes his head and repeats, "No, we cannot take U.S. traveler's checks, no credit cards except on Australian banks. U.S. cash, Aussie cash only. Sorry, company policy." Larry waits as I pocket my credit card, lay out the last of my Aussie dollars, and eye the small but expensive pile of fresh vegetables I want for the 3,000-mile voyage to Rodriques Island. He lets me suffer for just a few seconds before reaching into his wallet and handing over a dozen crisp US$20 notes.

It was neither the first nor the last time our hidden stash of cash has brightened a dark situation. Ten $1 bills rolled inside a $10 note smoothed our way through the Suez Canal. Two hundred dollars in cash got our boat moved to the safest mooring before she could suffer any damage when hurricane-force easterly winds swept 5-foot seas into the normally safe harbor at Falmouth, England, when *Taleisin* was being decommissioned. U.S. cash was all that worked in the Juan Fernandez Archipelago on our voyage north from Cape Horn.

For cruising, the well-known advertisement, "Your American Express Card—don't leave home without it," could better read, "Cash, never cruise without it." We try to keep at least $1,000 in smaller bills on board at all times. We have found that people worldwide know the exchange rate and feel confident accepting U.S. dollars. British pounds and euros work throughout Europe, Africa, and the Near East, but not worldwide.

Needless to say, don't hide this amount of cash in a drawer near your bunk, or in a clothes locker. These were the first places that boarding thieves looked when two cruising friends left their boat (and $5,000 in cash) on a mooring in the far corner of Knysna Lagoon, South Africa, while they went ashore for a weekend with friends. A safer storage place is inside some inauspicious package such as a cracker box or a cereal packet, stashed among the provisions in your food locker. Or consider a well-sealed plastic box under your engine beds or beneath the floorboards. I prefer this to a built-in safe. An intruder always assumes that safes contain valuables. Logical conclusion? They rip it out and carry it away to open with tools onshore. It is important to put this break-in risk in context. During 40 years of voyaging to 80 countries and probably 500-plus villages, towns, and pretty wild cities, we have had only one on-board burglary. Thieves used our dinghy to enter our wide-open boat when we went ashore to say farewell to friends. The farewell extended over five hours, until well after dark. Four days later, the majority of the valuables were recovered with the aid of the police (see *Seraffyn's Oriental Adventure*).

To back up our cash, we also carry another few thousand dollars in traveler's checks. In Brazil, this paid off. The government announced a 4-day bank holiday—i.e., it closed all banks, all electronic-transfer centers, and all money changers (the legal ones, that is) in an attempt to control hyperinflation. Local money changers would accept traveler's checks under the table and offered a very handsome bonus for them.

Banks don't like exchanging cash, which is bulky and must be shipped to a clearing house by secure, insured courier—i.e. expensive. And the bank charges you for the extra cost and hassle. Traveler's checks can be cleared electronically, as can transfers via ATM or cash advances, which offer the banks convenience and instant access to funds. Their rates reflect this.[1]

When we voyaged on *Seraffyn* before wire transfers existed, and we wanted to top up our on-board funds, we had to plan a 3- or 4-week stay near a major town or city and wait for a bank to clear a Bankers Trust check. Electronic banking has erased this problem and eliminated the check fees, and it allows our savings to earn interest until we need the funds. But we have learned that it is important to read the fine print and understand the terms before making electronic transactions of any sort.

Many folks have become comfortable with using ATM cards to get cash or as a substitute for handwritten checks (direct debit or eftpos—electronic funds transfer at point of sale) for life ashore. In the majority of first-world countries, a strongly regulated banking system, ease of access to statements via the Internet, and a knowledge of the normal security precautions for using ATM machines means there is little reason to be concerned with the difference between using a credit card or a debit card. As soon as you head to third-world countries, however, the difference becomes very important.

When you use a credit card such as MasterCard or VISA (the two most widely accepted ones), it is the card company that pays the merchant and then bills you on a monthly basis. By law and company policy, these companies offer 60 days from the date of your statement (not the date of purchase) to challenge any charges or purchases you feel were not yours. The disputed amount is deleted from your account until the claim is fully investigated. In other words, no money comes out of your bank account. A debit card, on the other hand, gives the merchant direct access to funds in your account. In the case of a money market account with a brokerage firm, this also can include your margin account. Money to cover the transaction is withdrawn immediately. You get your statement, notice that funds are missing, and have to wait until your financial institution investigates the situation before the money can be refunded.

. . . .

1   Exchange rates provided by Bank Direct, New Zealand on October 26, 2005.
    To buy New Zealand dollars using U.S. cash, the exchange rate is .7367—i.e., US$1,000 buys you NZ$1,357. To buy New Zealand dollars using traveler's checks, the exchange rate is .7212—i.e., US$1,000 traveler's checks will buy you NZ$1,386. To buy New Zealand dollars using electronic transfer, the exchange rate is .7155—i.e., US$1,000 will buy you NZ$1,397.

Some cruising friends in the Southern Caribbean used their debit card to buy provisions at a small island shop, after which they obtained a cash advance at a small bank. Either the merchant or the teller noted the card numbers and the PIN and then took cash advances against all the funds they had—literally stealing their whole cruising kitty. For the next nine months, while the bank investigated, these cruisers had to take any jobs they could find in order to cover day-to-day living costs. They did recover all of the stolen funds, and their credit rating was cleared, but they could never recover those months of lost cruising, those nights lost to worrying about money.

This is in direct contrast to our own experience in Rio de Janeiro, where—due to our own carelessness—our VISA credit card was stolen by a pickpocket during a rush-hour ride on a crowded bus. Although we reported this within 45 minutes, more than $20,000 in charges were made against our card, which had a $5,000 limit. The VISA New Zealand people did not even request payment on transactions that could have been made by us until we had been given a chance to see all of the paperwork. Not one penny went out of our bank account, and, as the VISA manager told us, "Since it is our company's money, we have a lot of incentive to solve this problem fast."[2]

Although credit cards may be the better choice for general purchases,[3] cash advances can be costly, with fees ranging up to 3 percent of the total, plus 1 percent for FOREX conversion, plus interest. With a debit card, cash-advance fees are rarely more than $2. So what is a workable solution? You can keep a separate account for your direct-debit card and deposit only the amount that would not affect your lifestyle should something go wrong. Or ask your card issuer to block any purchase over a set amount without telephoned approval. Another option is to consult with your credit-card issuer to see if your account can stay in credit. The Bank of New Zealand VISA card that we use pays interest on credit balances. So when we know we will want a large amount of cash—such as when we arrived in South Africa and wanted to purchase a $15,000 4WD Nissan for a 7-month foray into Bushman land—we transferred funds to our credit account a few days in advance. With our passports and credit card as identification, the $15,000

....

2   Some banks have recently made it a policy to return disputed funds to debit-card holders until investigations have been completed, but until this is arranged, you are out of pocket.

3   Credit-card companies are now charging at least 1 percent for each foreign purchase or cash advance in addition to normal credit-card charges. The bank issuing the card may also be charging 1 or 2 percent. The bank charges may not be shown separately, but rather as part of the total purchase price. The credit-card company will usually show its charge separately. The excuse given for this is the need to cover the cost of fluctuating currency values between the time you make the purchase and the time you make your payment. There are no extra fees for foreign purchases or for cash advances if you use a debit card.

transaction at the biggest bank in Durban took less than 20 minutes. We were charged only the credit-card cash-advance fee, and we paid no interest, as we were simply withdrawing our own money. There is one caveat: Our card has a 2 percent cash-advance fee with a maximum charge for each transaction of NZ$10. Some cards have a far higher maximum fee. Before you set off, discuss this with a representative at your bank and ask to see the fee schedule in print.

Charges for clearing foreign checks have become astronomical. The waiting time for clearance can be anywhere from three to eight weeks. So, before you set sail, it pays to discuss using wire transfers or bank-to-bank transfers. Some banks will provide you with a secret password or code in addition to your PIN to be used by telephone; others may provide you with forms that must be returned with your signature via FedEx or other courier before they will wire funds. This may seem a nuisance, but remember that they are trying to protect your money.

In countries with currency control, be sure to keep receipts for each cash advance and bank transfer. If—as we did when we sold our 4WD safari machine—you wish to convert local currency back into dollars, you will need proof that you brought funds into the country legally and did not earn them under the table.

With e-mail and Internet access, plus affordable telephone calling cards, it pays to handle all of your financial transactions and payments yourself. Keep track of your charges and pay accounts in advance if you do not have regular access to your mail. Keep a list of any payments you must make and check your statements to make sure they were covered. Also, once yearly, confirm the contact information you left with your bank and important vendors. A friend moved on board two years before she and her husband actually set off cruising. She sold her home and put her favorite possessions in a storage unit. When she finally set sail, she paid her storage bill each month and, as most of us do, received her mail about once a month for another year. Then their voyage took them across an ocean. In the excitement of preparing for the passage, she did not think to pay ahead for her storage unit. At her destination six weeks later, she found her mail had not been properly addressed and had been returned to her mail handling service. It was another month before the missing package reached her. Almost the first letter she opened was a notice: "You have 10 days to pay overdue storage fees before all items will be sold to recover costs." Frantic telephone calls revealed that the storage company had tried to reach the contacts provided, but her sister (listed as the emergency contact) had moved a year previously, so her telephone number and mailing address were no longer correct. The only good news was that the storage people still had all of her family photos and a check for the extra money received for selling the antiques and clothing from her unit.[4]

Now to the nitty-gritty. You have covered all the general financial considerations, set sail, and reached a new country. You row ashore, eager to sample the local foods and buy some fresh bread. A word of caution: Avoid changing more than a few dollars until you learn the ropes. Hotels and banks right at the harbor often give less advantageous exchange rates. ATMs also have different charges near major tourist spots. People who come up to you and offer to exchange money may be con artists.

Until we know the situation, we only exchange money where we see the rates posted and can get a receipt. In some countries, there are strict laws against changing money except with authorized dealers. We have sometimes sold currency to black-marketing locals, but only where this was very common practice and the penalty for a first-time offense was a warning. In Israel, this was illegal but it was done openly at a special plaza where you could get up to 25 percent extra for dollars. In other countries, you may forfeit your boat and spend time in jail if caught. Be sure you know the risks before you take a chance.

Before you make any large funds transfer or exchange, ask about fees. These can change from bank to bank and even branch to branch. At one Namibian bank, there was a US$6.30 fee for all foreign transactions, in addition to the compulsory government fees; at another, there was no transaction fee. The same was true in Australia: One bank charged US$15 for changing as many traveler's checks as we wished, whereas another charged $5 per check. In countries with stable, internationally convertible currencies, banks always give you the best exchange rates. Hotels and private currency-exchange services sometimes take commissions as high as 5 percent.

You'll avoid a lot of frustration when you deal with foreign banks if you put yourself in the teller's position. Remember that you have no local address, the teller may never have handled a foreign conversion or seen a foreign passport, the amount of money you are asking to have handed over to you may be more than the teller's monthly salary, and a mistake could cost him/her the job. So be extra patient and ask for the manager before you lose your temper. In fact, if our transaction is large, we often ask to speak to the manager first to discuss the best way to handle the situation.

. . . .

4   We do not have anyone in the United States handling our credit-card payments or financial transactions. We have seen the conflict that can be caused by this. Instead, we keep track of our expenditures and pay accounts in advance if we feel we will not have regular access to our mail or the Internet.

We also carry extra identification with us: our passports, a copy of our ship's papers, plus a credit card and driver's license. For security when we voyage to more isolated areas, we have color copies of our driver's licenses and the relevant pages of our passports. We paste these on thin cardboard and carry the pasteups with us. That way, if our wallet is stolen or lost, we still have positive IDs back on the boat. Only when a bank demands it do we carry the originals with us and leave the copies on board for security.

Choose a quiet time to change money; be careful to avoid local paydays. Do not put your cash in a pants pocket. Pickpockets hang out around banks on payday and often watch where you put your cash. For men, the European custom of carrying a small clutch bag is a good idea, or buttoned-down shirt pocket can work well: for women, don't exchange large amounts alone in cities with bad reputations. Manila, Mexico City, Acapulco, Rio, Rome, Hong Kong, and Jakarta are ones about which we've been warned. In Manila, a local friend arrived at the yacht club with slashed pants and no money after cashing his monthly paycheck and putting the cash in the buttoned front pocket of his pants.

Avoid carrying more cash than you need for the day. Not only does this make any potential loss less painful, but some shopkeepers will increase their prices if they see you handling more cash than their monthly incomes. I have a small change purse that I use at the marketplace. I put some small bills and change in the purse and keep the extra in the bottom of my handbag. Periodically, I find a quiet place and recharge the change purse. An extra advantage to leaving most of your cash on board is that it will reduce impulse buying of the beautiful handmade souvenirs you see in the marketplace by giving you time to reconsider while you return to the boat for more money.

Never put down your wallet on a counter as you pay for a purchase. In 40 years of cruising to more than 80 countries, we only once had our pocket picked (actually, it was my purse, as mentioned above), but Larry's wallet disappeared from an Australian newsdealer's counter in the seconds between handing his money to the shopkeeper and reaching down to pick up his wallet from the counter.

I learned another lesson in Australia. To avoid totally self-induced hassles, carry your wallet in a handbag that has a secure buckle, or in a front pocket with a button-down flap, especially when you are climbing on or off boats. I slipped as I clambered on board a friend's boat and watched in horror as my handbag fell from my shoulder and started to sink. Quick boathook work by my host saved the bag and nothing was lost, as the buckle kept everything inside.

Shipyards have had some bad experiences with cruising people—ranging from those who sailed out at night without paying to a customer paying with traveler's checks and later claiming the checks were stolen. To counter this, we offer to leave a deposit as soon as we are hauled out. Then we run a tab. The deposit establishes our legitimacy and saves time when we run in for one roll of masking tape or a few sheets of sandpaper. In exchange, we often receive a discount for this prepayment.

Finally, spend any remaining local currency before you leave for a new country, or toss it in a jar to give to other yachting people going the opposite way. Money changers will not accept coins or small bills.

Handling currency and financial business as you cruise can be a hassle. I sometimes long for those simple days on *Seraffyn* when Larry and I worked on the box system. We had a 3-inch-high box just the right size to store US$1,500 worth of $20 traveler's checks (six months' worth of cruising funds). Halfway down the box was a 3/4-inch peephole. We'd work on boat-repair projects or yacht deliveries, and when the box was full, we would set off exploring. As long as we could only see money through the hole, we were carefree. When we could see a bit of light, we began looking for work. When we could not see any bills through the hole, we'd take any jobs we were offered—to keep from eating up our reserve. But times and our lives have changed, and we find that ATMs, the Internet, and electronic transfers are a real boon.

Bear in mind, though, that no matter how often folks reassure you that your ATM card is all you will need, our experience has taught us to carry backup cash and some traveler's checks. Thus, when we sailed among a wonderful maze of 365 islands inshore of Isla Grande, Brazil, and local sailors called out, "Come on over and join us, the best grilled fish in the world is right there at the café on the sand," it didn't matter that the nearest bank or ATM was a 30-mile beat to windward, that the café on the sand only took cash. I reached into our secret cash cache and we then rowed ashore to join the party and savor the delights that make cruising such a memorable and addictive affair.

. . . .

Day 4

Noon to noon: 185 miles (90 miles due to Japanese current)
Miles to date: 280
Smooth broadreach
Sunny and warm

Breakfast
　　apple, orange juice
　　bread and jam
　　coffee, tea

Lunch
　　scrambled eggs
　　tomato-and-cabbage salad with mayonnaise
　　coffee, tea

Snack
　　potato chips and cheese

Dinner
　　Chinese-style shrimp over instant *mee* noodles

. . . .

CHINESE-STYLE SHRIMP

Sauté (until onions brown lightly)
　2　tbs. butter
　5　cloves garlic, chopped
　1　onion, cut into chunks
　½　bell pepper, cut into chunks
　　▼

Combine

1	tbs. soy sauce
2	tbs. cornstarch
¼	cup water
	lemon juice to taste

Pour soy-sauce mixture over onions

Stir gently until gravy thickens.

Add

1	unpeeled tomato, cut into chunks
1½	cups uncooked shrimp

Cover and cook 1 minute. Remove from heat and allow to sit 3 or 4 minutes. Then toss and serve over mee (rice) noodles.

. . . .

Preparing for the First Few Days at Sea

During the first three or four days of every offshore passage, I feel tired and clumsy. We're usually recovering from farewell parties, the mentally exhausting job of shopping for stores, and the physically tiring job of storing them away. Then we need to get used to the motion and the rhythm of the changing watches. This has been a calm voyage so far; the sea is almost glassy. Even so, because of the swell, other ships' wakes, and *Seraffyn's* motion, we have to brace ourselves as we move around. All night our bodies tense, then relax, as the boat rises and falls over each wave, and though we've slept like rocks on each of our off-watches, six hours of sleep never seems like quite enough. I think this initial tiredness—which in my case causes me to lose most of my initiative—is even worse than seasickness. For these first days at sea, I have to force myself to do something besides lie in the bunk and read. Cooking is about the limit of my self-starting ability, and the idea of opening up the egg locker and checking over 120 eggs doesn't appeal to me at all.

Had the Sea of Japan been noted for heavy winds or rough seas, I definitely would have prepared several meals ahead of time. When we sailed out of Cartagena, Colombia, eight years ago, bound north for Jamaica, I'd known and worried about the fact that we'd be close-hauled and contending with 20-to-25-knot trade winds. At Larry's suggestion, I cooked up several main courses before we left: beef stew, chili and beans, a pork roast. These stayed right in their pots when we left port. Thus, in spite of a rude bout of seasickness and rough seas, I was able to heat up something Larry enjoyed even though I was having trouble just keeping down dry biscuits.

Reprovisioning as You Voyage

It is relatively easy to fill your food storage lockers as you prepare for your first ocean passage. You'll probably know the layout of the town, products will be familiar, and you'll know where to get the best prices. But what do you do when your stores lockers begin to empty, when you open the second-to-last jar of mayonnaise, or when you notice that there are only three packets of pasta left? Reprovisioning your floating warehouse can be either an affordable pleasure or a budget-destroying traumatic exercise, depending on how you plan your cruising route.

It is impossible to list the prices and products you'll find in each port or country you will visit, but I can provide guidelines based on our observations of the past 40 years, plus advice from cruising friends who are currently exploring other parts of the world.

As your stores begin to dwindle, the most important thing to remember is that everyone, everywhere, needs to eat. So even if you cannot find the foods you prefer, even in the most isolated villages you'll find enough to keep you going: corned beef, canned fish, cooking oil, jams, flour, pasta. The less developed a country is, the more the people will depend on canned and dried food. We've bought food supplies in more than 70 countries and in some of the most-isolated villages in the world, and though there have been times when we found shelves that were bare except for a few dozen cans of bully beef and a stack of noodles, we could have survived. But survival is not what makes cruising interesting and enjoyable.

When we cruised in 24-foot *Seraffyn*, a 5-ton boat with locker space for about 40 cases of provisions, we found we needed a good provisioning port every six months to ensure interesting eating. On 8-ton *Taleisin* (which displaces more like 9 tons right after a full reprovisioning), we carry closer to 75 cases of provisions and go nine months between major reprovisioning stops. By choosing these stops carefully, we have found we can cut our food expenditures by 30 to 50 percent and save several thousand dollars each year.

Prices for canned and packaged provisions will always be higher on islands than in a mainland country. The farther offshore an island is, the higher the prices will be. Transportation costs are the main reason for this. Your choices will be more limited on islands.

French islands worldwide have very high prices but an excellent range of goods. The supermarket on the island of Réunion (in the Indian Ocean) had a truly stunning display of cheeses, pâtés, sausages, wine, and condiments. In that case, I could afford a selection of these because we'd been cruising in very inexpensive places the previous six months.

In less-developed countries, any locally produced goods will be inexpensive and more often organically grown than those from developed countries. But imported goods will be expensive.

Costs in European Union countries will be about double those in the United States, although fresh food in the Mediterranean countries is still reasonable.

Countries with controlled currencies, such as South Africa, have high prices on imported goods and low prices on local goods. The same is true of countries with high inflation rates.

You'll find a more limited range of canned, dried, and packaged goods in tropical countries than in areas with more temperate climates. This is because the local people have easy access to fresh food year-round. Also, because the climate causes cans to rust, packaged goods to decay, and bugs to multiply in grains and cereals, shopowners keep only limited supplies on their shelves.

In countries with a limited selection of provisions, check out shops in the major tourist areas and near wealthy retirement communities. This is where we often find the specialty items that enliven offshore cooking. But keep in mind that prices in these shops will often be higher than in regular supermarkets.

Your best reprovisioning stops will be near major shipping ports in countries with diverse economies, such as Singapore, Los Angeles, Sydney, and Gibraltar. But of course these ports may not be anywhere along your route when you need them. Therefore, below you'll find a list of the most dependable reprovisioning ports that we and our friends have found as we cruised. I am listing only those countries or ports about which I have current information.

One of the lessons we have learned the hard way is that if you see something you need or something that is a real favorite, buy lots of it immediately—even if your lockers are still pretty full or the price is a bit high. You probably will not find it the next time you walk into the shop. Even in the progressive economy of Sydney, Australia, supplies of nonessential packaged goods can be sporadic. One time, I bought only three jars of Larry's favorite blueberry jam because I didn't feel like carrying anything extra. I didn't find more of it until we reached Fremantle, seven months later.

Don't be ashamed about appearing constantly cost-conscious as you look for reprovisioning ports. It is essential to research and find the best value for your money, especially if you are on a cruising budget, because your single largest expense will be for food and drink.

The very best prices for dried legumes can be found at the stalls in public markets, such as this one in Guadalajara, Mexico.

Joan Reynolds, on board the yacht *Utahna*, had a final comment: "Don't take a food list from someone else unless you know and like and eat everything they eat. Would you do that at home?" I can't help but agree, and after looking at different people's food lockers, I find that most long-distance cruisers soon come to the same conclusion. So overstock on your favorite things. Buy more every time you see things you like. Use your boat as a pantry-warehouse. Preservable food is never a waste; you can use it a year later and probably find it was like a savings account. But always remember that you will be able to find food to eat anywhere you find people, even when the local eating style is vastly different from yours. I think that this is one of the joys of cruising; it's either feast or famine as far as stores shopping goes. But when it's feast, you really appreciate and remember it.

Good Places to Reprovision

This list is arranged according to routes normally used by voyagers.

SPAIN AND PORTUGAL

Lower prices than most EU countries, good variety. Excellent fresh food at reasonable prices. Good African dried fruit and nuts.

CANARY ISLANDS

Good variety, prices slightly higher than in mainland Europe but lower than most Atlantic islands. Avoid reprovisioning when any sailing rally is in port, as supplies can be depleted.

BRAZIL

Good variety. Prices on local foods are very low. Imports can sometimes be found at bargain prices due to black-market currency exchanges.

TRINIDAD

Lowest prices in the Caribbean outside of Puerto Rico. Half as expensive as Antigua. Good variety.

ST. THOMAS, U.S. VIRGIN ISLANDS

Excellent variety if you are patient. The requirements of the charter fleet keep suppliers on their toes. It can be pricey here, so shop carefully.

PUERTO RICO

U.S. variety and prices with about 5 percent extra cost due to freight. Many local specialties at reasonable prices.

U.S. MAINLAND, ESPECIALLY FLORIDA AND CALIFORNIA

Excellent shopping at half of European prices. But fresh vegetables should be bought at produce stands, as supermarket produce can be pretty tasteless and far from fresh. Look for large retirement communities where residents demand variety plus good prices.

MEXICO

La Paz, Baja California, Guaymas, and Acapulco. You'll pay extra for favorite U.S. products, but this is the last place you'll see many of your favorites in the Pacific.

PANAMA

Ship chandlers carry excellent supplies here. Prices can be good if you buy in case lots.

PAPEETE

Excellent variety of French products, expensive by any standard. But you'll probably need to replenish here unless you are heading right to American Samoa.

AMERICAN SAMOA

Prices are similar to those in Hawaii—i.e., about 10 percent higher than on U.S. mainland. Variety is pretty good, but you must visit each shop in town to find what you want, as each one stocks different items.

FIJI

Low prices on good local and Chinese products. Products from Australia and New Zealand can be good buys. Variety may be the best of the South Pacific island nations.

MANILA

A good range of local and imported products can be found here. U.S. specialties are often on the shelves. Prices are excellent for local goods but high for imports.

NEW ZEALAND

Good quality, low-priced local goods. Large selection of canned and packaged fruit and vegetables; small selection of canned meats. Imports are a bit high and supplies can be sporadic. You will need to go to Auckland for real variety. One special canned item found only here and in Australia is called "cucumber slices." These are the finest sweet-pickle slices I have found, at a fraction of the price for fancy-looking bottles.

AUSTRALIA

The food halls at the entrances to major supermarkets have to be seen to be believed. Shopping is easy and adventuresome in Sydney and Fremantle, with prices that seem very affordable to U.S. and European budgets. Unfortunately, supplies and prices in Darwin—the port most often used by voyagers as a reprovisioning spot—are not quite as good. But they are still better than you'll find anywhere to the west of Darwin.

SINGAPORE

A shoppers' heaven if you can stand the hustle and bustle. Shopping takes longer here than elsewhere, as shops are more specialized and harder to reach due to heavy traffic.

GUAM

Good supply of U.S. goods at U.S. mainland prices because of the presence of a large military base. Low-cost local produce is also available.

INDIAN OCEAN

Supplies and prices are not good anywhere in the Indian Ocean, so stock up seriously before leaving Fremantle, Darwin, or Singapore. You can get what you need at Grand Baie, Mauritius, or on Réunion, but you will pay very high prices.

SRI LANKA

An interesting cruising destination but a necessary evil for those who are in charge of reprovisioning. Variety is limited, and prices for any available imports are high. But you'll have no other dependable reprovisioning ports before South Africa or Israel. The 2004 Tsunami took a terrible toll on the small ports south of Colombo. But according to cruising reports, facilities for cruising boats are mostly restored in Galle as are ships chandlers and small provisioning shops.

SOUTH AFRICA

Durban and Cape Town are your best choices for reprovisioning before heading across the Atlantic. The variety is excellent, with local goods at prices that seem low or modest to Europeans and fair to Americans. Imported goods are available at larger supermarkets in almost every city. We also found exceptional fresh produce at low prices at the farmers' market in Langebaan, a lovely bay with a friendly yacht club, 45 miles north of Cape Town.

KENYA

Good supplies, but prices are higher than in South Africa.

MEDITERRANEAN

The most affordable, easiest reprovisioning ports are at Malta, Cyprus, Rhodes, and Spain. The variety is better in mainland Italy, but prices can be higher. Israel, because of its wide range of immigrants, has surprising variety but sometimes at surprisingly high prices. If you are headed east through the Mediterranean, it doesn't pay to stock up heavily unless you are bound down the Red Sea, as you will not be long between good shopping ports. Westbound, shop as you go, buying the bargains that each country offers, and then do your final provisioning in Spain or Gibraltar before you set off across the Atlantic.

SOUTHERN SOUTH AMERICA

Brazil—The supermarkets of Rio and the public market all have an abundance of fresh vegetables and excellent meat and cheeses. We could not find many of the canned products we were used to carrying, so we had to do a lot of tasting before finding items to fill our lockers for a long passage north to the Azores. There were almost no supplies available at Isla de Noronha, the only easily accessible stop on our route. Coastal villages have very limited supplies.

Uruguay—Punta del Este, a duty-free port, is a favorite shopping spot for Argentineans, who come here on day trips. Therefore, the markets are filled with foreign delicacies. A good place to stock up on canned and packaged goods from Europe.

Argentina—Buenos Aires and Mar del Plata are the only ports with full access to the provisions you will need if you are sailing toward Tierra del Fuego or the Chilean canals. Prices and variety tend to be better in Mar del Plata, which caters to wealthy Argentinean holidaymakers. It pays to search out the wholesale food distribution warehouses for wines and general provisions, and then visit the small specialty shops in the fancier neighborhoods for treats such as pears in Marsala wine (excellent). The public market is definitely the best choice for fresh produce. One item we could not find at all was canned meat. Although Argentina is a major producer of canned corned beef, it is all for export. We did, however, find some in the isolated ports of Patagonia and Tierra del Fuego. Good supplies are available at Punta Arenas. Limited provisions are available at Ushuaia. Excellent fresh meat is available everywhere, even in tiny villages—the best we have ever had.

Chile—Valparaiso, Valdavia, and Puerto Montt are the best provisioning ports for those headed into the Pacific or toward Patagonia. Though there are no formal public markets in Puerto Montt, you will find excellent fresh produce at the stalls set up by farmers in the center of town. We found a far larger assortment of canned and packaged goods here. If you are headed south, it is imperative to carry everything you will need, as there are only three small villages along the Chilean canals, and often the shelves of the tiny shops are completely bare. Limited supplies are available at Puerto Williams, mostly frozen goods and basic canned products, plus the usual excellent wines.

. . . .

Day 5

Noon to noon: 90 miles
Miles to date: 370
Close-hauled, just making our course in an 8-knot breeze;
cloudy

Breakfast
- whole tomatoes
- Japanese pastries
- coffee, tea

Lunch
- chef's salad with shrimp, cheese, ham, tomato, onion, lettuce, cucumber, and Thousand Island dressing

Dinner
- pork chops in sweet-and-sour sauce
- boiled potatoes
- steamed cabbage
- Camembert
- red wine

 PORK CHOPS IN SWEET-AND-SOUR SAUCE

Sauté lightly in oil
- 4 pork chops

Add
- ½ cup ketchup
- 1 tbs. vinegar
- 3 tbs. sugar

Simmer slowly 15 minutes if chops are thin, longer if they are more than ½ inch thick. The same sauce can be used for any sweet-and-sour dish.

Cooking Ahead

We were becalmed when I was preparing dinner, but there was a large swell from the east, dead on our nose. A swell like that can be the forerunner of a good blow. There were no other signs of a storm; the barometer was high, the clouds settled-looking, But just to be safe, I put several extra potatoes into the pot when I was making dinner. Then, after we'd eaten and before I cleaned up the galley, I made the extras into a potato salad for the next day. I've learned the lesson the hard way about preparing food ahead whenever there are signs of a storm. In fact, I've come to the conclusion that whenever I am in the mood to do a bit of extra cooking, it pays to make up something fancy for the days ahead. If the weather stays fine, I end up with some free time to enjoy it. If the weather deteriorates, Larry (and whatever crew I'm with) thinks I am a magician when I produce something more than soup in a mug.

Rudi, the Filipino cook on *Deerleap*, a beautiful cruising power yacht, told me, "It is always calmer in the morning at sea. Either that or you have more patience in the morning. So if you want to cook up something elaborate, do it as soon as you get up or before you wash up the breakfast things."

One other hint he mentioned came to mind as I was preparing the potato salad. "I only peel the potatoes when the owner is on board or when we are entertaining fancy," Rudi told us. "When we are at sea, I think the crew needs all the vitamins they can get, and the vitamins in a potato are all near the skin." I agree wholeheartedly, and I also feel the skins add flavor to any salad. Besides, peeling potatoes is a drag.

Special Provisions

Certain nonfood items are vitally important to long-term cruising people. These include toiletries, medicine, paper products, and cleaning and boat supplies.

Most people who have traveled in foreign countries already know that toilet paper in almost every country other than the United States, England, Australia, and Singapore is rough, poorly packaged, and very expensive. In some places—such as India, Sri Lanka, the South Pacific islands, Africa, and the poorer South American countries—toilet paper is almost impossible to find except in the largest cities. The same is true of that indispensable item, paper towels. So I would advise finding someplace in your boat where you can store a case of toilet paper and a case of paper towels. We find that the odd-shaped area around the water tank under *Seraffyn's* cockpit can hold

36 rolls of plastic-wrapped paper towels plus 80 rolls of toilet paper. These last us about five or six months. Every time we are low, we start looking for another case.

Special cosmetics, shampoo, and lotions should also be bought in quantities to last for at least a year. These, along with sun-protection lotions, are most easily found in resort areas—if necessary, in the fancier hotels. But if there is a brand name you vastly prefer, stock up when you see it. I know that between Israel and Malaysia there are absolutely no places to find toiletries we recognize, and the quality of such local products as hand soap and shampoo is poor. Tampons and sanitary napkins are the one exception. Mary Baldwin, who hitchiked around the South Pacific islands for a year on board three different cruising boats, laughed when she told me how she'd given up valuable space in her rucksack for a year's supply of sanitary products—only to find that they were easily available even in more primitive places. One comment on tampons: Be sure to store any opened package in a sealed plastic bag; otherwise, the cotton will absorb moisture and the whole tampon will be useless.

Birth-control pills and medications for your medical kit are actually easier to find and buy in primitive countries than they are in the United States, England, or continental Europe. They are also much cheaper. Be sure to have your doctor give you the generic names of any drugs you may need, as brand-name items are rarely available in foreign ports. Then go directly to the pharmacy in almost any country; you'll find you can buy drugs without prescriptions at about 1/4 to 1/2 of the American price. I have asked doctors from various countries about the advisability of buying medicine in foreign countries. They all assure me that drugs worldwide are carefully manufactured and packaged, mostly by American, British, French, German, and Swiss companies. Ask to see the package before you buy your pills. The generic names are the same no matter where the pills were packaged, so you can make sure you are getting the right one. At the same time, check the expiration date on the label, if there is one. Carry a written prescription for any narcotic-containing drug you have on board. This way, officials will know your drugs are for legitimate uses.

Standard household cleaning products such as scouring soap, dish soap, and scouring pads are easy to find worldwide, though you'll often have to use local brands, which may smell different from those to which you are accustomed. Scotch-Brite pads are available worldwide; in less-developed areas, they are sold by the square meter. Bleach is one item that you should buy when you see it—especially in the South Pacific and Indonesia, where you'll probably want some for water purification.

One of the real curses of the cruising sailor's life is buying boat supplies and parts. Even in the United States, it is difficult to find the specialized items needed for yachts in any ports that don't specifically cater to sailors. Stock up with spares before you leave; carry a magnet with you whenever you shop for any nonferrous items. The only places where you have a good chance to find items such as stainless-steel bolts or screws, bronze or stainless rigging items, bronze screws, sailmaker's dacron thread, and sailcloth are Southern California; eastern U.S. yacht harbors; Puerto Rico; Antigua and St. Thomas in the Caribbean; England; the Baltic countries; northern Italy, Gibraltar, and Malta in the Mediterranean; Singapore; Australia and New Zealand in the South Pacific; and Hawaii in the North Pacific. With boat parts and supplies even more than with food items, it's a real case of "it's cheaper to carry extra." And we've found that any spare bits and pieces we haven't needed have made great gifts or trading items as we cruised. Spare thread and scraps of sailcloth earned us several new friends in both Malaysia and the Philippines.

Basic electrical repair gear is much easier to find. Electrical tape, simple connections, and various gauges of wire are available worldwide. But any boat specialties—such as electronic taffrail logs or the special circuitry to keep them running and 12-volt lightbulbs—are difficult to find when you go foreign. Simple batteries for flashlights and such are cheap and available in the more out-of-the-way places. But if you use any sizes other than C, D, or square 6-volt batteries, carry spares.

Don't depend on being able to get any engine parts as you voyage. Even engine oil can be a problem, and you should definitely buy transmission oil by the case and carry it with you. Write to the manufacturer of your engine before you set sail and request a list of parts dealers in the area in which you plan to cruise; if there are no dealers, find out whom you can contact to have parts shipped when you require them. Then visit a shop that repairs engines such as yours, ask what parts are likely to give trouble as you voyage, and stock up on spares and any special tools required to change them. *And then double-check to make sure you have purchased the right spares and tools.*

I know this list seems to have gone beyond the scope of this book. But I know of several hundred sailing people who spent three times as long looking for engine-repair parts as they did shopping for all the food for a 2,000-mile voyage. Some foresight in this area will free the whole crew for that sightseeing tour during the last few days before you set off from another interesting port-of-call.

E-mail and fax machines have definitely improved a cruiser's chances of locating and purchasing special spare parts and reducing (to some degree) shopping hassles. Before you set sail, make a list of e-mail and snailmail addresses and fax numbers of each parts supplier and each maker of any equipment that may be vital for your voyaging style. Once offshore, even if you order by e-mail, it pays to send a backup fax. Not only is it easier to do a sketch of the product you are ordering this way, but your fax back up serves as a hard copy which can be presented to customs officials and also is easy for you to access without the need to boot up a computer. To order accurately with a fax, be sure to include as much information as possible: the make, the model, the serial number of the machine you are repairing, and a sketch of the broken part. Or, if you have a parts diagram, include a photocopy with the required part circled. Be sure to request a confirmation of receipt of the order, plus the exact posting date, shipping method, and shipping address used. It may cost a few dollars extra, but it could prevent a long, frustrating delay. A couple in the Cocos-Keeling Islands kept expecting their new GPS, ordered from a major U.S. mail-order firm, to arrive any day, as they had specified shipment via air-freight express. After waiting three weeks, they spent $60 telephoning the United States, only to be told, "Your fax did not definitely order a GPS; it only asked whether we could supply it at the price quoted. We've been waiting for your order." This delay made our friends late for a voyage to the Chagos Archipelago and up through the Red Sea, and deteriorating weather gave them a far rougher trip than they normally would have had.

There are two companies that we have used for special spares over the years. They handle mail, online or fax orders and ship them to overseas destinations very competently. There are probably several others, but these are two about which we have heard absolutely no complaints:

Jamestown Distributors
17 Peckham Drive
Bristol, Rhode Island 02809
Phone: 1-800-497-0010, 1-401-253-3840
Fax: 1-401-254-5829
Website: www.jamestowndistributors.com

West Marine International Direct Sales
P.O. Box 50070
Watsonville, California 95077
Phone: 1-800-262-8464 (from North America), 1-831-761-4800
Fax: 1-831-761-4020
Website: www.westmarine.com

(West Marine has toll-free phone numbers for many countries. These are listed on their website.)

Both companies will send you complete catalogs by airmail (or you can download catalogs in PDF format from their websites). Jamestown is more of a builders' supply house, specializing in fastenings of all sorts—from stainless steel to bronze to alloy, from exotic bolts to common rivets, plus a wide assortment of electrical parts. West Marine carries everything found in the biggest marine stores—from books and charts to sailing clothes, electronic gear, and outboard motors—but does not have a comprehensive supply of fasteners. On the other hand, we have found that both companies will scout out things you require that are not part of their regular inventory.

West Marine has compiled a list of guidelines for those who wish to use their services as they voyage offshore. A few are definitely worth quoting:

> Out of stock items. Due to high shipping costs resulting from separate shipments, we prefer not to ship backordered items at a later date. Please tell us when you order if you wish to have us hold all items until the order is complete. Otherwise, we will cancel the item, refund your money and notify you of the cancellation.
>
> If you wish to have a large order sent by sea please designate a freight forwarder and provide the following: Freight forwarder's full business name, address, phone and/or fax number along with the complete forwarding address and phone number.
>
> Hazardous or toxic items such as paint, flares, fire extinguishers, batteries, epoxies, compressed gas and some cleaners cannot be shipped to international destinations [due to restrictions by couriers].
>
> Current recommended methods of shipping are:
>
> Federal Express Economy Air:
> Fast, traceable service. Usually less expensive than airmail.
> Average delivery to major overseas cities, 4 to 5 days.
>
> DHL:
> Fast, traceable service. Usually less expensive than FedEx.
> Average delivery, 5 days.
>
> Air Parcel Post:
> 2 to 3 weeks delivery, not traceable.
>
> Surface Mail:
> 1 to 5 months, not traceable.
>
> Customs procedures and charges vary from country to country. West Marine is not responsible for any costs, delays or problems caused by shippers or customs once the shipment leaves our warehouse. Please check with local officials to get a cost estimate before placing your order.
>
> We will gladly exchange, replace, or credit items. The customer will remain responsible for shipping costs when returning goods.

The same general guidelines apply to any reputable mail-order house with whom we have dealt. A final important rule to remember is to have any package clearly marked, "For the yacht [insert your yacht name] IN TRANSIT. [insert your yacht's country of documentation] documented yacht." By doing this, you will usually eliminate all customs clearance requirements and customs duties. Small packets with this written on them are usually sent through just like regular letters.

Although e-mail and faxes have made ordering spare parts and communicating with sales and tech people easier, they have not solved the problem of customs clearance or lessened the hassles of freight forwarding. Restrictive trading practices, tighter security policies on airlines, and antiterrorist precautions have added new considerations. Therefore, more than ever, it pays to take along spare parts and/or make sure you can sail onward and have nonworking gear repaired when you reach a port with easy communications.

We know of one cruiser who paid US$238 for freight and clearance to have 3 pounds of spare parts shipped from the United States to Nuku Hiva in the Marquesas. Meanwhile, he waited three weeks for the parts to arrive. Had he sailed about 600 miles downwind to Tahiti, the cost would have been $128, delivery time four days. Had he sailed another 600 miles to American Samoa, the freight would have been $28, the wait time two days.

We learned an interesting lesson in Bermuda when our main compass developed a worn bearing. There were no compass experts on the island, so we contacted a firm in Boston that offered overnight-turnaround repair service. The local FedEx agent recommended that we take the compass to Bermuda Customs and have them issue a certificate indicating that the item was being repaired and returned. We had the repair people in Boston attach a copy of the certificate to the outside of the package. Our compass, with this document attached, came through customs without delay and without charge, and it was back on board only four days after we sent it off.

. . . .

Day 6

Noon to noon: 40 miles
Miles to date: 410
Becalmed; warm and sunny

Breakfast
melon
cheese
coffee, tea

Lunch
hard-boiled eggs
potato salad
tomatoes and lettuce
orange juice and nougat candies

Teatime
last of the Japanese pastries

Dinner
homemade tomato-vegetable soup
Salisbury steak (i.e., thick seasoned hamburger patties, no bun)
canned potato chips

. . . .

TOMATO-VEGETABLE SOUP

Put in soup pot
4 large (or 6 medium) tomatoes

Add
1 cup saltwater
1 cup freshwater

Boil
Bring to a boil for 5 minutes.
▼

Remove tomatoes and let them cool until you can easily remove skins and stems. Return tomato "meat" to pot.

Add

12 small cloves garlic, chopped
4 carrots, scrubbed and sliced
1 large onion, chopped
¾ cup shredded cabbage
1 tsp. oregano
3 tbs. sugar
3 cubes beef bouillon

Boil an additional
15 to 20 minutes until
carrots are tender.

....

On Weight Loss

DAY 6. *For the first 10 days at sea, you feast on fresh food, trying to use perishables before they go bad.*

I spent part of this morning checking over the vegetables in the forepeak. We had all of the hatches open, the sea was very smooth, and I'm starting to get my energy back.

One thing of which I'm sure is that I'll never buy vegetables of any kind from a ship chandler unless there is simply no other choice. The cabbages the chandler sent are already starting to show signs of rot where they became bruised in handling. I peeled off one layer of outer leaves on each cabbage,

84

cut a thin sliver off the bottom of the stem, and turned them so they rested on a different spot in their basket. I took careful count of my tomatoes. Because of the gift crate that arrived the morning we were setting sail, I know we will have too many to last. That's why I decided to make a soup.

I'm starting to lose a bit of weight now, just as I always do at sea, no matter how much I eat and no matter whether or not I have been seasick. Larry isn't quite so lucky, and when I read this last paragraph to him today during our cocktail hour, we got into a discussion of why some people lose weight on sailing voyages.

From the moment you leave harbor on a yacht, your body is moving, even though you aren't aware of it. Your muscles are tensing and relaxing according to each bit of motion. Even when you are sleeping, sitting, or lounging on deck, you are burning calories that you wouldn't use up on land. Of course, the amount of weight you'll lose, or the extra quantity of food you'll eat to maintain your weight, depends on how long you've been sailing, how big or complicated the boat is, how many sail changes you have to make, and what kind of wind and sea conditions you encounter.

On *Seraffyn's* first few voyages, we were busy all of the time we were at sea—changing, modifying, experimenting. Larry would be adjusting the sails every half-hour to get more speed out of whatever wind we had. He spent hours playing with the adjustments on Helmer, our self-steering gear, and tore through our collection of spare junk almost every day, looking for the right piece of gear to make a different adjustment lever or a better bracket for something on board. So he tended to lose weight on any voyage that lasted more than five days. Now, on board *Taleisin* almost four decades later, all the bugs are worked out of the rig. The windvane works perfectly, our spinnaker-pole arrangement is so simple I can handle it alone, the reefing gear is really "jiffy." Larry knows the exact adjustment that gets the most out of the sails. There is almost nothing to do on the boat at sea other than routine checking of gear and changing of sails. So Larry rarely loses a pound. On the other hand, when we were delivering a 50-ton ketch from the Mediterranean to New Orleans, Larry lost weight even though he ate like a horse—including egg, toast, and pancake breakfasts. He spent two or three hours a day in the engine room of that 60-footer; he varnished; he spliced up rigging replacements; he had to horse up a temporary 4-by-4, 22-foot-long, 60-pound whisker pole. And, after all that, he had to stand behind the wheel steering six hours a day, just like the rest of the crew.

When we did an Inland Waterway delivery, powering most of the way, both of us gained weight. We sat and steered all day, with no sail changing. There was no sea motion to keep our bodies active. Because of the constant steering necessary in the canals, meals were all that broke up the day, so we ate more snacks and meals.

One lesson we've learned the hard way is that an exercise program is essential when you've chosen cruising as a way of life. On any small boat at sea, your legs just don't get enough use. Your knees grow weak, while your arms and shoulders get stronger. It really helps to have a regular program of knee bends and leg exercises for 10 minutes each day on long passages. I do mine on my night watches on deck in calmer weather. If you are on a delivery and have to steer each watch, it's easy to exercise right at the helm. When you reach port after a long passage, try to get a bit of extra leg exercise—walking without carrying a big load, bicycle riding, or even dancing to the local band.[5]

Buying Meat in Foreign Countries

Jill and I were walking down the main street of Turtle Bay in Baja California, exploring while her crew took on diesel. She was on a northbound delivery trip; I was on one going south. Around one corner, we spotted the local equivalent of a butcher. A man stood on the dirt road in front of his home, using a hatchet to split a side of beef into chunks. The beef lay on an old wooden spool that had once held telephone cables. Only inches away from the pile of yellow and maroon meat, snarling dogs fought for chunks of bone and fat. "Sure glad I don't have to buy meat here," Jill commented. Both she and I still had loads of fresh food from the supermarkets of Southern California.

Turtle Bay's butcher was one of the worst I've seen. But as you cruise, you'll find that meat markets and butchers vary greatly from those you are used to at home. Some may be far fancier than you expect, while others, even well into this new millennium, may be extremely basic. But one aspect is universal: Butchers outside the United States do not use the same cutting methods, and almost none of them age beef beyond the time it takes to carry the slaughtered animal to the marketplace. Certain pointers will help you select usable meat no matter how primitive the marketplace.

PORK

Pork (see fig. 2) is by far the safest meat to buy in any country. I have never bought a tough piece of pork. Though foreign pigs rarely have as much fat as U.S. pigs do, the flavor is usually the same. Any cut of pork other than

. . . .

5   Over the 49 days this voyage lasted, I lost 15 pounds, arriving in Victoria looking wonderfully svelte. Larry lost about 8 pounds over the same period.

the lowest part of the leg can be barbecued or fried for tender, tasty chops. To keep the pork fresh for more than a day, rinse off any bone chips, blood, or foreign matter with freshwater. Dry the meat completely. Then store it in a loosely covered metal or ceramic container and set it right on the ice. I use a large salad bowl for all of the meat I buy at one time. I use sheets of aluminum foil to separate the various types of meat, then I cover the whole container lightly with a paper towel. Do not use plastic bags for any meat you plan to keep more than three days; it will hasten decay. Pork will last up to seven days at the 34- to 38-degree (F) temperatures that are close to the ice in your cold box. If the pork should get yellow slime on it, wash the meat in freshwater and rub it with a dishcloth dipped in a mixture of equal parts vinegar and freshwater. Pat the meat dry, and, if it smells fresh, cook it within 12 hours. If the meat takes on a green hue, discard it.

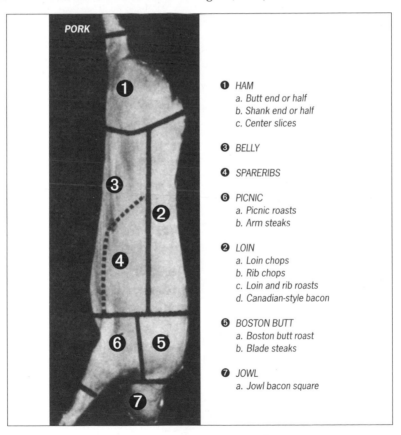

❶ HAM
 a. Butt end or half
 b. Shank end or half
 c. Center slices

❸ BELLY

❹ SPARERIBS

❻ PICNIC
 a. Picnic roasts
 b. Arm steaks

❷ LOIN
 a. Loin chops
 b. Rib chops
 c. Loin and rib roasts
 d. Canadian-style bacon

❺ BOSTON BUTT
 a. Boston butt roast
 b. Blade steaks

❼ JOWL
 a. Jowl bacon square

FIGURE 2. *Pork—Wholesale and Retail Cuts*

Section 2 would definitely be my first choice for barbecue or grilling. Sections 5 and 1 bake nicely. But 7, 6, 3, and 4 tend to be quite fatty.

Trichinosis bacteria die at 140 degrees F (60 degrees C). This is the same temperature as the middle of a piece of rare beef. So as long as you cook any pork products until the meat is white throughout, this disease is no problem.

BEEF

Beef (see fig. 3) lasts longer on ice than pork does, but it is far more difficult to get a piece that is sure to be tender enough to fry or barbecue. American and English cattle are usually grain-fed and confined in pens for at least a month before they are slaughtered. Everywhere else, including Australia and New Zealand, cattle is range-fed. I've come to really like the flavor and texture of Australian beef, which is what you'll find (frozen) in most of the Far East. But the uninitiated will notice the difference. Fresh beef from almost every other place we've been tends to be tough. Even the sirloin

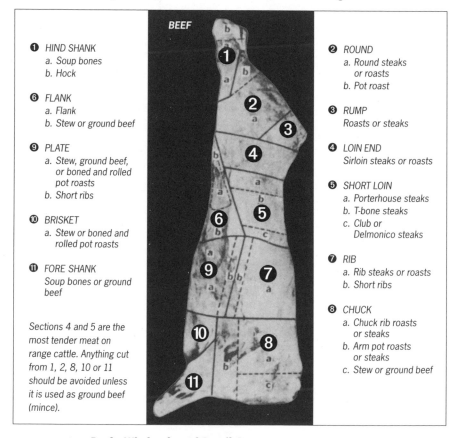

BEEF

❶ HIND SHANK
   a. Soup bones
   b. Hock

❻ FLANK
   a. Flank
   b. Stew or ground beef

❾ PLATE
   a. Stew, ground beef,
     or boned and rolled
     pot roasts
   b. Short ribs

❿ BRISKET
   a. Stew or boned and
     rolled pot roasts

⓫ FORE SHANK
   Soup bones or ground
   beef

Sections 4 and 5 are the most tender meat on range cattle. Anything cut from 1, 2, 8, 10 or 11 should be avoided unless it is used as ground beef (mince).

❷ ROUND
   a. Round steaks
     or roasts
   b. Pot roast

❸ RUMP
   Roasts or steaks

❹ LOIN END
   Sirloin steaks or roasts

❺ SHORT LOIN
   a. Porterhouse steaks
   b. T-bone steaks
   c. Club or
     Delmonico steaks

❼ RIB
   a. Rib steaks or roasts
   b. Short ribs

❽ CHUCK
   a. Chuck rib roasts
     or steaks
   b. Arm pot roasts
     or steaks
   c. Stew or ground beef

FIGURE 3. Beef—Wholesale and Retail Cuts

● Numbers in circles refer to wholesale cuts and major subdivisions of such cuts. Letters refer to retail cuts.

cuts can need 40 minutes of stewing or 24 hours of marinating to make them tender.

The only cut that is usually tender enough for frying is the filet, the 2- to 2½-foot-long, cigar-shaped strip of meat found inside the rib cage next to the backbone of the animal. Don't pay the price for filet unless you've actually seen the butcher remove it from the ribs. Otherwise, you might end up with a piece of extremely tough leg muscle that looks similar. Second choice would be the sirloin, which comes from the opposite side of the rib bones and is halfway back from the shoulder of the animal (where the saddle would sit). Anything else is bound to be stewing or grinding meat. Wherever possible, avoid buying leg meat unless you plan to cook it for a minimum of 1½ hours. Even if you grind leg meat, it can be stringy and tough.

Almost any cut of beef other than leg meat can be used for ground or minced beef. If you are having the butcher grind it for you, make sure he doesn't put it through the grinder more than once. Otherwise, it will be finer than the hamburger North Americans are used to. Also, ask the butcher to add some fat. If they don't grind at least 15 percent of fat into them, hamburger patties will not hold together and will tend to be much too dry. The fat adds more flavor as well. (For health reasons, be sure the butcher does not grind the beef using the same machine he just used for pork.) Hamburger or ground beef will not keep as long as whole pieces of beef. I find that regular beef keeps eight days on ice, ground beef only four or five. This is one of the reasons I recommend carrying on board a portable hand-operated meat grinder, which you can buy for less than $12 in the United States.

Beef will turn a darker color as it ages, but it is safe to eat as long as it smells good and has no green or mold on it. Cut off any green parts, and if the inside meat looks and smells good, use it. Beef liver and kidneys also keep very well. Try to buy pieces that come from a young-looking animal.

Occasionally, even in countries that usually slaughter only old dairy cows for meat, you'll find a good young animal whose sirloin meat will be very tender. Look for a carcass with very white fat and marbling or white streaks in the sirloin meat. To age the meat yourself, wash off any foreign matter, dry the meat, then place it in the ice chest on a cloth-covered tray or plate for four or five days, turning it over once a day. This will help tenderize the meat.

HORSEMEAT

Horsemeat is sold in many European markets, usually in a completely separate area from more common meats. The flesh is a deeper red than beef and has no fat at all. When cooked, it's much drier but tastes almost like beef. I haven't had much experience with horsemeat, but I did once purchase some by accident. It made a tasty but dry meatloaf.

LAMB

Lamb (see fig. 4) and goat both look the same once they are cut up. They often taste the same. Only the rib chops are sure to be tender enough for grilling or frying. Once again, try to get the chops that are near the saddle of the animal. Marinating other cuts in a mixture of 1/2 oil, 1/4 vinegar, and 1/4 white wine, plus any spices you prefer, for 12 to 24 hours in the icebox will make the tougher cuts tender enough for shish kebab. Otherwise, stew them at least 35 to 40 minutes. Ground lamb or goat is just as usable as ground beef.

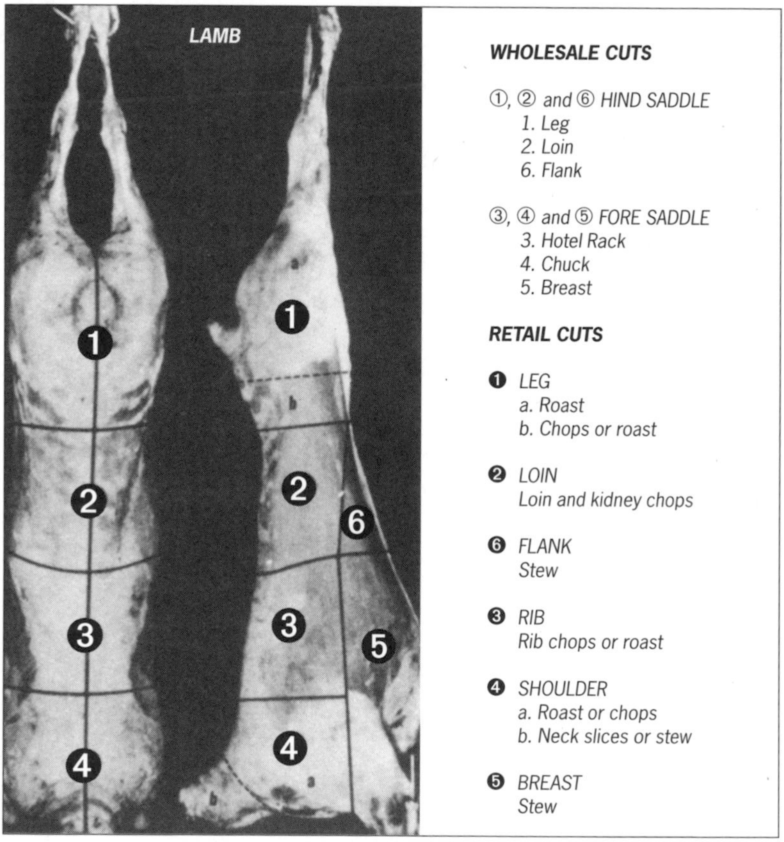

FIGURE 4. Lamb—Wholesale and Retail Cuts

● *Numbers in circles refer to wholesale cuts. Letters refer to retail cuts. I would prefer cuts from section 2, 3, or the top of 1, as these tend to be less fatty.*

CHICKEN

Although several countries now sell frying chickens already cut and frozen, you'll find that live chickens are normally slaughtered to your order. A chicken that weighs more than 5 pounds is probably too tough to fry. A live chicken loses a third of its weight when it is plucked and cleaned. They are sold with head and feet intact, since many foreign recipes use these for soup and gravies. If you buy a frozen chicken that is locally grown, don't be surprised to pull out the head and feet along with the liver and gizzards.

This is a typical sight in public markets through out South America, freshly plucked poultry complete with heads and feet.

If you are buying a ready-plucked chicken, don't be put off by the yellow color of the skin. This comes from different feeding methods. Test the chicken for tenderness by pressing on the end of the breastbone nearest the neck. If it is as flexible as the end of your nose, or only a bit firmer, the chicken is young and probably just what you want. If the end of the breastbone is tough, plan on using the meat for stewing, boiling, or slow baking.

Unless you want small, unidentifiable chunks of chicken, learn to cut up the birds yourself. You'll need a good chopping board and a very sharp, thick-bladed knife, plus only one or two birds for practice. I learned this after I watched in amazement while a Mexican butcher took his hatchet to my chicken. Before I could say a word, he handed me 25 or 30 1 1/2-inch chunks when I had planned to make Southern fried chicken. Chicken rinsed and dried keeps for five or six days on ice.

SAUSAGES

Cooking sausages in many countries are not seasoned in the same way as the ones at home, so taste the local ones before you invest heavily. On the other hand, as you travel, you'll discover many kinds of smoked and cooked sausages that are delicious. These keep well without refrigeration for up to two months. Hang them in any airy place; if mold starts to grow, wipe the sausage with a rag dipped in equal parts vinegar and freshwater; then let them dry. When we sailed from Poland, we had 40 pounds of smoked sausage hung in our chain locker. We ate the last ones in England two months later. On a delivery from Spain, we carried 30 pounds of *chorizo blanco* and 10 pounds of *chorizo rojo*—two types of tasty garlic sausage. They make great snacks, sliced thinly and served on crackers. Cut in bite-size chunks, the sausage added spice to stews and rice dishes. The last piece made a tasty soup 60 days later, as we approached the United States. When shopping for sausages, just indicate that you want a small sample. Almost any vendor will slice off a small piece for a serious-looking customer.

BACON

Sides of smoked bacon are a wonderful addition to an offshore crew's diet. We've bought complete sides, drilled a hole through one corner, and hung them from the beams in the chain locker for four weeks at a time. When mold formed on the outside, we left it until the time came to slice pieces to cook. A vinegar-and-water scrubbing removed the mold. The bacon was great fried, grilled, and added to mixed dishes.

If you don't have room to hang bacon or sausages, dip a rag in vinegar, let it dry, then use the rag to wrap the meat so it is covered completely. Wrap the resulting package in newspaper and store in a cool, airy place.

·······

In Australia, a land of heavy meat eaters, many butchers will vacuum-pack meat portions. This prolongs the life of all meats—corned, smoked, and fresh. Unrefrigerated but cool corned or salted meat will keep for up to five days in vacuum packs. Fresh vacuum-packed meat will last up to three days if kept below 60 degrees F. With refrigeration or on ice, vacuum-packed fresh meat can be kept for up to three weeks, and salted or smoked meat will last two months. Since we left Australia, I have found that at least one butcher in most larger towns will have a vacuum-packing machine. Ask the butcher to put one meal-size portion in each bag or pack. Choose meat that has not been previously frozen.

In South Africa, butchers will often add various premade marinades or spice combinations to your vacuum pack at little extra cost.

For new ways to preserve meat for voyaging, look at old farmers' cookbooks. I found great recipes for pickling, canning, and potting meat in a 1920 farmers' almanac in a New Zealand secondhand bookshop. When I try some, I'll pass them along.

Don't be shy about trying game meat and fowl as you cruise. In South Africa and Namibia, it is sometimes on offer at butcher shops for lower prices than more common meats. We've found game such as kudu, buffalo, and springbok—which are drier than beef but tasty. I always plan a marinade or sauce with game.

Wildfowl, such as guinea fowl and ostrich, are tasty, although drier than chicken. But duck of any variety, wild or domesticated, is fatter than chicken.

Biltong (dried meat made from beef or wild game) is extremely common in Australia and South Africa. Usually it is served as an appetizer—dry, salty, and chewy. But when fresh meat stores dwindle, it can be reconstituted by soaking it in freshwater for three hours. Then add it to stews or sauces. It can also be added as is and simmered 20 minutes for a different texture. Either way, it adds extra spice to rice or pasta dishes.

One final word on buying meat products in foreign ports. Few people in the world can afford to buy large pieces of meat as North Americans do. In most underdeveloped countries, meat is used as a seasoning to be added to rice or beans—or, as in Mexico, to be wrapped inside tortillas. So don't be surprised when you find most meat cut up into tiny chunks, or chops and steak sliced 5/8-inch thick. With patience and lots of sign language, you can persuade the butcher to cut your chops 3/4-inch thick, and to leave on some of the fat when he trims your steaks.

When you are stocking up for a passage, overbuy on meat just a bit. I find that we rarely catch fish during the first few days at sea, so we welcome the fresh meat for our main meals. The life of excess fresh meat can be extended three days beyond its normal limit or three days beyond the life of your ice. Just cook up any meat you have left and leave it in a pot on top of the stove. Reheat it each morning until the liquid in the pot comes to a full boil, simmer two minutes, and cover tightly. Then let the closed pot of meat sit until the next day. Even hamburger will last for three days without refrigeration. Two weeks after you leave port, the crew will be pleased to be served an Irish stew or spaghetti Bolognese that tastes just like the fresh food found onshore.

. . . .

Day 7

Noon to noon: 44 miles
Miles to date: 454
Light breeze from the south
Slight surge from the south
Afternoon: beam-reaching with 8 or 10 knots of wind

Breakfast
 biscuits
 cheese
 jam
 coffee, tea

Lunch
 fresh rye bread
 ham slices
 tomatoes
 hot leftover soup

Dinner
 tossed salad with last of our lettuce, tomatoes
 onion, shrimp, and cucumber in Lin's special dressing
 pork chunks in wine sauce
 rice (including extra for use tomorrow)
 white wine

· ·

SPECIAL DRESSING

Mix together
 remains of broken egg (about ½ scrambled raw egg)
 2 tbs. salad oil
 1 tbs. vinegar
 1 tbs. Parmesan cheese
 ▼

1 tsp. Worcestershire sauce
½ tsp. garlic powder
½ tsp. oregano
Let sit 10 minutes before using.

....

PORK CHUNKS IN WINE SAUCE

Sauté

    ½ lb. pork chunks
    1 tsp. slivered fresh ginger
    1 tsp. oil

Add

    ½ cup white wine
    1 tbs. soy sauce
    Simmer 10 minutes.
    Thicken with a bit of cornstarch and bring to a boil.

Add

    1 onion, sliced
    1 green pepper, sliced

> Cover and remove from heat. Let sit 5 minutes, then serve over rice. (Onions and peppers should still be crisp.)

....

DAY 7. *Sorting out the various fruits and vegetables only takes a few minutes every other day.*

I had to throw out a cantaloupe today—I didn't think they'd last too well. I should have invested in thicker-skinned melons, such as watermelons. I have had 3-pound watermelons that lasted up to four weeks in hot climates like the Red Sea in August.

We've been having very light winds since we left Yokohama, so we've only covered 454 miles in six days. Being a worrywart at times like these, I begin to do some arithmetic. If we continued at the same rate, we'd average 76 miles a day, and it would take 52 more days to get to Canada. Then I begin to wonder if I have enough food. Looking back at our worst passage ever, the time we drifted painfully across the Arabian Sea at an average speed of 62 miles a day, taking 32 days to cover 2,200 miles, I realize my fears are unfounded. Even if we do take 52 more days, there is lots of food. The variety might not be too inspired by the time we get there, but we'll keep right on eating.

Just before noon, the winds freshened, and we started making 5 knots through the water. There is a 3/4-knot current with us. Now I'm dreaming of 120 miles a day; if we could keep up that pace, it would mean only 31 days to go.

We ate lunch in the warm, steady cockpit. The fresh, hot bread smelled delicious and tasted even better when spread with well-salted Australian butter. Two Japanese fishboats passed us while we ate. Gulls glided over the sparkling swells, diving for any crumbs we threw them. All is right with my world.

Food for Thought

one potato, two potato, three potato, four,
five potato, six potato, should have bought some more

The childhood chant was in perfect rhythm with my chore. I'd brace myself on "four" as *Taleisin's* stern rose to each following trade-wind swell and then relax my body as her bow surged upward and a rush of water cascaded along the hull for "more." The "potatoes" I was counting were just that, perfect potatoes—red-skinned potatoes, new potatoes, Irish potatoes, sweet potatoes. They were part of the collection of the finest produce I'd ever had on board for a long passage.

Fremantle, Western Australia, had been a yacht provisioner's heaven. Because of its large and diverse European population, I had had a choice of grocery wholesalers. After a round of visits to two dozen ethnic shops, Australian canned goods competed with Italian, Greek, British, and U.S.

specialty items to fill my canned-goods locker spaces with color and variety. As a major fishing port, Fremantle's ship's provenders had lists of duty-free items that made me drool. But a careful check of their prices showed that the huge supermarkets, only a short bike ride from the sailing club, actually offered better prices—except for those items rarely used by shore-based families, such as canned butter and canned Camembert. But best of all, Fremantle had a true farmers' market each weekend, a huge tent-covered area filled with stalls selling the finest and freshest produce I'd ever seen—Chinese cabbages, spring peas, and kale organically grown by a local Chinese family; golden-yolked eggs gathered freshly that morning by a farmer who fed his chickens lettuce leaves he recycled from his produce-selling neighbors each market day; onions, potatoes, lettuce; and tomatoes unwashed, unbrushed, and fresh from the open-air market that morning so they'd keep for days extra as we sailed to the isolated atolls of the Indian Ocean. When we finally set off toward the Cocos-Keeling Islands in early July 1992, my forepeak looked like a miniature reflection of the produce market. Five large plastic laundry baskets nestled securely on the forward bunk, full to the brim with fruit and vegetables.

Ten days out of Fremantle, I was in the midst of my third inspection of the slowly dwindling selection of produce. I'd selected vegetables and fruit of varying degrees of ripeness for the voyage—a few almost-red tomatoes for the first days out, some with red creeping over the sides, most almost green. Avocados were the same—some already soft for the first few days of the trip, a few rock-hard for later in the passage. Now I inspected everything for bruises or signs of decay. I set aside an almost-ripe avocado, some tangerines, two glowing tomatoes, and an onion with the first sign of a green spout at its tip to use in the day's cooking. I laughed as I remembered how easy it had been to fill *Taleisin* to the brim and watch her boottop edge even closer to the water in Fremantle. It hadn't always been that easy.

I remember my growing concern when I inspected the empty shelves in Aden's markets in South Yemen after sailing down the Red Sea in August 1977 on board our 24-foot cutter *Seraffyn*. Although we'd stocked to overflowing in Malta and again in Israel, a month in Egypt and 15 days of sailing down the Red Sea had made serious inroads. My fresh provisions had dwindled to less than a dozen onions and half a dozen potatoes. Ahead of us lay 2,200 miles of Arabian Sea. Three days of searching onshore had turned up absolutely no fresh produce other than three rough-looking cabbages. The one ship chandler still in operation in the civil-war-torn, Marxist-run port opened the warehouse for us to provide an abundant stock of liquor and wine, stacks of English canned meat pies, and several cases of Skippy peanut butter. In turn, the chandler asked me if I'd sell him some sugar or rice from my supplies. In desperation, I sought help from the British manager of the BP oil company. His wife organized a collection among the ever-dwindling colony of expatriate oil workers and two days later presented me with a carefully packed basket containing two dozen fresh eggs. Imagine my horror as I turned to say good-bye, slipped on the smooth varnishwork of the elegant staircase, and fell. Somehow I survived the fall down half a dozen steps and sustained only a bruised elbow, skinned knee, twisted ankle, and one slightly cracked egg.

My final attempt at increasing our produce supplies required a mile-long row across the windswept harbor to the only foreign freighter in port. The cook, a Singaporean with a sorely tried sense of humor, explained that they too were suffering after being held in port by the political upheaval for more than two months. But the cook went through their dwindling stocks and traded us 20 onions and 15 potatoes for a few bottles of wine and some yeast I felt I could spare.

My meager supply of fresh provisions barely filled one small washbasin as we set out on a passage fraught with calms and slow sailing. Yet 36 days later, when we arrived in Sri Lanka, I still had two onions left for our first dinner at anchor. We both were in good health and I'd learned a dozen new ways to used the canned provisions, but I admit to being desperate at that point for a tomato, a piece of fruit, anything with the inimitable texture of freshness.

Our provisioning problems in Japan in 1978 presented an interesting contrast to those in Aden. An absolutely amazing variety of fresh produce greeted me when I visited the local market stalls. Each piece of fruit, each vegetable I saw was perfect. Many were nestled in protective individual baskets and laid out in magnificent, perfectly symmetrical displays. My mouth watered as I pictured the supplies I'd carry for our 4,600-mile passage to Canada. Then I asked the prices. "Apples are very low price right now," the young Japanese sailor who'd offered to translate told me. "Only $2 [U.S.] each. Last month they cost $5." I got out some paper and had him write down the prices, just to be sure I wasn't confused. Yes, tomatoes cost US$14 a kilo, lettuce $5 each, and cabbage about $7 each!

I took the train to Tokyo to find a ship chandler. The duty-free price list he showed me was extensive, and I ordered Philippine frozen prawns at US$1.80 a pound (the local people were paying $16 a pound), Australian beef sirloin at $1.50 a pound (the locals were paying $28 a pound), a Black & White whiskey at $3 a fifth. But the prices of fresh vegetables, even in 50-kilo sacks, were staggering; potatoes were still more than $3 a pound, onions the same.

Even though I couldn't speak a word of Polish, I still found ways to communicate at the marketplace.

After careful soul-searching I forked over US$400 (in 1978, that would have been enough for us to cruise for more than six weeks) for a carefully considered but adequate supply of fresh produce, including an extravagance on my part: 24 fresh tomatoes. I was glad Larry was otherwise occupied when the vegetables arrived the day before our departure. As I checked the items off the list, noting the perfection of each piece of fruit, each melon, each vegetable, my throat constricted when I read, "24 tomatoes, $56."

We weren't quite prepared for the farewell party that had secretly been planned for the next morning. Japanese friends we'd made during our month's stay mingled with yacht-club officials, and a dozen crews prepared their boats to sail out with us. My knowledge of local prices gave me a real appreciation for the six ears of perfect sweet corn one friend gave us and for the gift-wrapped cantaloupe another presented. But it was almost a week later—when we were 900 miles east of Yokohama and I was desperately trying to use up every single piece of ripening produce—that I finally showed Larry the receipts for what I had bought. Then he understood my tears and laughter when the commodore of the Yokohama Shimin Yacht Club had presented us with a case of perfect, glowing ripe tomatoes as a farewell gift.

Provisioning as you voyage is both an adventure and a challenge. I often have a bout of concern just before we set sail on a long passage (even after 38 years and more than 180,000 miles of passagemaking). Did I buy enough, or should I search the shops one more time for something more exciting? Will there be enough variety or will we get bored with what I cook up? Yet I know my concerns are basically unfounded. With 40 pounds of flour, 20 pounds of rice, 30 cans of meat, 30 cans of fruit, and some condiments, we could get by on a 30-day passage. Add three cabbages, some onions, potatoes, eggs, and apples and life would be okay. We find that by replenishing our lockers with the ever-changing variety of canned and packaged goods we discover each time we stop in more-industrialized countries, we've rarely lacked variety—if I use my imagination. I know this, but still I sort through the wonderful array of produce I found in Fremantle feeling happily satisfied. As we rush along with the fresh southeast trades, each day's menu is preordained by the produce that ripens to perfection as the miles pass quickly beneath our keel.

Choosing and Keeping Fresh Fruit and Vegetables

The following list of fruits and vegetables is based on my observations and actual experiences in far northern waters as well as in the deep tropics. The climate in which you will be sailing and the water temperature surrounding your hull will affect the longevity of your produce. Buying direct from the farmer or produce supplier is far better than buying from a supermarket. It is well worth having a chat with the farmer or produce supplier before you buy; he usually knows which vegetables last longer on his shelves. I know that every time I went to the trouble of doing this, I not only ended up with better fruit and vegetables but also learned new tips for how to keep them. Everyone loves to be asked questions about his profession, and the farmer or supplier with whom you will be dealing is no exception.

Whatever you do, don't buy from ship chandlers if you can avoid it. First, they think you are like a big ship and have a refrigerator or cool room for storing your produce. Second, they do not handle produce nearly as carefully as the retail man, since most ships are only keeping produce for two or three weeks between ports.

Mike Greenwald, in his excellent book *The Cruising Chef*,[6] recommends soaking all fruit and vegetables in a light solution of chlorine bleach and water to kill skin bacteria, then drying each piece before you store anything away. Although this works well in the temperate climates of the Mediterranean and North Atlantic, I don't recommend it for tropical climates. If any vegetable is not absolutely dry before you store it away, decay will set in even sooner than if you hadn't dipped the produce. The other problem with this method is that it is time-consuming just when you are busiest—the day before you set sail.[7]

The proper selection of the type of produce, a careful inspection of each item you buy, and proper storage on board are critical. The following guide to longevity or unrefrigerated produce is based on my own records for ocean passages in our two boats and on deliveries of a dozen others.

We have always been able to keep hard produce, such as potatoes and onions, unrefrigerated for at least two or three months. Recently, we discovered long-life produce bags, which help keep a larger variety of vegetables and fruits for up to three or four weeks (see below).

The time frames in this table are based on produce that is stored in secure, relatively dark areas of the boat with good ventilation. I have two large baskets that are permanently installed in an open-fronted locker under the stove. On passages, these baskets hold most of our onions and potatoes. During passagemaking, I store melons and large squash nestled in newspaper-lined plastic or straw baskets that I wedge securely with cushions and sleeping bags into the forward bunk, an area we don't use while underway. While we have never had a problem, in rough weather it would probably be a good idea to lash down the baskets and tie netting over the open tops to avoid fruit salad in the forepeak.

. . . .

6   Available through Paradise Cay Publications (www.paracay.com), or call 1-800-736-4509.

7   If you have purchased fruit or vegetables in any area prone to typhoid, yellow fever or other water-born infectious diseases, and do not plan to cook the item, it pays to soak the produce in a mixture of fresh water with one teaspoon of bleach per quart of water for 15 minutes before use.

It is vital to choose a storage area with good airflow and to make sure the baskets are well secured, because bruised produce rots more quickly. If you do not have a free bunk, you can hang produce baskets from the overheads in the forepeak, in an unused forward head compartment, or in the workshop area. You can also string hammocks for produce throughout the boat. Be sure, however, that they swing clear of everything—bulkheads, cabinetry, the hull. Otherwise, in rough weather the produce will bruise and rot. Below the floorboards and in the lazarette are my last choices for produce storage, because of poor ventilation.

All produce other than watermelons and hard-skinned squash must be kept absolutely dry. To ensure this, I inspect each item of produce twice weekly and use any that show signs of deterioration.

The following preservation times are based on buying almost farm-fresh produce of high quality that has not been in cold storage and is free from bruises. All times are based on tropical passages, such as our recent Indian Ocean crossing.

Long-Life Bags

Long-life plastic bags contain a natural mineral ingredient that slows the aging process of fruits and vegetables. Although the bags come with instructions for use with refrigeration, I have found that they also work well without cool storage, provided all produce is absolutely dry before being put in the bags. If produce has been refrigerated, allow it to dry and come up to air temperature for at least five or six hours in the open, away from direct sunlight. If available, however, it's best to buy same-day fresh produce that has never been refrigerated. We found we can reuse each bag twice if we rinse it well and turn it inside-out to dry for at least 10 hours. On our Indian Ocean passage, I waited to rinse the bags until we reached port in order to conserve freshwater.

	Days in Baskets	Days in Long-Life Bags
VEGETABLES		
Avocados	14	26
Broccoli	2	7
Brussels sprouts	4	10
Cabbage (large)	40	56
Carrots	15	22
Green beans (string)	2	7
Green peppers (bell)	8	23
Leeks	10	21
Lettuce (iceberg)	2	7
Mushrooms	2	7
Onions (brown)	90	not nec.
Onions (white)	40	not nec.
Potatoes (Idaho, thick-skinned)	70	not nec.
Potatoes (new)	100	not nec.
Potatoes (sweet, yams)	120	not nec.
Squash (hard, such as butternut; also pumpkin)	124	not nec.
Tomatoes	20-24*	32*
Turnips and parsnips	10	25
FRUITS		
Apples	10-12	24
Cantaloupes	16	not nec.
Grapes	3	9
Oranges	20	30
Tangerines (mandarins)	14	26
Watermelons (small)	40	not nec.

Based on selecting green tomatoes and slowing their ripening by covering.

Long-life bags are produced by Evert-Fresh at P.O. Box 5, Katy, Texas 77492 USA (www.evertfresh.com), and are available at West Marine and many produce shops. In Australia, Rob's Long-life Vegetable Bags are available through Gelpack Enterprises, P.O. Box 257, Noble Park, Victoria 3174 (www.gelpack.com.au).

Mal Mostert, who cruised with her husband and son for six years on the 45-footer *Mossy*, found quite a good substitute for long-life bags. She wrapped each item separately in dry newspaper and then stored them in loosely closed

Grapefruits tend to shrivel and dry up after two weeks afloat.

plastic bags, being sure that some air could seep into each item. She writes, "Carrots and cabbages kept in this way were still crisp and crunchy at the end of our 39-day sail from Brazil to Cape Town. The newspaper around each article gets moist from the veggies, but it keeps them fresh and stops them drying out, getting limp and soft or apples from going dry and powdery."

The following list gives more detail on selecting vegetables and fruits, plus longevity information on less-durable produce not included in the previous list.

Fruits

APPLES

Green ones keep the best; red, hard varieties, next; yellow, least well. Buy small apples without bruises. Wrap each one in tissue and store in a dark place. Check them over every week, cut off bruised spots, rub the spot with lemon juice. Use any bruised ones first.

ORANGES

Thick-skinned varieties keep best. Store them in a cool, dark place with lots of air. Check every three days.

TANGERINES

Great if you can get them. They last better than oranges. Leave the stems on them if they come that way. Keep them as cool as possible, and in a dark place, but give them lots of air. Be sure to inspect every three or four days and toss out bad ones.

MELONS

Cantaloupe, honeydew, and others with skins less than 1/4-inch thick are only good for up to 10 days. Check them carefully for bruises; keep them in a cool place.

WATERMELONS

The thick-skinned, red-fleshed variety keeps for up to a month if bought carefully. They ripen slowly. Buy the smallest ones you can find. In the Far East, 2-pound watermelons are readily available. They are perfect for two people at one sitting. Ripe watermelons sound hollow when you tap them with a knuckle. Store watermelons in a place with lots of air, where they can't roll around. I kept four in the chain locker on top of some newspapers when we sailed from South Yemen in September 1977. We ate the last one 21 days out. We cooled it by lowering it 20 feet over the side in a net bag. What a treat!

PEACHES, PEARS, GRAPES

Too much trouble because they bruise easily. I only buy enough for two or three days at the beginning of a voyage.

LEMONS

Real lemons with thick skins should be bought slightly green, wrapped in aluminum foil, and stored in a cool, dark place. They last 20 to 25 days that way.

LIMES

Small, green hard ones kept in a basket and turned over every four or five days will last 30 or 40 days and are still good for juice even when the skin gets hard and brown.

BANANAS

A cruising boat sailing off into the blue with stalks of green bananas hanging from the boom gallows—what a romantic sight. But the picture a week or so later has no romance at all. The crew is fed up with trying to eat the damn things before they go bad. Overripe bananas are falling off the stalk, making the afterdeck a danger zone at night. A stalk of bananas, usually consisting of up to 150 individual fruits, will all ripen within four or five days. Sunlight will hasten the process. It is better to buy individual hands of bananas from different sources and set them in a dark, cool place below decks. Large, thick-skinned varieties ripen more slowly. Very dark green, hard bananas can be kept for approximately 15 days. To avoid bringing spiders on board, hang hands of bananas overboard for two minutes, then rinse well in freshwater before storing them away.

PLANTAINS

These look just like bananas but aren't at all similar. I think they could better be classed as a vegetable, since they require cooking. Plantains need the same care as bananas, but they last twice as long. They can be cooked when green, yellow, or overripe (black). I've kept plantains for 30 days and then fried them in slices for a sweet treat with cocktails.

COCONUTS

These keep indefinitely but are bulky to store. The meat and milk taste great 30 days out.

PINEAPPLES

I have no luck keeping pineapples on board for more than six days without refrigeration. The same goes for mangoes, papayas, and starfruit.

MAMONES (RAMBUTANS, LYCHEES)

These delightful tropical treats will keep for 10 to 15 days if stored in a dark, dry place. They are all basically the same fruit. One has a red, hairy-looking skin, one has a smooth, green skin. Lychees, with bumpy green and rose colored outer skin, is the one you may have already tasted in canned form. It's fruit is slightly larger but has the same texture and flavor as rambutan or mamone and taste just like grapes when fresh. Store them right on the branch on which they have grown. Lay them in a basket or hang them in bunches. Once the skins become tough (eight or nine days), split them open with a knife instead of your thumbnail.

Vegetables for the Offshore Passage

LETTUCE

Choose tightly packed iceberg and romaine lettuce with as many outside leaves still intact as possible; store lettuce in a very open space wrapped in newspaper or a long-life bag.

CABBAGES

Buy these fresh from the farmer's field if you can. Preferably buy on a dry day, as moisture inside the cabbage from a recent rainfall will cause it to decay faster. Have the stems left as long as possible, and keep all of the outer layers intact. Store so that cabbages are not touching each other. Check every three days and remove any mildewing or rotting leaves, but don't remove leaves that are only getting dry. Cut 1/8 inch off the bottom of the stem if it is black or soft. I have kept cabbages as long as 35 days. They last better in hot, dry climates than in cold, damp ones. If the cabbage becomes dry, steam the leaves for half a minute to restore moisture, then cool to use in salads.

ONIONS

Before buying squeeze dry yellow or purple onions. If they are solid-feeling in all directions (test both vertically and horizontally), they should keep for two months or more. Store them in a dry, dark place. I use a plastic shopping basket for storing mine. Buy more than you think you will need; toward the end of a long voyage, they may be the only fresh vegetable you have. Check them every week.

POTATOES

New potatoes are best. Try to buy completely smooth ones. Irregular ones rot faster. Keep completely dry and in a dark place. Inspect once a week. Good for two months.

TOMATOES

The longest we ever had tomatoes keep on board without refrigeration was 34 days. We purchased them through Jurgensen's Grocery in San Diego, a specialist who used to outfit sportfishing boats bound for Mexico. They sent us a carefully packed crate of very round tomatoes that ranged in color from extremely green to ripe and red, with the greenest on the bottom of the crate. Each tomato was wrapped in tissue paper and fitted securely in the box so it couldn't roll around.

CARROTS

In the tropics, carrots go limp in about eight days' in northern climates, they stay crisp for two weeks and usable for about three. Select large carrots and keep them dry and well aired. Check every three or four days and remove any spots that are going black.

SQUASH

Butternut, acorn, pumpkin, and other hard squashes are great. They need no special care other than a secure location so they don't break. Buy small squash, ones you can use up at one or two meals; once you cut into them, they rarely last for more than four days. Squash has kept on Seraffyn for up to seven weeks.

TURNIPS

Good for four weeks if kept in a cool, dry place.

YAMS

Buy solid, regular-shaped ones. These last as long as potatoes with the same kind of care.

CUCUMBERS

Buy very dark green ones. Keep them out of direct sunlight and turn them over every four days. If any feel soft, use them right away. (They can be preserved in any pickling mixture, such as equal parts vinegar and oil.) Good for 12 to 14 days in the tropics, longer up north.

PEPPERS (CAPSICUMS AND CHILES)

Keep cool, avoid bruising. In the tropics, they last up to 10 days; in higher latitudes, up to 20 days. They may dry out a bit, but their flavor perks up most cooked mixed dishes. I find that the green peppers tend to last longer than other colors. Chile peppers of all types can be kept for as long as two to three months if they are turned occasionally and kept from getting damp. They will dry out and wrinkle up, but they can be used in all cooked dishes.

BEAN SPROUTS

These can be great fun. I've personally only used mung beans, which I sprout in bread tins in the oven. They only take four days to mature and are good when added to salads and Chinese-style cooked dishes.

BRUSSELS SPROUTS, CAULIFLOWER, GREEN BEANS, ASPARAGUS

These vegetables don't keep well, so enjoy them in port or during the first few days at sea.

JICAMA

This Mexican root vegetable tastes like sweet carrots. Great raw or cooked. Just like turnips, they will last up to a month if kept dry.

PLANTANO (PLANTAIN)

See Fruits, above.

. . . .

Checking and turning vegetables and fruit may sound like a tedious job, but in reality it only takes about 10 minutes a day. At the same time, you can be choosing the vegetables you plan to use for the next few meals. Evenwhen I was feeding a crew of seven on a fishing trawler offshore for 28 days, caring for our produce took less than 20 minutes a day on average.

How Much Produce to Carry

Fresh fruits and vegetables are almost always cheaper than their canned equivalents—not to mention that they are tastier, more nutritious, and more versatile. They take up less storage space than canned goods and require less freshwater to prepare than dehydrated vegetables. So when we get ready for a passage, we overstock on produce. We figure that we will lose 10 to 15 percent to spoilage and that it is better and (in most cases) relatively inexpensive to have too much rather than too little. We have found that on tropical islands—such as the Tuamotus or, the Cocos-Keeling Islands—simple items such as potatoes and onions that cannot be grown in the climate or soil of coral atolls will cost three to five times more. It pays to overstock on these items before setting sail.

My recommendations for quantities to carry on a passage are based on our style of cooking and eating. Larry and I both have come to prefer calorie-conscious cuisine, with salads and vegetables for two meals a day and meat, fish, or fowl once a day. We also find that our at-sea lunches—bread, cheese, and fruit or a mixed salad—are more casual than lunches we might eat in port. We assume that pasta and rice will be substituted for potatoes

50 percent of the time and that one or the other will form part of our main meal each day.

We recommend that you allow a 50 percent safety margin for provisioning, in case of a slow passage. Carry at least 15 days' worth of provisions for what should be a 10-day passage, 45 days' worth for a projected 30-day voyage. The tables of quantities below have that margin built in. In Maritius we saw a South African yacht as it sailed slowly in under jury rig after having been dismasted. It took the crew 35 days to sail from Cocos Keeling Islands, a passage that most cruising boats complete in 14 to 20 days.

The quantities of fresh, unrefrigerated produce in the table below are per person (double the portions for two), based on average appetites.

per person	10 days*	20 days*	30 days*
LONG-LIVED VEGETABLES ++			
Cabbage (large, 2 lb.)	1	2	4
Onions (medium assorted)	7	20	35
Potatoes (¼ lb. each, assorted)	8	15	30
Potatoes (sweet, yams/small, smooth-skinned	2	6	15
Squash (hard/small, one or two meals' worth each)	1	2	5
SHORT-LIVED VEGETABLES §			
Avocados (different stages of ripeness)	4	7	+
Brussels sprouts (servings)	2	5	+
Carrots (carry extra for snacks)	12-15	25	+
Green peppers (bell)	2-4	7	+
Leeks (servings)	2	5	+
Tomatoes (medium)	10	25	+
FRUITS //			
Apples	8	25	+
Cantaloupes	1	3	+
Oranges (double these amounts for juice)	10	25	+
Tangerines (mandarins)	5	10	+
Watermelons	1	1	3

NONPRODUCE PERISHABLES

Beans and peas, dried (supplement with canned)	None	2 lb.	5lb.
Eggs (fresh, never washed or refrigerated, turn daily to extend longevity)	8	24	40
Flour (⅓ whole wheat, ⅔ white, includes bread making)	3 lb.	9 lb.	20 lb.
Pasta	2 lb.	5 lb.	8 lb.
Rice	2 lb.	5 lb.	8 lb.
Yeast	2 oz.	5 oz.	14 oz.

NOTES

* Quantities per person, 50 percent safety margin included.

+ Same quantity as for a 20-day passage; will not last much longer than that.

++ For long passages, buy long-lived vegetables in quantity because they will become your staple fresh food when short-lived vegetables are gone.

§ In addition to the above, select three or four short-lived vegetables such as lettuce, beans, or broccoli and plan three to six servings per person for each type. This will add variety for the first week of your passage. To extend their life, use long-life bags or place these items in cold storage as space becomes available in your refrigeration unit.

// Besides the fruit listed above, carry a small selection of softer fruit for the first week of the passage. To extend their life, put these in your refrigeration unit as space becomes available.

I stock pasta, rice, and dried beans and peas in generous quantities, even beyond the built-in 50 percent margin, because in an emergency these staples will last much longer than other produce.

Fresh cherries are in season in Abo/Turku, Finland.

I almost hated to disturb the symmetry of the stacks of fruit at this stall in Puerto Montt, Chile.

....

Day 8

Noon to noon: 108 miles
Miles to date: 562
Beam-reaching, sunny and warm

Breakfast
orange juice
bread, peanut butter, jam
cheese
coffee, tea

Lunch
soup
shrimp salad on cabbage leaves
apples

Dinner
garlic-and-onion omelet
grilled tomatoes
rice salad
white wine

. . . .

RICE SALAD

1 cup leftover rice
½ small onion, chopped
½ green pepper, chopped
¼ cucumber, diced
3 tbs. mayonnaise
1 tsp. granulated sugar
½ tsp. garlic, minced
½ tsp. dried dill weed

Mix well and let sit
1 hour in a cool place
before serving.

. . . .

This morning, Larry had to add 5 gallons of water to our header tank. That means we've used about 8 gallons so far—not bad. We have 60 gallons on board and only 4,000 miles to go.

We ran out of ice, and at noon I cleaned out the icebox and wiped it down with bleach so that it wouldn't take on any odors. Normally our ice lasts 10 to 14 days, but the price of meat was so high in Japan that I only bought enough to last a week. Then I bought 40 pounds of plain ice and 25 pounds of dry ice instead of our usual 50 and 50. After 10 years of cruising on *Seraffyn*, I'm sold on an icebox. (See discussion of refrigeration, below.)

Well, from now on, it's sea cooking. No more fresh meat. We're moving well, the sailing is unbelievably smooth, the sky is clear. Canada doesn't seem too far away.

Just before dinnertime, the wind freshened, the seas built up on the quarter, our speed was up to almost 6 knots, and the motion was definitely getting uncomfortable. Larry suggested I hold dinner for a few minutes, and together we took down the nylon drifter and set the smaller number-two genoa in its place. Cooking and eating was more pleasant. That is one of the big differences between cooking on a cruising boat and cooking on a racing boat. No racing skipper would give up a half-knot of speed just to gain a bit of comfort.

In spite of changing sails, the building seas created more motion than we'd had the previous seven days. Tomatoes slid off the plates, my omelet tried to crawl over the end of the pan. Larry put a damp towel on the table before I set out dinner, and we used coffee mugs for our wine instead of our pewter goblets.

To Ice or Not to Ice

Refrigeration on board a cruising boat is one more subject on which opinions range from extreme to extreme. The average English sailing person, used to shopping daily and a climate where the idea is to keep warm as possible, looks on any form of refrigeration as a nuisance, a waste of time and space. The average American, pampered by freezer foods, can't imagine living without at least a small freezer. Somewhere in the middle lies the long-distance cruiser, who spends much of his/her time in the tropics, where fresh food spoils in a day if it isn't kept cool.

I was chatting with an English couple who had just started cruising on board a 35-footer and were wintering near us in the Mediterranean. The husband asked, "Is an ice chest really worth the bother? Doesn't it just take up good storage space?" Larry answered, "Lin only has to go shopping once a week if she has ice, and if someone asks us to join them for dinner, the food we have on board can keep until the next night. Most important, fresh food costs less than canned and is certainly more interesting. If you do run out of ice, the box can still be used for storage." His answers must have impressed them, because they were building an ice chest the last time we saw them.

On the other hand, Larry and I were lounging comfortably under our sun awning in La Paz, Mexico, about nine years ago when the launch from a luxurious 50-foot cruiser approached. "Do you like roast lamb?" the owner asked. "Who doesn't?" we replied. He handed us a semifrozen leg of lamb and explained, "My freezer broke down two days ago, and we can't use up 200 pounds of thawing meat, so I'm giving it away." That was only the first time we were on the receiving end when someone's freezer gave out. It happened again in Acapulco, Panama, Gibraltar, and the Suez Canal. We were told about the crew on *Windward Passage* threatening to mutiny when their freezer gave out three days after the start of the Bermuda-to-Spain transatlantic race.

Like everything else aboard a long-distance sailing yacht, your food-cooling system should be extremely simple to repair. We were having dinner with a couple who had just taken delivery of a 35-footer the previous month. They were moving on board, and the wife looked at us in exasperation and stated, "I've had refrigerators in my house all my life. Not one has ever given any trouble. What is so special about a refrigerator on a boat?" Larry answered, "Onshore, the electricity company makes sure the power gets to your house at a constant and steady voltage. The electricity company stores the power for you when you don't need it. The community household wiring codes ensure that your electrical system is properly installed. And, in the past few years, there must have been 30 to 40 million household refrigerators built. That is enough to make sure all the bugs are worked out. Compare that to the refrigeration unit on a sailboat. *You* personally have to convert the power to run the refrigerator. *You* have to store it in your own batteries to run your compressor twice a day. *You* have to be sure power is available on demand. *You* have to wire it all up or be sure that the shipyard does it correctly. And there are few companies that have built more than 1,000 refrigeration units of the same model for sailing boats. Most have probably built fewer than 100 of the same type in the past year. So the actual units aren't as tried-and-true, or as reliable. And, finally, not one household refrigeration unit is asked to stand up to saltwater corrosion, constant motion, and unlevel working conditions. You'll have to face it—there are a lot of links in the chain that can break down and leave you with a freezer full of thawing meat. No fuel, water in the fuel lines, broken-down alternator, unreliable generator, broken compressor, coolant leaks—all mean no refrigeration. When this happens, *you* have to provide the servicing and repairs. There are few professional refrigeration mechanics in primitive places, and almost none at all at sea."

Refrigeration on long-distance cruising boats is just as much of a problem in 2006 as it was back in 1980, when I wrote the first edition of this book. We did an informal survey of voyagers reaching New Zealand in 2006 and found that almost 80 percent had had problems with mechanical or electrical refrigeration units during the course of their cruises. Discussions with Nigel Calder and a review of questionnaires filled out by various cruising-rally members confirm these numbers; in fact, several people said refrigeration was the biggest problem they'd had on board. Though modern advancements have lowered the electrical draw of some units—so it is now possible to power a 5-cubic-foot freezer using four 30-watt solar panels if the box is well insulated—no one has been able to make a constantly successful, can-be-used-on-any-boat, full-time-tropical-use-proof, simple-to-install unit.

On *Taleisin,* as on *Seraffyn,* we chose an ice-chest system. Her larger size gives us room for more insulation and more ice. On *Seraffyn,* we could carry about 85 pounds of ice and keep food cold in the tropics for about 10 days. Now, with 135 pounds of good-quality ice in a box (constructed as discussed below, under "Hold That Cold"), we find that we can keep food cold for up to 15 days in the deep tropics and three weeks in cooler climates—such as found around New Zealand in the summer. (Remember that the clearer the ice, the better it lasts.) During the past 20 years, we have been able to buy ice or have it made in every port we have visited. We pay an average of $5 for 100 pounds. Our yearly ice costs run about $150. The original cost to build and insulate *Taleisin*'s chest in 1982 was approximately $300, including the stainless-steel liner. Since refrigeration repair people now charge up to $75 an hour, we still find the ice chest financially practical.

We have found a way to have very inexpensive block ice even in places where ice is normally hard to find. We carry three rectangular plastic washbasins nested together. They store neatly in the bilge and have a dozen other uses. When we need ice, we have found that most merchants or fish-processing plants are willing to let us put these in their freezers for a small fee. A large store freezer makes 20-pound blocks of ice in each basin within 12 hours. A normal shop or home freezer will make blocks in about 36 hours. In Moorea, at Rodriques Island (Indian Ocean), in the Cocos-Keeling Islands— it seems that everywhere we have asked, shopkeepers or local people have solved our ice problem for $1 per block or less if we bought food at their shops.

Since we, as most voyagers, spend up to 90 percent of our time near ports, we are rarely far from icemaking sources. So it is only when we are on passage that we go more than a few days without cold facilities. For long-distance ocean passages, we buy all frozen meat and bring it on board as late as possible. We ate our last lamb chops 10 days out from Bermuda and had only five days of eating from cans before we reached the Azores on *Seraffyn*. On *Taleisin*, we have had fresh iced meat right across the Indian Ocean, where passages averaged 14 to 16 days each. But,even if we can't get ice, the box is still useful. A frozen 3-pound chicken will cool down a bottle of wine and be fresh and perfectly thawed three days after it is bought in most temperate climates. And because the icebox lid seals well, fresh food and leftovers stored in it will be safe from flying and crawling insects in tropical ports.

For those willing and able to have a slightly more complicated system—one that requires more maintenance—the second most successful refrigeration unit is a top-loading box with a holding plate and a refrigeration unit run off a compressor on your engine. By using your engine to drive this compressor (many home builders use one from an automotive air-conditioning unit), you avoid the energy loss of converting mechanical power to electricity, which is stored in a battery and then converted back to mechanical power to drive a compressor to cool your refrigerator. Your freezer holding plates can take up very little space, and, with a properly insulated box, you should only have to run your engine twice a day, for 30 minutes each time, in the tropics.

There are, however, three problems with this system. First, you must be around the boat to start the main engine that drives your compressor. If you decide to go away from your boat on the spur of the moment to explore Madrid for four or five days, you have to arrange for someone to come on board twice a day to run your engine and protect your frozen food. Second, diesel engines and many transmissions wear out faster if they are not run under a constant load—i.e., with the propeller engaged. (Excessive wear occurs because unloaded engines actually rattle themselves to an early death. Many transmissions must be in gear to achieve proper lubrication. They also last longer if they are kept under load as much as possible.) Finally, generator sounds are not particularly welcome in an otherwise-serene anchorage or, even more important, in a crowded marina. Since considerate generator or motor use when there are other boats moored nearby is confined to the hours of 9 a.m. to noon and 1 to 4 p.m., people who have engine-driven refrigeration systems must schedule their day around those hours or risk alienating other sailors.

A butane refrigerator does not belong on a boat. Even if the burner has an emergency heat-activated shutoff, it is dangerous. I have seen these shutoff valves fail in household refrigerators. Consider that to meet the demands of a butane refrigerator, you must leave your butane tank and lines open all the time. It is just a matter of time before your system develops a leak, or a gust of wind puts out the pilot flame. As opposed to stoves that don't have pilot lights and can be checked easily each time you use them, a butane refrigerator system is too dangerous to use on a boat.

No matter what type of refrigeration you choose, the design and insulation of the food box will determine how well your unit works. Following is an article that Larry wrote for *Boating* magazine, *Seacraft,* and *Practical Boat Owner.* In it, he describes how to build and insulate your own ice chest.

Hold That Cold

When I asked, "What is the best way to build an ice chest?" everyone I spoke to said, "Ask Vic Berry." Vic's sheet-metal shop in Newport Beach, California, had made hundreds of stainless-steel liners for ice chests, refrigerators, and deep freezes on local yachts and also on the sportfishing boats that went south to Cabo San Lucas, Mexico, for marlin. Vic told me how he made deck freezers for some of these sportfishing boats that could hold the cold so well that the compressors would only run for 20 to 30 minutes a day, even though these freezers were sitting out in the Mexican sun.

Vic said, "The trick is the design and insulation of the chest, whether you use ice or a compressor." He told me the chest should first and foremost be top opening. A front-opening design just pours all of the cold on your feet and rarely seals perfectly—the cold leaks out all day long, melting your ice or causing your compressor to work overtime. Even with a top-loading chest, the cold will seep out if the lid doesn't have a good, airtight seal. A top-loading chest is definitely safer at sea. Unlike the side-opening box, things can't come sliding out just because you are on an unfavorable tack.

Your chest can be built with a complete top-opening lid, with or without a wedged access plug—or a combination of both, as shown in figure 5. The combination is best for large freezers or ice chests, as it makes cleaning and storing items like blocks of ice easier, while the smaller plug for everyday access allows less cold to escape each time you go for a drink. The complete lid should have good seals with firm latches so you can't feel any cold escaping when you put your hand at the lid-to-ice box joint. The wedged plug should also be well sealed with two or three soft, compressible gaskets.

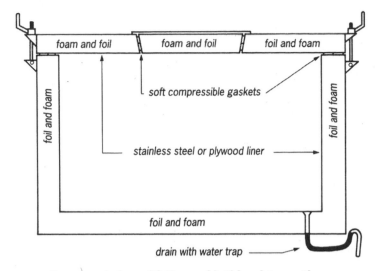

FIGURE 5. *Freezer or Icebox with Removable Lid and Access Plug*

A good-size drain (³/8-inch inside diameter minimum) with a screen to catch food particles is essential. It will allow you to wash the chest and drain off ice water easily. A water trap or valve in the drain will stop cold air from leaking away into the bilge (fig. 5). The water from the ice chest shouldn't be allowed to drain into the bilge in any case, as it will soon cause odors. In wooden hulls, it causes rot; in glass hulls, osmosis; and in steel hulls, corrosion. On *Seraffyn,* we used to drain the water from our ice chest into a bucket, then use the water to chill our wine, champagne, or bottled drinks. On *Taleisin,* this drain leads directly into the sump tank we use for our shower/tub.

Vic went on to say, "Next to top opening, the most important thing is the thickness and type of insulation you use." He recommended several layers of 1/2-inch-thick closed-cell polyurethane sheet foam, with ordinary household aluminum foil between each layer—ideally resulting in a 4-inch insulation barrier. First put in a layer of foil with the shiny side to the outside of the chest, then add a 1/2-inch layer of foam, another layer of foil, then foam, and again foil—until you have a 3-to-4-inch insulation barrier. The shiny side of the foil tends to reflect the initial heat and creates a barrier between each layer of foam. Half-inch-thick Styrofoam sheets can be used, but closed-cell polyurethane is better, as it is denser than Styrofoam and each cell holds a tiny dead-air pocket. Dead air is a great insulator.

Several companies make commercial equivalents to this insulation system, but the cost for the materials is much higher. If I did consider using these products, I would err toward the pessimistic and still use at least a 3-inch insulation barrier comprising several layers to make sure no potential

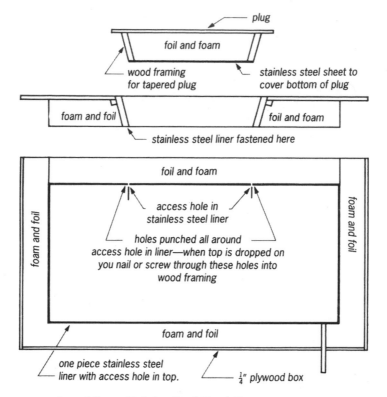

FIGURE 6. *Assembling a Stainless-Steel-Lined Chest*

heat or moisture-transmitting gaps existed between the outer airtight box and the inner liner of the chest.

Poured-in, 2-part foam is problematical as an insulation choice. First, it does not have the same insulating qualities as the 2-part system described above; second, the chest and liner have to be built extra strong just to support the expanding foam. There is also the matter of health problems associated with handling the toxic chemical combination. And with poured-in, 2-part foam, there is no way of knowing whether or not all the areas between the liner and the ice chest are properly filled with insulation.

To build the chest, first decide on the outside dimensions and make it as big as possible. Plan to slope the bottom of the chest toward the drain hole. The lowest corner of the chest should have space under it to fit a water trap or valve. Now build a 1/4-inch-thick plywood outer chest. This chest should be capable of holding water. To achieve this, use 3/4-inch by 3/4-inch corner pieces fastened with screws and glue. Or use a simpler method: Fasten the corners of the plywood chest with copper wire and seal each joint inside and outside with 2-inch-wide fiberglass tape.

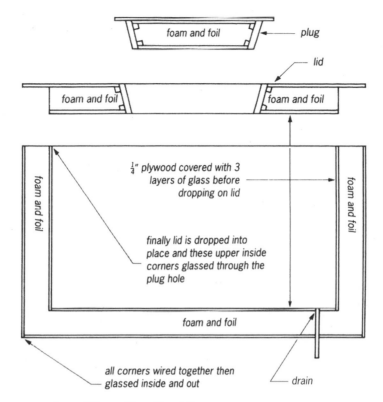

FIGURE 7. *Assembling a Glass-Lined Chest*

Use glue to secure the first layer of foil to the plywood chest, then cut the 1/2-inch sheet of foam slightly oversize and jam it snugly against the sides. A handsaw and a plane will shape the foam easily. Alternate layers of foil and foam until you have the desired insulation thickness.

Vic used eight layers of 1/2-inch polyurethane foam, with foil between each layer, to get 4 inches of insulation on his Mexican freezers. You can use as little as two inches of foam and foil for refrigerators, and this is usually enough, but the cold-holding efficiency will drop proportionately.

The chest liner comes next. To fit a professional-looking stainless-steel one, you'll have to make an accurate pattern that suits the inside dimensions of your insulation. A cheaper liner for the home builder is 1/4-inch plywood fitted to the inside of the insulation. Glass the corners with tape and drill a hole at the lowest corner of the chest through the liner, insulation, and outer chest wall. Make a mold for a fiberglass drain tube by rolling thin cardboard into the desired shape and size and then covering it with cellophane tape, as illustrated in figure 8. Fiberglass around this mold and form a flange at one end. When the glass tube is set up, you can remove the cardboard mold by soaking it in water. Fit the tube into the drain-hole position in the chest, then glass the whole inside of the chest, bonding the flange to the bottom layers of glass. If you choose a stainless-steel liner, have your sheet-metal man solder a drainpipe connection to the liner. The pipe should be long enough to extend through the bottom of the insulated chest so you can clamp a plastic drain hose to it.

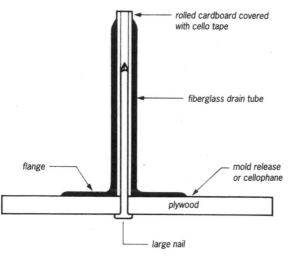

FIGURE 8. *Molding a Drain for a Glass Liner*

The liner for your chest should be strong and slightly flexible. If it is glass, it should have three layers of heavy cloth and resin. Otherwise, when you drop ice or heavy frozen food into the box, it could crack the liner, and polluted water will leak into your insulation and foul it. I would use epoxy resin for this job, as it is more flexible and less likely to crack than polyester resin.

When all the cloth is bonded in, sand the inside of the chest smooth and paint on a flow coat of finishing resin to give a smooth, odorless, easy-to-clean interior surface. Then fit the top and glass the upper corners. Whatever type of top you decide to use, it must be as well insulated as the sides and bottom.

In addition to being easier for the home builder, a plywood-and-glass liner has other advantages over the stainless-steel one. For instance, it is simple to screw wooden supports on the inside for sliding food trays. It's also easier to drill and seal snug, airtight holes for refrigeration pipes.

Proper placement and usage of your cold chest or freezer can help hold the cold. If you want a deck or cockpit freezer chest, paint it white to reflect the sun's heat; if the chest is located below, try not to position it next to the stove, heater, or engine. If possible, place it below your load waterline, where

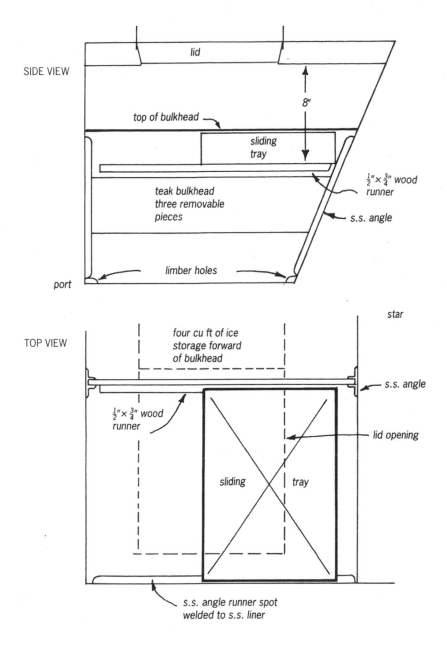

SIDE VIEW

lid

8"

top of bulkhead

sliding tray

$\frac{1}{2}" \times \frac{3}{4}"$ wood runner

teak bulkhead three removable pieces

s.s. angle

limber holes

port

TOP VIEW

star

four cu ft of ice storage forward of bulkhead

s.s. angle

$\frac{1}{2}" \times \frac{3}{4}"$ wood runner

lid opening

sliding tray

s.s. angle runner spot welded to s.s. liner

FIGURE 9. *Inside of Ice Chest, Side and Top Views*

the boat is kept cooler by seawater. On long passages, plan your meals so that you open the lid to your chest only once or twice a day. With an ice chest, arrange the drainage so you can put it into a bucket and use the cold water to chill beverages so that guests don't open the main ice chest every time they want a cool drink. Don't leave the melted water standing in the bottom of your chest in a seaway—it will melt your ice faster. If you have spare room in your compressor-driven refrigeration box, fill it with blocks of ice. This will help keep the temperatures down. For safety, if you have a freezer, carry extra nonfrozen stores in case your unit quits working.

The ice chest on *Seraffyn* had one of Vic Berry's stainless-steel liners, a double seal on the plug, and only two inches of foil and foam insulation. On *Taleisin* we have 3 1/2 inches of foil and foam insulation and a stainless steel liner made by Vic's son.

We made two changes in the ice-chest system we use on *Taleisin*. After 20 years of living and cruising on her, I would say that the first was extremely successful, the second a slight compromise.

Inside the stainless liner, we had a channel built to let us insert three teak boards, each 1/2-inch thick. The boards are topped by a slider for a separate tray (see fig. 9). The divider keeps ice from sliding around in a seaway. It also lets me use one section for ice and the other for perishables, so the ice stays clean and the perishables dry and easy to find. When we go on passage and I want the ice to last longer, I fill both compartments with ice and put the perishables on top. The divider lifts out to make cleaning simple. The stainless-steel tray, which is shaped so it can be lifted out through the ice-chest opening for cleaning, is used to hold soft or breakable items such as cheeses. Since the tray is watertight, I use it for milk storage, as it will contain accidental spills.

The second change was to lead the drainpipe back to the sump tank we use for our bathing facilities. This means I do not have to drain a separate ice-chest sump. But I no longer have access to the ice water to cool a bottle of white wine. I also find it is important to be able to remove this drain hose from the sump tank for a yearly clean-out. Tiny bits of food, plus natural bacteria, cause mold to grow inside the drainpipe. If the mold is not flushed out with a strong solution of chlorine bleach and warm water, it eventually causes the hose to become clogged.

. . . .

Day 9

Noon to noon: 106 miles
Miles to date: 668
Sunny and warm, reaching in 7 or 8 knots of wind;
seas very calm

Lunch
tuna salad sandwiches
leftover rice salad
soft drinks

Dinner
spaghetti Bolognese
red wine
Camembert
canned peaches

....

TUNA SALAD

Combine
1 can tuna, drained and flaked
½ onion, chopped
2 tbs. pickle relish
1 tsp. vinegar
3 tbs. mayonnaise

Mix well and let sit for a
while before serving.

....

BOLOGNESE SAUCE FOR SPAGHETTI

Place in deep saucepan

3 very large tomatoes (pulp and seeds only)
10 small cloves garlic, crushed
1 onion, chopped
3 tbs. sugar
2 tsp. oregano
1 tsp. marjoram
Simmer slowly, 30 minutes,
    stirring occasionally.

Add

1 can corned beef (in small chunks)

> Stir well and serve over pasta. Sprinkle with Parmesan cheese.

Meal Schedules and Division of Labor

This afternoon, I found some tomatoes that had split because they rolled out of the basket. I used them to make a spaghetti dinner, a real at-sea favorite for us. I love spaghetti; Larry loves the chili and beans I make with the extra sauce. If we have ground beef, we use that, but the corned beef tastes almost as good. When I'm not trying to use up overripe or bruised tomatoes, I use a can of peeled tomatoes plus a can of tomato paste for this recipe.

After I cleared up dinner dishes, I put a cup of dried beans in freshwater to soak for tomorrow. I prefer canned beans—not only because they are already soft and ready to use but also because they don't take extra freshwater to prepare. You can't soak or boil dried beans in saltwater—their skins stay tough. So preparing three cups of beans requires a quart and a half of freshwater plus a cup of dried beans. But I couldn't find any type of canned beans in Japan for under $2 a can; dried pinto and brown beans only cost 50 cents a package and yield as much as four cans of beans would have.

As you may have noticed, Larry and I don't have any formal breakfast plan at sea. There are several reasons for this. When we are making a passage on board *Seraffyn*, there are just the two of us. We always stand night watches of three hours on, three hours off, usually starting about 2000 hours. Larry sleeps the first three hours, so his day starts at about 0500, while I sleep on until 0800 or 0900. Rather than wait for me to get up and feed him, he makes a snack for himself—coffee, bread and jam, a piece of fruit. He usually makes a cup of tea for me when he sees me stirring.

This casual breakfast works well for us, since it eliminates one set of dishes and gives our mornings at sea a more leisurely schedule. The rest of the day's schedule goes like this: After the casual breakfast, Larry takes a morning sight and checks the rigging while I spend some time cleaning up the boat. Then, just after Larry takes a noon sight, I record the noon-to-noon run on our small-scale passage chart and enter it in our log. Then I serve lunch.

We have tea at about 1600 if neither of us feels like taking a nap. Then, at 1730 or so, we have cocktail hour, when we get together and practice the guitar, watch the birds fly by, or play our favorite tapes on the cassette stereo. This is an important part of each day because, as surprising as it may sound, it may be the only time we really get to discuss our plans and schemes.

We eat dinner about 1830. Then Larry helps me wipe the dishes and goes on deck while I clean out the sink and galley. After a final check around, he brings in the oil lamps and I clean the chimneys as he fills and lights each one.

On days like this, I enjoy serving lunch in the cockpit. This photo was taken on board Seraffyn *during our North Pacific crossing.*

All of the cooking at sea on board *Seraffyn*—including taking care of stores, baking, doing the dishes, and cleaning up the galley—rarely takes more than three hours of my time per day. On delivery trips when we hire crew, we serve a formal breakfast, lunch, tea with snacks, dinner, and snacks for the night watches. If there is no self-steering on the boat, meals have to be staggered, so cooking, cleaning, and so on, will take five to six hours of my day, even though one of the crew helps in the galley each day.

I stand no watch during the day if we have two extra crew on a delivery. This works well because it means each member of the crew gets six hours of uninterrupted sleep, while I end up with a good four or five hours of uninterrupted rest before my watch and again before it's time to start breakfast. With only one extra crewperson on shorter deliveries, I stand two 2-hour watches, which means nine hours of my day are full. But these deliveries rarely last more than two weeks.

When we are at sea on *Seraffyn*, Larry takes care of all of the navigation and most of the sail adjustments during the day, while I do the cooking and care for the inside of the boat. At night, we each take care of any sail trimming that is necessary during our own watch. If there is a sail change because the wind is dropping, we almost never wake the other person. But if the wind is increasing and a sail change means going out on the bowsprit, we usually wake the person who is off watch, just to be safe. The noise of my changing the big genoa for the small one would wake Larry anyway.

This schedule seems to give both of us plenty of time for reading and doing any little tasks we want to do during the day. With the vane steering, the night watches are a great time for writing letters or reading—or even doing projects like this one.

· · · · · · ·

Day 10

Noon to noon: 68 miles
Miles to date: 736
Very light winds, calm seas, cloudy

Lunch
chili and beans
bread, butter
soft drinks

Dinner
huevos rancheros (scrambled eggs topped with ranchero sauce)
bean salad
Camembert, saltines

. . . .

CHILI AND BEANS

1½ cups leftover Bolognese sauce
1½ cups boiled beans
1½ tsp. chili powder
2 small green peppers, chopped

> Simmer 15 minutes, then serve in bowls.

. . . .

BEAN SALAD

2 cups cooked beans (or canned if available)
1 small onion, chopped
4 cloves garlic, chopped
½ cup salad or olive oil
¼ cup vinegar
1 tsp. sugar
½ tsp. oregano
½ tsp. dill
salt, pepper to taste

> Mix and let sit at least 4 hours.

To keep longer than two days, put the bean salad in a clean jar until ¾ inch from the top. Add equal parts oil and vinegar until the jar is full. Secure the lid tightly and store upright. It will last 15 to 20 days and works great as an addition to any kind of salad.

RANCHERO SAUCE

2 tbs. butter
1 onion, cut in strips
1 green pepper, cut in strips
3 cloves garlic
1 whole tomato, chopped
1 tsp. sweet basil
1 tsp. lemon juice
1 tsp. Worcestershire sauce
½ tsp. chili powder

Simmer all ingredients, stirring occasionally, 15 minutes. Serve over scrambled, fried, or poached eggs.

In the morning, while we did our usual chores, I boiled the beans that had been soaking since the night before. They took about 35 minutes to become tender. Half went into the Bolognese sauce and half became bean salad, which I made just after lunch and left to soak up the flavors of the spices until dinner. Then I checked the egg supply and turned them over. Three of the eggs had cracks in their shells that hadn't been there three days earlier. A bit of investigation showed that those eggs were slightly larger than the rest, so they must have cracked when I closed the plastic cartons more securely. One of today's meals has to be eggs so that I can use up the cracked ones.

With more than 3,700 miles still to go, the last two days of light winds have been wearing on our nerves. Today was muggy, cloudy, and hot; our moods matched the gray color of the sea. I must admit that I'd have given anything for a restaurant to run to. Cooking dinner was the last thing I felt like doing. Paul Simon sang sad songs on the stereo. The mainsail slatted back and forth in the windless swell. I was nearly crying by the time dinner was over; the idea of scrubbing up a sink full of pots had little appeal. Larry offered to wash them on deck and rinse them below. A bunch of Mother Carey's chickens fluttered and chattered near our taffrail log spinner. The clouds turned crimson as the sun set, and Larry broke the day's gloomy spell when he said, "We sure have small problems; we could be commuters fighting our way onto a train home from Tokyo everyday."

DAY 10. *The secret to successful egg storage is buying them correctly.*

On Preserving Eggs

Every cruising cookbook will mention some way of preserving eggs on long voyages. I've personally heard of five basic ones; the choice depends on your pattern of thinking.

1. Grease each egg carefully and thoroughly with Vaseline.
2. Paint each egg with sodium silicate (water glass).
3. Boil each egg 10 seconds.
4. Deep-freeze the eggs.
5. Turn over the eggs every two or three days.

The first three methods are slightly messy and consume time when you are busiest—preparing to leave port. Greasing must be done carefully, as any void in the coating will allow the eggs to rot. Overboiling will cook the eggs so they are not good for cakes or baking, and you won't find this out until you actually break open an egg you are about to use. These methods require no extra maintenance once you are at sea other than removing the Vaseline if you choose method 1. Neither Vaseline nor sodium silicate is dangerous to your health if a small amount should get into your food while you are breaking an egg.

Freezing works perfectly, and that is how eggs are kept in many countries where they must be imported. You can tell an egg has been frozen if it has a pale yellow yolk. If your freezer fails and the eggs even begin to defrost, they'll start going bad in five or six days.

Turning the eggs is the method I always choose. All I have to do before we leave port is store away the eggs in regular egg cartons. Then at sea, it's necessary to remember to turn over each carton three times a week. There is a chance of failure with this method. If the eggs aren't turned over because you forget, or because you are too seasick, they'll start to deteriorate. If they sit for a week without turning, they'll start to go bad after 25 days or so.

The reason all these methods work is that they keep air from entering the semiporous eggshell. When an egg is absolutely fresh, its shell is well coated inside by the clear egg fluid, and air can't get through. As it ages, the shell dries out inside where the air space sits, and then the shell becomes more porous. Vaseline and sodium silicate add an airtight barrier to the outside of the egg. A 10-second boil adds an internal barrier. Turning the eggs works the same way—it keeps the whole inside of the shell moist.

Whichever method you choose, buy the freshest eggs you can find—ones that have never been refrigerated or kept in an air-conditioned room. Two- or 3-day-old eggs tend to have lumpy shells that are absolutely white and opaque. After five or six days of storage, even in refrigeration, the shells start to develop small, slightly gray spots that are easily visible if you hold the egg up to a strong light. Supermarket eggs are a poor choice: (1) these are usually bought from a central egg distributor and are at least three days old when they reach the store, and (2) they are almost always transported in air-conditioned trucks. This is vitally important. A 20-degree increase in temperature will drastically affect the keeping quality of eggs. If you are sailing from a cold climate such as England, New England, or Canada, bound for the tropics, your eggs won't last much longer than 25 days. So buy just enough to last until you reach warmer waters, such as in Spain, Bermuda, Hawaii, or Mexico. Then buy your egg supply. Going the other way, there is no problem.

Don't wash your eggs before you store them away. They have a natural protective covering, and it's water-soluble.

Store your eggs in the coolest part of the boat, somewhere below the waterline if possible and close to the hull but away from the heat of the engine. Water temperature in the tropics rarely gets above 76 degrees, and eggs keep naturally at this temperature; with no preserving methods at all, they will last nicely for two or three weeks.

No matter how you keep your eggs, they will change slightly as they age. After 12 to 25 days (depending on the temperature of your storage locker),

It was obvious that these eggs at the marketplace in Gdynia, Poland, were fresh off the farm..

thc yolks will become fragile, and making sunny-side-up eggs will be a challenge. After 25 to 30 days, the eggs will only be good for scrambling, boiling, or baking. After 30 days, the whites of hard-boiled eggs may have a slightly yellow or brown tinge and the yolks will be pale in color. This doesn't change the eggs' cooking value, nor does it affect the flavor. But if the egg is cracked, or has a dark appearance right through the shell, I wouldn't use it. After you've kept eggs 15 days, I'd also suggest breaking each

133

egg separately into a cup so that a bad egg won't spoil a whole cake mix or a 10-egg omelet.

The longest I've had eggs last by turning them over three times a week is three months. Then I ran out of eggs. Out of the 144 eggs I'd started with, only five went bad—the first one 25 days out, the second after 45 days. But either of these eggs could have had a small crack in its shell.

Don't throw away egg cartons. They might not be available in the next country you visit. Save any Styrofoam ones you get; they'll last better than pressed paper ones and can be washed if necessary. Pressed-paper egg containers also seem to promote mold on the eggshells. In Mexico, the Mediterranean, and the Far East, you can buy plastic egg carriers in 1-dozen and 2-dozen sizes. These are great. They're sturdier than Styrofoam, have a good carrying handle, and are quite crush-resistant. I still have one I bought in Mexico nine years ago.

As for quantity, I take as many eggs as I have room for. Eggs are a real bargain worldwide. A dozen of them cost less than one 12-ounce can of corned beef, yet they can be a main course for five or six people. I figure on a minimum of two eggs a person per day on real long passages, one and a half a day on 1,000-mile voyages. When most of your other perishables are an ancient memory and cans are the reality, eggs in all forms still taste fresh—eggs and egg salads, deviled eggs, omelets, custards, soufflés, cookies.

For our voyage south from Virginia and then around Cape Horn, I wanted provisions to last for up to 60 days at sea. I purchased small packets of powdered whole eggs from a camping supply store. They have since become a staple on board—not a substitute for fresh eggs, but a supplement. They are easier to handle than fresh eggs for baking projects—i.e., just add tablespoon of egg powder and 1/4-cup of water to any recipe calling for a whole egg. They make fine scrambled eggs if you add a few drops of vinegar to the recommended mix plus some fresh or dried parsley, then beat well with a wisk before cooking. One caveat: The soft paper and foil packets are susceptible to leakage, so I store my spares in Ziploc bags until I need them. With powdered eggs on board, I can reduce my fresh egg supply by about a third.

. . . .

Day 11

Noon to noon: 73 miles
Miles to date: 809
Light north breeze, close reach, cloudy skies

Lunch
liver pâté sandwiches with tomato slices
cabbage salad

Dinner
pork stew
bread, butter
red wine

....

CABBAGE SALAD

Combine
1½ cups chopped cabbage
½ tomato cut into cubes
½ cup bean salad

> Toss together and let sit for a while before serving.

....

PORK STEW

Prepare
3 carrots, scrubbed and cut in chunks
4 potatoes, scrubbed and cut in chunks
1 onion, cut in chunks
2 bay leaves
½ cup saltwater
½ cup freshwater

> Bring to a boil, then reduce heat and simmer until potatoes are tender.

Add

    2 cans (small size) pork chunks
        (Chinese Great Wall brand)

    1 tsp. sweet basil

    Bring to a boil.

Combine separately

    3 tbs. gravy mix or 3 tbs. flour

    ½ cup red wine

> Thicken stew by slowly adding wine-and-gravy mixture. Stir constantly 2 minutes.

We are moving along a bit better today, and our noon sight confirmed that the Kuroshio (Japan Current) is giving us an extra 20 or 25 miles a day. So at worst we could take 36 or 38 days more to reach land. That's well within our planned, good-eating stores list.

Several years ago, we read a delightful true sailing story in *Sail* magazine called "The French Nudist and I." In it, Kay Cartwright describes Rosie, a hitchhiking French sailor who joins the Cartwrights on board their ketch in the Canary Islands for a voyage across the Atlantic. Rosie comes complete with her own sextant, life raft, and a bag of 99 spices with the ability to use them. I wonder if Rosie brought her own wine, too. Every bit of spice and wine magic you can think of is necessary when it comes to cooking from cans. Even if we didn't carry drinking wine on board, I'd still want some for cooking.

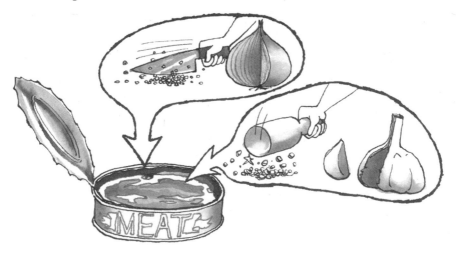

DAY 11. *Dressing up canned meats will require all the spices and imagination you possess.*

136

Wine and Liquor around the World

As we look back over 40 years of voyaging, many of our fondest memories seem to have connections with wines or liquors. There was the time two families of local fishermen adopted us as we explored the upper reaches of the Ria de Arosa in northwestern Spain. Late one evening, as we sat on the porch of their shoreside hacienda savoring a heaping broth-filled bowl of oysters and mussels, one of the fishermen began strumming minor-keyed melodies on his guitar. Our hostess, Marisa, blew out each candle on the table and then went into her simple kitchen. Moments later, she turned off the lights in her house. For a few minutes, we sat quietly contemplating the perfectly still evening, the glint of stars on still waters with *Seraffyn* backlit by the moon, the warmth of companionship that seemed to require no common language. Then Maria came out and set a large bowl on the table. Pedro, her husband, lit a match and touched it to the liquid in the bowl. He began lifting the burning brandy with a ladle and letting it stream back like ribbons of flame. As he poured warm brandy into small pottery cups for each of us, I felt like I had been witnessing some ancient ritual. Just as I began to lift the cup to my lips, the last flames flickered out. The heady fumes seemed to flood my senses. In the darkness, Marisa began to sing a song so haunting that tears began flowing from every eye.

Other memories are of expeditions with a dozen South African friends in the Cedarburg Mountains, four hours north of Cape Town, to find the best new harvest wines for our voyage across the Atlantic; and of Argentinean friends competing to introduce us to the wines they were sure would suit not only our tastes but our pocketbook for our voyage south toward Tierra del Fuego. Afloat, there were the wonderful evenings where, with or without friends on board, we watched hopefully for an ever-elusive green flash and raised a glass of wine or rum punch to toast the promise of many more sunsets to share.

Though we are not wine or liquor connoisseurs, we have found discovering the new wines of each country to be one of the delights of cruising. Almost every country we've visited has its specialties. Since voyaging yachtsmen can often buy beer, wine, and liquor duty-free at prices that are 50 percent lower than in the stores, few cruising people sail with a dry ship. Even when we live ashore, wine has always had its place on the table. So it is natural that it is the same at sea. Cocktail hour is a special part of our offshore day. We turn on the stereo or play guitar and sing. I enjoy a sherry or rum-and-Coke while Larry has scotch or rum and water. On cold days at sea, a hot buttered rum sets a nice tone for the evening. At dinner, Larry will usually have a glass or

137

two of wine, which definitely helps him sleep while I take the first watch of the night. (See Day 1, above, for our hot buttered rum recipe.)

On delivery trips, we include one drink before dinner and a little wine or beer with dinner for the crew who will not be standing the first night watch. On long passages, especially ones such as described in this book, there are lots of small inconveniences and discomforts. The custom of wine with dinner adds a special sparkle to meals and brightens days that might otherwise be pallid.

The following list of wine and liquor provisioning information is arranged alphabetically by country or territory. As you read it, please remember that these are our opinions only, and they are based on our tastes. Larry tends to like his whiskey straight and his wines red and full-bodied; I enjoy lighter, sweeter wines and liqueurs instead of liquor. Sometimes we tend to choose quantity instead of quality when it comes to wine for cruising get-togethers.

For voyaging, we have learned that bottled wines keep far better than any we buy in bulk and put into our own bottles. Boxed wines are an excellent choice for storage afloat; they are lighter, better shaped, and less breakable. The quality of wines being put in cartons has improved tremendously. Since no air gets into the bladder containing the liquid, your wine will not oxidize and will keep its flavor far longer than it would in a bottle that is opened and closed time and again. But a word of warning: Do not remove the bladders from their cardboard boxes to save storage room. The constant flexing of the unsupported bladders will make the foil lining deteriorate and contaminate the wine.

It is important to consider customs requirements when you are provisioning to sail to a new country. We have found that there are few restrictions on yachts carrying alcoholic beverages for the crew's consumption. In some countries, sailors arriving with more than the legal quantities on board are allowed to put the overage in sealed lockers to be consumed on departure. In a few, you can pay a minimal import duty fee. We make note of the few exceptions in the following list.

ARGENTINA

This is a red wine connoisseur's paradise, a sweet white wine lover's dream—with an overwhelming selection at prices that made us wish we could carry more than the normal 120 bottles our wine cellar in *Taleisin's* bilge can comfortably contain. It paid us to shop around here, as prices for favorite wines varied by as much as 50 percent between one wholesaler and another. Larry found the brandies to be bold and smooth. Only the reminder that our next destination, Chile, also had a reputation for good wines kept us from overloading *Taleisin*.

AMERICAN SAMOA

The local shops carry a good variety of Australian, New Zealand, and California wines at affordable prices. Definitely stock up here for the journey through to Singapore or Australia. Prices are far better than you will find in most of the islands to the west (including New Zealand). The same applies for liquor.

AUSTRALIA

Both red and white wines are very good, and many have won international prizes. Prices can be excellent. This is the country that created boxed wines (called "Chateau de Cardboard" by cruisers), and we found several very nice boxed wines in 2-liter casks sold at discount by larger chain stores. Australian brandies rival their French counterparts at half the price. We found the local rum and whiskey copies to be pretty rough. But beer-loving cruisers find a lot to like.

AZORES

When we sailed here in the early 1970s on *Seraffyn,* we found the wine to be unique and interesting. Grown in volcanic soil in a cool, damp but very sunny climate, the reds were hardy if a bit rough; the white wines were gold-colored and extremely potent; the local brandies were crisp but not worth remembering other than for their low prices. During a more recent stay (30 years later), the local shops were filled with very cheap wines from the mainland ($1.20 a liter in 5-liter bottles), and it was only at the homes of local friends that we were served the island wines we remembered. On the other hand, since we were headed south to Brazil with at least 5,000 miles of sailing ahead of us and no definite plans to stop at the Cape Verde Islands, we bought a good supply of 750ml bottled, corked Portuguese wines at reasonable prices (about 50 percent lower than U.S. prices).

BERMUDA

There are no indigenous wines in Bermuda, but this is a good place to purchase duty-free liquor from around the world. All of the ship chandlers carry different wines, so shop around if you are headed toward the Caribbean islands, where wine is often quite pricey.

BRAZIL

Wine is expensive here. Most is imported from Chile and Argentina and then heavily taxed. We were glad we had stocked up in South Africa before sailing to Rio de Janeiro. Most people enjoy the local clear *cachaça*— a liquor somewhat like vodka and made from sugar-cane juice—which is inexpensive and potent. The favorite drink is *Caipirinha,* which seems to be served almost everywhere from noon to midnight.

CAIPIRINHA

Use a large glass pitcher.
Wash and quarter at least a dozen limes.
Squeeze the limes lightly, then put
each lime and its juice into the pitcher.

Add

¼ cup of sugar for a 1-quart or 1-liter pitcher.
Fill the pitcher to the brim with small ice cubes.
Add *cachaça* to top up the pitcher.

Stir

Stir lightly with a wooden spoon, mashing the
limes a bit to release the flavor from their skins.

> Serve before the ice melts, spooning some of the limes into each glass along with the *caipirinha.*

BRUNEI

We were amazed to find a large supply of pleasant Australian wines available here. This is a strictly Muslim sultanate, and the door of any business that offers wine and liquor for sale has a sign that says, "It is against the law to sell alcoholic beverages to any person of the Muslim religion." The huge numbers of foreign oil-company employees are the main purchasers. Prices are about 25 percent lower than in Singapore.

CANADA

A word of warning for those arriving from overseas: Foreign yachts may only bring in two bottles of wine per crew. Any overage will normally be confiscated or taken into storage (for which you will be charged a monthly fee). If you are arriving from an offshore voyage, such as when we sailed from Chile to Victoria a few seasons back, and you declare a larger amount, officials will often bend the rules and allow you to keep a few extra bottles to save them the hassle of arranging storage. Cruisers who regularly sail back and forth between the United States and Canada often have separate lockers for Canadian-purchased wine or liqueur.

Wine and liquor is sold primarily in government stores, though this is slowly changing in many provinces. Prices are 25 to 50 percent higher than for the same wines purchased just across the border. We are impressed with the improvement in Canadian-grown wines over the past several years, but the prices for the good local wines are high when compared with their imported counterparts. Sherries made in the Okanagan Valley wineries (in British Columbia) rival the best of those from Europe.

Taleisin's bilge "wine cellar" holds up to 120 bottles (or the equivalent in boxed wines).

141

CAPE VERDE ISLANDS

Though the selection of wines available here is limited, the prices are similar to European ones, with no local taxes added. Local people do not have the money for any but the least expensive of wines, so many of the wine bottles in the cruisers' price range may have been stored for a long time in less-than-ideal conditions. We would not plan to stock up here.

CHILE

We had looked forward to sampling Chilean wines ever since the captain of a Chilean tuna clipper in Panama befriended us during the second year of our cruising life. He gave us a gift of his favorite wine—a 10-liter bottle covered in beautifully woven wicker. We lashed it to the base of our mast, where it stayed for the six weeks required to fully savor its delightful contents. When we reached the San Blas Islands, we traded the empty bottle for a handsome mola. We finally got to explore the wines of Chile after sailing *Taleisin* around Cape Horn a few years ago. We were not disappointed, but the abundance of Argentinean wines had spoiled us, as had the prices. Even in main centers, Chilean wines of similar quality—though inexpensive by European or American standards—tended to be twice the price of those we'd purchased in next-door Argentina. Given the choice, I would choose to put the extra money into higher-quality Argentinean wines if I were filling up my wine cellar. But since we were heading into the Pacific, with our supplies from Argentina depleted, we topped up on Chilean reds from the districts just north of Valdivia and fine dessert wines from the mountains near Santiago.

COLOMBIA

There is a surprising collection of imported wines available here at affordable prices. The local rums can range from very inexpensive (acceptable for mixed drinks) to very high-priced boutique products. Mixers can be inexpensive if bought by the case; the bottle deposit fee is almost as high as the price of the liquor.

COSTA RICA

There are few locally made alcoholic drinks other than white rum, which is coarse and expensive. Mixers are also expensive, so it pays to bring bottled or canned beverages with you from Mexico or Panama.

EGYPT

There are no locally produced wines. This is mainly a Muslim country, so few shops carry alcoholic beverages. Duty-free liquor is available for yachtsmen transiting the Suez Canal.

ENGLAND

If you like beer, this is the place for variety. Guinness stout, on draught, in a fire-warmed 600-year-old pub, must be tasted to be appreciated. Though England is part of the European Union, all alcoholic drinks are taxed £1 sterling a bottle, plus GST. We found that it paid to top up at the huge wine warehouses in Calais, France, where we bought fine European wines at half the United Kingdom prices. There is no problem taking as much of it as you want back to England with you.

FIJI

The only locally produced beverage is kava, made from the root of the pepper tree. It is actually a mild narcotic. When you visit a new island in this group, you are expected to take along a gift of kava roots to present to the local chief. He will have the roots prepared and ceremoniously welcome you to his district. Partaking of kava from the communal drinking bowl is part of your initiation. I am told kava tastes like slightly muddy water and leaves your tongue and lips feeling numb. Reports are that wine and liquor are hard to find except in main centers, and prices are relatively high.

FRANCE

Some of our favorite wines are those we have bought directly from farmers as we toured by motorcycle. Prices are lowest at large wine warehouses on the outskirts of larger towns. Surprisingly, a specialist at one of these gave us an hour-long tasting tour to try to find a hearty red wine to please Larry. Then he finally admitted that he himself found imported Chilean Cabernets to be the best buy for a good wine at a good price.

FRENCH POLYNESIA

Wines from France and the EU were among the only reasonably priced goods we found in this area. Stock up in Papeete; you will pay double in other islands. Chateau Plastique—as cruising sailors call the French table wine sold in crude-looking, 1-liter bottles—is cheap, and to me it tastes that way. Beer is pricey. But several brands of Cognac are offered at affordable prices.

GREECE

Many wines here are sold in bulk, but, unlike in Spanish *bodegas*, wine dealers usually have only two or three varieties to offer. So in Greece it is a matter of visiting each of the local dealers, tasting their wines, and then trying to remember which dealer's wines you liked best. Retsina, the most common wine in the islands, is aged in resinous pine barrels; to me, it tastes like turpentine. Even when it is well chilled, I find it is just barely drinkable. Larry likes it—chilled or not.

IRELAND

Another fine place for beer drinkers. Whiskey lovers will enjoy comparing the local distillery products to those of Scotland. Wine is all imported from the continent; prices are kept high with local taxes designed to try to limit alcohol consumption. There are no limits on bringing in alcoholic beverages, as it is assumed they all come from European Union neighbors.

ISRAEL

The local wines are excellent, but we found prices in Israel to be the most expensive in the Mediterranean. There were no duty-free provisions available in Tel Aviv, though we heard you could make arrangements through ship chandlers in Haifa.

ITALY

Wine here is sold only in bottles unless you visit very small villages. We found some wonderful wines by asking local people for recommendations. But we also learned that wines you come to love in one part of Italy can't be found just a hundred miles away. Prices are about 50 percent higher than in Spain. Table wines come in returnable bottles with high deposits to ensure that you recycle. On the island of Lampedusa, we first encountered a lovely dry white wine called Porto Palo, produced in Sicily. We bought two cases to tide us over to Malta. A month later, we sailed to Sicily, landed in Porto Palo, and found that their entire supply goes to Lampedusa. Never found another low-priced wine as nice anywhere in Italy.

Almost 30 years later, I noticed a few bottles of this same wine in a government shop on Gabriela Island, north of Victoria, Canada. Just for old times' sake, I bought two bottles. Without showing Larry the label, I poured him a glass of the chilled wine and asked him what he thought. "This is good," he said. "Reminds me of that wine from Sicily, the one we liked so much when we were cruising around Malta."

JAMAICA, CAYMAN ISLANDS, AND CARIBBEAN IN GENERAL

Finest rums in the world. Mount Gay Eclipse Rum is an international favorite among sailors. At the source, it costs about $1.50 a bottle. In Jamaica, Appleton Estate Gold Four-star Rum was Larry's choice. I mix mine, so I can't tell the difference.

JAPAN

We had quite a surprise here. We knew about sake (rice wine), produced by the Japanese, but we never suspected that the local breweries would be copying European wines and whiskeys. As usual, Japanese copies are excellent, with prices low compared to most items here. Sake takes getting used to. Served warm, it is extremely intoxicating. But the local custom of drinking warm sake from tiny cups while seated barefoot on cushions in a house made of paper screens in the company of six Japanese sailors is a special treat. Thank you, Sanae.

MALAYSIA AND SINGAPORE

There is no local wine or liquor, but some pleasant beers are brewed here. Duty-free beverages are readily available in Penang, Klang, and Singapore through ships' suppliers.

MALTA

This is the only place we have visited where wine was delivered to our door (the ship's boarding ladder) just like milk. Unfortunately, the local wines can be of poor quality—good enough for washing down a meal, but not much to remember. Fewer than 100 acres of grapes grow on Malta. As one local story goes, an old Maltese winemaker is lying on his deathbed. He calls over his oldest son and whispers, "Son, I want you to know my secret. . . They do make wine from grapes, too." In fact, Maltese wine is fermented from grape juice shipped in from Sicily. Excellent duty-free imported wine is available when you set sail.

MEXICO

Tequila, rum, and gin are half the price you would pay for them in the United States. There are some interesting brandies to sample, plus chocolate liqueurs. Rough red wine is now being produced in Mexico's northern states, but in 2002 we found few that were worth remembering. Be careful of the frozen margaritas and daiquiris offered in cafés and bars—they are much more potent than they taste. If you are not used to drinking tequila, go easy.

NEW ZEALAND

Some grand beers, excellent white wines, and, recently, moderate- and high-priced red wines are comparing well to those from Australia and even Europe. Prices are higher than in Australia, and customs officials are lenient with cruisers arriving from overseas, so don't be afraid to stock up in American Samoa or Australia before sailing here. You can buy duty-free at good prices if you depart from Whangarei.

NORWAY

Prices here are outrageous. We were told to take along some whiskey when we sailed from Scotland's Outer Hebrides. We found there was no better gift to bring; in Norway, the same bottle sold for four times the price.

We never tire of sampling new wines as we cruise. Here we are trying out Kiwi specialties.

PHILIPPINES

Excellent selection of rums and gin. Filipino businessmen we got to know at the Manila Yacht Club preferred the expensive 5-year-old rums. But after careful taste tests offered by the bartender, we decided our favorite was the unaged, gold-label, 1/4-the-price rum. A local drink—calamansi-and-rum over ice—is a treat. Calamansi (or calamancy) is a tiny citrus fruit that has a flavor somewhat like a cross between a lemon and an orange.

POLAND

Wines from the former Iron Curtain countries are available here at exceptionally low prices. We found Bulgarian red wines to be excellent; in fact, the red Gamza wine we had on board for the North Pacific passage described in this book is one we first tasted in Poland. Pink sparkling wine from the Crimea (Ukraine) is a particular favorite of mine.

PORTUGAL

No cruise in this area is complete without a visit to Oporto. Visitors can choose from five different *cavás* (wine warehouses in caves along the river) and take a delightful tour that ends with a chance to sample the cave's supply of port wines. Eat a good meal before you go. There will be at least 20 different varieties offered; the sample glasses are small. The samples and tours were free, the prices for bottled port irresistible.

Vinho verde ("green wine") is a favorite wine on the coast; the wine is called green because it is not fully aged or as potent as most wines. Supply your own bottle at the local café for good wine at low prices.

SAUDI ARABIA

If you visit any port here, all your liquor must be put in a sealed locker. The seals will be checked frequently, and the consequences can be very grave if you are found with illegal alcohol. Do not be tempted to smuggle liquor to oil-rig personnel or locals in this area. You may earn $50 or $60 a bottle, but you could possibly lose your boat.

SCANDINAVIA

Liquor and wine in all countries in this area, including those within the EU, was very expensive—even the local aquavit, a potent vodka-like drink. Duty-free liquor can be bought when outward bound in the Kiel Canal. Inward bound, it would pay to stop at a French port and load up before exploring the Baltic.

SCOTLAND

No cruise through the Hebrides would be complete without visiting the various distillers, most of which are situated next to fine anchorages. A favorite stop before beginning the tour is Campbelltown, just inside the Mull of Kintyre, where a 500-year-old pub features hundreds of different malt whiskeys. Prices ranged from about US$3 a shot to more than $500. We are told that some aficionados visit once each year for a tot at this price.

SPAIN

Wine-tasting adventures start here. Every town has a *bodega* where wine and liquors are sold from the barrel. If you arrive with five or six empty bottles, the proprietor usually will hand you a small glass and invite you to taste some from each barrel. In some *bodegas* we visited, there were as many as 15 different wines with prices varying from unbelievably cheap to moderate. Liquors—especially a good selection of brandies—were also included in the array. Different regions had distinctly different specialties. Some we preferred were:

Galicia (northern Spain)—People here preferred a very young white wine that is drunk from low, handleless cups. I really liked it.

Costa del Sol—Even if you don't like sweet wines, you must try the local *medio-medio,* a half-and-half combination of muscatel and young white wine. A wonderful aperitif. Spanish sparkling wines are a bargain, with two of our favorites being Carta Blanca Sec and Freixenet Cordon Negro.

Mallorca—In Puerto Andraitx, a well-loved local wine is available from the tobacco shop. Called *vino de verano* ("summer wine"), it is a light red wine with only 10 percent alcohol content. Smooth, perfect chilled for lunch on a hot summer day.

SRI LANKA

Arak, made from coconuts, is similar to white rum and usually is served straight or with ginger ale. A potent punchlike drink is also made using arak, papaya juice, and lemons; it's delicious over ice. Local soft drinks are excellent, with Elephant brand ginger ale being the best of the lot.

UNITED STATES

Although there are limits on the amount of alcoholic beverages you can bring with you as a tourist or returning resident, officials clearing yachts in from overseas are somewhat lenient as long as you declare what you have on board when asked. Surprisingly, though we fly the Canadian flag and have, several times over the year, cleared in both by telephone and by arriving at a customs location and meeting with an official in person, we have never been asked to provide a list of stores. We were, however, asked if we were carrying banned substances, drugs, or large amounts of cash. State laws govern the cost of alcoholic beverages. Local usage governs the quality and variety available in shops.

Wine prices on the West Coast are excellent, with real bargains from big wine outlets such as Trader Joe's, where we stock up on their specials-of-the-month. A wine-tasting trip should be part of any visit to the area around San Francisco. On the East Coast, some of the wines, brandies, and sherries from New York state are well worth a try. Beer is relatively inexpensive. Liquor can be costly but is available duty-free at major shipping ports.

. . . .

Of necessity, the foregoing list is incomplete; it only mentions the highs and/or lows of our round-the-world cruising adventures with wine and liquor. If it sounds like a lot of drinking, remember that the list is gleaned from nearly four decades of cruising. Shopping for interesting and affordable local wines can be a delightful adventure.

A wonderfully informative incident happened while we were delivering a 54-foot ketch from Palma, Mallorca, to New Orleans. On board, we had found a 5-gallon pine barrel marked "Grog Keg." It had never been used, and you could see light through its staves. So we filled it with water and set it in a large plastic bucket in the shower stall for the three weeks it took us to prepare the boat and sail from Mallorca to Madeira. By then, the keg was good and tight.

I didn't carry the keg with me when I did my stores scouting in Madeira, so it took quite a humorous mixture of Spanish, English, and hand signals to explain to the Portuguese-speaking taxi driver that I was looking for a wine shop that sold bulk wine. When he started driving away from the market district and straight up the hills toward the outskirts of town, I started getting a bit concerned. One mile later, he drew to a stop in front of a vine-covered stone warehouse. He led me inside, where I was surrounded by beautiful old oak barrels and the aroma of wine.

A gentle-faced, middle-aged man in a gray business suit saw us and came down from his office. He spoke English, and when I explained my quest, he said, "Bring me the barrel. If it is sweet, I will sell you some good wine to go in it. But if it has been used for bad wines, that will ruin it."

The next morning, Larry and I carried the keg with us. As soon as we arrived at the wine warehouse, the same gentleman appeared and called to a diminutive, gnarled-looking man who was working around the huge barrels at the back of the warehouse. Together they removed the bung in our little barrel; each smelled it carefully, conferring seriously in Portuguese for several minutes. Then the proprietor turned to us and said, "Yes, it is a sweet barrel. What kind of wine do you prefer?"

Larry asked for a dry, hearty, red wine, and we were led along the rows of barrels until the proprietor pointed to one of them. The gnarled wine taster climbed a short ladder and pulled the bung from the top of a 5-foot-diameter barrel. Then he dipped into the barrel a long, thin-handled ladle. It was made from a 4-foot length of bamboo, with the bottom 6 inches left round to scoop up the wine through the bung hole. The wine he brought out was excellent, like a hearty French Burgundy. With our approval, he climbed down and opened the spigot on the huge barrel, poured a liter of wine directly into our small keg, swished the keg around for a minute, and then, to our horror, poured the wine out onto the floor. Then he proceeded to fill our keg, taking wine from the large barrel and measuring it in 2-liter bottles. As we watched, the proprietor explained that these wines were from his family vineyards, which were 8 miles outside the city on the hills of southern Madeira.

"Now you must be careful about how you decant this wine," he told us. "Do not take off one bottle at a time. Instead, keep four or five bottles with you and decant a whole week's supply. Then take a small square of clean cotton and dip it in pure alcohol; a piece 12 centimeters by 12 centimeters is enough. Place it just inside the bung hole, light it on fire, drop it into the wine barrel, and seal the bung. That small fire will burn all of the oxygen out of the barrel and your wine will last perfectly for up to a year, even on your ship."

As we were thanking him and paying the 47 cents a liter he charged for his wine, I asked, "Do you have a real fine bottle of Madeira that we could buy?" He excused himself and climbed the steps down to the cellar below the warehouse. A few minutes later, he emerged with two unlabeled bottles marked with hand-painted numbers. Their tops were sealed with a heavy ceramic coating. As his taster finished wiping off our barrel and finding a box to carry the two bottles of Madeira, the proprietor ran his fingers down the pages of a much-used notebook. Finally he pointed to some numbers, turned to us, and said, "Each year our family stores away 200 bottles of the finest wine from our vineyards. These were bottled 24 years ago. Please take them as a gift and listen carefully to the radio as you sail. In seven days, there will be the first Portuguese election in 50 years. If we do not become a communist country, then open this wine and drink to our success. If our people choose the communists, then please do not drink this wine until Portugal is again free."

Eight days later, 1,200 miles from Madeira, we heard the BBC radio reports of Portugal's election results. Larry opened our first bottle of Madeira, and as the mellow, full-bodied, sweet wine first began to work its magic inside my throat, we toasted the winemaker who cared so much about his family's product and the now-free country from which he came.

. . . .

Day 12

Noon to noon: 96 miles
Miles to date: 905
Cloudy, occasional drizzle; 8-knot headwind

Lunch
leftover stew
bread, butter
hot chocolate

Teatime
raw carrot sticks
Cheddar cheese, biscuits

Dinner
Greek salad
canned ham, sliced and fried
canned sweet potatoes
white wine

....

GREEK SALAD

Arrange on a plate
tomato slices
thin onion slices
green pepper slices
cucumber slices

Sprinkle with
feta cheese (if available)
olive oil
oregano, salt, pepper
chopped garlic

> If possible let sit in a
> cool place for one
> hour before serving.

....

On Catching Rain

Larry woke me during the morning off-watch with a shout: "It's raining!" He struggled into his wet-weather gear, and I soon heard the sounds of the raincatcher being tied in place. I looked out the companionway and saw only a slight drizzle. But when I awoke three hours later, Larry told me he'd caught 3 or 4 gallons of freshwater. Once again, we laughed about the eight years we'd spent experimenting with all sorts of ideas for raincatchers until the day Larry come up with the obvious solution. He tied our mainsail boom cover under the main boom and it acted like a rain gutter, catching almost every drop that ran off the mainsail. Larry sewed a rope grommet into the part nearest the mast, and we insert a length of hose into the grommet. During a tropical squall lasting 15 minutes, we've caught more than 35 gallons of water. The raincatcher is also handy because it can be left right in place on any point of sail, as long as the winds don't surpass 30 knots. (See following section.)

By dinnertime, we were close-hauled, heeling about 15 or 20 degrees, beating into a short chop. Dinner was definitely not as elaborate as it would have been otherwise.

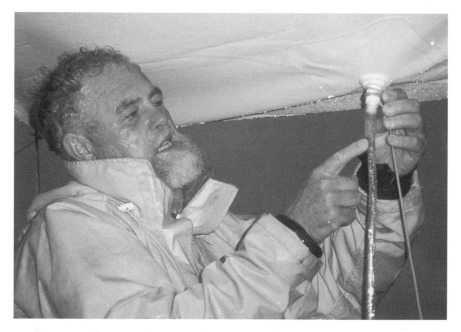

We use our large awning to catch rainwater when we are at anchor. Just like our at-sea, under-the-boom raincatcher, it has udders built in at the four lowest points.

Sweet Water from the Skies

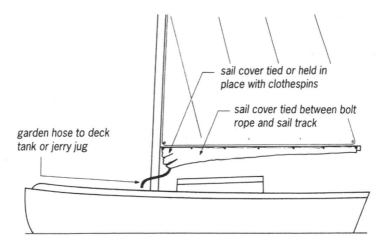

FIGURE 11. *Pardey's Unpatented Nearly Perfect Passagemaking Raincatcher*

Throughout our cruising years, we've seen and tried several different raincatchers and found that they all fall into three categories: deck-collection systems, sun-cover systems, and sail or mast systems. As you look over your boat for potential rain-collection ideas, you'll want to keep four things in mind. First, a well-thought-out system can augment your regular tankage. If you have a watermaker, it can help conserve fuel and engine running time. It can cut down on the number of trips to the fuel dock for freshwater and can allow your crew to shower more often, wash clothes on board, and generally be more relaxed about one of the irksome aspects of life afloat—control of water usage. But since the system will only be used when there is a chance of rain, it should be unobtrusive yet easy to set up quickly. At sea, an efficient raincatcher should work while the boat is heeling, tossing spray.

If the sails can be incorporated into the at-sea system, even the condensation of fog or mist can add a bit to your water supply. In port, any system you design should be workable in fresh winds. Rainsqualls around tropical islands are often preceded by force 8 or 9 gusts. If you have to lower and reset your collection system for each squall, chances are you'll say, "The heck with it." So the best solution would be a catcher that can be set in place and left unattended for much of the time, or a combination of systems for various conditions. Finally, only if I were on board and able to taste the water running out of the collection hoses would I feel good about letting it drain directly into our main water tanks.

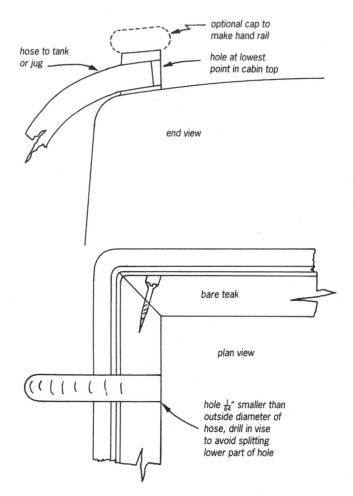

optional cap to
make hand rail

hose to tank
or jug

hole at lowest
point in cabin top

end view

bare teak

plan view

hole $\frac{1}{64}$" smaller than
outside diameter of
hose, drill in vise
to avoid splitting
lower part of hole

FIGURE 12. *Cabin-Top Water Collector*

One of the simplest systems we've seen is a cabin-top collector (fig. 12). On some English cruising boats, the grab rails (or cabin trim) are modified to act as a rain gutter along the whole length of the cabin. At the lowest point on port and starboard sides, a hose jams or screws tightly into the wood. At sea, a length of hose can then be led from either side to a plastic jug to collect water on calmer sailing days. In port, hoses can be inserted in both sides, and once the water is tasted, it can be safely fed directly into your water tanks during heavier rainfalls. A few cruisers we've met have extolled what sounds like an even simpler system—blocking off the scuppers in the boat's toerails or bulwarks and letting the water that gathers on deck flow directly into the open deck fill plates. With this system, there is a real risk of contaminating your water supply with bacteria and dirt carried on board by

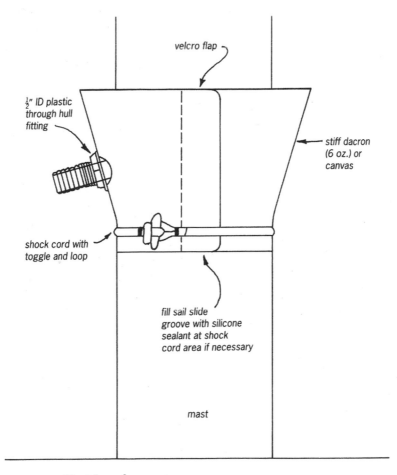

velcro flap

½" ID plastic
through hull
fitting

stiff dacron
(6 oz.) or
canvas

shock cord with
toggle and loop

fill sail slide
groove with silicone
sealant at shock
cord area if necessary

mast

FIGURE 13. *Mast Funnel*

guests and crew. The thought of the bacteria that cause athlete's foot, plus the shore dirt carried on by bare feet, makes this system seem less than tasty.

Another very simple, easy-to-construct system is a mast funnel. Since the funnel skirt can be unobtrusive and not affected by wind, it can be left in place whenever you wish. To collect the amazingly strong stream of water that runs down your mast once the rain sets in, you need only have a semicircular skirt of stiff canvas and a piece of shock cord, plus hose to reach either a jug or your water tanks, as figure 13 shows. As a temporary or trial mast collector, you can wrap a short piece of 1/2-inch-diameter line around the mast just above the gooseneck, secure it together lightly with a lashing of twine, and then let the end dangle into a funnel. The funnel will guide enough water into your waiting jug to encourage you to build a more efficient mast catchment system.

Sail-based water-collection systems can be the most efficient choice at sea. But they only work in port if there is little wind or if the sail used is a riding sail. We've seen several different ways of catching the water that runs down a mainsail. Pete Sutter, a veteran San Francisco racer/sailmaker-turned-offshore cruiser, showed us the simplest sail-based system we've seen—one that he used on his Wylie 37, *Wild Spirit*. He stitched a double layer of fabric along both sides of a mainsail seam, just above the first reef. The flap was tacked in place along the upper edge to produce a water trap that funneled rainwater forward to a small, 1/2-inch-inside-diameter plastic through-hull fitting (fig. 14). This system worked well even during fairly brisk sailing conditions as salt spray rarely reached the area above the first reef. For boats with high booms, it might be best to secure the flap below the reef points to take advantage of as much area of the sail as possible.

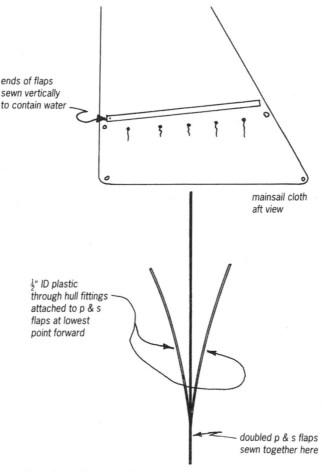

ends of flaps sewn vertically to contain water

mainsail cloth aft view

$\frac{1}{2}$" ID plastic through hull fittings attached to p & s flaps at lowest point forward

doubled p & s flaps sewn together here

FIGURE 14. *Pete Sutter's Super Gutter*

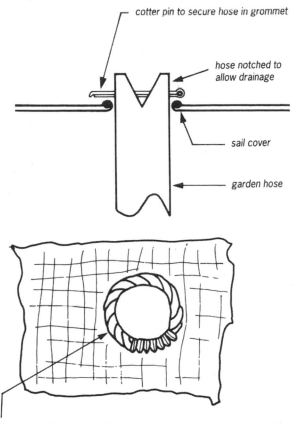

cotter pin to secure hose in grommet

hose notched to
allow drainage

sail cover

garden hose

3-strand marlin laid back into a grommet and sewn to sail cover at the
lowest point—should fit snugly around the garden hose

FIGURE 15. *Details for the Passagemaker's Raincatcher*

Only slightly less simple is the system Larry invented during our 49-day
voyage from Japan to Canada on board *Seraffyn*. He turned our mainsail
cover upside down and secured it to form a trough under the boom.
His trough caught almost every bit of water that rolled down the sail and
then funneled it forward to a reservoir area he created by lacing the head
of the mainsail cover securely. As we sailed closer to Canada, he added
one simple modification that helped us arrive in port with full water tanks.
As figure 15 shows, he stitched a grommet to act as a hose-holder at the low
point of the reservoir. What amazed us most was that during days when fog
obscured the horizon, we caught up to 3 gallons of condensation during
each 24-hour period. We liked this system, and we had the people who
made our new mainsail cover for *Taleisin* sew a fabric udder into the head
area. The udder folds out of sight inside the cover, except when we need it

as part of the rain catchment system. Then a hose slips inside and is held by a lashing of marlin (fig. 16).

Andy Peterson, a Chicago sailmaker who is now cruising on his floating sail loft, a 57-foot ex-offshore racer named *Jakaranda*, originally showed us these cloth rain-funneling udders on his sun covers. We had him sew similar udders in four places near the edge of our sun cover, once we determined the best collection spots, and we found they contributed to an excellent in-port rain-collection system. But for any sun cover to be part of a collection system, it must be strong enough to set in winds of up to 25 knots. We had to reinforce our cover battens and batten pockets to make this workable. In stronger winds, the cover must be taken down and replaced with a smaller cover.

For those with a soft-top bimini, either udders such as those in figure 16 or a cloth gutter similar to the one Pete sewed onto his mainsail can be secured along the outer edges of the top. This will work both in port and at sea.

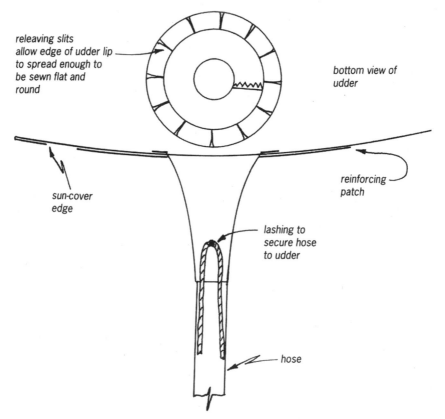

releaving slits allow edge of udder lip to spread enough to be sewn flat and round

bottom view of udder

sun-cover edge

reinforcing patch

lashing to secure hose to udder

hose

FIGURE 16. *Rain-Funneling Udder*

Whatever rain-collection system you experiment with, it pays to have spare jugs to hold the water you catch (see Day 13, "Water"). Even though the first runoff from a rain shower will probably produce water that is slightly brackish from the accumulated dust and salt being flushed off sails and rigging, this could still be useful for bathing and rinsing clothes in areas where rain is in short supply. Without spare jugs, you'd have to let it run off into the sea.

As you enjoy your first months of cruising, look around and consider the raincatching ideas here. Next time a shower or squall comes by, put on your wet-weather gear and spend some time watching the rain flow off your boat. Follow the track of the heaviest flows and think of ways to form a dam or entrapment area. Try rigging a small cover to see how much extra water this will catch. We were amazed to find a 4-foot-by-6-foot sailing sun cover caught 5 gallons of rainwater for us during a 15-minute squall, so remember that the catchment area need not cover your whole boat to be a helpful addition to your water supply.

Some people will say, Why not just add a mechanical watermaker to your want list? But those on small budgets will find that a water-augmenting system that works at almost no cost, uses no electricity, and requires little maintenance will allow the budget to be stretched to cover a few more months of cruising. Even those who do have watermakers on board should look toward collecting the free rain that falls on board, especially in a tranquil harbor. That way, their generators will get a break and they will be doing their small bit for the environment by using less fossil fuel and minimizing noise pollution.

Water Jugs Afloat

It is difficult to imagine the importance that water jugs assume in a cruising life. If you have spent the majority of your sailing life along the coast of Europe or the United States, chances are you have rarely had to cart every gallon of water you use from shore to ship in a dinghy. But once you set off for long-distance exploring, there will be few dock hoses accessible to deep-draft vessels, and fuel docks where you can lie alongside for top-ups will be rare except for major charter-boat areas. So a careful look at jugs before you set sail will have more beneficial effects than you'd first imagine.

For years, we used clear hard-plastic jugs; we secured them on deck near the shrouds when they were full and under the dinghy once they were empty. Full or empty, they always seemed to be underfoot, taking up far too much deck space, scratching the paintwork if they slid across it, stubbing toes at

Once the water tanks are full, Larry funnels rainwater from the upside-down mainsail cover into our collapsible water jugs. With this system, we rarely have to fret about water usage on our voyages.

night, and breaking open if one of us accidentally dropped a full one against something hard. All the solid jugs we tried—whether the cheapest or the most expensive—began to crack and deteriorate after a year in the tropics. And no matter how securely we tied them, one always seemed to slip loose from its lashings during a rough beat to windward—it would bang against the bulwark and drag one of us forward into the leeward scuppers just when we didn't particularly want to be there.

Next we tried the clear, soft-plastic folding jugs that we found in a fishing shop. These had definite advantages. We could carry half a dozen of them folded away in a locker until we needed them. Since they took up little space, we could leave two in the dinghy and grab a bit of water each time we went ashore—instead of making a major foray in order to top up our tanks. The soft jugs conformed to the shape of the bilges and so gave us instant extra internal water tankage separate from our main tanks for passagemaking. Their ability to conform to different shapes meant we could fill and secure one inside the dinghy when it is stored at sea, so if ever we had to abandon ship in a hurry, we'd have an extra water supply to augment that provided by our Survivor reverse-osmosis hand-pump watermaker. Though these soft jugs didn't burst or crack if they accidentally hit a cleat or metal fitting, they were susceptible to chafe and cuts where they lay against hose clamps or threaded bolt ends in the bilge. So we took care to store them clear of sharp objects. As with the solid jugs, the ultraviolet rays of the sun made these jugs brittle if we left them on deck for more than two months in the tropics. But because they could be folded and stowed below, we could reduce their sun exposure to a minimum.

After a chat with a plastics engineer, we finally found a way to improve on this aspect of jug performance. In his words, "Carbon black inhibits the transmission of UV rays into plastics and slows the breakdown of the plastic molecules." He recommended black plastic jugs such as those used by photochemical companies. We used hard, black-plastic chemical jugs for water storage during our last three years of voyaging on *Seraffyn*. Not one broke down due to UV light exposure. Then, during a shopping trip to a camper-supply house in California (Grant Bros. Camp Supplies, Harbor Boulevard, Costa Mesa), we found a fine compromise solution that has made our tussle with water jugs a far fairer one. Reliance Products L.P. (1093 Sherwin Rd., Winnipeg, Canada R3H 1A4, www.relianceproducts.com) produces tough black-plastic folding jugs, which they fit out to be used as solar showers for backpackers and campers. They are available in two sizes: 5 gallons (20 liters) and 2½ gallons (10 liters). We carry both sizes on board. The smaller one is easy for the lightweight crewperson to carry, so we can both help with the transport of water. This smaller size also takes up less space on deck, so we don't mind leaving one under a rain-collection hose even if there is no immediate sign of rain. These jugs seem impervious to the sun and have lasted six years at a time, in spite of hard use both on deck and below as we cruised on *Taleisin*. And, as a bonus, we find we often used them as they were originally intended—for on-deck, solar-heated showers after a day of skin diving near the coral reefs of tropical cruising grounds.

. . . .

Day 13

Noon to noon: 46 miles
Miles to date: 951
Brisk east wind, close-hauled
It's a dead muzzler (wind dead against us), but skies are sunny

Lunch
fried ham slices
fried tomato slices
bread, butter
canned rambutans stuffed with pineapple
(a Chinese Malaysian treat similar to lychees)

Teatime
butter cookies
pot of Earl Grey tea

Dinner
chicken in sage sauce
mashed potatoes
white wine

. . . .

 ## CHICKEN IN SAGE SAUCE

Sauté until onions start to lose opaqueness
1 onion, cut in strips
8 cloves garlic, chopped
2 small green peppers, in chunks
1 tsp. butter

Add
1 tsp. rubbed sage
1 14-oz. can Chicken in Supreme Sauce
(an English product similar to chicken in white sauce)

> Heat slowly 5 minutes, stirring lightly to avoid breaking up chicken chunks. Serve over mashed potatoes.

. . . .

DAY 13. *Some days, nothing seems to go right in the galley.*

Can Openers

Larry was in a fix-it mood when I woke up this morning, and almost before I'd really opened my eyes, he asked, "Need anything done?" "Can opener isn't working well," was the only thing that came to mind. Larry disassembled it, greased the moving parts with Lubriplate waterproof outboard-motor grease, and sharpened the inside edge of the cutting wheel with a fine file. It works like new. Ours is the same handheld, chrome-plated, heavy-duty $2.98 Sears, Roebuck Swing-Away can opener we've used for years. It has a replaceable cutter and plastic-covered handles. I find it much handier in a seaway than a wall-mounted model, because I can operate it right in the sink, so any overflows go down the drain. Besides, bulkhead models are subject to being ripped off in a seaway if the boat lurches while you are using them.

We are beating again, and it's a time for spills. Yesterday it was one rum-and-water and a deck of cards. We lost one of the cards somewhere in the bilge. Today it was half a bottle of Coca-Cola and the tea leaves from the teapot. The spills were only an additional irritant. Just beating to windward bugs me.

Water

Some folks say modern, efficient, reverse-osmosis watermakers have revolutionized voyaging, eliminating the need to worry about strict conservation of water, saving the weight and space of extra tankage for crossing oceans, eliminating the health concerns and hassles of taking on water in foreign ports. This may be true in that best of all worlds—the one where all electrical and mechanical devices work all the time, where there is enough sunshine to keep solar panels producing most of the day, and where the water around your boat is clean and oil-free. Unfortunately, however, none of us sail in this mythical world. So even if you have space, funds, and the desire to include a watermaker in your voyaging plans, it is important to start with the basics: good water storage, a well-designed tankage-and-pump system, conservation, and purification, which are covered here, along with some thoughts on integrating a watermaker into your system.

We've seen offshore sailors run out of water more often than they run out of food. When we were on the race committee for the Long Beach-to-La-Paz Race several years ago—a race that everyone expected to be a run but turned out to be a beat—two boats came in without freshwater. One crew just hadn't had enough water on board; the second had a broken pressure system and couldn't get at the 40 gallons stored in the bilge tank. We've met cruising people in the Med, Mexico, the Bahamas, and the Indian Ocean who had to cut short their stay in fish-laden, magically deserted anchorages when their water supply ran short.

But the people who must be most concerned about water are the ones bound across the oceans, where there are no escort vessels to come to their rescue, no nearby ports for replenishing water supplies. The passagemaker bound for the Marquesas or across the Indian Ocean must be able to carry water to last the crew for 30 days or more. As with food stores, you must carry 30 to 50 percent extra water for such unforeseen possibilities as unfavorable winds, storms, or gear failures. But unlike food stores, water needs special taste-proof containers. It is also far bulkier and heavier than food.

The average island-hopping onshore voyager needs 1½ gallons of freshwater per day per person. This is higher than for offshore passagemaking—first, because water supplies can be more easily replenished and therefore it's hard to convince people to ration themselves as carefully; second, because the surrounding saltwater in port may not be clean enough for use for washing or cooking.

On most passages, 2½ to 3 quarts per person per day is the minimum for safety and comfort, even though many cruising manuals—recommend

1/2 gallon per person. But most of these guides were written by Britons and Canadians such as the Hiscocks, the Smeetons, and the Guzzwells. They refer to the imperial gallon, which is 20 percent larger than the American gallon.

The average daily use of water per person on an offshore passage is: 1 cup per day for tooth brushing and morning washup; 2 cups per person per day for cooking; 4 cups for coffee, tea, hot chocolate, or fruit punch. With 2 1/2 quarts (or 10 cups) of water, this leaves less than a quart for other uses, such as a twice-a-week rinse-down and the occasional rinse-out of clothes that are necessary on a passage.

During particularly warm-weather passages, you need more freshwater. When we ran down the Red Sea in August, the temperature never fell below 95 degrees F, even at night, with 10 days at 110 degrees. We drank a gallon of water a day just to keep up our perspiration.

It's important to carry beer, soft drinks, and canned fruit juices, but it's safest to figure these items as additional liquid sources, not part of your freshwater supply. But if you are on a very weight-conscious boat, or if your water-storage capacity is extremely limited, it is acceptable to carry 2 cups of water less per day for every quart of other drinks you carry.

The most dependable and often least expensive water-tank building material for any boat other than a steel-hulled one is marine-grade stainless steel. Manufacturers of some glass boats don't use stainless steel because it is easier for them just to glass a cover over some section of your boat's keel, or to glass up a portion of the area under a bunk. They also complain that separate tanks can't be fully shaped to fit each curve of the boat, so they end up with a slightly smaller water capacity. But, unlike fiberglass tanks, stainless steel doesn't impart a flavor to your water supply. It is relatively easy to build with the proper baffles; it is lighter than a separate, properly constructed glass tank, and, surprisingly, it is less expensive. Stainless steel is subject to electrolysis. If your tank shows signs of pitting on the outside, check to see if wet, salty items are lying against the metal. Also check for electrolysis. When you are wiring your hull fittings together, it may be important to include your water tank, to avoid electrolysis.

One of the most reputable fiberglass molding shops in California's Newport Beach/Costa Mesa area, Crystalliner Corporation, explained that fiberglass water tanks can be constructed so that they are taste-free. To do so, they must be coated inside with finishing resin. The only problem is that when you secure the top of the tank in place, you have to use laminating resin. This 2-to-3-inch-wide strip, which goes completely around the inside of your tank, will impart a flavor to your water unless you cut an inspection plate in the top of your tank and then cover the inside joint with a coating of finishing resin over the appropriate epoxy sealant. If the tank has baffles in it, this can be a difficult job.

If you have fiberglass tanks on board right now and your water tastes bad, Crystalliner recommends steam-cleaning the tanks. In the United States, there are often outfits that bring a steam-cleaning unit right to the dock to clean bilges and engines. They'll know how to help your situation. A product called Aqua-Chem disguises the fiberglass flavor in water. There are also water-filtering systems that can be installed in your water-pressure line. But for the discriminating water drinker or the person who brews mild tea, there is no real answer if your fiberglass tank isn't properly built in the first place. Even after two or three years, your water will still taste bad.

Steel boats, of course, use steel tanks—the cheapest way to go and the best way to avoid electrolysis. For the first 10 years of a steel boat's life, tanks welded right in place work great for water. But after that, you will wish you had separate tanks, as you may start to suffer from rust-red water or holes caused by corrosion and electrolysis.

While I was preparing this chapter, I spoke with Vic Berry's sheet-metal shop in Newport Beach, California, the people who built all of *Seraffyn's* successful stainless-steel tanks a decade ago. Tom Berry, Vic's son, who now runs the shop, made a comment that surprised me. "We use 5052 marine alloy, the Coast Guard-recommended, saltwater-corrosion-proof aluminum," Tom told me, "and it is absolutely no good for freshwater tanks. The aluminum builds up calcium deposits that not only make the water taste bad, but after six or eight months these deposits will start to foul up your plumbing." These tanks are slightly cheaper to build and lighter. They cost the boat manufacturer less and are great for some purposes—but not for storing freshwater.

Molded polyethylene tanks have become popular with some production boatbuilders. They are seamless and have molded-in fittings. Such tanks can be fabricated in complex shapes to take more complete advantage of available space. They may cost less than other tanks to produce, since they are made in molds. They are lighter but they must be carefully supported—not only on the bottom but also on the sides—or they will work-harden and eventually crack. Baffles cannot be installed in molded tanks; for this reason, we would choose another type of tank material. Though polyethylene tanks can be repaired by heat-sealing right on the boat, you must have the tank absolutely dry and oil-free to do so. Taste should not be a problem with polyethylene tanks, but the hoses and fittings used in your system might impart a plastic flavor. Be sure to use all high-quality vinyl and polyvinyl chloride (PVC) hoses and fittings to produce the taste-free results. Tanks should not be stored in the sun before installation, or they will deteriorate and work-harden sooner than normal. We personally have had only one experience with polyethylene tanks during a 5,800-mile delivery from Palma, Mallorca, to New Orleans. The connections leaked and the tanks bulged badly. We lost more than 100 gallons of freshwater during a 2,800-mile passage. This convinced us that the tanks weren't strong enough, should have had baffles, or needed extra external support.

Flexible water tanks are light and easy to install, as they are form-fitting. They are also quite affordable, at less than a third the cost of custom-built metal tanks. In spite of these advantages, they should not be used for your main tankage, except on smaller local cruisers. Though they can be amazingly tough, they are prone to chafe, even if extremely well secured, since the water inside the bladder is constantly in motion, flexing the soft sides of the tanks. On the other hand, to extend your water supply for longer voyages, they are an excellent choice. In 2002, when we headed down the Atlantic from Bermuda toward Argentina and onward around Cape Horn on board *Taleisin*, we wanted the ability to be at sea for up to 60 days at a time. We purchased a flexible tank made by Vetus and carried it, well secured in the bilge, clear of all potential chafe points. We used the water from that tank first and then depended on our normal stainless-steel tanks for the rest of the voyage. As soon as we were finished with the flexible tank, we rolled it up and had the bilge free for its more normal use as a wine cellar. Later, when we were headed north through the tropics from Chile to Canada, we didn't want to give up the wine storage space, but we still liked the idea of having extra water on board, so we decided to try storing the tank on the cabin top and again use the water from it first. This worked well, especially because we were able to gravity-feed this water directly into our 10-gallon day tank.

Whatever type of tank you use, make sure it has sufficient baffles or cross plates built into it to prevent sloshing at sea. Eric and Susan Hiscock had water tanks welded into the large space under their sea berths on their 49-foot steel *Wanderer IV*. The builder did not put in proper baffles, and the water in their tanks sloshed around so much in a seaway that they couldn't sleep on those bunks. Baffles help prevent the oilcanning that half-empty tanks cause and cut down the flexibility of the tank. Stainless-steel tanks that aren't properly baffled and supported will eventually work-harden and crack. Tom Berry recommends a baffle every 16 inches on tanks 24 inches by 24 inches by 48 inches—and slightly closer if the tank is much larger. I saw tanks in their shop as small as 8 inches by 10 inches by 18 inches with baffles built in (see fig. 17).

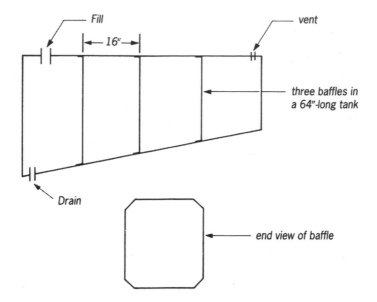

FIGURE 17. *Proper Water-Tank Construction*

If you have either solid or flexible water tanks amidships or under bunks in your accommodations area, be sure they are secured directly to structural members of the hull. The cabinetry supporting bunks or settees is not strong enough to support the stresses that could be exerted during a knockdown by a full tank of water with a capacity of more than 10 gallons (or a fuel tank of the same capacity). A bad situation became even worse for a family on a Valiant 40 during a storm in the Coral Sea when one of their 35-gallon water tanks broke through the settee cabinetry during a knockdown. As the water-laden tank flew to leeward, it shattered the galley table and the lockers on the far side of the boat and injured one member of the crew. There was no way to secure the tank once it was free. This, on top of shredded sails and a blown-away life raft, forced their decision to abandon ship when help was offered. The yacht was later recovered at a salvage cost of US$50,000. This did not cover the cost of repairs to the interior.

If your tanks are in the bilge, be sure you have an alternate way of getting them. If your pressure or pump system breaks down, you could be stuck without freshwater even though there might be 50 gallons of it beneath your feet. A large inspection plate and portable hand pump are the best bet.

If your water filter is on deck, be sure that it is clearly labeled. A dose of diesel in the water tanks will take months to clear out. One way of avoiding contaminating the water tank is to have a large opening such as a 3-inch bronze inspection plate on deck, then the opener to the water-tank fill below that (fig. 18). That way, the dirt that builds up around the edges of the opener won't go into the tank each time you fill it. Also, by having a type of opener different from the normal fuel fill, accidents will be less likely. On a long ocean voyage, contaminated fuel would be an inconvenience, but contaminated water would be a disaster.

If your water tanks do not have easy-to-reach deck fillers, consider changing them now. When water is not easily available from a garden hose at the dock, you'll find those under-the-bunk fillers a nuisance. I know that Mary Baldwin, who crewed on *Peloris*, resented catching rainwater because they had to channel it into 5-gallon jugs, carry the jugs below, move the cushions, siphon the water from jug to tank, then wipe up the spills before going on deck for another jug of water.

Most of us bound on a long voyage resort to carrying extra water in 5-gallon plastic jugs. Smell the jugs before you buy them. Avoid any that aren't specifically made for water. We learned this the hard way when we bought four 5-gallon jugs in the Philippines. Our water was almost undrinkable if it stayed in the jugs for more than 24 hours. We cured much of the problem by adding one cup of chlorine bleach to each 5 gallons of water and letting it sit for a week, then rinsing the tanks four or five times. (See Day 13, "Water Jugs Afloat.")

Even if you don't need spare jugs to supplement your water supply, plan on carrying at least two 5-gallon ones for those times when the nearest freshwater is three blocks or more from the waterfront. Once you leave North America, I'd estimate that you'll find a watering dock in less than 10 percent of the ports you visit, even when alongside a fuel dock.

When it comes time to fill your water tanks, sample the local water supply first. If you are bound on a long voyage, it may be worth your while to go somewhere else to fill your tanks. In Malta, for example, the water in the city mains tasted terrible. In fact, people collected rainwater in their

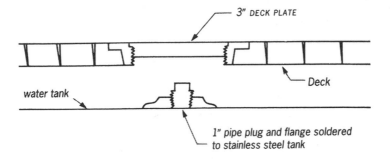

FIGURE 18. *Dirt- and leakproof water-tank fill*

roofs or off awnings to drink. Yet a friend told us about one of several small artesian wells on the island, and there we found superb springwater. Though we had to tote our 5-gallon jugs 1/4 mile, we felt it was worth it. In Gibraltar, most water is made by converting seawater, and it is extremely brackish-tasting. Ceuta, only 16 miles away on the tip of North Africa, has excellent drinking water. If you are bound for the Canaries or Madeira, plan to stop there. But there are times when you have no choice. In Aden, we had to put up with water that was safe but tasted as bad as any we'd ever sampled. We had to drink it halfway across the Arabian Sea before we were able to replace it with rainwater.

One subject that worries many new cruisers is the matter of taking on water in a foreign country. They have heard the warnings issued by travel agents about drinking only bottled water or boiling water for five minutes, or adding tablets to the water to purify it. For the average tourist whose resistance is low because he or she is usually rushed and tired, eating all meals in restaurants, and sleeping poorly in a strange bed every night, this may be a good precaution. But for the cruising family, the best solution is to check for any cholera, bilharzia, or typhoid warnings. If there are none, and the local people drink the water, then drink it yourself. If you are concerned, chlorinate the water. (See Table 1.) Add 1 teaspoon of any 5.25 percent solution of sodium hypochlorite—such as Clorox, Purex, Sani-Chlor, Hy-pro or Super-X—to every 5 gallons of freshwater. Let it sit with the cap off your tank for at least 30 minutes so that the chlorine has a chance to work and the fumes dissipate. This not only kills almost all bacterial contamination but also helps keep your tanks free from green or brown slime. When I called the Orange County (California) Health Department seeking to confirm these facts, Elizabeth Mazer, who works in the environmental health agency in charge of water sanitation, confirmed that this simple chlorination is equivalent to boiling your water for 5 minutes. She also told me some interesting facts about water worldwide. "Most people who get upset stomachs from water in a place they are visiting really are reacting against the different trace chemicals and elements, not any bacteria. Water in some places has more selenium, or more magnesium or more calcium. This doesn't make it dangerous, just different. Children notice the changes because of their smaller body size. People who travel a lot grow more used to the changes. Don't think that bottled water is going to prevent problems. There is no way of knowing how sterile the water containers are, or how good the water in the bottle is. What it comes down to is, you can't be sure of the water purity even in the United States." She went on to tell me about two Orange County health officials who went into the San Joaquin area of California, part of the watershed for Orange County. "They were there to test our water's primary sources. There was no problem at the source in the mountains of San Joaquin, the water that reached us here was fine. But both officers picked up a water-borne bacterial disease from the San Joaquin county water supply.

TABLE 1:

Purifying Freshwater

··

CHLORINE BLEACH

Use unscented liquid chlorine bleach. Read label to determine percentage of chlorine the product contains.

Available chlorine	Number of drops to add per quart	
	Clear water	Cloudy water
1 %	10	20
4-6 %	2	4
7-10 %	1	2
percentage unknown	10	20

1. Mix thoroughly.
2. Let stand 30 minutes with maximum ventilation.
3. If you cannot detect slight chlorine odor at end of 30 minutes, repeat process and let stand 15 minutes more.
4. Water is safe to use.

··

TINCTURE OF IODINE

Available iodine	Number of drops to add per quart	
	Clear water	Cloudy water
2 %	5	10

1. Let stand 30 minutes, then water is safe to use.

··

Information courtesy of U.S. Department of Health and Human Services, Public Health Service.

To enjoy cruising worldwide, you have to avoid being a hypochondriac about water. People fully adjusted to a cruising life rarely suffer from stomach upsets—at least no more than they would have at home.

Rainwater makes the best drinking water in the world. If you are in a tropical area, your sun awning could probably catch all the water you'll need with only a bit of conversion (see Day 12).

No matter how you get your water, fill your tanks and keep them topped up every chance you get. If you are at sea, this is really important.

Catch every bit of rain today, because tomorrow it might be blowing too hard, or the rainsqualls might pass you by. Island- and harbor-hoppers soon learn that water isn't always easy to get in the next port.

To preserve the water you carry and to extend your cruising range, turn off your pressurized water system when you leave port. Use a hand pump or gravity day tank or daily jug to make people aware of just how much water they are using. We speak from experience. We were delivering a large ketch with two extra crew who were not used to ocean passages. The boat had 10 40-gallon water tanks and a pressure system. Twenty days out from Madeira and 210 miles from Antigua, the pressure system ran dry. Fortunately, we had 30 gallons of water in a separate shutoff tank. Where did the water go? The crew had let the tap run while they brushed their teeth. They had showered for five minutes with the taps on full. We'd used only freshwater in the galley. That wastefulness used up an average of 5 gallons of water per day per person. In the United States, the average person uses 65 gallons of water a day. So the measures necessary to conserve water for an ocean passage are far from the average shore dweller's experience.

On a long voyage where the tank capacity is near the minimum requirements, we find it works well to figure consumption as a ratio of gallons to hundreds of miles left to go. If the ratio drops, we tighten our water usage. If it increases, we take a shower. In other words, if we start out with 68 gallons of water for a 4,500-mile passage, that's 1.5 gallons per 100 miles. Fifteen days later, if we've covered only 1,200 miles and consumed 22 gallons of water, our ratio becomes 1.4, so it is time to cut back. If, on the other hand, we've covered 1,900 miles during the same time, our ratio becomes 1.77, so we can indulge just a bit. This way, our water conservation happens all through the voyage, not just toward the end.

To save freshwater, install a saltwater tap conveniently placed right in the galley area. The simplest way to do this is to put a 3/4-inch through-hull fitting below the waterline with a hose to a convenient tap near the cook. This will only work if the waterline on your boat is near knee level or higher. On *Taleisin*, our saltwater tap has a hose fitting on it so we can use it for scrubbing and rinsing out the bilges.

If your boat floats too high for this method, you'll have to install a pump in the galley. Choose a pump that is obviously different from the freshwater pump, or a complete meal can be ruined when a new cook adds a pump full of saltwater instead of fresh.

Saltwater can be used for cooking. One cup of saltwater has approximately 2 round teaspoons of salt in it. For bread baking, substitute 1 cup of saltwater for 1 cup of freshwater. When boiling vegetables, use $1/4$ saltwater and $3/4$ fresh. Boil eggs in 100 percent saltwater; cook rice in $1/3$ saltwater, $2/3$ fresh. For dried beans, don't use any saltwater, or they'll stay tough.

Wash all your dishes and pots in saltwater. We often do this right in the cockpit instead of below decks. Then we rinse them in a basin with 1 or 2 cups of freshwater. This is important, as salty plates or pans not only will flavor other foods but also will start to grow mold after a week or so in the tropics.

Wash yourself in saltwater, then rinse in fresh. Liquid dish soap and hair shampoo work fine as a body soap in saltwater. My thick, long hair feels great if I wash and rinse it with saltwater and then shake out the excess and rinse over a bucket using a quart of freshwater. I run the freshwater through my hair three or four times, then use it to rinse my body.

Some people don't feel the need to rinse with freshwater at sea, but this can be unwise, as it leaves you susceptible to skin diseases. Salt attracts moisture; moisture on your skin attracts fungus. Several types of skin problems—ranging from itchy rashes to skin discolorations—can develop quickly in the tropics. Almost all are aggravated by salt deposits on your skin, either from perspiration or from saltwater.

Washing clothes in saltwater doesn't work well at all. If they aren't thoroughly rinsed in freshwater, they won't dry completely, they'll be stiff, they'll soon smell, and they'll cause salt rashes, especially on your bottom and under your arms. If it is necessary to wash out some clothes or towels during your long voyage, use a small amount of dishwashing liquid in freshwater, then rinse the clothes just once. The small bit of soap left in the fabric won't hurt at all.

Don't try to conserve freshwater by drinking saltwater. Alain Bombard, the scientist who tried to prove that man could live on saltwater and cross an ocean, did survive his Atlantic crossing, but he obtained most of his liquid from the raw fish he ate.

Freshwater is the most important store you carry on board. If your food supplies run out because you lose your mast and have to limp along under jury rig, or if you hit a bad weather system, your water supply could save your life. The average healthy person can live for 30 days with no food and only $1\frac{1}{2}$ pints of freshwater to drink and still suffer no irreparable body damage.

Watermakers

Some years ago, we had the interesting privilege of helping test the original hand-operated, energy-recovery, reverse-osmosis watermaker being developed for use by the navy and the air force in their abandon-ship packs.

Prior to this time, the military had depended on inflatable plastic water-distillation units, which had only an 80 percent success rate even if used within two years of manufacture and produced no more than a quart of water per eight hours of midlatitude sunshine. The military and, I must say, we too, were intrigued by this original unit, as it offered the possibility of yacht-size watermakers at prices far more affordable than the engine-driven evaporation units previously used on luxury yachts and ships. By the time *Taleisin* was ready for sea, the first Survivor watermaker was available. The price at that time was 50 percent more than for an EPIRB. We figured it would help us survive in an abandon-ship situation, and it also could work to extend our on-board water supplies in an emergency. So we opted for the Survivor watermaker instead of, at that time, an EPIRB. This hand-operated unit is about the size of a large novel, weighs less than four pounds, and after 20 years is still in fine condition. It does require yearly flushing with a biocide to maintain its usability. (Leave it two years without flushing and the membrane dries out and needs replacement at a price that is almost as high as the cost for a new unit.)

The relative price for these units has dropped dramatically over the years. So has the price for the larger units inspired by this first simple water-conversion unit. With the decline in prices, the proliferation of watermaker choices, the desire to be free of water restrictions, and the increased financial wherewithal of many cruisers we meet, I would estimate that 45 percent of the cruising boats we see offshore now how have one on board. Newer units are relatively easy to install and far more dependable than refrigeration units.[8] Currently, many cruising advisers say that watermakers are a must-have item, and that they will increase your safety while offshore. We find both of these statements misleading.

Manufacturers and suppliers urge you to buy a watermaker to save you the cost of installing extra tankage. They say it will eliminate excess weight on board because, in their opinion, you will no longer need to carry as much water on board. This concerns us, as on our recent encounters with cruisers who have fitted watermakers, we have met several who either removed most of their tankage or converted the tanks to be used for fuel. They have

....

8   Between 2001 and 2006 We did a survey of the most frequently requested repairs at four different voyagers' crossroads: Horta, in the Azores; Papeete, Tahiti; Opua, Bay of Islands, New Zealand; and San Diego, California. Mechanics there told us that autopilots, refrigeration, and radios were the most frequent problems that came to them, with watermakers a close fourth. This is not the same order as shown by the 2005 SSCA equipment survey which is sited in the January 2006 edition of Cruising World Magazine. In their list of Products Most Prone to Breakdowns, watermakers came first, with 36.1% failing each year, followed by water generators, heads, wind generators, autopilots, and refrigeration.

then been caught short by the failure of some component in their electrical system, engine, or watermaker.

Another sales argument we hear is that a watermaker will save you money because in some ports it is necessary to pay for potable water—because of either short supplies or concerns about quality. In 40 years of voyaging to more than 80 countries, we have spent less than US$200 total for potable water. Most of this was in Rio de Janeiro, where, during our visit, cholera was a problem. Had we planned to stay, a simple water-filter system (at the cost of approximately $200) would have solved the problem.

Does this mean we would not install a watermaker if we were on a less budget-minded voyage? I am not sure, although given the choice between mechanical or electrical refrigeration and a watermaker, I would lean more toward the watermaker. We were delighted to be able to stay for a few extra days at a lovely secluded bay in the Marquesas before going on to a main center. We could only do this because, after a 31-day voyage from Chile had depleted our water supplies, another yachtsman invited us to top up from their almost unlimited watermaker-produced supply. We could imagine the pleasure of having guests on board without being concerned when they wanted to take a shower after each swim. It would be nice to forget lugging water jugs ashore. But convenience always comes with a price. Before you purchase any unit—or, if there is one on board, before you set off voyaging—carefully read up on the correct installation and maintenance of these units, plus their actual power consumption. (A good source of information is Nigel Calder's *Boatowner's Mechanical and Electrical Manual,* 3rd edition, published by International Marine in 2005.)

The newest watermakers still require approximately 2.2 amps to make a gallon of freshwater. For most, this means adding an hour of generator time per day. More engine-running time means more fuel consumption.

For any watermaker to work well, it must be carefully installed and considered part of a system, not a stand-alone unit. It is best to have not one, but two filters on the intake line to eliminate all foreign matter from the saltwater before it reaches the actual membrane of your reverse-osmosis system. You will also need to create a simple system for flushing your unit with fresh, clean, nonchlorinated water or with biocide. Unless you use it daily, there is a chance that growth, if not removed promptly, will ruin the membrane. Another potential problem with these units is that seawater contains chloride ions, which are highly corrosive. The concentration of salt in the water of the intake lines increases during the watermaking process. Thus, corrosion is a problem that must be considered, along with electrolysis prevention, both in the watermaker itself and in its connection to the other electric components of your boat.

The maintenance costs must also be considered, and spare parts must be purchased. You will need to carry spare pre-filters to replace existing ones after about every 100 hours or so of use (depending on the silt content of the saltwater you are using), plus O-ring seals to replace existing seals once a year. For extended voyages, it also pays to have a spare membrane unit on board and the tools to replace it, as even a trace of oil in the intake water can destroy the existing membrane.

If you cruise in colder waters, be sure you have a reminder system to ensure that you close the seacock for the watermaker intake whenever you plan to leave the boat. John McConnico, who ran Yankee Point Marina in the Chesapeake Bay for many years, told us of two boats that came close to sinking because of ice that formed in their watermaker lines. Freshwater freezes sooner than saltwater, so even if locals tell you the bay always remains ice-free, a sudden frost could burst a hose in your watermaker system and sink your boat if any of the lines are installed below the waterline.

One very important reminder: Even if you do carry a watermaker on board, it is vital to have sufficient tankage to ensure at least 1/2-gallon of water per person per 100 miles for the proposed length of any passage, plus 50 percent more for a safety margin.

....

Day 14

Noon to noon: 32 miles
Miles to date: 983
Sunny but very cool
Still beating against 15-to-18-knot headwind

Lunch
hot dogs
baked beans topped with onions

Cocktail time
biscuits, cheese
rum-and-water

Dinner (cook's night off)
cold canned corned beef and canned beans
crackers

....

We are still beating to windward with the reefed jib, staysail, and main set. It's a dead muzzler, a cold east wind right out of Vancouver. Larry took down the staysail just before dinner to reduce some of the violent motion. But still I felt just on the edge of seasickness. The thought of cooking dinner made me blue, and my culinary imagination deserted me completely. So when Larry suggested, "Cook's night off," I took two seconds to agree. He opened a can of corned beef and another of beans and ate right from the cans. I ate a few saltines and cheese. Primitive, yes. Nice rest for the cook, though. On average, the need for a cook's night off on board *Seraffyn* seems to happen after about 12 to 14 days at sea.

I'd say that only once or twice a year have I been too seasick to enjoy cooking. Only twice in 10 years have I been too sick to cook anything at all—and both times were during the same voyage south down the Adriatic in winter. (See the discussion on handling seasickness that follows.)

Meanwhile, back to tonight. Larry took care of his own dinner and produced no dirty dishes. Then we cuddled together under a blanket on the settee and listened to Beethoven's Fourth Piano Concerto on our stereo. For a little while, beating over the cold, gray sea didn't seem so frustrating.

Seasickness Prevention

It never fails. Every time we get into a discussion with a new or would-be cruising sailor, there comes a moment when a concerned look crosses his or her face and the question is blurted out, "Do you ever get seasick?" I don't think any aspect of sailing causes more worry, and certainly nothing is more demoralizing, than being seasick. I know; I'm one of the sufferers.

There we were, finally on our way after more than three years of scheming, planning, and building. I'd sailed lots of times before, but when we set off from San Diego into a confused cross sea, I was so sick that I finally ended up lying on the cabin sole praying for land. "All my dreams ruined," I said to myself. And even more morbid thoughts rushed through my head. Larry tried joking with me, holding me, teasing me, but nothing helped. Then, to my amazement, the second day out, my seasickness began

DAY 14. *If only once Larry would get seasick! Then he'd know what the rest of us feel like.*

178

to fade away. By the end of that day, I was more than making up for my lack of interest in food. Even more amazing, after three days, I had forgotten that I had been seasick.

I still get uncomfortable occasionally, and every time it happens, I am just as unhappy as the first time, but I have learned to minimize the problem. I don't include Larry in the problem because he is one of the outrageously fortunate 10 percent who don't even know what seasickness is. Put him in a boat with bilges full of diesel, odoriferous food on the counter, and a vicious sea running and he'll ask where the butter and jam are so he can make a sandwich. But about 90 percent of all people who go to sea do suffer at one time or another. So, an active program of prevention is worth considering.

I'm convinced that 30 to 50 percent of the problem is psychological, and other long-time sailors have supported me in this belief.

Curiously, I never get seasick when we are working, delivering other boats—only when Larry and I are sailing alone, on our own boat. When I am being paid to cook on a delivery, I have important responsibilities and don't want to let the crew down, so I guess I'm busier or trying harder. On board *Taleisin*, I know Larry will take care of any problems, and he handles the boat easily by himself with the aid of our self-steering gear, so I can relax and it doesn't matter. Peter Phillips, who owns the 50-foot *Voyager*, reports the same thing. When he is captain and has a crew on his own boat, he's never seasick. But daysailing as a guest on friends' boats is a different matter. I'm not in any way saying that our seasickness is any less real for being psychological. But by accepting the fact that sometimes it is caused by mental processes, we can more actively fight it.

Drug companies are forever coming up with new pills to fight the problem. Unfortunately, they often forget to put the most important instructions on the package. To work at all, any anti-motion-sickness pill *must* be taken one hour before the motion starts. Once you are sailing out the marina entrance, it is too late. It takes an hour for some pills to dissolve and spread through your body. If you vomit before then, you lose the medicine.

After 40 years of voyaging, I still have to deal with a day or two of seasickness every time we set off into a fresh wind with sloppy sea conditions. Even when I have been at sea for a while with gentle weather, I have had bouts of head-in-the-bucket seasickness when the weather turned stormy. When we were exploring the Gulf Islands near Victoria, British Columbia, I fell prey to that dreaded wish-I-didn't-have-to-cook-for-anyone feeling when we had three friends on board for an afternoon dash across a tide-driven 4-foot chop. Unfortunately, I, like many long-term voyagers, in the excitement of getting underway, usually forget to take pills before we set sail. Or, if I do, it turns out to be lovely, easy sailing and I have to suffer with the drunk, sleepy feeling that the pills often create. But I have continued to try the different methods recommended by sailing doctors—ranging from drinking ginger beer to using a wristband to taking a mild tranquilizer. (Although other sailors have found tranquilizers to be a solution, they only worked for me in some situations.)

After much experimentation, I now use Stugeron, a children's motion-sickness tablet (cinnarizine, 25 mg). I take a child's dose one hour before leaving port—with good results and very little of the feeling of lethargy associated with other remedies. Surprisingly, I have found that this medication tends to work even when I am already feeling a bit off—as long as I take the tablet with a dry biscuit or two and a small glass of fruit juice and then lie down for an hour. This is especially helpful when a voyage starts out calmly and deteriorates after a few days.

Wristbands supplied by acupuncturists have been very successful for several friends, and so has the patch (Scopoderm-TTS, Transderm Scop, 1.5 mg). But if you are allergic to the adhesive used on most bandages (as I am), you will have a skin reaction at the site of the patch. Some people have tried reducing the dosage from the patch by cutting it in half. This is definitely not recommended, as most people will get a rash where the cut edge of the medication-dispensing gauze touches the skin. Furthermore, the slow-release mechanism of the patch will no longer function correctly.

Whatever medication you choose, consider the potential side effects carefully, especially if you plan to use the medication for more than a day or two. Some people who have depended on using a patch for the whole length of a voyage have had hallucinations after a few weeks at sea. Even after removing the patch, this continued for a few days.

Dosage is another problem often overlooked with seasickness remedies. Overdosage causes doziness and dry mouth and can impede urination. It tends to occur more often in women than in men—for a simple reason. The average weight of adults used to determine medicinal dosage is 140 pounds. If you weigh 110 or less, you should probably be taking a young person's dosage.

If you do find a medication that works for you, take along at least a year's supply on your cruise. It is often difficult to find an exact duplicate in the countries you'll visit. Furthermore, a medication that is available over-the-counter in one country might require a local doctor's prescription in another.

Whether you want to use anti-motion-sickness pills or tranquilizers, or go without, there are other measures you can take to minimize seasickness.

1. Keep your boat very clean. Eliminate any odors you can. It's the odors that do the final trick. A person can be fine until he opens the ice chest and gets a whiff of blue cheese or sour milk. In fact, we've found that people get seasick less easily on a boat with no engine. There are fewer unusual odors in a nonauxiliary vessel. If you do have an engine, be careful of overfilling the tanks; check for any diesel leaks and wipe excess oil off the engine itself to eliminate odors.

   Ventilate the boat well, and remember that odors you live with day in and day out may not upset you, but they may do the trick for a guest. If anyone on your boat is prone to seasickness, don't allow anyone to smoke on board while underway. If you are embarrassed to ask your friends to snub out their cigarettes, put up a sign, "Smoking allowed on deck forward of the mast."

2. If you or your guests have a tendency to feel queasy, try living on board at anchor for a few days before you head to sea. There always is a slight motion afloat, and this seems to help you get acclimatized. People who live on board constantly suffer less when they head to sea.

3. Rest well before you set off. I know now that my first real bout of seasickness was brought on by too many farewell parties and an excitement-induced sleepless night before our departure. At sea, get all the rest you can. This will help your body to cope better with weather changes, and mentally you'll be less annoyed if some queasiness does occur.

4. If you happen to be in charge of cooking, prepare enough meals for two or three days before you leave port—or, if you are on a long passage, when it is calm. I usually make up an 8-quart pot of stew or spaghetti-and-sauce or a really thick soup. I mix sandwich fillings and bake fresh bread before each long passage. Then, once we set off, I don't have to put up with the unsettling smells of cooking if it's rough. And if I do get seasick, I don't have to worry, for Larry can turn on a fire under the pot and scoop out a bowlful for himself. If you have prepared several meals beforehand and you don't get seasick, you end up with a bit of extra free time at sea for sunbathing or reading a good book.

5. Once you are underway in a rough sea, avoid going into either the forepeak or the engine room, where the motion is more pronounced. Also, if possible avoid using an enclosed toilet. Head areas are rarely

ventilated well enough, and the odors multiply when you are in a seaway. Instead, use the lee rail—or try a bucket if it's really rough. Even fishermen and seamen on small fishing boats prefer not to use a cramped enclosed head.

6. Keep warm and active and stay out in the fresh air. Because seasickness is partially psychological in many cases, if you don your foul-weather gear, get out on deck, and actually join in the sailing of the boat, you won't have as much time to think about the motion. Very few people who sail dinghies get seasick; they are just too busy.

7. If you have a tendency toward seasickness, avoid hot, spicy food. Choose such easily digested items as bread, oatmeal, apple juice, and saltines rather than citrus fruits, lasagna, and bacon.

8. On a very hot, still day, try to keep cool. It's amazing how many people become upset on glassy, calm days when the sails are slatting. To prevent this, find some shade, pour seawater over you, or drink a cool glass of juice.

9. If you do become ill, try drinking some sweet fruit juice, such as well-chilled apricot or peach nectar. This seems to settle well and provides almost all of the nutrition necessary to keep you from becoming weak or dehydrated.

10. In really bad conditions, if a crew is very seasick, try changing the motion of the boat by easing the sheets a bit and reaching, running, or even heaving-to. We know one tough-looking 6-footer who becomes as weak as a baby as soon as the sheets are hauled up hard. He lies in his bunk until the sheets are eased. Then he makes up for lost time—and food. He just can't take the motion of being hard on the wind in anything more than 12 knots or so. But he loves sailing and traveling so much that he is willing to put up with the inconvenience.

Finally, if you have a first-time sailor on board who becomes seasick, don't discourage him or her from sailing. One of our best friends spent years learning about boats and building beautiful dinghies, which he sold with the goal of someday having his own yacht. When he was asked to crew on a 40-foot hot racing machine, he accepted excitedly. In 20-knot winds, he became helpless. The regular crew of the boat teased him, and he never went sailing again. It's rather sad, because he would have made a good sailor with his quick mind and strong frame. But to him, sailing wasn't worth the discomfort and the ridicule.

I think that is one of the big secrets: You have to *want* to sail and cruise so much that you'll put up with one or two days of discomfort for the reward of new ports and new people.

Normally, few people stay seasick for more than two or three days except in most extreme storm conditions. I did hear of one person who reported that she was seasick the whole way across the Atlantic. But it turned out she was suffering not from seasickness but from a problem that can be caused by seasickness. I learned about this when I spoke to Dr. Isola, the port doctor in Gibraltar. He told me that in the previous two years he had had to assist in the delivery of nine unplanned babies conceived by cruising people who were using the pill.

As Dr. Isola explained it, an oral contraceptive must stay in your stomach for four to eight hours to spread into your bloodstream effectively. He advises that if you have been seasick for more than a day and want to be sure of avoiding pregnancy, use other means of contraception such as condoms or abstinence. Pregnancy in its second and third month will cause almost the same symptoms as seasickness.

No one enjoys being seasick, but for most of us it is an integral part of going to sea. If there's anything to be said on behalf of seasickness, it might be that it definitely helps me shed some of the pounds I gained in the previous port. But—far more important—the discomfort is quickly forgotten the minute you reach a new port or sail out of a storm into beautiful weather.

. . . .

Day 15

Noon to noon: 49 miles
Miles to date: 1,032
Pounding to windward with single-reefed main and staysail
Just after noon, wind dropped and sun came out

Lunch
> hard-boiled eggs
> tomato pudding
> hot chocolate

Dinner
> fresh rye bread with butter
> salmon loaf with lemon sauce
> baked potatoes
> sliced tomatoes

· ·

TOMATO PUDDING (AN OLD ENGLISH SIDE DISH)

Put in small saucepan
> 2 large ripe tomatoes, cut in chunks
> 1 tbs. butter
> 2 tbs. sugar
> 2 tbs. finely chopped onion
> 1 tsp. oregano
> Simmer 20 minutes, stirring often.

Top with
> layer of bread crumbs
> light sprinkling of salt
> grated cheese

Put into small baking tin. Bake 20 minutes at 350 degrees.

· ·

SALMON LOAF

1 large can salmon, drained
(mackerel can be substituted)
2 eggs
2 tbs. lemon juice
½ cup bread crumbs

Mix well, then form into
a loaf on a baking sheet
or tin. Bake 35 minutes
at 325 degrees.

LEMON SAUCE

Put in small saucepan

½ onion, chopped fine
2 tbs. butter
2 tbs. water
2 tbs. lemon
½ tsp. minced garlic
½ tsp. salt
Simmer 10 minutes, stirring occasionally.

Combine

2 tbs. flour
½ cup milk
Pour slowly into onion mixture, stirring constantly
until sauce becomes very thick.

As soon as the wind died down and my seasickness went away (this happens almost immediately), I set some rye bread to rise. The temperature on board is well below 70 degrees F, so I warmed the oven for three minutes, then put the dough in to rise. Since I was using the oven to bake bread, I planned a dinner that could all be baked at the same time.

By dinnertime, the old sea was lying down and a light breeze was moving us almost directly toward Canada for the first time in three days.

Tips on Baking Bread

Bread baking doesn't require very much actual work. In fact, preparing the dough only takes about 10 minutes once you learn the basic tricks.

With two extra crew to help stand watches, I had lots of time to bake bread as we delivered this racing boat up the coast of Mexico.

But the rising and baking process requires your presence in the vicinity of your galley for a minimum of 2^1/$_2$ hours. If you are involved with the complications of a job onshore, this may be difficult. But on an offshore passage, bread baking fits the rhythm and time schedule perfectly. You're never more than 20 feet from the galley. There's almost no chore on the boat that can't be interrupted for three or four minutes while you check your rising dough. The motion of a yacht at sea doesn't seem to bother bread dough at all; give it any temperature over 75 degrees and below 110 and it rises merrily away, oblivious to whether you are beating, running, or reaching, whether seas are 1 foot or 15 feet high. If you are heeled and don't have a gimbaled stove, your final loaf might have a tilt, but it will still taste fine, and the homey atmosphere created by the aroma of baking drives away going-to-windward blues.

For the uninitiated, bread baking is almost magical. One English crewman on a delivery trip was so fascinated by the process that he insisted on watching me make the dough for each twice-weekly baking. After two weeks, he tried his own batch. As soon as he'd set the dough to rise, it was his turn on the wheel. Chris was like a kid watching for Santa Claus. He opened the engine-room inspection hatch, which was right next to the helmsman's seat, about 20 times an hour, and he shouted out when the towel on top of his bowl of dough began to take on a rounded shape.

His first loaf was slightly browner on one side, but the sandwiches he proudly served at lunchtime tasted great. For the next 4,000 miles, I had to fight with him for the right to bake the crew bread.

The ingredients for bread are available worldwide. With a bit of care, they will keep quite well, and toward the end of a voyage of more than 20 days, you'll find fresh-baked bread one of the highlights of your menu.

Dried yeast—purchased either in individual packages or in 1-pound cans—will keep for up to one year if unopened. I prefer the cans, and once I open a 1-pound can, I store the yeast in a Tupperware container. The individual packets of yeast should be stored in strong plastic bags as the packaging tends to deteriorate after three or four months on board. Two pounds of yeast will last us for about a year of average cruising.

Keeping flour is much more of a problem, especially if you are voyaging in warm waters. Enriched, unbleached flour in 5-pound or 2-kilo factory-wrapped packages rarely gets weevils, while whole-wheat flour usually does. So I've found it pays to buy the enriched flour and put each 5-pound sack into two separate plastic bags, one inside the other. Then, to get the healthy flavor of whole-wheat flour, I add granola or wheat germ, which I buy in the cereal section of the market. This usually comes in vacuum-packed jars and never gets weevily. I have kept vacuum-packed jars for up to a year with no problem.

If you are shopping in a foreign country where the only flour available comes from 50- or 100-pound sacks—or if you suspect the flour you are buying has been shipped into the country in large sacks and repackaged locally—try to find large, airtight containers for the flour. One-gallon glass jars are my first choice. Fill the jars to within two inches of the top. Put in an egg-size lump of dry ice. Fasten the container top in place so it's not quite airtight. When the dry ice dissipates, seal the container well. Put a tight ring of tape around the lid to insure the seal is air tight. The chemicals in the dry ice will kill any weevil larvae.

If dry ice is not available, chloroform is a good substitute. To use it safely, cut several small holes in a 35mm film container or a small plastic jar such as those used for asprins. Fill the container with cotton and put six or seven drops of chloroform on the cotton. Put the closed container in with the grain and seal the whole works. Chloroform is available from most chemists or drug distributors. A 1/4-pint bottle will last through a 5-year voyage. Bay or laurel or eucalyptus leaves are also supposed to act as weevil repellents. I have used these on a short-term basis, and others claim they work for up to a year. A final recommended idea for those with access to a microwave oven is to put each package of 2 pounds or less in the microwave oven at high power for $1^1/_2$ minutes before storing it away. I do not believe this changes the properties of the grain, but it does kill any weevil eggs before they can hatch.

If you do get weevils, a flour sifter will get rid of most of the ones you can see. If you miss one or two, they will die when you bake your bread. At this point, I can hear Larry joking, "Who cares about a few weevils? They just add a bit of protein to your diet." This may sound a bit flippant, but unfortunately weevils are a fact of life in some Mediterranean countries and most tropical ones. The flour you'll buy in such places as Sri Lanka, Egypt, Barbados, and Brazil will have weevils in it, or larvae ready to hatch. They are a nuisance, but once dead, they are not harmful.

On the other hand, weevils do have powerful teeth. Before we left Sri Lanka for Malaysia, we had to buy some local flour from 50-pound sacks to supplement our supplies. We stored it in two separate Tupperware containers under a quarter berth. Two weeks later, in the middle of the Bay of Bengal, we both started getting sharp bites from something that left a small, red, itchy pimple. A thorough search showed that weevils had eaten right through the Tupperware—boring perfectly round $1/_{16}$-inch-diameter holes in the plastic. They'd also attacked several packages of lasagna noodles. Fly spray killed them easily. But after that, I put any suspect flour in glass containers.

A few extra words about flour should be added to help voyagers over a few of the hurdles I've encountered. First, you should test your yeast if it is more than four months old. To do this, let your yeast-and-water mixture stand for about four minutes before adding other ingredients. If it begins to foam even a little, the yeast is fine. If there are no bubbles at all on the liquid, the yeast is dead.

Flour can also become dead. This usually happens when it becomes slightly moist or is kept unsealed for too long. Dead flour will feel lumpy and heavy when you handle it; your bread will not rise well or will taste slightly nutty. If you cannot replace the flour, you can perk it up by sifting it and laying it out in bright sunlight on a flat tray. This has only happened to me with flour I kept more than a year in paper flour bags.

I do not normally carry self-rising flour because of the limitations of stowage space on a small boat. I find it quite easy to add the necessary baking powder or baking soda to ordinary flour rather than carry both kinds of flour on board.

When it comes right down to it, baking bread is simpler than storing the ingredients. People in the most isolated corners of the world do it daily on open fires, in stone fireplaces, and on top of old sheets of metal heated by butane torches.

The first thing I learned about most bread recipes printed in American and English cookbooks is that they insist you knead the bread 300 times but they don't tell you that all the kneading does is produce a loaf textured like store-bought bread. This just isn't necessary, and in fact, most people prefer the coarser, almost cakelike texture of unkneaded bread. So on the day when you'll be around the boat for three hours doing other chores or projects, try this basic recipe.

BASIC BREAD RECIPE

In large salad bowl, put
  ⅔ cup saltwater
  1⅓ cups freshwater
or
  2 cups freshwater
  2 tsp. salt
Add
  2 heaping tsp. (or 2 packets) dry yeast
  Stir until yeast dissolves.
Add

> Water should be between 90 and 100 degrees F, baby-bath temperature. If you put your bare wrist in it, the water should feel comfortable. Too hot and it will kill your yeast; too cool and the yeast will work too slowly.

  ¼ cup sugar (honey, maple syrup, or brown sugar can be substituted)
  5 or 6 cups flour

Stir the flour with a spoon until the mixture is too stiff to stir, then start working in the last cups of flour with your hands, adding more flour until the dough stops clinging to your hands. There is no exact measurement on the flour because humidity affects the amount you'll use. It's difficult to work in too much flour; just keep adding it until the dough feels smooth and doesn't stick to a clean finger when you press it firmly.

At this stage, it will appear smooth and feel almost satiny. This usually takes 2 or 3 minutes. If you want to knead your bread, do it now. But if you are slightly lazy like me, you won't. Form the dough into a ball in the middle of the bowl, cover the bowl with a clean towel, and put it in a warm, dry place to rise. The engine room—right after you've been running the generator—is great. Or if you are engineless like us, a sunny spot that is out of the wind works well. You need any temperature between 80 and 110 degrees F at this stage. If you are in a cool climate, turn on your oven for 3 minutes. Turn it off and let your dough rise in the oven.

▼

189

In 30 minutes, check the dough. If it hasn't started growing, it is in too cool a location. If it's starting to get a crust, it's too warm. In 40 to 45 minutes, the dough should be about double in size.

When it has doubled, you can punch it down (yes, hit it with your fist four or five times) and let it rise again to get a smoother-textured loaf. Or, if you have it scheduled for a meal and don't feel like waiting, grease some bread pans or line them with aluminum foil, cut the dough in half, form it into two loaves, and place them in the pans. If you rub your hands with salad oil before you handle the dough, they will stay cleaner. Let the loaves rise again until they are double. Then place them in a cool oven. Turn the oven to 350 degrees and bake until the loaves are golden brown, or 30 to 35 minutes. (You can preheat the oven, but I prefer not only to save on propane by putting the dough in a cold oven, but I find the slowly warming oven encourages the bread to rise to its full potential. Dough put into a pre-heated oven will tend to produce a more evenly browned loaf.) Turn the bread pans at least once during the process to ensure an even brown color. If your oven doesn't control perfectly, don't worry; the bread may bake faster or more slowly, but it is quite forgiving. To be sure it's done, rap it with a knuckle. If it sounds hollow, it's ready.

Remove the pans from the oven and let them cool five or six minutes. Then remove the loaves from the pans and rest them on their sides. Or set the loaves on a cake rack so the steam escapes from the bottom.

Don't try to cut a loaf for at least 15 minutes. Not only will it burn your fingers, it will ball up around your knife. This recipe gives you a crusty loaf. The more you knead it, the less crusty it will be.

There are endless variations on this recipe, most of which can be used with the pressure-cooker bread or batter-bread recipes that follow.

. . . .

For variety, add one of the following

1 cup wheat germ
1 cup rye flour
1 cup granola
1 cup flour
1 cup dried potato flakes
1 cup oatmeal
¾ cup raisins and 2 tsp. cinnamon
¾ cup chopped onions
¾ cup grated or chunked cheese
▼

½ cup sunflower seeds or pine nuts

2 tsp. garlic powder, 2 tsp. sage, 2 tsp. oregano

Substitute

1 cup fruit juice for 1 cup water.

Instead of making a loaf, make a dozen individual rolls; they bake in 12 to 15 minutes.

Divide the dough into three pieces and roll out each piece into a long worm like you did in play school when you made clay pots. Then braid the pieces and let them rise. Just before you bake the braided loaf, brush each lump with the white of an egg. (I use my fingers for this job, rubbing the egg white lightly over the loaf.) The egg white will add a nice gloss to the top of the loaf.

For a real treat, take a third of the dough after it has risen once. Put it on an oiled cookie sheet and press it out to form an oval about 12 inches wide, and 18 inches long. With a knife, spread a thin layer of butter over the oval. Sprinkle liberally with brown sugar and raisins, or nuts and chocolate chips. Roll from one side to the other. Roll up the ends and bake as for a normal loaf then serve at teatime. You can also use the same dough, but instead of the sweet filling, make a savory filling with chopped meat, onions, garlic, green peppers, and seasonings.

And, finally, this dough makes a good pizza base.

. . . .

Several people have given me recipes for oven breads that don't need to be shaped into loaves. They are quite foolproof because the measurements are exact. The problem with both of these recipes, however, is that they require not only careful oven control but steady sailing conditions—and, in the case of the beer bread, very slow baking.

CELIA VANDERPOOL'S BATTER BREAD

1 pkg. or 1 heaping tsp. dry yeast

1¾ cups warm water

2 tbs. shortening

2 tbs. sugar

2 tsp. salt

2⅔ cups flour

▼

Add one of the following

1 onion, grated
¾ cup grated cheese
¼ cup sesame seeds or
2 tsp. cinnamon and ¾ cup raisins

Dissolve the yeast in water. Add shortening, sugar, salt, and flour. Blend, then beat for 300 strokes. Scrape sides of bowl. Cover and let rise until double (about 30 minutes). Stir batter down by beating 25 strokes. Spread in a greased loaf pan. Smooth out the top, cover, and let rise again until double.

Bake 45 minutes at 375 degrees F. Remove from oven, brush top with melted butter, and allow to cool.

. . . .

Nina Mann from Virginia gave me a recipe that doesn't even need yeast. It makes a heavier loaf that is better with some fruit or nuts to liven it up. The basic recipe is simple.

. . . .

NINA'S BEER BREAD

2 cups self-rising flour
3 tbs. sugar
1 can beer
Mix well, then bake immediately
1 hour at 350 degrees F.

The recipe needs no salt. The beer must be fresh—any brand will do—and there is no beer flavor left when it's finished baking.

. . . .

Pressure-cooker bread is one of the three solutions for people who don't have ovens. Another solution is a folding stove-top oven, which may be hard to hold in place in a seaway. This recipe was thoroughly sea-tested by Janice Taggert on the 35-foot ketch *Labi Labi* during a voyage from Malaysia to Greece. I tasted one of the first loaves Janice made; it was good and nicely browned.

. . . .

PRESSURE-COOKER BREAD

1½ cups lukewarm water or
1 cup freshwater and ½ cup saltwater
2 tbs. dried yeast
▼

2 tsp. salt (if you don't use saltwater)

4 cups flour

2 heaping tbs. oatmeal or coarse cornmeal

Stir and let rise

Combine water, yeast, salt, and sugar and let stand 5 minutes. Stir in flour and let rise in a warm place about 90 minutes, or until double in size. Stir down and let rise again.

Bake

Grease pressure cooker thoroughly, add cornmeal or oatmeal, and shake to coat the cooker evenly. (The oatmeal or cornmeal adds an insulating barrier so the dough can brown.) Pour in the dough and let it rise once more. Lock the lid but do not use the pressure-regulator valve. Cook over low heat with a flame tamer (asbestos pad) for 40 minutes. Steam will escape through the vent. Do not remove the cover while baking.

. . . .

Twice in the past couple of years, we've had to travel without access to an oven or a pressure cooker—first while we were crossing the wilds of Tasmania on horseback, and second when we spent six months on a 4WD photo safari through southern Africa. In both places, the local people taught us new ways to make excellent pan breads. Since these can be made on the top of the stove in about 20 minutes, they could be useful additions to a seagoing menu.

DAMPER: STOVE-TOP PAN BREAD

Combine

2 cups white flour

1 tsp. salt

2 tsp. baking powder

1 tbs. milk powder

enough water to form a very thick batter

Fry

Grease a cast-iron or cast-aluminum frying pan liberally with butter. Heat until butter sizzles and then add batter. Over medium heat, slowly fry the bread until bubbles begin to burst through the top of the batter. Now the difficult part: Work a spatula under the pan bread and turn it over.

▼

193

Add a bit more butter from the sides of the pan and spread some on top of the cooked side to keep it moist. Test with a knife to be sure the inside is cooked through.

Serve it hot. This makes enough for four people.

In Australia, it is called "damper." We had it spiced up with fried fruit or cheese or nuts as the mainstay of each lunch. Cooked over a wood fire on the beach, it is wonderful.

. . . .

The two years we spent exploring the coast of Mexico—first on *Seraffyn* and later on *Taleisin*—made me a fan of tortillas as a substitute for bread. Unfortunately, I never learned the art of making the flour ones I liked best. But Robyn Rogin on *Mintaka,* whom we first met in the Marquesas as we sailed north from Chile, provided this easy-to-make recipe when I told her I was working on a new edition of this book. To prove it worked, she made us a batch when she arrived at our home base in New Zealand. It's tasty—and grand as a quick treat for bread-short days.

FLOUR TORTILLAS

Combine

4 to 4½ cups wheat flour
1½ cups water
1½ tsp. salt
2 tsp. baking powder
½ cup oil
Combine all ingredients, adding only 1 cup water at first, then gradually adding more water only if necessary.

Prepare

Let tortilla dough sit 15 minutes. Twist off enough dough for one tortilla. Roll out flat. Fry in a dry, hot frying pan (i.e., no oil). When it starts to bubble, flip the tortilla and fry the other side.

. . . .

If you bake more than one loaf of bread or more tortillas than you can use at one meal and wish to put away the extras for more than a day, wait until the loaf is completely cool. Then wrap it first in aluminum foil, then in a plastic bag. It will keep fine for three to five days.

We have found that fresh-baked bread never seems to get wasted. In fact, on deliveries or with crew, I rarely seem to end up with the 2-day-old bread I like to use for some of my favorite recipes. Two- or 3-day-old bread makes better French toast. I float 3-day-old slices on top of onion or beef soup, top the bread with grated cheese, and bake it.

But my favorite use for 3-day-old bread is English-style bread-and-butter pudding.

BREAD-AND-BUTTER PUDDING

Combine in a bowl

3 eggs
¾ cup milk (½ can evaporated milk plus ¼ cup water)
½ cup sugar
1 tsp. vanilla
½ tsp. cinnamon
½ tsp. salt
½ cup raisins, sultanas, or chocolate chips

> Let cool completely, cut into squares, and serve as a treat for the night watches.

Add

8-10 slices old bread, in ½-inch cubes (approx. 3 cups)
Toss in with egg mixture.

Add

15-20 pieces butter (½-inch cubes)
Toss again.

Bake

Pour into well-greased baking pan and bake 25 minutes at 350 to 375 degrees F, until the top turns brown.

To preserve bread once you've baked it, or if you purchase it from a bakery, paint each loaf all over with a light coating of white vinegar (a clean paintbrush or a pastry brush will do the trick). Then double- or triple-wrap the loaf in plastic wrap or well-sealed plastic bags. The bread will keep mold-free for 10 to 14 days in the tropics, longer in cool climates. When you unwrap the bread to use it, there will be no hint of the vinegar. (This trick also works for cheeses—the same type of mold must attack both cheese and bread.)

For those times when it's too rough to bake bread, or when the bread supply runs out and you haven't time to bake, I've found several handy substitutes. Baking-powder biscuits take only 20 minutes to make. You can use a biscuit mix or the following recipe.

. . . .

BASIC QUICK BISCUITS

Combine

1 cup flour (not sifted)
1 tsp. baking powder
1 tsp. salt
1 tbs. sugar
2 tbs. cooking oil
2 tbs. milk
Mix until batter is very stiff.

> These are really only good fresh as they get hard as a rock about two hours after they are baked.

Bake

Drop by spoonfuls onto a sheet of aluminum foil or greased cookie sheet. Bake at 325-400 degrees F, 12 to 15 minutes, until the tops turn brown.

. . . .

Leftover pancakes are a good bread substitute. Larry loves them cold, buttered, and jammed as a late-night snack. Cornbread biscuits go well with meals or as a snack, but they are best served very fresh.

For treats, I like to carry some canned Boston-style brown bread, but this is hard to find outside the United States. Biscuits—or what Americans call crackers or saltines—are available worldwide. They come in large, round patties throughout the Far East and the South Pacific. Packed in wonderful airtight metal tins, they usually are called cabin biscuits. We use biscuits or saltines for after-dinner cheese or for morning peanut butter and jam, with soup, or crushed as a substitute for bread crumbs on fish cakes and meatloaf. When you are buying biscuits or saltines in countries where they aren't sold in tins, buy small packages so they can be kept individually sealed. The salt on the biscuits attracts moisture, and an open package will go limp after one night. To revitalize stale biscuits, place them on a baking sheet and heat in the oven until they are crisp once more.

In recent years, I've come to enjoy the convenience of long-life breads available from shops in more sophisticated ports. These, along with refrigerated pastry sheets, can be very helpful for the first part of a voyage, or when you do not have the patience (or the stomach) to bake fresh bread.

My top favorite is flour tortillas. I carry at least a dozen packets of them, even for local cruising. Wrap a few in aluminum foil and warm them in an oven or a covered frying pan. Wrap them around any sandwich filling for a quick meal. Or make quesadillas, which are essentially a Mexican version of toasted cheese sandwiches. Once opened, unused tortillas can be kept by resealing them in a Ziploc bag to be stored in a cool (but not necessarily cold) place for up to five days.

Vacuum-packed, prebaked bread will keep for up to six months afloat. For those unwilling to try their hand at baking fresh bread, they are a definite plus. Many come with the suggestion that you bake the loaf in a hot oven for up to 10 minutes before serving. I would bake any vacuum-packed bread, even ones marked "ready to eat." Five minutes in a prewarmed 350-degree oven will give you a crispier crust and make the bread taste fresher. Unfortunately, once opened, these prebaked breads do not seem to keep for more than two days without becoming rock-hard.

．．．．．．．

Day 16

Noon to noon: 58 miles
Miles to date: 1,090
Fog patches; close-reaching over a smooth sea

Breakfast
   canned mandarin oranges in juice
   biscuits, jam
   coffee, tea

Lunch
   salmon-loaf sandwiches with tomato and mayonnaise
   hard-boiled eggs

Dinner
   spaghetti Bolognese
   red wine

. . . .

During vegetable inspection today, I found that two tomatoes had gotten loose while we were beating the past few days. They were badly bruised. Two others were overripe, so dinner tonight was planned by circumstances.

Galley Arrangements

The average long-distance cruiser spends less than 15 percent of the hours in any one year at sea. When you've been beating to windward like we have for the past two days, it may seem different. But to plan the galley of a cruising home only for seagoing is a potential mistake. On the other hand, since the galley on a boat is in a much smaller area than that in a house, and since the amount of foot traffic per square foot must be 100 times that of the average house, traffic planning is extremely important—not only for times at sea but also for when you are in an anchorage.

The idea that your galley must be right next to the companionway to be useful in a long-distance cruising boat must be a bit of rebellion against those pre-1940 yachts in which the crew all worked forward of the mast. I've sailed on one 50-year-old, 60-foot Alden schooner in which the galley was next to the foremast, dividing the crew's quarters from the guests (fig. 19A). It was only 10 feet from the chain locker. The motion was appalling, the ventilation even worse. A cup of coffee for the helmsman usually arrived cold and half-empty after being carried through 40 feet of boat. But fortunately for the cook, if not for the romantics, those days are gone for good.

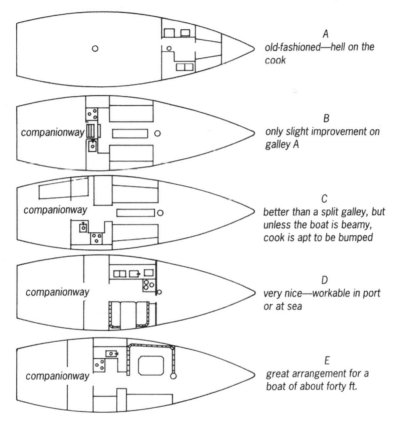

A
old-fashioned—hell on the cook

B
only slight improvement on galley A

C
better than a split galley, but unless the boat is beamy, cook is apt to be bumped

D
very nice—workable in port or at sea

E
great arrangement for a boat of about forty ft.

FIGURE 19. *Galley Layouts*

Putting your galley right next to the companionway also has its disadvantages (fig. 19B). This has the cook right in the busiest part of the boat. Unless the boat is very beamy, the cook must dodge anyone coming for a sail bag or going to the WC. If the cook's working counter is next to the companionway, a crewman rushing below stands a chance of putting his foot in his own half-prepared sandwich. Underway, the cook loses the very ventilation he/she needs because the companionway must be shut to keep spray and gusts of wind from putting out the stove. And finally, in most cruising boats the engine is under the forward end of the cockpit, right next to the aft galley. The poor cook who has to dish up a meal in the tropics standing right next to a hot engine has my sympathy.

Although a galley set off to one side of the companionway is a vast improvement (fig. 19C), the most serviceable arrangements I've seen are ones where the galley is more toward the middle or forward end of the main cabin (figs. 19D, E). With a large Dorade vent or an opening hatch just above the stove, your cook has the ventilation she needs. She is out of the crew's way and in the part of the boat with the best motion. The table on most cruisers is near the mast so the cook can easily reach the table from the midships galley. One final improvement on this midships galley is an opening portlight right over the sink. Then the cook can enjoy the view or cool off and can also get that fresh air that prevents nausea.

When I started writing about galley arrangements, I spent a day visiting four different cruising boats. All the couples on these boats had cruised for almost a year, and all four cooks were unanimous on one recommendation: They all felt that the galley sink should be as close as possible to the stove. It really makes sense when you consider cooking at sea. A pot that is hot and boiling over can be quickly transferred into the sink without making a mess. Mugs can be lined up in the sink so that soup can be poured with little lost motion or few spills. If you have to carry a pot of water from the sink on one side of your boat to the stove on the other, there are bound to be mishaps.

If possible, the stove should also be several feet away from the heads of any bunks or settees. Sleepy people are often careless about where they put their hands when they are climbing out of the bunk. And, with the inevitable spills on a heavy-weather passage, your cook has one less worry if there is no one sleeping or sitting just inches from the stove. If, on the other hand, the stove must be near a bunk, a dividing bulkhead 18 inches above stove level will solve the problem.

A real must for cooking in a seaway is a backstrap for the cook to lean against while the boat is heeled. This strap should be made of 2- or 3-inch-wide strong webbed fabric with easy-to-use clips on each end. It pays to have an adjustable lanyard on the strap so it can be changed easily to fit various crew members. I also like the adjustment as, when we are going to windward on one tack, I like to lean away from the galley sink with the strap around my buttocks. On the other tack, I need the strap to help me stay close to the sink, so I secure it around my waist. So this means two very different length requirements. The attachment points for the strap should be easy to clip into and secured in place with bolts, not wood screws, as they will, at times, take the cook's total weight (fig. 20).

FIGURE 20. *Adjustable Lanyard for Galley Strap*

We found it pays to be able to lengthen or shorten the galley strap so either one of us can use it at sea. This simple lanyard-and-lashing system works well.

In a U-shaped galley this strap is easy to arrange. Not only does it give the cook support but it also keeps the crew out of the cook's way. On larger boats, where the galley may be 10 or more feet from the cockpit, I've seen an extension of this strap the length of the main cabin. The cook could carry a cup of coffee directly from the stove to the companionway without having to look for a handhold.

Galley floors deserve much more consideration. It is impossible to avoid splashing a bit of grease on them during everyday cooking, even in port. On a long voyage, the floors are guaranteed to get wet when your thirsty crew clambers in for a quick cuppa. So, floors must be made of some material that is not only nonskid when dry but also nonskid when wet and greasy. It should be easy to clean, because it will be the most stood-on 3 square feet of space in your boat. Only one material really meets all of these requirements: bare, edge-grained teak. It is always nonskid. Hot water and detergent and a quick scrub with a plastic pot scrubber will keep it bright. It wears like iron and always looks smart. Iroko, afromosia, or hard or pitch pine can be substituted if necessary. A nonskid patterned fiberglass surface will get slippery the minute any oil gets on it. If you don't believe me, spill some diesel or cooking oil on your glass deck, add water, then step on it. Dirt will work into the cracks and scratches after a year of use. Although carpets are nonskid, cheap, and easy to install—and they hide rough or shoddy workmanship—they have no place in a galley. Carpets stain easily, pick up odors, and are almost impossible to keep dry, especially at sea. As soon as linoleum gets wet, it isn't nonskid. Every way I look at it, scrubbed teak is the perfect galley floor for the long-distance cruiser.

If you are buying a new boat, building a new interior in yours, or simply looking at improvements you can make, consider your galley arrangements carefully. What works beautifully tied up in a marina can be useless in a rough anchorage or in a seaway. And even though you don't spend all of your time at sea, the cook spends almost a quarter of her/his day in the galley, whether in sea or in port.

. . . .

Day 17

Noon to noon: 100 miles
Miles to date: 1,190
Close-hauled, smooth sea, not quite laying our course
Gray day

Lunch
chili and beans
bread, butter
cola

Dinner (picnic style)
fried canned sausage
bean salad
Larry's favorite seagoing cabbage salad

. . . .

 ## LARRY'S FAVORITE CABBAGE SALAD

Combine
2 cups chopped cabbage
¼ cup chopped onion
⅛ cup raisins (or sultanas)
3 tbs. mayonnaise
2 tbs. lemon juice
1 tbs. sugar
½ tsp. dried dill

> Allow to sit 1 hour
> before serving. (When I
> have fresh tomatoes or
> carrots, I add those.)

. . . .

After tea this afternoon, we got out *Ocean Passages for the World* to see if the headwinds we've been experiencing are normal. They are not! But careful reading informed us that rain is possible for the next 800 miles or so; after that, it's rare. Right now, we have 45 gallons of water left, or 1.4 gallons per

100 miles. Winds should improve, but still we discussed the water situation and reminded ourselves not to waste any. We've had very light drizzle most mornings, so we have left the raincatcher on the boom, just in case. Maybe that is why there's no rain. The minute we take down the catcher, the rain will come.

DAY 17. *Galley burns are the most common and dangerous accident at sea.*

A Good Stove, a Good Cruise

I've never met a crew on any offshore passage that didn't hope for two or three hot meals a day. When cruising, this becomes a 52-weeks-a-year proposition. If cooking isn't easy and enjoyable, then neither is cruising. Good food conveniently prepared is one of the joys of life, and the most important tool the cook uses is the stove.

I'm sold on propane. Why? It lights instantly. Just turn on the safety valve, light a match, and it's burning. No priming needed; if there's fuel, it works. The flame is hot and extremely clean. The stove requires very little maintenance other than a monthly check of the valves and connections.

Since you can use either propane or butane in the same bottle, supply is no problem. We have now been in about 80 countries and have been able to have our tank filled in each—though sometimes we needed to provide our own transfer hose (described later in this section).

Our 20-pound (10-kilo) tank keeps us in cooking fuel for an average of three months, including the fuel needed for baking our own bread. When we use our gas heater also, it lasts three weeks during an English winter. To fill one tank costs between US$5 and $9, depending on the country. Our tank has a level gauge on it, which is extremely handy, but two smaller tanks work just as well. When one runs out, we switch tanks and refill the empty.

The biggest advantage to a gas stove is that only with gas can you get an efficient, clean oven. Is an oven essential? One day we were moored in the estuary behind Punta Arenas, Costa Rica. A glorious 58-foot, Herreshoff-designed ketch flying a French flag anchored near us, and we were invited for cocktails. We were dazzled by the polished bronzework and traditional teak finish of *Denebola*. We invited her owner to bring her youngsters for tea the next day. I baked fresh cookies for the children. Our very gracious guest said, "I know I am richer than you are, but which one of us is wealthier? You live on a 24-foot yacht, yet you can serve fresh-baked pastries. I serve only what can be cooked on two burners, and we have a 58-footer."

She missed the enjoyment of cooking with an oven. So do many other boat wives I meet. Life without baked potatoes, roast beef, or grilled pork chops just wouldn't be the same for us. Trade-wind sailing 10 days from land with fresh-baked bread and casseroles is only possible with an oven. Besides, a diet of fried foods is just what a sailor doesn't need—too much fat and not enough variety. I know that stove-top ovens work, but they require steady sailing conditions and time to set up and dismantle. The stove-top oven will almost always have a hot spot, so to keep the bottoms of cakes and breads from burning, you will have to use a flame spreader and a slow baking method.

Two of the most common reasons we hear for not using gas are: It's not safe and it weighs too much. As to the first, I can only say, butane can be dangerous, but so can sailing—both require care, planning, and prudence. The problem with gas afloat is that it is heavier than air; therefore, it sinks to the lowest possible level if it is not fully burned. In a home ashore, this is not a major problem, as it is hard to get enough gas concentrated into one space to cause an explosion. And the minute you open a door, the gas runs out of the house or caravan. But in a boat, this gas will go right to the lowest part of the bilge, where it is concentrated into a very small space and has no way of dissipating short of being pumped overboard by a bilge pump backed up by a bilge blower. For this reason, even if a stove is equipped with automatic gas shutoffs on each burner, it shouldn't be left unattended. If a pot boils over and you return a few minutes later to find your flame out, you shouldn't relight the stove until you have checked and aired the bilges. A butane stove must be well installed with the tanks on deck. There must be a convenient tank-shutoff valve right near the stove. Connections through the deck should be heavy-wall bronze piping. We use a nylon ball swing valve. If the handle is perpendicular to the piping, the tank is off. It is much quicker and easier to check a swing valve than a gate valve (see fig. 21).

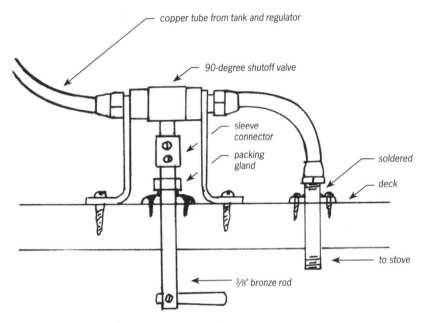

FIGURE 21. *Through-the-Deck Shutoff for Propane Stove*

We have sailed on boats with solenoid switches to shut off the butane right at the tank. Although these can be very conveniently installed with the switch right next to the stove and a bright, hard-to-miss indicator light, they have certain disadvantages. The solenoid switch requires constant electricity to start the stove, so it drains batteries if the stove is used frequently when the engine isn't running. If the ship's electrical supply is out of order, you must bypass the solenoid switch* before you can cook. The wiring and switch itself costs $160 excluding labor, while a direct swing valve can be purchased

. . . .

* If you choose to have a solenoid shutoff switch, be sure you have arranged for a bypass system and backup propane shutoff system for those times when—due to engine, alternator, generator, or battery problems—the house batteries are not available.

for about $12. And finally, to ensure complete safety, your solenoid system should have an explosion-proof switch in the cabin or a gas sniffer and alarm, which will add another $150 to your stove costs. If your tank must be several feet from your stove, a swing valve and a mechanical Morse-cable arrangement would be cheaper and safer than a solenoid switch. (Prices and information are courtesy Coastal Propane, Vancouver, British Columbia.)

This bears repeating: *The tank must be on deck.* So-called waterproof cockpit lockers are not safe. A friend of ours on a well-built Swedish yacht was running from Trinidad to Cartagena, Colombia. His propane tank was in the cockpit locker with two overboard drains near the stern of the boat. After running for four days in heavy wind, Eric went below to start the engine and charge the batteries. His boat contained the explosion, blowing the skylight right through the bottom of his dinghy and burning and partially blinding him. The vapor-proof propane-locker drains had been covered by his quarter wake. The tank developed a leak, and propane, flowing like water, had overflowed the locker, filled the cockpit, and poured over the companionway, filling the bilges. With the tank on deck, butane will run out the scuppers, flowing harmlessly overboard.

When we had a small leak in our butane tank, we just asked everyone not to smoke on board. We used the stove and the oil lamps until we were able to repair the damaged tank three months later. Ours is stored in a bottomless deck box forward of the cabin.

On *Seraffyn,* our 20-pound (10-kilo) galvanized tank kept us in cooking for an average of three months. When we used a gas heater during two winters in Europe, it lasted three weeks. The tank had a level gauge, which we found essential, but we often wished we had two smaller tanks so that when one ran out, we could switch tanks and refill the empty one. When we built *Taleisin,* we opted for two separate 10-gallon tanks and paid extra for lightweight aluminum. The rust-free tanks are far easier to hoist on board, and they have lasted twice as long as steel ones. In fact, we would still be using the original tanks, except that regulations in North America have changed and we had to have tanks with upgraded safety valves.

I particularly like having the smaller tanks, as they can be carried easily on the racks of our folding bicycles for refilling. When we set sail for the long haul toward Cape Horn and into the Pacific, we knew we would be using propane for heating when our kerosene cabin heater was not sufficient. We purchased an extra tank, which, because of its small size, nestled under the dinghy stored on the cabin top. Once the tank was emptied, we left the valve open for several days, and then we were able to find space inside a locker to store the spare tank for future use.

Our bottle is the type used for propane in the United States, Canada, and England. It has a reverse-thread female fill fitting. The bottle is rated to 250 psi pressure and has a plate stating this. This is well in line with the safety standards of every country we have visited. The tank has a pressure-release valve, and we carry a transfer tube with a male reverse-thread fitting on one end plus hose clamps to secure the appropriate local fitting to the other end. By upending a full bottle of butane, hoisting it above the level of ours, connecting the two tanks securely, and opening the valves on both tanks, plus the pressure-release valve on ours, we can get a full refill from a tank the same size or slightly larger.

At Rodriques Island in the western Indian Ocean, no tank-filling facilities are available. We paid the deposit on a 50-kilo propane tank, purchased a local fill fitting for the equivalent of $6, took it down to the jetty, and transferred fuel into our empty tanks as well as those of the only other visiting yacht, *Patience*. The remaining propane was transferred to the tank of the local tailor, who was so delighted with this gift he sewed a free courtesy flag for each boat. We have accumulated a selection of five different fill fittings, which seem to cover us everywhere we have been in recent years.

What's wrong with kerosene (paraffin), alcohol, diesel, wood, electric, and compressed natural gas? I've used alcohol, kerosene, and electric, but not wood or diesel. I think the disadvantages of wood are obvious for long-distance offshore sailing. I have been told that diesel is great for northern climates but it roasts you out of the cabin when you head south. It also means waiting for the first cup of hot coffee in the morning or leaving the stove on all night. I dread electricity, because generator failure means no hot food.

Kerosene smells just enough to make a queasy cook seasick. So does alcohol (methylated spirits). Kerosene and alcohol need priming, and using kerosene means carrying two separate fuels. Priming requires waiting before you can cook. So the person on watch can't just dash down and warm a cup of coffee quickly. With an alcohol stove, the packing glands dry out and must be adjusted frequently, or else they will leak. Both alcohol and kerosene must be pressurized; that requires remembering to pump the tank before your fire goes out; otherwise, you have to go through the whole repriming-and-relighting procedure again. I'm often caught when I'm on a boat with a pressurized stove because the fuel in the pressure tank runs out just at the wrong moment. Both fuels must be burning perfectly or they will cause soot. Over a few months, your nice white cabin overhead will turn gray or yellow. Overpriming causes fires. I know you can put them out with water, but any fire is a nuisance unless it is the perfect blue glow of a gas fire under a bubbling fish stew.

Each time Larry hears the debate about what fuel to burn, he sits smuggly back and says, "Alcohol is made for drinking, not burning." Considering the cost of methylated spirits (as they call it in Europe), I can't help but agree. It's $10 a gallon.

Why can't a kerosene or alcohol stove have a good oven? A proper oven needs a fire the whole length of the enclosure (fig. 22). A small, round burner in the center doesn't radiate properly and causes a central hot spot. Using priming cups creates more difficulties. With propane, the oven can have a properly shaped burner with a heat-controlling thermostat. Fiberglass 1$\frac{1}{2}$-inch insulation makes our oven super-efficient and produces evenly browned breads and cakes with no burned bottoms. A grill or broiler under the oven burner gives us space to toast six sandwiches at once.

After almost 40 years of cruising, Eric and Susan Hiscock finally installed a gas stove. Susan's only comment after 8,000 miles of voyaging with her new stove was, "We should have had it 25 years ago."

We do carry a single-burner Primus kerosene stove to use as a backup in case we run short of propane. We also carry it with us if we go ashore for a camping trip. In extremely hot climates, the kerosene-burning Primus can be set in the cockpit so the cabin isn't overheated. In boats larger than *Taleisin*, Primus stoves in a sea swing mounted on a bulkhead can be quite handy for slow-cooking soups and stews.

If you like microwave ovens, portable ones are convenient to use in marinas when you are on shore power. Keep in mind, though, that these units require a lot of energy. Most people find they have to run the generator when they microwave out at anchor. Since most microwaving is done just when neighboring sailors are enjoying a sundowner in the cockpit, you might (in this environmentally sensitive era) find yourself becoming known as a source of noise pollution. You'll also find your microwave less useful afloat, since time is not as important as it was when you worked onshore. Quick-defrosting ability is not relevant when you have all day to plan your meal as you savor the slower pace of life afloat.

If you are worried about the space for a stove that has an oven, consider not gimbaling it. Except for boats designed and used for long-distance ocean racing—races in which the boat may be on the same tack, bashing to windward for days at a time—gimbaled stoves are a waste of space, an extra expense, and potentially dangerous.

I'm sure no one will argue about the extra space required to gimbal a stove properly. The extra expense incurred involves the gimbaling brackets, flexible piping, and (most necessary of all) a proper lock for the stove when it is being used in port.

208

Burns are the number-one hazard at sea, and gimbaled stoves can be the cause of dangerous burns in two different ways. First, the stove is free to swing. A person accidentally losing balance and falling against it in a seaway can cause a pot to tip off. This happened to a friend of mine during a transpacific race several years ago. The boat lurched and she bumped the stove, spilling the contents of a boiling pot of coffee inside her oilskin pants. She had to be evacuated by helicopter for treatment of third-degree burns. Cruising people don't have the support of a Transpac Race committee and escort vessels, so a burn like that could potentially prove to be fatal.

Even in port, a free-swinging stove can cause burns. A friend was tied to a mooring in Avalon harbor at Catalina. On top of the stove was a pot of boiling water for the corn on the cob she was preparing. She bent over and opened the oven door, which changed the center of gravity of the stove. It tilted forward, the water in the pot poured out, and she received third-degree burns over most of her forearm. The same thing happened during the 1979 Newport Beach-to-Cabo San Lucas Race. Help couldn't be found for two days, and the unfortunate crew on *Maverick* had extensive scarring.

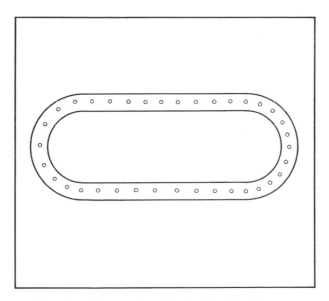

FIGURE 22. *Plan View of Proper Oven Fire for Even Heating*

The second danger of a gimbaled stove is that few come with quick-to-use, individual clamps for each burner. A pot is set on the stove top and expected to stay in place. A sudden lurch, a change of tack, and the free pot slides across the stove, bumps the rail, and pours on the cook or the cabin sole. Larry really noticed this when he sailed in the 1974 'Round Britain

2-man race. He was on a 30-footer with a gimbaled stove that had a sea rail. Yet when they were beating out to the Shetland Islands, he had to tie down the teapot with marlin or it flew off the stove, adding one more bit of racket to keep the off-watch awake. If you must have a gimbaled stove, please have good seagoing pot clamps (fig. 23), a solid, 3-inch-high rail, and a warning for each crewman: Don't grab the stove for support! And consider gimbaling the stove athwartships so it is bulkhead-mounted.

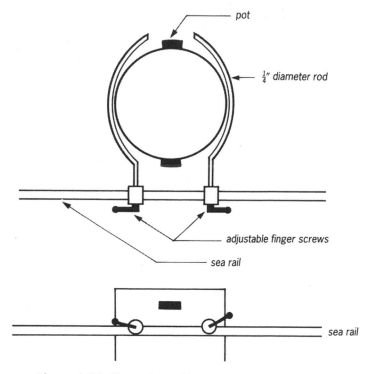

pot

$\frac{1}{4}$" diameter rod

adjustable finger screws

sea rail

sea rail

FIGURE 23. *Plan and Side Views of Good Set of Pot Clamps*

I have a passion for commercial boats, and I've never been on one that was fitted with a gimbaled stove. I had the dubious but interesting privilege of being cook on a 100-ton Costa Rican shrimp trawler for a month. I fed our crew of six with little difficulty, using oversize pots clamped to a 3-inch-high sea rail on a solidly attached stove. A shrimp boat may not heel like a sailboat, but it sure can roll.

On *Seraffyn,* we bolted our oversize cooker amidships to the aft side of our forward bulkhead. We had a 3-inch-high solid bronze sea rail with great, easy-to-use clamps. Twice we were on our beam ends—once because of an unexpected williwaw and the second time because of a hurricane. Both times our high-profile, 6-cup coffee percolator stayed put.

What did I do when we were beating to windward? Luckily, *Seraffyn* was a beamy boat and didn't immediately assume a 30-degree heel. About 15 to 20 degrees is right. More than that and it's time to shorten down. *Taleisin*, her five foot longer big sister, is the same. So, deeper pots solve the problem. Since we rarely race *Taleisin* long distances, I could usually get Larry to shorten down for mealtime. During an ocean passage, five minutes lost means little. Living on board means about 80 or 85 percent of our cooking is done in port. That leaves only 15 percent to be done at sea, and odds are that half of that should be with fair winds and calm seas. (Odds have been against us at times, I will admit.)

One special advantage of having an athwartships-mounted nongimbaled stove—i.e. the cook is facing either fore or aft when using the stove—is that if the liquid in a pot does overflow or boil over, it usually spills either to port or to starboard, not toward the cook.

In 1985, we met Doug and Joanna Watson in Tonga when they were heading home from a cruise on 36-foot *Ben Hall*. As I was showing them the safety features of *Taleisin*'s athwartships-mounted stove, I remember Larry saying, "If we had another 8 or 9 inches of beam, I'd gimbal our stove athwartships and have the best of all worlds—the safety of keeping the cook clear of spills, no fear of the oven door overbalancing the stove when it was opened, and the advantage of taking up less space than a normal gimbaled stove."

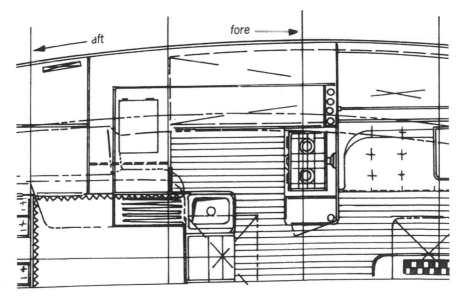

FIGURE 24. *Athwartships Gimbaled Stove on* **Ben Hall II**

Five years later, we visited Joanna and Doug in Sydney and had a tour of the almost completed *Ben Hall II*, designed for them by Rodger Martin. There was the stove exactly as we had envisioned it, taking up far less space than a side-mounted gimbaled stove (fig. 24).

Rodger Martin took his stove idea a step further when he designed *Katie G* for the well-known U.S. East Coast boatbuilder Eric Goetz. In Eric's words, "The stove lives in its own module, which gimbals as a unit. This enables the cook to stand aft of the stove, never downhill from the hot soup. The module also provides level surfaces, which are covered with stainless steel, on which to place the hot kettle. The funny-angled face outboard of the oven allows one to open the oven even heeled." (See figs. 25 and 26, plus photographs.) *Katie G* is 40 feet in length. I think her stove arrangement nears perfection.

If space for a large stove and oven is a problem on your boat, consider installing the oven separate from the top burners. Although this means additional plumbing, it worked wonderfully for Bill Townsend on his 40-foot light-displacement cruiser, and it led to a safe, easy-to-clean gimbaled burner arrangement. Bill's oven was mounted against the bulkhead at the aft end of the galley. The burners were set on gimbals in a stainless-steel-lined depression along the side counter of the galley. A drain leading from the depression into a Y connection on the galley sink drain made it easy to flush away spills. Bill had three burners on his gimbaled stove. The front of the depression created a good handhold for the cook and made it impossible for anyone to bump into the stove in a seaway.

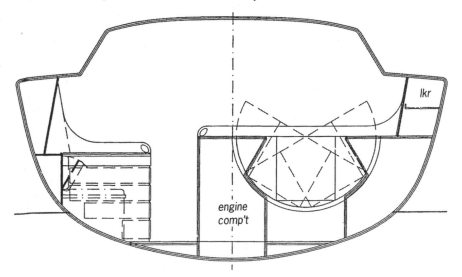

FIGURE 25. *Forty-foot* **Katie G:** *Section in Way of Galley*
(Roger Martin Yacht Designs)

A. This is the galley on Rodger Martin's Katie G—*when the boat was on even keel. Note the locking device at the lowest point of the gimbaled stove cabinet.*

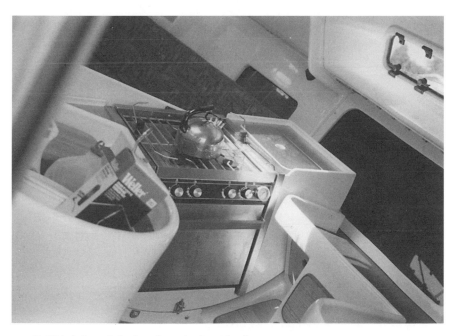

B. This is how it looks when the boat heels.

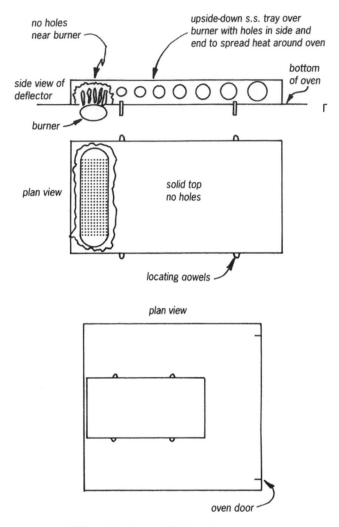

no holes near burner

upside-down s.s. tray over burner with holes in side and end to spread heat around oven

bottom of oven

side view of deflector

burner

plan view

solid top no holes

locating aowels

plan view

oven door

FIGURE 26. *Heat Diffuser for Ovens with Hot Spots*

An important safety addition for a gimbaled stove, whether it is mounted athwartships or fore-and-aft, is a permanently installed grabrail slightly above and inboard of the stove. This will give the cook and crew something to grab in a seaway instead of the hot, swinging stove. It also keeps the cook from falling against the stove and unbalancing any pots that are bubbling away on it.

For any gimbaled-stove arrangement, you should have a locking device to use in port. But some of our friends have found that an additional sea lock is also useful, especially when you will be on one tack for a long time. Tom and Harriet Linskey installed a bolt on the lower edge of their side-gimbaled stove on *Freelance*. On the side of the gimbal enclosure, they drilled holes in a semicircle, each of which allowed a change of about three degrees of angle. This stopped the stove from swinging wildly in a seaway when it wasn't in use.

A question we are still wrestling with is, Does it pay to spend $1,200 to $2,000 for a specially built stainless-steel stove for our boat, or would it be wiser to buy a $250 enameled caravan (trailer) stove with oven and replace a few parts after three years of salt-air abuse? On *Seraffyn*, we chose the caravan-stove route, as no special yacht stoves were available. The oven was excellent, and the stove worked well for at least 15 years, but some panels did rust out. We replaced them as necessary and found it easy to buy burner parts. Total cost for the 12 years we had the boat never came close to the price of a specialty stove. When we built *Taleisin*, not only did we have a better cash flow but also a choice of two different brands of specially built, rustproof stoves. We opted for the expensive route. The stove definitely looks more elegant. But the oven has a hot spot. (See fig. 26 for the solution to this problem.) When, after 11 years of use, the grill burner and top burners needed replacing, we found it difficult to get parts since they were specialty items made only for the particular stove model we purchased. A six month search turned up the parts we needed in a second hand supply house. Conclusion: It is a toss-up. But in all cases, I'd opt for the safety features of the marine stove (safety thermocouplers and a locking oven door).

Stainless-steel propane barbecue grills—which usually are mounted on the stern rails of many types of boats—can be a definite boon in hot climates. By cooking out on deck, you keep from overheating the galley and the interior of the boat, you share the cooking responsibilities, and you even have a stove to carry ashore for parties. Yet, in spite of their popularity in marinas along both coasts of the United States, it is surprising how few offshore cruisers use them once they leave on a long voyage. Part of the reason is the need to store away the barbecue and its gas bottle during passages and also when anchored in big cities, where it could be a temptation to light-fingered types. This is one item I would not put on the predeparture list as a necessity. But if you already have and enjoy using one, it's well worth trying to find an easily accessible, below-decks storage space for the barbecue.

. . . .

Day 18

Noon to noon: 73 miles
Miles to date: 1,263
Hazy; wind fresh from SE
Sheets eased just a bit

Lunch
tuna salad sandwiches
cabbage, carrot, and bean salad

Dinner
Larry's Heavy Weather Hash

. . . .

LARRY'S HEAVY WEATHER HASH

Boil (until almost soft enough to eat)
3 potatoes, diced

Put in large frying pan with
2 tbs. cooking oil
1 onion, diced
10 cloves garlic, diced

Sauté 5 minutes.

Add
1 can corned beef
Cover and simmer slowly 5 minutes more.

Add
1 tomato, in chunks

Cover and remove from heat.
Serve 4 minutes later.

. . . .

DAY 18. *Onions, eaten daily, not only give the cook a good chance to shed some tears but also add vitamins to canned foods.*

We had a fine mist all night, and this morning we were surprised to find that our raincatcher had added more than a gallon of freshwater to our supply.

Right now, we are making 5 knots but slamming into a leftover head sea. The boat is heeled about 20 degrees. Chopping onions and getting them safely from cutting board to pot is taking a lot of patience. It's so tempting to ask Larry to shorten sail. But we'd lose almost a knot of speed if he did. We've had so little fast sailing this trip, and Canada is such a long way ahead. Besides, I know the wind is starting to ease.

Just after I wrote that, Larry noticed that I was getting impatient with something I was trying to cut. "Come on, sit down and have a drink," he insisted. "So what if dinner is a bit late tonight?" An hour later, the motion seemed easier, or my patience a bit stronger, and the last of my dinner preparations went along much better.

Health and the Cook

For the past few days, Larry has been complaining about a sore tooth. My first thoughts were of vitamin deficiency, but last night, a small abscess formed at the base of the offending tooth. Out came the medical chest and our medical guidebook, *Being Your Own Wilderness Doctor* (Stackpole Books, Harrisburg, PA). We started Larry on the recommended course of antibiotics. This morning, there is a definite improvement. But I still don't rule out a possible vitamin deficiency. This is a real problem on board cruising boats—not only those making long passages such as we are, but also on board those visiting unusual ports of call. It seems that our bodies adjust to the vitamins we eat during our normal shore life, and when our diets vary drastically—whether it's because we are using mainly processed and canned goods or because we're eating tropical fruits and vegetables instead of apples and pears—then vitamin deficiencies can crop up. The symptoms and results can be drastic.

The late Peter Tangvald wrote about an incident that occurred when he was crossing the Atlantic on his 32-footer *Dorothea* several years ago. He started having tremendous pains around his heart. He was unable to leave his bunk for several days while *Dorothea* steered herself though storm and calm. When he landed in the Caribbean islands, his pains disappeared almost immediately. The same thing happened again during his 40-day passage across the Indian Ocean. He assumed it was a heart attack or some problem connected to the rheumatic fever he'd had as a child. On reaching France, he went into the hospital to find that in both instances he had been suffering from beriberi, a vitamin-deficiency disease. Some years later we spent a week moored alongside Peter and his wife, Lydia, in Manila. He told us that before he'd met Lydia, his complete at-sea diet came from cans. "Vitamins," Peter commented, "I thought they were something for hypochondriacs to worry about." But now Lydia plans offshore meals that include whole-grain breads, wild rice, and as much fresh food as possible, plus vitamin supplements. Peter, who, when we met in Manila was 56, had the vitality of a 36 year old. I know Larry and I may sound like health-food nuts, but we have both been surprised to find that problems we developed at sea were caused by vitamin deficiency. I arrived in Florida after two years in the tropics with small ulcers on my gums and bleeding around the edges of my teeth every time I brushed them. When I went to a local dentist for a routine checkup, he informed me that I was suffering from the first stages of scurvy. I am not keen on tropical fruits, so I had missed out on the necessary quantity of vitamin C.

Even with a bimini, it pays to have movable side curtains to create sun-sheltered, at-sea lounging areas.

During our Baltic cruise, Larry developed pains that first were diagnosed as kidney stones. A Polish doctor finally told us he was suffering from vitamin B12 deficiency. An overnight miracle cure brought on by one injection of B12 convinced us. Larry had been avoiding bread, noodles, and potatoes to try to keep his weight down. We'd been unwilling to pay the price for fresh meat in Scandinavia and had been using our canned meats. Grains, potatoes and meat are the main sources of vitamin B12.

We still do not go running to the health-food store for our provisions. But we do take a multiple-vitamin tablet every other day at sea, one that contains thiamine (B12), A, and C, plus magnesium. We add wheat germ or other natural grains to the bread we bake, and we carry fortified orange juice concentrates to provide extra vitamin C.

On deliveries, we provide vitamin tablets for the crew. So far, no one has objected to taking them, and we've never had a serious health problem among our crew.

Vitamin tablets are easy to store. We purchase them in glass bottles of 200 at a time and keep them out of the light in a cool place. They have a shelf life of one year if they are kept perfectly dry.

In the tropics or in extremely hot summer weather, there is an additional health concern for the cook—salt deficiency. When people sweat profusely, their bodies use more salt than normal. If this isn't replaced, headaches, severe muscle cramps, and irritability may follow. During our recent visit to French Polynesia, I found more signs of salt deficiency among cruising sailors than in previous years. Probably 20 percent of the sailors from northern climes made comments about feeling lethargic, short-tempered, slightly faint, or clammy-skinned. (A check will often show lowered blood pressure—first sign of potential heatstroke.)

Several modern trends seem to have contributed to this problem. First is the use of watermakers, which remove almost all traces of salt from drinking water. Second is the current medical recommendation that people avoid unnecessary salt to help lower blood pressure. Third is the use of dodgers, which reduce the breezes that typically would flow through cockpit areas. This breeze normally combines with the sweat your body produces to cool your skin. Eliminate the airflow and you have created a high-humidity steam room that forces your body to sweat more than it otherwise would, depleting its salt supply more quickly. Salt deficiency can creep up on you. During our voyage down the Red Sea, I developed cramps that were beyond the limit of most pains I'd had before. Both of my legs were affected, and for 30 hours I was unable to leave the bunk to stand watches. We'd had 10 days of 110-degree-F weather before the cramps developed, and I am not naturally a heavy salt user. Clouds covered the sky the day my cramps developed, and as the cooler weather reduced perspiration, the cramps slowly went away. But their weakening effects made walking difficult when we reached Aden three days later. When we spoke to the doctor there, he immediately pointed to salt deficiency.

Drinking alcoholic beverages also can contribute to salt deficiency. The ice-filled, cooling drinks taste so good that cruisers often forget to drink enough nonalcoholic beverages to compensate for the dehydrating affects of the alcohol.

One way of knowing whether or not you are drinking enough liquid in the tropics, and replenishing your salt supplies sufficiently, is to keep a casual check on how often you or your crew urinate. A safe average to shoot for is once every 2 to 2 1/2 hours during waking hours. The color of urine also is a good indicator. If you notice that it's becoming darker yellow, you need to add liquid to your diet.

If you do see signs of salt deficiency, the cure is simple. Add 1 teaspoon of salt to a cup of natural, sweet-flavored juice—it will act almost like a miracle cure. The headachy feeling will usually begin to recede within half an hour. But prevention is better than cure. In the tropics, add salt to your diet. Drink lots of liquid. Provide lots of ventilation inside the boat and use a bimini-type top for shade (or add opening windows to your dodger arrangement) to increase airflow.

Slightly off the subject but of great importance, since many of you reading this will be women: Don't wear nylon panties or nylon bathing suits in the tropics. They will cause or aggravate cystitis, which is extremely painful and irritating. (Symptoms: pain when urinating, blood in urine, pelvic discomfort, slight fever, possible pain around kidney area.) Nylon does not absorb perspiration, so it creates the hot, damp atmosphere next to your skin and private parts that will allow bacteria to incubate. For the same reason, men should also avoid wearing nylon trunks and shirts. Cotton is cooler and healthier.

Keeping well-hydrated also helps prevent cystitis, as does taking vitamin C or capsules containing cranberry extract. Cranberry juice or extract will definitely ease the discomfort of cystitis. As we meet many women with this problem, I carry dried cranberries (which we also enjoy using to spice up salads.) About three tablespoons of dried cranberries to a cup of boiling water plus a spoonful of sugar, produces a pleasant tasting infusion that quickly alleviates the discomfort of urinating.

Skin cancer is a concern for people who sail. Those with light-colored eyes and fair skins are particularly susceptible. Staying out of the sun under a bimini, a dodger, or a sun cover is not a complete solution, as the reflected rays of the sun hitting the water can also cause skin damage. A combination of proper sunscreens; light-colored, loose clothing; and a selection of sun hats will help mitigate skin damage. Unfortunately, choosing a sunscreen is problematical. There now seems to be some controversy about whether sunscreens prevent melanoma. They definitely can prevent sunburn and squamous cell carcinoma, but the jury is out on more serious types of skin cancer. There is even some concern that sunscreens might increase the risk of melanoma by allowing people to spend more time in the sun. The current recommendations are to use a broad-spectrum sun block that blocks both UVA and UVB rays. (UVA doesn't cause sunburn but still causes skin damage.)

Mary Jane Gilmer, a nurse practitioner and university professor who is currently doing a doctoral thesis here in New Zealand on the long-term health of cruising sailors, has vetted this health section. She has recommended adding the information that many medications can cause photosensitivity—i.e., cause your skin to burn more easily. These include several that are in all cruising medical kits, such as tetracycline, sulfa drugs, many antihistamines, even such over-the-counter drugs as ibuprofen. She also lists certain perfume oils, such as bergamot, citron, lavender, sandalwood, cedar, and musk. It's crucial to be aware of the contraindications for any medication you use.

With all this talk of skin cancer and avoiding the sun, you might ask, Is it safe to go sailing? I had an interesting experience when I consulted a noted California dermatologist during my biennial checkup. He removed a few small sun-damaged spots (keratosis) on my hands and face and, in answer to my questions, said, "You have two choices. You can avoid all sun, wear gloves, a large sun hat, a long light-colored dress, etc., etc., or you can get out and enjoy life, wear a sun hat, apply sunscreen, and come and see me every two years." I burn easily, as I have light gray/green eyes and fair skin. After 40 years afloat, I have some scars on my skin, and possibly a few more wrinkles than my indoor-sports friends, but I feel comfortable with my choice of his second option.

A wide-brimmed hat, a pareau to keep the sun off my legs, the sails to shelter my back—perfect protection for enjoying trade-wind sailing as we run toward Mauritius in the Indian Ocean.

If you are cruising in mosquito-prone areas, Mary Jane suggests a simple repellent you may already have in the galley. Soybean oil will, according to the *Annals of Internal Medicine,* repel mosquitoes for three to four hours. The best way to prevent mosquito bites is by using DEET-containing repellents (10 to 30 percent concentration for adults, and no more than

10 percent concentration for children). A secondary line of defense is to spray your clothes with products that contain permethrin. This insect repellent is effective for up to two weeks, even with laundering. As Mary Jane states, the very best way to avoid diseases such as malaria, dengue fever, and yellow fever is to prevent mosquito bites.

Dental care is one real cruising problem. American and Canadian dentists are the best in the world. Therefore, have your teeth checked and cared for before you leave home. A good program of flossing is worthwhile, but carry a supply of floss with you. It can be hard to find once you're underway.

The cruising life is normally an extremely healthy one if you can avoid dietary problems. Contagious diseases such as those that might be contracted by people working in crowded offices and schools just don't happen at sea. Because cruisers cook the majority of their own meals on board, they are far less prone to stomach problems than other travelers. Colds are rare, injuries less likely than onshore, and tension-caused ailments seldom exist. But boredom on long passages can be a problem, and this is where the cook can contribute tremendously to the health of the crew. A smash-up meal when the ship is slatting, becalmed in a fog for the fourth day; a steamy, hot mug of rich, creamy chocolate when the crew is wet and cold from a sail change; a surprise cake to break up the sameness of a trade-wind passage— all contribute to mental stimulation and therefore to the health of the crew.

It may seem as though the cook is being burdened with a lot of jobs— medic, psychologist, dietitian, purser, bottle-washer—but if you are at sea with only two or three on board, many jobs come your way that never would have occurred to you before. But in return, everything you do will be appreciated, and you'll rarely be bored.

NOTE: A wealth of information is available regarding many health topics of interest to cruising sailors at www.cdc.gov, under Travelers' Health.

. . . .

Day 19

Noon to noon: 104 miles
Miles to date: 1,367
Same fog and gray but fresh wind
Close-reaching over a lumpy sea
By Dinnertime, the wind drew aft, and we eased sheets
until we were beam-reaching

Lunch
scrambled eggs
leftover corned-beef hash

Teatime
cheese, biscuits
last chocolate bar

Dinner
Chinese-style ginger chicken
mee (Chinese-style rice noodles)
white wine
Camembert

....

 ## CHINESE-STYLE GINGER CHICKEN

Sauté (until cabbage and onions lose opaqueness)
1 cup large chunks of cabbage
½ cup onion, in chunks
1 green pepper, in chunks
¼ cup sliced cucumber (with rind)
1 tbs. chopped fresh ginger
10 cloves garlic, chopped
2 tbs. cooking oil
▼

Add

    1 can chicken meat with natural juice
    Heat until sauce starts to boil.

Dissolve

    1 tbs. cornstarch in 1 tbs. soy sauce

    Add to sauce to thicken, and stir constantly
    until all vegetables are coated.

> Serve over *mee*
> (rice noodles).

We are moving faster than hull speed. The sea is a bit lumpy but starting to even out as the wind holds steady from the south. There's a light drizzle, and in the past two hours we've caught about 4 gallons of freshwater. If it drizzles all night, we could fill our tanks. Then all we'd need is a sunny day so I could splurge and wash my hair completely in freshwater.

Keeping Clean

Scene: midocean, trade-wind clouds, running sails pulling hard, the setting sun modestly silhouetting a nude sailor who cavorts under a cascade from a bucket of seawater. Soap and towel complete the picture we've seen in dozens of voyaging stories.

This idyllic snapshot belies one of the realities that must be faced by cruising sailors who venture outside warm trade-wind routes or who live on board in crowded ports between passages. Keeping clean afloat is a complex problem, one that few yacht designers consider. Most designers seem to assume that on-board showers will rarely be used. And they are probably right for the majority of cases—those in which boats are sold to people who usually spend only one or two nights away from onshore shower facilities. Furthermore, getting efficient on-board bathing facilities is difficult, since both space and water are limited, especially on yachts under 40 feet. But if you plan to voyage offshore for extended periods, you need a good shower—one that will be easy to use (both at sea and at anchor), easy to tidy up and keep clean, and, most of all, water-efficient. Otherwise, you'll find yourself choosing anchorages, harbors, even cruising routes on the basis of the proximity of yacht-club or marina shower facilities. Your perception of the ports you visit will be heavily colored by the quality and cleanliness of the onshore showers, and your cruising costs will be increased by the need to pay to tie up where hot showers are available. Lost towels, facecloths, and soap, plus the fungal foot infections (athlete's foot) that are often acquired in communal showers, could mar an otherwise excellent visit to a romantic port. So, rather than relying on shoreside facilities once you set sail, carefully consider ways of becoming "self-sufficient" bathers before you set off.

The location/design of your bathing facilities depends on the size of your boat. But one choice, as simple as it seems, is usually less than satisfactory in the long run. That choice is the commonly seen stand-up shower set in a toilet compartment with a shower-curtain surround. Although this works for occasional in-port cleanups, it has several drawbacks. It is muggy and close-feeling even if there is a hatch directly over the toilet. Both overspray from the shower and condensation from hot water will cause the enclosed toilet to become wet. Everything—the toilet seat, the floor, the toilet paper, the walls—will become soggy. Few of us enjoy mopping around toilets just after we've gotten ourselves clean, yet this is vital in a small enclosure or mildew will soon form. Finally, if the toilet area is forward of the mast, showering below decks during cool-weather passages will be difficult, if not dangerous. Within the motion-exaggerating enclosure, crew could become seasick or disoriented and then slip and fall. Even if the toilet-shower enclosure is situated aft, it can be difficult to use in a seaway without a secure seat and a handheld shower head on an extension hose.

So what could be better? For small boats (those under about 28 feet), there are a few other possible solutions. The first is to improve on-deck shower facilities. The manufacturer of Sun Shower solar water-heating bags makes a windproof plastic shower enclosure that can be hung from a halyard on the foredeck or from the boom over the cockpit to provide privacy. The framework to shape the enclosure is inflatable. You can make a similar enclosure using nylon shower-curtain material and a collapsible frame from a circle of black plastic water pipe. We rigged up a windproof enclosure for autumn cruising on board showerless 24-foot *Seraffyn*. We found we could use it comfortably in sunny weather with temperatures as low as 55 degrees. But our setup was a real hassle to use, as it took an hour to rig. I remember resorting to a visit to the local tuberculosis sanatorium in the Dalmatian islands of Yugoslavia—just for the luxury of a hot shower on a cold autumn day. Had we sewed together a hanging shower enclosure such as the SunShower, we could have suspended it just beside the companionway over a waterproof canvas containment basin or a children's plastic bath basin and then hung our solar-shower bag from the boom to provide comfortable warm showers on a cold day.

One small-boat cruising family we met had made a collapsible canvas bathtub to fit the cockpit area of their 28-footer; it also fit at the bottom of the companionway ladder. Four hooks were positioned on interior joinery to line up with grommets on each corner of the 30-inch-high "instant tub." Gracie said the two children (1 and 2 1/2 years old) could play in the bathwater she heated on the stove, yet they didn't splash the boat interior. She and Irwin sat on an upturned bucket inside the canvas and used a solar-shower bag for very satisfactory washups below deck. The water in the tub was simply poured overboard; the collapsible tub was hung out to dry and then folded away.

Another satisfactory shower arrangement for a small-to-medium boat is to use the companionway area between the toilet compartment and the storage lockers that are often placed opposite each other on many boats. There is usually a hatch close by or over this area to help it dry quickly after it is used and to provide good ventilation, so condensation is not a major problem. If you install a shower-curtain ring, you can clip a curtain in place to protect the cabinets in this area and then remove and air the curtain on deck after each use. A small shower pan can be built below the floorboards to contain the water and direct it into your sump tank for later disposal.[9] A final improvement on the amidship's shower is a small, secure seat of some sort, either fold-out or fold-down. Showering in a boat that can lurch at unexpected times will be safer and easier if the bather can be seated.

On boats over 28 feet, it becomes easier to have permanent bathing facilities that are quick to use, easy to clean, and safe in a seaway. I emphasize this seaway use because experience has proven that a warm shower, a good towel-off, and fresh, dry clothes can take away many of the frustrations of rough, cold sailing weather. I remember how good a shower felt after setting *Taleisin's* parachute anchor and trysail to ride out storm-force winds off the Queensland coast of Australia. Although we lay hove-to for 60 hours in those raging winds, I reminded myself that life would have been a lot worse without the sit-down shower tub that had been one of Larry's prime desires in our new 29-footer. I might have been uncomfortable, but at least I was clean, unsalty, and warm.

Once a boat reaches this size, it is no longer absolutely necessary for the shower to occupy part of the toilet area. Furthermore, there is usually space to move the shower, and even the toilet, aft near the companionway, where crew can have almost direct access from the cockpit. The direct access is

. . . .

9   A gray-water sump tank is an important part of any bathing setup. Shower or bath water should never be allowed to settle in the bilges of a boat. This mixture will eventually smell, and it can cause rot in wooden structures. It will promote osmosis in fiberglass boats and corrosion in steel ones. And if that isn't enough, the hair and grease can clog most bilge pumps. The sump tank should be big enough to hold wastewater from at least the total number of showers your crew will take in one day. On Taleisin, our sump tank holds 10 gallons and is emptied by use of the main bilge pump (a gallon-a-stroke bronze diaphragm pump with 2-inch outlet made by Edson) joined to the sump tank exit line by a swing valve.

great for warming up skin divers in moderate climates where wet suits are imperative. The diver can climb below wearing the wet suit without fear of trailing saltwater all though the boat. The diver can then strip off right in the shower area, away from chilling winds. The shower area situated near the companionway can serve as a drip-off spot for foul-weather gear, wet boots, soggy sailing gear, or garments from guests arriving on rainy evenings.

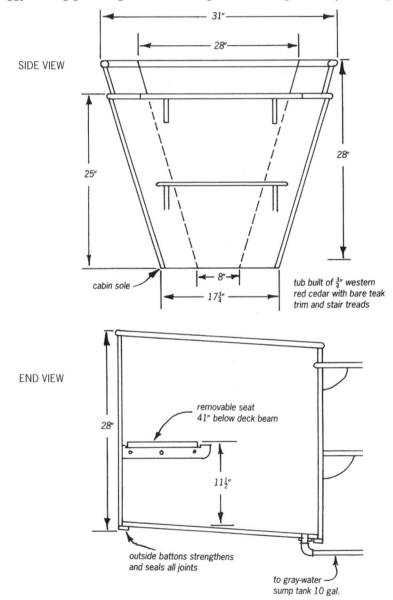

FIGURE 27. **Taleisin's shower/tub**

A good way to get excellent bathing facilities near the companionway without using the vital space in the middle of the cabin to provide headroom is to use a sitz bath (Japanese-style tub). A seated bather requires 2 feet less headroom than a standing one. A tub that reaches to midchest height contains the spray, so a shower curtain or door is unnecessary. An amazingly small space allows the bather free movement. The tub we have used for more than 20 years on board Taleisin is considered very generous by visitors who have used it (see fig. 27). It is right under the bridge-deck area and is tapered to fit the general shape of the hull. Because we have no engine, we can use this space for bathing. But this same space could be available on boats with engines installed amidships under the galley table or saloon area. With other interior arrangements, this type of tub can be fitted under the side deck, as shown in figure 28. The seat inside the tub should be hinged or removable for easy cleaning. The tub can be made from a wide range of materials. Ours is splined western red cedar finished with 2-part polylinear varnish. It seems to disappear into the general scheme of the boat's interior, even though it is completely open to the main cabin. Friends have had equal success using fiberglass sealed with gelcoat or 2-part polylinear paints.

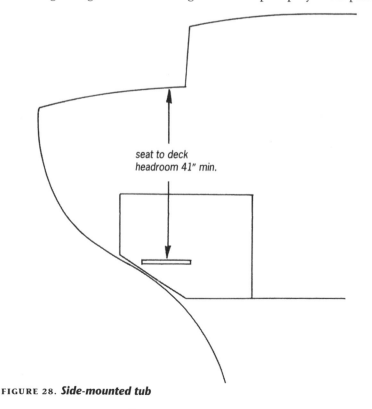

seat to deck
headroom 41" min.

FIGURE 28. *Side-mounted tub*

Even though we have never filled this tub to have an actual soak-type bath, we have used it as a very handy and successful laundry tub, one that is large enough to rinse small sails and sleeping bags. Since the tub is open to the rest of the boat, it dries quickly and the bather never feels claustrophobic or sweaty. (In fact, the bather can have a brandy and talk to the cook while bathing.) Cleanup is simple: After every five or six uses, one of us wipes down the tub with dish soap or shampoo on a washcloth before the bather has a final rinse-down. The tub space is not wasted between baths, as it makes a temporary storage spot for visitors' duffel bags, an excellent drip-off area for foulies, and a safe place for stashing last-minute provisions before you set off for a passage.

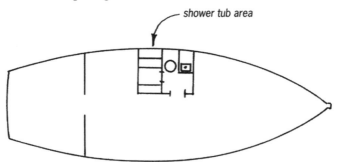

shower tub area

B. inside Whalesong's shower looking forward

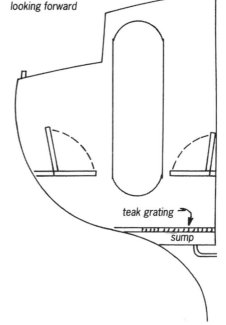

This drawing is done from memory, so we cannot give exact dimensions. One very good idea suggested by Cecil Lange, a boatbuilder and voyager from Port Townsend, Washington, is the raised grating over the sump area. This sump holds 3 gallons of water. As soon as the showerer sees water lapping the grating, he or she knows it is time to ease up and rinse off. The grating can be removed easily to make the tub area larger when necessary. Water from the sump is pumped overboard after each use.

teak grating

sump

FIGURE 29. **Whalesong's *bathing area***

On *Whalesong*, a 45-foot custom-built boat, the shower is set just aft of amidships, next to the head but in its own separate stall. It has two seats—one on the bulkhead close to the centerline of the boat and the other against the hull—so the bather is safely seated on the leeward side of either tack (fig. 29). The step into the shower stall is 18 inches high—enough to provide a tublike containment area that can be used for washing clothes. A hatch is installed directly above the shower area to try to combat the mildew that can gather within weeks on any shower curtain that is not dried perfectly after every use. *Whalesong's* shower cubicle is used only for bathing purposes. It is luxurious but occupies a lot of interior space.

A big-boat idea that works wonderfully if you have unlimited water supplies, or if you are cruising along waterways where freshwater hoses are available every two or three days, is a pressurized cockpit shower—great for rinsing down after a swim, great even for rinsing feet to keep sand from creeping on board. Unfortunately, these tempting showers consume too much water once you head offshore. In fact, one of the major reasons given for rowing ashore to use the rather primitive showers of many small yacht clubs along the world's cruising routes is, "It's easier to shower onshore than to cart water to the boat for showers."

Once you leave North American or European waters, you'll find yourself at anchor most of your cruising time. To get water, you'll either have to fill water jugs and carry them to the boat or lift your anchor and go alongside docks that are often difficult to reach, dirty, and threatening to your topsides. So I can sympathize with this problem. But metering the water used by showerers could help alleviate the problem. The truth is, unless pressurized water is metered in some way, unwary bathers can use 15 to 20 gallons for one cleanup. Even among experienced offshore bathers, unmetered showers tend to take 3 to 5 gallons.

Before you set off cruising with an on-demand or pump-type shower water system, it is vital to separate your water tankage so showers are curtailed before they cause a water shortage. Some sailors close off one tank with sufficient water rations for half the length of a proposed voyage and say, "When we get down to that tank, no more showers until we close the land." Others have one tank set aside just for bathing; when it is empty, no more showers. This is the system we use; we take shower water only from *Taleisin's* 24-gallon port tank at sea, at anchor, and even in a marina berth. To further control usage, some voyagers have a header tank with a limited capacity near and above the shower area. They pump water up to the header tank just before showering and then add a kettle of water heated on the galley stove or by the engine heat exchanger. Others, including us, use a plastic insecticide sprayer with hand pump to provide metering, hot water, and pressure. Two gallons of cold water, plus 1 gallon of water heated to boiling in a large kettle that nestles in the foot of the bathtub between uses, gives perfect-temperature water for two satisfying showers.

We met the captain of a larger charter boat who used a solar-heated variation of this header-tank metering system. He installed a handsome, black-sided deck box topped with clear lucite. The tank inside the box was warmed by the sun during the day to provide warm showers for guests. For people cruising anywhere that has sunny days, the simple solar showers sold in many camping and marine stores are excellent for not only heating but also metering shower water, as you can watch the water level through the clear sides of the bag and judge just how much more rinsing you can do before exhausting your supply.

Whatever system you use to supply pressure water, it is most efficient if the bather is seated. To work well, a header tank or solar-shower bag should be at least 2 feet above the bather. With a pump-type shower sprayer, the bather will need a shorter shower hose and can reach the pump handle more easily from a seated position.

Most important of all, every on-board shower system needs a demand-type shower head. I vastly prefer shower heads which have spring loaded on/off levers. Because the bather has to actively hold the level down, water conservation is more likely. (On/off pushbutton-type shower heads are not nearly as effective as spring-loaded ones.) If you combine an on-demand head with a flexible hose to allow the bather to direct water flow efficiently, you can get a dramatic decrease in water usage. Even with a pressure system, water usage can be cut by using this spring-loaded demand shower head with a mixer-type shower valve—i.e., one that lets you set water temperature separately from the hot- and cold-water valves so you can turn off the water temporarily and have it come right back on at the same temperature. Otherwise, an amazingly large amount of water will be wasted each time you let it run to mix the hot and cold to get the right bathing temperature.

For those times when freshwater is in very short supply, or when bathers want to luxuriate under hot running water, a primary saltwater shower and then a final rinse-off with fresh can be a good answer. Peter Brown, a 10-year cruising veteran we met in South Africa, told us of a quite inventive system. Pressurized saltwater is running to the line feeding a demand-type propane water heater. By placing a swing valve in line—to close off the saltwater and open the freshwater hose to the heater—the bather can stand under a stream of continuous hot, salty water and scrub to his or her heart's delight. Most shampoos or liquid dish soaps work well in saltwater. There are also

We put the kerosene-fired heating stove right next to the tub, below the companionway. It keeps the bather warm and also is next to the watch-keeper's seat, where it works as a hand warmer/dryer.

special saltwater soaps that lather well and clean skin and hair efficiently. A swing of the valve and instant hot freshwater is used for the final rinse-down with this system. Since freshwater is used last, it flushes out the lines of the demand heater. Peter says this system has worked for 10 years with no noticeable salt damage to the heater. A word of warning, however, for those who install a demand propane or butane heater: Make sure there

233

is good through-ventilation in the shower area, as these units consume a tremendous amount of oxygen and could asphyxiate a bather. They also must be installed with the same care taken for any propane unit on a boat—i.e., with a shutoff valve, such as those used on galley stoves, to prevent propane from filtering into the bilges.

How much water does a water-conscious showerer use? A consensus seems to be: For trade-wind, on-deck saltwater scrubs followed with a thorough freshwater rinse of body and hair, 2 quarts of freshwater is okay. For those with metered demand systems and spring-loaded demand shower heads, here are some reasonable estimates: 1 gallon for non-hair-washing showers, 1 1/2 gallons for a 2-shampoo-and-cream-rinse shower with short hair, and 2 gallons for someone with long hair such as mine. For nonmetered systems, and for bathers who are taught to wet down, turn off the water, use a small bowl of water for intermediate soaping, and rinse with the shower spray, 2 1/2 gallons per shower seems to be the norm.

Once you are passagemaking, bathing every day is rarely possible, or even something you will want to do, even if this is your habit ashore. On passage, we find ourselves quite content with a twice-weekly shower in any but very hot climates. During hot passages, daily on-deck saltwater scrub-downs, followed by freshwater rinses, feel great and let us extend our water supply. It is in port—especially in cities, which, worldwide, tend to be windless, sooty, and often sweaty—that daily freshwater showers become almost imperative. Consumption will go up, but access to freshwater will be easier. Two other times when it is exceptionally handy to have good shower facilities on board, with an extra water allowance for their use, are when you must be in a shipyard and when there is work to be done on board. Few shipyards have really clean shower rooms. Few busy harbors are perfect for work on board, as passing traffic can cause the boat to move just when you are trying to fit a difficult nut or bolt. But we've seen people put off engine repairs or sweaty jobs that could best have been done in an isolated bay because they wanted access to hot showers. As I wrote this paragraph, Larry was working aloft sanding our mast while we lay in a quiet lagoon. His last words were, "Sure looking forward to a shower when I get down." During these work times, a daily bath is imperative, and easy-to-use on-board shower facilities will make life more elegant.

The space, cost, and time required for good below-decks bathing arrangements might seem excessive when you are faced with the seemingly endless predeparture list. But during our cruising years, we've saved many times the cost, trouble, and time and gained a sense of independence by being able to choose our destinations and work stops without regard to shoreside bathing facilities. When we visit a port with a yacht club, we decide to stay because we like the people, the access it gives us to local sights, or the racing activities. If the showers are grotty, we don't use them. If they turn out to be utterly luxurious, we can indulge in a long, hot soak for pure pleasure, not out of necessity.

An Unorthodox Idea for the Interior

I must admit, I was skeptical, dragging my heels like a plowshare in the mental ground of plans for 29-foot *Taleisin's* interior. "I want a sitz tub, watch seat port and starboard," Larry kept saying. "I want a wet area where I can come below in my foulies without worrying about getting water on anything important, and a toilet I can use in rough weather, one right next to the companionway." I looked around inside the seemingly cavernous hull we'd just finished building. The watch seats, the permanent place for the toilet bucket right aft, made sense and fitted easily as we mocked up bunks, seats, and galley arrangements with bits of plywood, cardboard, and planks. But a bathtub? Why? Where? We'd cruised successfully for more than a decade with on-deck, bowl-and-sponge, and yacht-club showers. Sure, this boat was 5 feet longer and 20 inches wider, but did we really need a tub? What about a canvas enclosure like Gracie and Irwin used? But Larry persisted, despite my protests, and I found myself sitting inside variously shaped cardboard boxes, pretending to scrub my toes. We determined the smallest possible space a tub could take and then placed a box that size in various positions in the hull (see fig. 27 and 30).

The final results have me saying, "I'm glad you told me so," even now, more than two decades and thousands of miles later. Our final interior setup might be of interest to those of you planning to embark on an extended cruise. It was amazingly successful for us (see fig. 30).

The watch seats on each side of the companionway have bare teak lids. The bare teak is easy to wash, is nonskid, does not absorb salt, and can handle rough usage. The low bulkheads just forward of the seats provide an armrest and salt barrier to protect the velvetlike draylon upholstery of the main settees. This way, people in foul-weather gear can come below and rest without worry about removing the salty gear. Swimmers or guests who arrive with salty, wet bottoms have a place to sit, and a hatch that is left open accidentally during a rainsquall is no big problem, because the wooden seats dry quickly.

Our kerosene vented heating stove is tucked under the bridge-deck area to give warmth not only for normal winter days but also for those

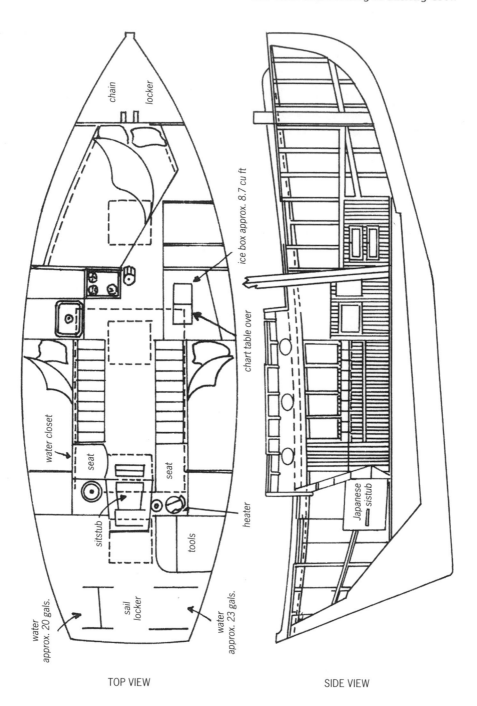

chain locker

ice box approx. 8.7 cu ft

chart table over

water closet

seat

seat

sitstub

tools

heater

Japanese sistub

water approx. 20 gals.

sail locker

water approx. 23 gals.

TOP VIEW

SIDE VIEW

FIGURE 30. **Taleisin** *Interior* *(29'6" Falmouth Cutter)*

times when we want to use the shower/tub on cooler evenings at the edge of the tropics. The upper half of the companionway ladder lifts away to give access to the small tub. The shower pressure-spray tank is hidden from view under the small counter behind the sink, to port and right next to the tub. To take a shower, move the ladder away and lift the lid over the shower tank. Add cool water directly from the gravity-fed hose leading to the bottom of the 24-gallon storage tank, which is aft near *Taleisin's* transom. Top it up with a kettle full of hot water from a perfect shower.

On the deck beam above the tub are four bronze hooks to hold wet-weather gear. During nonwet periods, the foulies are stored in the large locker under the starboard watch seat. The port seat covers a permanently installed toilet bucket with hinged teak seat. This bucket-and-chuck-it type of toilet is one of the few ways small-boat owners can comply with the complexity of discharge rules currently causing confusion in several parts of the world. (See page 260.)

The one drawback to this arrangement is that it affords little privacy unless we rig the modesty curtain right across the aft end of the interior.

Larry's insistence on good bathing arrangements has definitely led to an unusual open-plan, multipurpose toilet area. But it is one that has worked exceptionally well. Even when we have had guests on board for three to five days, they (and we) have quickly adapted to the open-plan bathing area. As one guest said, "Sure beats being closed up in a stuffy, windowless telephone-booth-size box when I'm already feeling a bit queasy."

A final advantage is that the absence of toilet/shower-enclosing bulkheads has made *Taleisin's* interior seem larger than it otherwise would. Also, it has improved ventilation and given the whole area lots of natural light.

....

Day 20

Noon to noon: 151 miles

Miles to date: 1,581

Foggy, running wing-and-wing with the lapper on the pole, smooth sea

Seraffyn at her best

Lunch
crab bisque with mussels (packaged bisque mix, canned mussels)
liver pâté sandwiches with tomatoes

Dinner
pork ragout
baked potatoes
squash with honey sauce

....

SQUASH WITH HONEY SAUCE

Cut in half and scoop out seeds
1 small acorn, butternut, or pumpkin squash

In center of each squash half, put
1 tbs. butter
3 tbs. honey
1 tbs. brown sugar
1 shake of cinnamon
1 tsp. lemon juice

Bake 40 minutes at
350 degrees F.
Eat carefully, as squash
stays very hot inside.

Prepare
Place in baking dish with aluminum foil
crumpled around squash to hold it upright.

....

PORK RAGOUT

Combine in casserole pan

2 small cans stewed pork
(Chinese Great Wall brand)

1 onion, sliced
3 carrots, sliced
¾ cup red wine
¼ cup Bisto instant gravy mix
1 tsp. sweet basil

Bake, uncovered,
30 minutes.

Storage Arrangements

We are moving beautifully, but as we come over the top of some waves, the motion is enough to make things in the oven scoot from side to side. A spare bread tin holds the pots in place; a nest of crumpled aluminum foil keeps squash and potatoes from rolling around.

The rain increased this morning. With the runoff from the mainsail collection system, we filled our water tanks completely. We now have as much freshwater on board as when we left Yokohama—and only 3,000 miles to go. The rain continued after our tanks were full. The seas were quite calm, so I decided to collect some extra rainwater in my big cooking pots and spare buckets and give both us and the boat a cleanup and a wipe-down.

As usual, I started by inspecting our stores locker. *Seraffyn* has four main food-storage lockers, one under each quarter berth, holding about 10 cases of food each, and a larger one under the head of the forward bunk, plus one smaller locker under one settee, which I use for all of our eggs and daily supplies (rice, flour, sugar, and so on). Larry has the opposite settee locker for tool storage, and I often have to fight him when he tries to encroach on my stores lockers with things like a new transformer/converter for his electric drill.

I don't use any kind of stores list. Instead, in the two quarter-berth lockers, which are subdivided naturally by the boat's frames, I have certain areas for categories of stores. Starting from aft on the port side, I fill the locker with condiments (vinegar, ketchup, spices, mustard, cornstarch, bread crumbs). Forward of that go the noodles, then there is a section for canned tomato products, then canned and packaged vegetables, then fruits, then milk products, and finally treats (cake mixes, candy, dried fruits).

On the starboard side, from aft to forward, are packaged beverages (tea, coffee, cocoa), soups, beans, main-course items, toiletries, flashlight batteries.

When I stock up, I put six of each item in the quarter-berth lockers. The others, along with the large supply of rice, sugar, and flour, go in the big forward bunk locker.

Once every week I try to check the quarter-berth lockers, making sure no packages are split. If any cans are showing signs of rust, I try to use them as soon as possible. I note what items are in short supply and "go shopping" in the big bin forward.

I prefer to plan my meals the same way once we run out of fresh food. I look over the cans and packages in the locker until something catches my eye.

Many people prefer a stores list, and that would probably be a good idea with a larger boat and larger crew for extended cruising. When a boat has 25 or 30 possible storage lockers in which items can be hiding, many will be forgotten. If you do use a stores list, only one person should be in charge of taking items from lockers and crossing them off the list. And a systematic schedule has to be arranged to make sure each storage locker is checked at least every two weeks. It doesn't take more than that for a slow drip from condensation to create havoc with a case of packaged noodles or for a rusty can to stain the paintwork.

One final warning if you use a stores list: Don't start preparing a meal until you have all your ingredients out of their various lockers. Zillah, who worked as cook on the magnificent charter schooner *Carina*, told me of one near-disaster when she planned an elaborate Cordon Bleu dinner for the discerning pair of charterers who were paying the equivalent of US$7,000 a week for their cruise. Because of 60-foot *Carina*'s multitude of lockers and exotic supply of stores, a stores book is used religiously. Unfortunately, however, when it came time to put the wine-filled casserole in the oven, topped with a special cheese, Zillah checked her book to find that the cheese was in the locker under the charterers' bunk. The female charterer was in her bunk sound asleep. Dinner was two hours late that evening— the time fortunately filled by an unusually good sunset and a prolonged cocktail hour.

On most cruising boats, this wouldn't be a problem, but you might plan a meal only to find the one can that you need has already been used and not crossed off the list, or it has been ruined by rust.

We don't prepare our cans in any way before we store them on board or when we are delivering boats. On deliveries, the cans are rarely on board more than three to five weeks, so they don't have time to rust. There usually are more than enough lockers so that we don't have to worry about their getting into the bilges and losing their labels. On *Seraffyn*, which had a wooden hull with no leaks and little condensation, we rarely found more than one or two cans during any year that had to be tossed overboard. And that was usually because I forgot to check one corner of the locker for too many days. To further help keep cans from rusting, we washed each locker thoroughly with freshwater once a year.

On *Taleisin*, with its larger storage lockers, I actually find I lose more cans to rusting than I did on *Seraffyn*. This is due to the larger quantity of packaged and canned goods we carry. I don't use up canned products as quickly, and, with the added depth of the larger lockers, I don't notice the first signs of rust in the lower layers and thus use the affected cans first, as I did before. Another easily avoidable problem intruded into my storage planning on board *Taleisin* because of the bronze flooring and strapping we used in her construction. I found that beer cans, which are made of aluminum, developed holes within two weeks if they rested against the metal. An insulating barrier of plastic matting solved that problem.

If, on the other hand, your boat has fiberglass or metal storage lockers, rust and soggy labels could be a problem. The first solution is to line your lockers with plastic, open-weave matting, which will insulate the cans from the hull. If this is not enough and your cans start to show signs of rust (not just slight discoloration, but real rust), then, before the next trip, line up the cans with the labels secured tightly and spray each can and label with varnish spray or lacquer before storing them away. This is extremely time-consuming, but if you are laying on stores for six or eight months and your boat is a damp one, it could prevent a lot of waste. I do not believe in removing labels—not only does this take time, but it also means that all the cans look alike, and a quick survey of your can locker won't tell you where your deficiencies are.

To protect our lockers and hull from being chafed or stained by canned goods, I line each one with the nonskid plastic matting that is sold as an underlay to keep small carpets from skidding on wooden floors (purchased from Wal-Mart or Target stores in the United States). This material is thicker material than the plastic nonskid sold for use on galley tables, and it has two extra advantages: The matting lets condensation or moisture filter down into the bilge without touching cans, and it stops them from rattling and shifting, so their labels stay intact.

241

Avoid storing cans of any sort in the bilge unless your bilges are so large that the cans can be stored right in their cases. There is nothing more unappetizing for the cook than having to reach into a dusty, greasy bilge and sort through wet cans. If you must store individual cans in the bilge because of lack of space, then it is best to remove the labels from the cans, mark the tops, and varnish each can before you set sail.

Canned goods are safe to use for up to 1 1/2 years if they show no signs of rusting through. If the ends of any cans bulge or become puffy, discard them. But if every can in your locker gets puffed ends within the space of a few days, figure out whether there has been a large temperature increase in the seawater. If there has been, the canned food is safe and the puffing has been caused only by internal expansion. We learned this when we sailed out of the 72-degree waters of the Mediterranean into the 88-degree waters of the Red Sea. Every can in the below-the-waterline lockers puffed up within two days. We used them anyway, with no ill results. Three weeks later, in the 78-degree Indian Ocean, they all resumed their normal sizes and shapes.

． ． ． ． ． ． ．

Day 21

Noon to noon: 128 miles
Miles to date: 1,709
Foggy and rough, running under just staysail
Late afternoon: wind dropped and set full sail

Lunch
    leftover crab bisque
    leftover pork ragout
    instant mashed potatoes

Dinner
    tossed cabbage salad, Thousand Island dressing
    mashed-potato salad
    garlic-and-onion omelet

· ·

 MASHED-POTATO SALAD

Mix well
    2 cups leftover mashed potatoes
    ¼ cup chopped onions
    ¼ cup chopped green peppers
    ¼ cup leftover green peas (optional)
    1 tsp. dill weed
    1 tsp. sugar
    4 tbs. mayonnaise

> Let stand at least
> 2 hours in a cold place.

· ·

DAY 21. *Going to windward, you need three extra hands.*

Cooking in Rough Weather

On days like today, a successful meal is anything that's hot and stays on the plate until it gets eaten. This is when I'd really like a gimbaled eating box like the old Cal 40s had. Their table had enough room over it for a long tray that had holes for drinks, a section for condiments, and room for one bowl for each member of the crew (see fig. 31).

Some boats have gimbaled dining tables, but this is space-consuming and doesn't work well in practice. A gimbaled table has all of the drawbacks of a gimbaled stove. If a person leans on it at the wrong time, everything slides off. If the table starts swinging when someone walks past, it can give them a whack, especially if it is properly ballasted with 100 pounds of lead. A table that tilts to different angles and bolts in place would be a good solution if you were going to be on the same tack for a long time. But in running conditions like these, you need something to hold things in place not only for heeling but also for the surging as you run off the top of a wave.

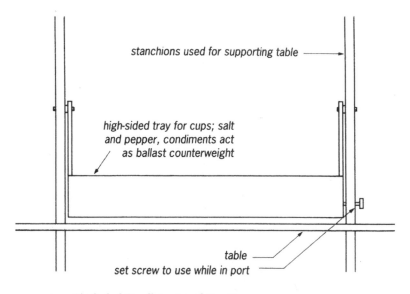

FIGURE 31. *Gimbaled Condiment and Cup Tray*

Annabelle and Gordon Yates have a good cup-and-plate-holding tray on their Great Dane 28, which they've cruised from Denmark to San Francisco. It clamps onto the tabletop and has compartments for glasses, bowls, condiments, and silver. If the same could be incorporated with holders right in the galley, the cook could load the tray there, then bring it ready to the table.

As it is right now, even with a damp towel rolled up on the table, the salt rolls just out of reach when you want it. Your coffee can't be poured until you are finished with your main course or it will spill.

Weather like we had this morning is the ultimate test of a sea cook. The crew is dying for hot, spicy food; the cook, if she is not prone to seasickness at all, isn't feeling too inventive. If the weather is really bad, the crew wouldn't expect so much, but as long as we can hold canvas and sail on our course, it's hard to go into storm rations. Luckily, most of our cruising is in fair weather.

A Rough-Weather Galley Table

There are few completely new ideas around the marine scene. Every first-time item you see on someone's boat or at a boat show is really an adaptation that evolved from a dozen hints, what-ifs, and wouldn't-it-be-nices. Each innovation we use seems to grow from chance encounters as we visit aboard or deliver boats, or as we chat with sailors in their saloons or at

This is the underside of Taleisin's *table. Here you can clearly see the hinge mechanism and the slide-out table-leaf support.*

some favorite watering holes in ports around the world. This is definitely the case with the most-often-noted items in *Taleisin's* otherwise-simple interior.

Years ago, we sailed on an elegant Sparkman & Stephens racing yawl with a gimbaled table. I liked the general idea but found it wouldn't fit well in a small boat, and its constant motion made me seasick as we surged and rolled in a running sea. The gimbaled table also could be dangerous if an unwary crewperson fell against it accidentally while hot soup was being served. But my comments set Larry's mind in gear. By the time we were dreaming of building a new boat, he said, "I would really like a table that tilted to make eating easier at sea."

When we began building *Taleisin*, we took a day off to visit *Spike Africa*, the impressive 65-foot coaster-type schooner being built by the late Bob Sloan, one of the most successful commercial yachting sailors of our time (and, incidentally, the man who introduced Larry and me). Bob, too, had grown tired of the problems of eating at a tilt during long passages. For *Spike's* galley, he had come up with a table that could be tilted and locked into position to approximate the average angle the boat assumed on each tack. His arrangement was relatively simple. The fore-and-aft table pivoted from a rod secured through the bulkhead at the forward end of the galley and through a strong wooden stanchion at the aft end of the table. The stanchion reached to the cabin top and provided an excellent handhold for crew climbing into the booth-type settees. A stout, semicircular bronze plate with holes drilled along it was secured to the bulkhead so a locking bolt on the table could secure it in various positions for each tack. To make the table easy to clean in port yet practical at sea, 2-inch-high fiddles dropped into brass-lined pinholes in the $1^1/8$-inch-thick table top (see fig. 32).

This idea proved very successful, and when we sailed on *Spike Africa* after her launching, we sat at that table and tried to figure out a way to make one to fit the much smaller space on our boat, especially because we had no handy bulkhead to support the end. Furthermore, we needed a folding table to give us space to move fore-and-aft in the boat—a table that would not dominate the whole interior yet would be large enough to let us serve four or, in a pinch, six people on generous dinner plates. The final table did not happen until we'd launched *Taleisin* and eaten off our laps for a few weeks on board—all the while thinking, measuring, and drawing ideas. But when we finally built our own tilting table, it did fill all the criteria and more: it was relatively simple to build, it used hardware available from most household building-supply companies, and it will fit in a variety of boats.

First we set two $1^3/4$-inch-diameter brass pipes 32 inches apart, $9^1/2$ inches from the port settee. This puts the pipes closer to the port side of the main saloon so the passage from the companionway to the galley could be $16^1/2$ inches wide when the table is folded. The pipe stanchions are bolted to the floor timbers. (These structural members connect the frames to the keel in a wooden boat. In a fiberglass boat, these stanchions should be attached to the framing above the keel.) They reach through the floorboards to the cabin top, where they are secured into pipe flanges. (*Taleisin's* table is demonstrated in the DVD *Getting Ready to Cruise,* available at www.paracay.com.)

The brass pipes are strong enough to serve as excellent handholds for people moving through the boat in a seaway. They also act as support for the cabin oil lamps we use during mealtimes. At sea, we attached a gimbaled telltale compass to the forward stanchion. The table pivots on two brass,

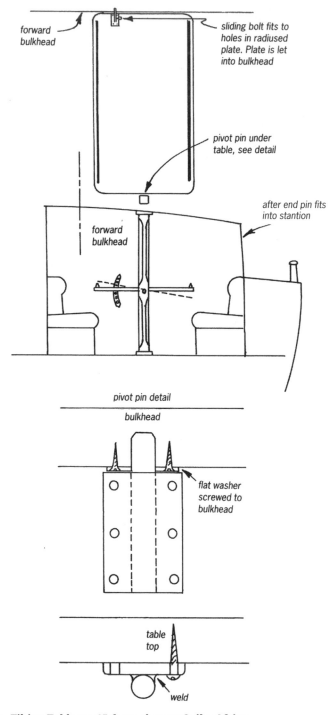

FIGURE 32. *Tilting Table on 65-foot schooner* **Spike Africa**

locking, barn-door-type bolts set into holes in the stanchions. The tilting device is simple—two brass transom window sliders. One end is screwed to the underside of the table and the other is secured to a bolt that is threaded into the stanchion. A large wing nut on the slider locks the table into position—square to the waterline in port or angled to match the boat's heeling angle at sea.

The resulting table is 15 by 32 inches in its closed position—perfect for two people to use at sea or for a simple meal in port. For guests or for more formal dinners for two, the table doubles in size with a leaf that swings open using three double-acting table-top hinges, the same as are used for sewing-machine table tops (see fig. 33). We find this arrangement far better than the normal drop-leaf arrangement used on other small yachts, as the folding top does not bang or rattle in a seaway. Also, it gives a more open appearance inside the boat and lets each leaf overlap its respective settee by two inches. The overlap means that diners can sit back while they eat instead of having to be on the edges of their seats to reach the table. Seating is more comfortable, as there is no drop leaf that interferes with legroom or clutters the area under the table. This is especially nice if you, as we do, use your bilge area as a wine cellar. With no drop leaf in the way, access is definitely easier. A final bonus to this fold-over leaf is that no one has to move his or her knees out of the way to open the table for dinner.

This fold-over leaf provides the base for an easily removed but very strong at-sea fiddle. Because we don't like the appearance of brass- or copper-lined pinholes in a table (besides, we doubt their strength) and because we like the idea of permanent fiddles even less, a completely different idea evolved.

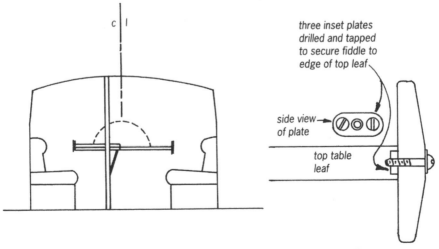

FIGURE 33. Taleisin's *Foldover Tilting Table with Removable Fiddle*

Larry set three ovals of $1/8$-inch bronze into the edge of the top leaf. (This leaf is $3/4$-inch-thick ash.) He then made a 5-inch-wide fiddle board, $3/4$-inch thick and tapering toward each edge. Three bolts go through the middle of the bare-teak board and thread into the bronze plates to hold it in place at sea. When we are on the starboard tack, the table is used in its closed position, with the fiddle over the port settee (downhill side). On the starboard tack, the table leaf is opened; the fiddle is now over the starboard settee. This puts you in the best-supported and most comfortable eating position at sea—downhill with a good backrest and nowhere to fall.

Removing the fiddle takes less than a minute. This means that in port it can be stowed away to leave a clear expanse of varnished ash. Even at sea, removal is easy enough that I am willing to remove the fiddle to clean away crumbs that inevitably collect in table corners.

This tilting table with removable fiddles has cut food spills to a minimum and works wonderfully for letter writing and chartwork at sea, as it holds onto pencils, dishes, and cups. In anything but the roughest seas, I feel good about leaving Larry a cup of hot soup sitting against the fiddle on the tilted table.

It is important to make the wing nuts on the sliders easy to reach and positive to secure. At sea, we have learned to loosen the nuts just enough to let us slide the table slowly to the required position. We've also learned to resist the temptation to leave cups or dishes on the table when we are not using them. That way, any sudden decision to tack can be acted on immediately, instead of after we have cleared the table. We had to learn this the hard way because the tilted table with fiddles does such a good job of keeping coffee in the cup and food on the plate that we often left things there all afternoon as we reached steadily across the trade winds.

To keep our china from sliding fore-and-aft, and to protect the varnished finish at sea, we use nonskid, expanded-plastic placemats, which we cut from material sold in many marine stores and camping and automotive supply houses. It looks like bumpy lace and feels slightly spongy. The matting is hand- or machine-washable, but beware of placing hot coffee pots on it; it does melt.

Is a tilting or gimbaled table imperative? No. We ate on our laps many times at sea and occasionally I still do when the going gets rough. But the luxury of setting out a complete lunch or array of nibbles as we close-reach across a stretch of ocean, or the ease of making sandwiches for six people on one work surface that lets me lay them out without chasing the ingredients around a counter that is tilted the wrong way, adds to my feeling that our life afloat is improving with age.

. . . .

Day 22

Noon to noon: 115 miles
Miles to date: 1,814
Fresh wind, running wing-and-wing over a lumpy sea
Very cold and light drizzle
By evening: force 7, reefed main and staysail

Lunch
pancakes and maple syrup
canned mixed-fruit salad

Dinner
tuna casserole (the old standby)
cranberry sauce
white wine

....

TUNA CASSEROLE

Combine
2 cups cooked macaroni (or pasta twists)
1 can solid tuna (drained, broken into chunks)
1 can cream of mushroom soup (condensed)
½ cup milk

Bake
Put in casserole, top with grated cheese, and
bake 25 minutes at 375 degrees.
Serve with cranberry sauce or chutney.

....

One of the main reasons I decided to make tuna casserole for this dinner was to use the oven and warm up the boat. It is less than 50 degrees on deck. With the oven going, it's cozy down below. I think Larry liked my choice of meals tonight because it was pretty rough by the time we ate. His comment: "This tuna casserole is good rough-weather eating; sticks to your plate and to your ribs."

Instant Foods

Instant foods definitely have a place on board during ocean passages, even though they are often more expensive than the uncombined ingredients. For the pancakes I served today, I used a Singaporean variety of Bisquick. If I'd had to make the pancakes from scratch, I'm not sure I would have. Other instant items I've found indispensable at sea include instant mashed potatoes. These can be used several ways, and with only a dash of garlic powder and some evaporated milk, they taste better than fresh potatoes. Instant mashed potatoes can be used to thicken fishcakes, as a topping for a meat pie, or as a thickener for vegetable soup. An additional use for the instant potato flakes we carry is to lighten the texture of bread if you run out of white flour or find your flour becoming moist and less prone to proper rising. Half a cup of instant potatoes per 5 cups of white or whole-wheat flour gives a loaf with a pleasant texture and only slightly different flavor. Though freshwater is needed to prepare instant mashed potatoes, it's less than what's required to boil regular potatoes. I buy instant potatoes in 2-pound cans and then store them for up to a year in a plastic, 2-quart fruit-juice pitcher with a tight-fitting cap. When I'm planning a stores list, I don't consider them a substitute for fresh potatoes.

I discovered instant noodles in the Far East; they are now available in the United States in supermarkets and discount stores. These packages of rice noodles contain just enough to serve two people for spaghetti or other pasta or noodle dishes. Unlike regular noodles, they require only three minutes to cook. In heavy weather, they are great. I still carry a good selection of regular noodles, however, as their texture is definitely different.

MINUTE RICE

I wish I had some on board right now. Minute Rice isn't as tasty as brown rice that has been boiled for 25 or 30 minutes, but on days when the sea is frolicsome, it is worth its weight in gold.

GRAVY MIX (BISTO)

We carry three or four 8-ounce packages of the English gravy mix, Bisto. This is now available in the foreign-food section of supermarkets. It has far better flavor than the average individual packages of gravy mix. I use it not only to make gravy quickly but also to thicken stews and soups and to add flavor to the gravy from canned meat. It is best to add the gravy-making powder to a bit of liquid, then pour it slowly into the cooking pot. I often use wine instead of water for this. Be sure to store Bisto inside a sealed plastic bag, or open the cardboard package and empty it into a glass container, as the salt in the mix will attract moisture and ruin both packaging and contents.

FREEZE-DRIED PEAS AND BEANS

The Surprise brand from England is excellent; we buy two dozen 2-serving packages at a time.

FREEZE-DRIED AND DEHYDRATED SOUPS

Although current research has shown that these soups contain fewer vitamins than do canned soups, I carry a variety of packages on board. With the addition of a few vegetables or a can of meat, a packaged soup can become a complete meal. Instant onion soup makes a fine gravy if it is mixed with 1 cup of water and brought to a boil, then simmered 10 minutes.

For cruising in cold climates, I also carry instant soups, such as Lipton's Cup-a-Soup. I find we enjoy these as on-watch warmers, much like a cup of tea or hot chocolate. I prefer the varieties without noodles, such as tomato, split pea, or cream of mushroom, as they can be sipped from a mug without any need for a spoon.

INSTANT SAUCES

Packets of these definitely are helpful afloat. A favorite is instant white sauce, which I use as a thickener for chicken or fish soups. For a fast at-sea meal on a rough day, I make up a cup of the sauce; add lemon juice, oregano, and a dash of white wine (if the wine is in easy reach); then mix in chunks of tuna or any other cooked fish and serve over toast.

SPICE BLENDS

Katie Braun, who cruises on 74-foot *Interlude,* loves her hoard of instant spice packets. Chinese style, Cajun style, a dozen different Indian styles—she chooses one, pours it in a plastic bag, adds chicken pieces, shakes them well, and then creates an appetizing sautéed dish with a zesty flavor. No need to rummage through the spice racks when the sea is running high.

PACKAGED CAKES AND COOKIE MIXES

These are invaluable, and I keep an assortment at hand. The hassle of getting out measuring cups, spoons, beaters, flour, and milk to make a cake in a seaway on a small boat usually means that I don't. I choose a variety of mixes that need only eggs and water added. On long voyages, I store these mixes in plastic bags, since the packages are not too water-resistant.

INSTANT PUDDINGS

My favorites are crème caramel (flan) and instant butterscotch pudding. These require milk, and we've found that powered milk doesn't work well, but evaporated canned milk mixed one part water to two parts milk is good.

. . . .

I have never tried instant meals of any sort; they have always seemed too expensive. But if they are within your budget, try some onshore beforehand.

With the advent of ecotourism (the latest buzzword for backpacking, camping, and other wilderness pursuits), more and more freeze-dried and instant foods are available. The Round the World racers are taking full advantage of what some call space-age foods. For a crew of 16 on a very weight-conscious boat, this is a tremendous advantage. According to the late Peter Blake, freeze-dried foods on *ENZA* weighed almost a ton less than canned and frozen food would have for their longest leg. However, the crew did complain about the flavor (or lack thereof) of the foods they ate, and few of us have the watermakers necessary to provide enough liquid to reconstitute a diet made up mainly of dehydrated products. Still, as you plan your provisioning, you might enjoy trying some of these items and comparing them in price and weight. As with canned foods, you should try each variety before you invest. Furthermore, be careful about buying in bulk, as many of these products begin to deteriorate soon after their individual packages are opened. In every case, I would chose foil packages over plastic ones for freeze-dried foods that I planned to keep for longer than a month. I have had plastic-pouched freeze-dried peas go moldy in six weeks, even though the packages were sealed. I have never lost a foil pack of any product.

. . . .

Day 23

Noon to noon: 118 miles
Miles to date: 1,932
Almost no wind, seas calm
It's cloudy and cold, but Larry was able to get a sight
through a break in the clouds

Lunch

canned tomato soup
Greek salad
Camembert, biscuits

Teatime

lemon pudding cake
Lapsang souchong tea

Dinner

leftover tuna casserole
peas (Surprise brand) and butter
whole-wheat bread

....

 ## LEMON PUDDING CAKE

1 package lemon pie filling
1 small package white cake mix

Prepare

Put pie filling into bottom of
greased bread tin.

Cover with cake batter.

> Bake 20 minutes at
> 350 degrees, or until
> cake is done. Let cool
> 15 minutes, then serve
> in bowls.

....

We used our last tomato today. Not bad, considering none of them were as green as they could have been. In 23 days, we used 35 large tomatoes.

One of the cabbages rotted from the inside out—first time that has ever happened. But I'd been forewarned: The cabbages had been picked at the height of the Japanese rainy season from a field that was probably 3 inches deep in rainwater. We now have only one large cabbage left, but there are lots of potatoes and onions.

Since we had a lovely calm after several days of boisterous weather, on went the oven. I set bread to rise and we had a scrub-down in the oven-warmed galley. Larry came up with a good idea. He took the galley table out of its sliders, placed it between the two settees, used two of the quarter-berth cushions and two bunk boards, and made a nice square bed. We took our big blanket and lay together in the warm, cozy cabin. Outside, it was less than 50 degrees F; the forward double bunk was covered with vegetables, but Larry's little square bed was a delightful place to spend part of our afternoon.

Luck stayed with us today. A fresh wind came up late in the day, and by dinnertime we were bouncing into a leftover slop. But I'd had time to bake bread and finish making lemon pudding cake before that happened.

Milk

After two years of cruising in Mexico and Central America, how I longed for sour cream. Larry dreamed of a glass of ice-cold real milk as we roasted our way down the Red Sea. And I didn't have any whole milk to bake a double devil's-food birthday cake as we approached Costa Rica.

When you head offshore, milk products do become a problem. There is little powdered milk available in Mexico, Central America, or any African countries. Fresh whole milk will not keep on board a cruising boat for more than a week, and canned evaporated milk just doesn't taste quite right in puddings.

Fortunately for cruisers, there is a product called sterilized or long-life milk, available in cans in the United States under the Dairygold and Parmalat labels. In all Commonwealth countries, long-life milk comes in cardboard cartons of various shapes and sizes. This milk will last up to six months in its sealed containers, and it tastes quite good when well chilled. For cooking or baking, only the most discriminating can tell the difference. Only one warning, however: Always open the cardboard containers of long-life milk in the sink, and then transfer the contents to a pitcher with a tight-sealing top. Otherwise, you'll get messy spills and the milk will spoil quickly. Once opened, this milk must be stored in an icebox, or below 70 degrees F.

Powdered milk has a definite place on board. Unless you drink it daily, stay away from large-size containers. The milk powder will stay usable for as long as it is kept perfectly dry, so small containers will ensure better flavor and fewer lumps. I use powdered milk for such things as pancakes and baking. Other cruising friends report that powdered milk makes excellent yogurt. (There's a recipe in *Joy of Cooking*.) For the best quality, stock up on powdered milk in the United States or the Commonwealth countries.

Canned evaporated milk is available worldwide—in fact, most foreign babies are raised on it. We have a Mexican friend whose mother ran out of names after her seventh child and named him for the only milk she could provide for him—canned Carnation. For baking or drinks, I add 1/3 water to 2/3 evaporated milk. The flavor is a bit different, but many friends claim to prefer it in hot chocolate or clam chowder. Again, transfer evaporated milk into a glass or plastic container once it is opened. An evaporated-milk spill in your icebox will cause a real stink.

Two very useful milk products we carry are condensed sweetened milk and Nestlé's double cream. The first is a very common canned milk mixed with sugar. Drunk right out of the can, it's delicious; mixed into hot chocolate, it's great. A book of recipes, available from the producer, will really add to your dessert list. This milk product is available almost worldwide.

Nestlé's double cream (on the can, it's simply called cream) is available in Commonwealth countries and on the specialty shelves in U.S. markets. The 6-ounce can contains cream so thick it has to be spooned out. I mix it with a bit of brandy and powered sugar for topping cakes and fruit. It blends into eggs to make wonderful omelets. Add a teaspoon of vinegar, let it stand two hours, and it substitutes well for sour cream in dips and stroganoff dishes.

Before each ocean passage, I plan on buying 12 liters of long-life milk, 12 small cans of evaporated milk, 2 pounds of milk powder, 6 cans of condensed sweetened milk, and 4 cans of double cream. That usually lasts the two of us for three months. We do not drink milk more than twice a week. So if you are a family of milk drinkers, I'd add a case or two of long-life milk to your list. Except in a few developed nations and large seaports, you'll rarely be able to buy fresh milk.

. . . .

Day 24

Noon to noon: 20 miles
Miles to date: 1,952
Cold, force 7 headwind
Can head for the Aleutians or Hawaii but not Canada
By Dinnertime, hove-to

Lunch
peanut-butter-and-jam sandwiches
lemon pudding cake
raisins and nuts

Dinner (hove-to and served)
chicken and rice

. . . .

CHICKEN AND RICE

Combine
1 can braised chicken
(Great Wall-Chinese canned variety)

½ cup leftover peas
1 onion, sliced
8 cloves garlic, crushed
2 tbs. gravy mix

Simmer 10 minutes, then serve over a bed of rice.

. . . .

I don't know if this tasted as good as we thought it did; but when hove-to, cold, and depressed, it sure hit the spot.

The cook is feeling lower than a snake's belly. I hate beating, especially when there are more than 2,500 miles to beat if this wind doesn't change! The pilot charts promised me a run!

Trash

Trash at sea can be even more of a problem than it is onshore. Even using the most conservation-minded attitude toward waste still leaves me feeling as though I am leaving a trail of waste to mark my path. But certain tips can help reduce waste. And your care and concern will definitely be appreciated by people who visit the isolated atolls and shorelines that would end up as depositories for the items that would otherwise be washed up by currents and winds.

DAY 24. *After a while, you feel as though you are leaving a trail of trash behind you as you sail.*

As you are putting your provisions on board, remove as much packaging as possible and leave it behind. The cardboard boxes and plastic blister packages protecting small store-bought items just take up space on board, so remove them. Toothpaste, disposable razors, batteries—all can be put in their appropriate lockers without their packaging. Use glass jars or reusable plastic containers for leftovers instead of plastic bags or plastic wrap. Buy vegetables loose and store them in baskets instead of plastic bags.

At sea, do not be concerned about throwing food scraps overboard if you are in deep water. Think carefully, however, about nonbiodegradable items. Paper and cardboard will rejoin the food chain in deep water. But all plastics are a possible danger—not only to marine life but also to other sailors and shipping. Plastic bags float just below the surface and can clog seawater intake valves. They will eventually float ashore. So rinse them in saltwater (if they would otherwise turn smelly) and then stash them in a locker to be disposed of onshore. Tin and aluminum cans will deteriorate quickly in saltwater, so if you are well offshore, poke holes in both ends to be sure they will sink quickly. But if you are in the enclosed waters of a gulf or in among islands, crush them and carry them to a shore station for disposal. Glass containers are more of a problem. The majority of sailors dispose of them offshore, filling them with saltwater to make sure they sink. Near shore, it is again best to keep them on board for later disposal. We find we end up with about one garbage bag full of waste for every 15 days at sea. We double-bag this and store it under the dinghy while underway.

But it is when we reach the shores of less-developed countries that a new problem often occurs. In many of these countries, there are no formal rubbish-disposal systems. We remember paying a young boat boy in Mexico 25 cents to take our garbage. He visited each boat to collect the trash. A few hours later, we saw him emptying each bag about a mile down the beach. He searched through for useful items and shoved the rest right into the water. In many African countries, and along some of the rivers of South America, the same thing is still happening. This, of course, makes you feel terrible. The solution? We are not too sure what should be the perfect solution, but we have decided to take our own garbage ashore in situations such as these, find a safe place well above the highest tide line, and dig a hole. Then we burn everything that will burn and bury the rest.

Fortunately for all of us, a great number of people are being more careful about trash disposal, and beaches are cleaner worldwide now than they were only 15 years ago. But even in the most environmentally aware communities, we find the most offensive rubbish abuse caused by plastic shopping bags, which are often blown into the water in spite of the efforts of all concerned. So be careful to secure these potential balloons well if you use them to carry food on board.

Handling of human waste (black water) is becoming an ever-increasing concern for voyagers. All ports in the United States, all of the Great Lakes, several enclosed lakes and bays in Canada, and many ports in Europe have been designated "no discharge" areas. In New Zealand, the rule is no discharge of black water within 500 meters of shore. Several New Zealand marinas now have staff put seals on toilet-discharge valves upon arrival.

Holding tanks are standard on most American cruising boats and many European ones, and they offer a solution in areas where there are pump-out stations. In Canadian waters, where it is legal to discharge human waste once you are beyond the "no discharge" areas, there are very few pump-out stations. Outside the Great Lakes, only a few large marinas in main centers have pump-out facilities.[10] Pump-out stations are rare or nonexistent in most other parts of the world. Furthermore, the vast majority of human waste going into coastal waters and inland rivers does not come from boats with installed toilets, but rather from fishermen and people in small open boats, as well as kayakers and day sailors with no toilet facilities at all. (More than 99 percent of the boats registered in the United States are under 18 feet and powered by outboard motors.) Most of these folks use some variation of the "bucket-and-chuck-it" system. (Even in the United States, where black-water-management laws are the most stringent, you are only required to have holding tanks if you have an installed marine head with through-hull discharge.)

Bucket-and-chuck-it may be okay in open areas, but we find it a discomforting choice in pristine anchorages or in enclosed marinas anywhere in the world. We have no installed head due to our dislike of holding tanks, so we have made an enclosure with seat and lid for a bucket and have come up with solutions that we feel work well. Offshore, we use the bucket-and-chuck-it system. Near shore or in enclosed anchorages, we use Wag Bags in the bucket. These fully biodegradable bags—familiar to dog and cat owners—contain special powder (called Pooh-Powder) that turns urine into a gel and deodorizes the waste. The special enzymes in the gel also kill bacteria and promote the breakdown of waste and bags. After using the bag (one bag can be used five or six times), we simply seal it into the separate biodegradable pouch supplied with each kit. Then it can be deposited in the trash for disposal at landfills. In Peru, where these bags are required for anyone hiking the Inca Trail, the waste product is allowed to break down in compost heaps; within four months, the compost can be used safely for gardening. They also are used for emergency waste management, such as during the aftermath of Hurricane Katrina, when more than a million of the bags were used in the area around New Orleans. In the absence of these bags, many small boat racers use a bucket with a fitted lid and plastic-bag liners. The bags and simple bucket with toilet seats are available through West Marine and most camping outlets. A folding toilet plus Wag Bags can be purchased directly from the manufacturer, Phillips Environmental Products (tel. 1-877-520-0999, www.thepett.com).

. . . .

10   Though the chemicals used to control odors in holding tanks are, by law, biodegradable, I learned from conversations with government marine biologists in the Gulf islands that there is growing concern that these chemicals, when dumped offshore, may do more harm to marine organisms than untreated waste.

Day 25

Noon to noon: 3 miles
Miles to date: 1,955
Set sail again just before Lunch
Wind force 6, sheets eased a bit
Seas lumpy; heavy fog

Lunch
  tuna salad
  rice salad
  bread, butter

Dinner
  mock party ham
  baked potatoes
  squash with honey sauce

....

 MOCK PARTY HAM

Arrange in baking pan
  1 can Spam, in ¼-inch slices

Decorate with
  maraschino cherry halves and
  pineapple chunks

Combine
  ¼ cup honey
  2 tbs. Dijon mustard
  Spread over top of fruit.

> Bake for 20 minutes
> at 375 degrees F.
> Baste twice during
> baking.

....

Being hove-to sure beats bashing into those head seas, but our 3-mile noon-to-noon total is hard to take.

Now we are moving again—it feels great. On the other hand, this heavy fog is a bit spooky. We know there is shipping out here somewhere, but what is the use of keeping a careful watch? Fortunately, we have an exceptionally good radar reflector, a 35-foot-long roll of aluminum foil crumpled inside our hollow wooden spar.

Outfitting a Galley

Larry and I were formally married just three weeks before we moved on board *Seraffyn*. We'd had no guests at our wedding, no formalities, and the only gift came from Larry, who handed me US$200 and said, "Outfit *Seraffyn*'s galley with things you'll enjoy using every day. She's going to be your home for quite a while."

In those days (1968), $200 represented half a month's pay packet for a boatbuilder, so I felt I had a pretty splendid budget to work with. I bought a set of Revere Ware stainless-steel, copper-bottomed pots; a set of English ironstone dishes; and Tupperware plastic containers. Each was the best I could find at the time. It is amazing how much this gift influenced my pleasure at living aboard through the years.

Ironstone dishware is heavy and relatively expensive. It will stand a lot of rough-and-tumble, but it is still breakable if handled too roughly. It has the appearance (if not the feel) of nice china, and it can be heated, so food served on it stays warm. I'd choose it anytime over any kind of plastic dishes I've seen. To me, plastic dishes, mugs, and bowls mean camping out. If a boat is to be your home, nice dinnerware counts. After all, you are going to be using it three times a day, all year.

On 24-foot *Seraffyn*, I chose to have ironstone coffee mugs, which doubled as soup bowls for rougher weather. I purchased ones with large handles to make it easier for Larry to get a secure, 3-finger grip. With the added space on *Taleisin,* I enjoy the luxury of carrying both mugs and teacups with saucers to complement our tableware.

For rough-weather meals, I carry a few flat-bottomed, plastic soup bowls with plastic nonskid rings on the bottom. These also double as serving bowls to use in the cockpit when we are sailing in milder conditions.

I am not fond of plastic drinking glasses, and on *Seraffyn* I found pewter wine glasses to be a good substitute. They definitely are safer than glass, although still not as satisfying. Once again, with the extra space of a larger boat, we have secure places to store both wine and water glasses. I purchase relatively inexpensive ones, as breakages are more common afloat than onshore. Glasses that fit our wine-glass rack (which nestles in a drop-down drawer between the deck beams) are not available everywhere, so I tend to purchase two dozen at a time to guarantee a 3-year supply.

For cutlery afloat, I have found that even the best-quality stainless steel will develop rust pitting if it is stored in a drawer. Therefore, forks and knives are stored in an open tray in the galley, where they stay in better condition longer. For knives, I have found it definitely pays to buy quality—I store mine in the simple knife rack Larry built right into *Taleisin's* countertop (see fig. 34). The stainless-steel blades have kept well in this rack, with little rusting. But when we plan to be away from the boat for more than a month, I rub a coating of cooking oil on their blades and on the metal parts of the sharpening steel.

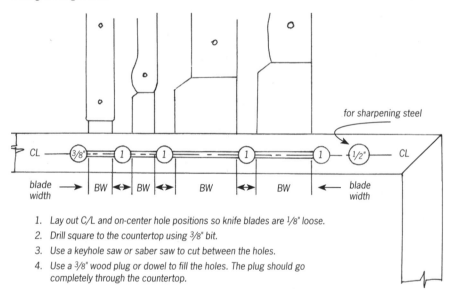

1. Lay out C/L and on-center hole positions so knife blades are 1/8" loose.
2. Drill square to the countertop using 3/8" bit.
3. Use a keyhole saw or saber saw to cut between the holes.
4. Use a 3/8" wood plug or dowel to fill the holes. The plug should go completely through the countertop.

FIGURE 34. Taleisin's *Simple, In-Counter Knife Rack*

Plastic storage containers are essential on a boat, and only one brand lasts year in, year out—Tupperware. It seems to be more heat-resistant than other plastics and doesn't tend to distort if I pour hot soup into it, although it will melt if exposed to direct flames. It doesn't get brittle or crack with age or saltwater contact. Nor does it stain too easily, and it keeps an airtight seal. I may sound like the Tupperware lady as I say this, but I've tried other brands and found they only last three or four years at a time. The Tupperware I purchased when we launched *Taleisin* some two decades ago is still working well.

I am, by nature, on the conservative side, and for most of my sailing life I chose top-brand stainless pots and pans. But last year at the Miami Boatshow, after listening for the umpteenth time to the sales pitch from a pot salesman at the booth across from ours, I broke down and bought a set of his wares. What sold me were the detachable handles plus the set of extra plastic lids that came with the heavy-duty cookware. After using them for a season on *Taleisin*, I am really impressed. The pots not only store more compactly in the locker, they also fit more easily on the limited space of the sea-rail-bounded stove top. With the handle removed, I can use them in the oven. By fitting the tight-sealing plastic lid, I can easily carry my soup or stew ashore for the frequent potluck dinners that are an integral part of cruising. I have a spare handle—not only as a backup but also because I have found it sometimes is nice to put two handles on the largest pot to make it easier to carry when it is full of pasta or seafood.

In addition to the basic cookware, I also carry two additional seagoing pots—an 8-quart soup pot and a 4-quart soup pot; both are 8 inches deep. Lobster, crab, a bucket full of clams—all have taxed the size of the biggest pot. In a seaway, the extra-deep 4-quart pot shines. If I fill it only halfway, even the sloppiest wave can't slurp soup or stew over its side. I also carry a large cast-aluminum frying pan, which is the best substitute I can find for a cast-iron one.

My collection of galley knives and the steel to keep them sharp are right at hand on the edge of the sink counter.

Though many cruisers swear by pressure cookers, I have not found the need for one afloat. I think that if you like one onshore, you'll love it afloat. Unfortunately, each time I am tempted to buy one, visions of the hole in the ceiling and the soup-blasted kitchen of my family home—caused when the steam-release valve of my mother's pressure cooker failed—come to mind. So, in spite of acknowledging the fuel savings afforded by pressure cookers, I have not convinced myself that I need one. I would estimate that one in two cruisers carry a pressure cooker. If you choose one, remember that it must be used with special care on board a yacht—both because your galley is small and because cruising cooks often wear a lot less clothing in the galley than normal cooks do. A good friend of ours was badly burned when she removed the top from her pressure cooker a bit too soon. She was wearing a bikini, and the steam burned her midriff in a 3-inch-wide patch. If you use a pressure cooker on board, be sure it is fully cooled before opening. Unless you can comfortably place your hand on the bottom of the pressure cooker, put a towel over the top as you are opening it so that any remaining steam is directed away from you. Offshore, don't fill a pressure cooker as much as you might normally do—in a rough sea, there is more likelihood of small bits of food (skins from beans, onion pieces, etc.) clogging the steam-escape valve than onshore.

On Taleisin, *I carry eight place settings of Mikasa ironstone dishes. They fit snugly into the holders outboard of the galley sink.*

Two stainless-steel bread tins, two different-size casserole pans, a cookie/baking sheet, and an oven-size grilling tray complete my cookware inventory. I also carry a 5-piece set of nesting stainless-steel mixing bowls that double as salad bowls. The largest is 18 inches across, and I use it for serving at large gatherings and also for mixing bread. Storage for these bowls takes up very little room, as Larry has adapted an idea from a Westsail 32 we visited years ago. They attached L-shaped holders under the middle of their galley table and stored the bowls there. Larry put similar holders under the shelf in my galley locker—an area that I otherwise wouldn't be able to use (see fig. 35).

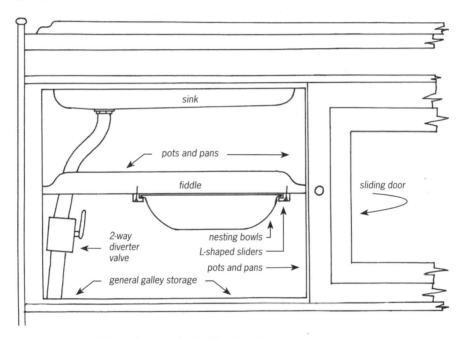

FIGURE 35. *Storage under the Galley Counter*

A stainless-steel cheese grater, stainless tongs, flexible plastic spatulas and spoons that won't scratch Teflon, along with a coffee percolator and a copper teakettle, make up the rest of my can't-do-without galley gear.

I have opted to carry some extras—more for luxury than for necessity. One item that I find especially good in less-developed countries is a meat grinder. Much foreign beef is too tough to use for anything but stewing. This is where a simple, home-style, plastic-bodied grinder that clamps to the counter top comes in handy. You can make delicious clamcakes if you run big, ugly clams through the grinder once. Bits and pieces of leftover meat, run once or twice through the grinder, become the beginnings of a delicious pâté. Any of your meat leftovers—run through the grinder once and mixed with an egg and some bread crumbs—can become the base for a good meatloaf.

Though the pots and pans we carry can double as serving "plates," I have opted to make life a bit more luxurious by including three oval stainless platters. When it is time for you to pack up your shoreside home and move afloat, select a few of your special serving items and make space for them afloat. They will spice up an occasional social affair and offer a bit of luxury in your life afloat. If you eventually find you don't use them, you can ship them home for storage—or they might make wonderful gifts for people who made you especially welcome or gave you a helping hand along the way.

·······

Day 26

Noon to noon: 129 miles

Miles to date: 2,084

Foggy, not so cold, beam reach, setting more sail

Lunch
rice salad
leftover Spam
hard-boiled eggs

Dinner
carrot and cucumber salad
mackerel cakes
lemon slices
canned sweet corn
white wine

· ·

CARROT AND CUCUMBER SALAD

Combine
1 cup thinly sliced carrots
½ cup thinly sliced cucumbers
2 tbs. olive oil
2 tbs. vinegar
2 tsp. sugar
½ tsp. dill

Let sit for 1 hour
before serving.

· ·

MACKEREL CAKES

Combine well

1 small can mackerel, well drained

1 egg

⅓ cup chopped onion

6 cloves garlic, minced

¾ cup mashed potatoes (very stiff)

If mixture is still wet-looking,
add ¼ cup instant potato mix.

Drop mackerel "batter" in large spoonfuls into hot, greased frying pan and pat down into ¾-inch-thick patties. Fry until crispy brown on both sides.

Stove-Top Food Preservation

Since the recipe above made more mackerel cakes than we could eat at one sitting, I cooked up the extras and left them sitting in the pan to be heated up tomorrow. Leftovers on an offshore passage can be a nuisance. We usually let them sit on the stove top and use them up in the next day's cooking. If I put them into plastic containers and store them in the icebox, I would probably forget about them. But highly visible, sitting on the corners of the stove top, leftovers make perfect snacks or the basis for the next day's meal plan.

This trick came from the captain of the Costa Rican shrimp trawler on which we worked for a month. I had been hired as cook and Larry as navigator for some offshore lobster exploration work. Johnson, the captain, was from Belize. He had previously worked as cook on trawlers, so we had some great impromptu cooking contests. Since most of the crew were Costa Ricans, I had to learn some of the local dishes. Johnson showed me how to boil up 2 gallons of pinto beans and spice them so the crew could then mix them in with some of the 2 gallons of rice I'd boiled to make the local favorite, *gallo pinto*. When I started to package the leftover rice and beans to store them in the ice room, he stopped me: "Don't waste your time. Leave everything on the stove top; after everyone is finished eating for the day, cover each pot, bring it to a full boil for two minutes, then shut off the fire and don't open the pot until you need it tomorrow. It will keep for seven days if you heat it every day." I followed his advice and found it to be correct. As long as there are no tomatoes in your soup, stew, or beans, they will keep for more than a week if brought to a full boil each day. This is handy when you want to make up a big soup or stew for the first few days at sea. Not only does it save icebox room; it also means only one pot to wash, once. The contents of the stove-top simmer pot seem to taste better day by day. In the case of beans, Johnson also taught me to add some new flavor each day. The first day, I boiled up the beans with just salt and garlic. The second day, I added chopped onions; the third, chunks of sausage; the fourth, a bit of fish and crab we'd had for dinner. Only on the day when I knew the pot would be almost finished did I add tomato chunks and loads of oregano. The crew loved it.

The trip we took with Johnson was in Costa Rican waters where the temperature never dropped below 80 degrees F. If the temperatures ranged around 50 or 60 degrees, I wouldn't be afraid to keep most stove-top dishes (again, excluding tomatoes) for up to 10 days. The signs that things have gone bad are obvious: Little air bubbles form around the edge of the pan and the pan smells sour.

. . . .

Day 27

Noon to noon: 102 miles
Miles to date: 2,186
Sun is out, but it's foggy and damp
We're beam-reaching; seas are regular; we're moving fast

Lunch
> packaged oxtail soup
> mashed-potato salad
> mackerel cakes (leftovers from previous night)

*Teatime (celebration for reaching the halfway mark
on our Pacific chart)*
> bottle of red wine
> Camembert, Cheddar, biscuits

Dinner
> chicken curry
> rice

....

CHICKEN CURRY

Sauté until onions are transparent
> 1 onion, chopped
> ⅓ cup raisins
> 10 cloves garlic, chopped
> 1 tbs. olive oil

Add
> 1½ tsp. curry powder
> 1 can chicken in supreme sauce or
> 1 can chicken meat and
> 1 can white sauce

> Simmer slowly, 4 or 5
> minutes. Serve over rice
> (or noodles).

....

DAY 27. *The first time we caught a fish, we were on our way down the Red Sea. Larry felt like a king.*

Catching Fish

Larry has doubled his fishing efforts. We are now towing two fish lines—one from our leeward quarter and one from the end of the vanged-out boom.

During the first four years of our voyaging life we never dragged a fish line, though we did carry one on board. I guess we had all the fish we wanted to eat from those we caught skin diving—or we bought fresh fish from fishermen. Besides, every time I thought of pulling a leaping, bucking fish on board and slaughtering him on our beautiful teak decks, I pictured blood and guts everywhere, scales in the sleeping bags, and a stink that would linger for days. During the first years of our cruise, we rarely made voyages longer than about 10 days, so we didn't have a great need to supplement our menu with fresh fish.

Then, in the Mediterranean, we started dragging a fishing line—200 feet of line with a leader and various lures, led to a shock cord that had a tin can with a couple of nuts and bolts in it. (This was supposed to act as an alarm if we caught a fish.) Well, we dragged that line for six or seven thousand miles with no luck, and we even had one massive tangle-up with the taffrail log. On the other hand, I found it fun to yank on the shock-cord alarm and then sit back and watch Larry's mad scramble as he tried to get out of his bunk to reel in the fish that wasn't there.

We asked every fisherman we could about tackle, lures, and so on. One would say, "Not moving fast enough." Another would say, "You're moving too fast." Or, "Too long a line," or "too short," or "too big a hook," or "too small, wrong color, wrong lure for the fish in our sea." We tried each new idea, but no luck.

We read stories of other sailors reaping a harvest of flying fish off their decks each morning in the trade winds. The ones that landed on *Seraffyn* were usually about two inches long, and they never landed in pairs; we were lucky to have one in a week. When we finally caught an 8-incher, we fried it up eagerly, but we disappointedly dumped it overboard when we found it bony and strong-flavored.

Then, in Rhodes Harbor, Greece, we were tied up next to two Australian yachts that had come through the Red Sea. The youngsters on both yachts raved about the fishing they'd had. While we were there, Larry spent two mornings teaching Simon, the 16-year-old son of Ross and Margaret Irvine on *Girl Morgan*, how to splice wire. Before we set sail, Simon came over with a gift—his own secret fishing lure and the promise that even *we* could catch fish with his tackle.

In mid-August, only a few months after the Suez Canal reopened following eight years of warring with Israel, we sailed into Port Said bound south toward the Red Sea. We sweltered in Port Said for three weeks, trying to convince the local authorities we could safely sail through the canal in our motorless yacht, as the wind was strong and favorable. Finally, after trying to hire a local boat to tow us through, another yacht appeared and the crew on *Vltava* offered us a tow from Port Said through the canal. We had only four hours to catch the tow; paperwork filled all of it. The prospect of bureaucratic hassles related to stopping at Port Suez on the far end seemed worse than sailing without fresh stores. So we set off down the Red Sea with plenty of canned provisions but only four days' worth of fresh meat on 30 pounds of ice.

Six days later, we pulled out Simon's lure, an extremely simple affair— 2-ounces of lead with a 1-inch, 3-prong hook covered by a skirt of dark-pink plastic cut from a shopping bag and secured around the bullet-shaped lead with a fine piece of string. Just after lunch, we put it overboard on the end of 200 feet of 100-pound-test, green monofilament line. Just before sunset, we were running wing-and-wing at close to 5 knots while we had a cool drink. Just after I suggested that we reel in the line so it wouldn't foul up the taffrail log at night, the tin-can alarm went off only inches from my head. Larry rushed over and grabbed the fishing line. "We've really caught one!!!" he shouted. Then, as he began pulling in the line hand-over-hand, he shouted out a string of orders so quickly that I am still not sure I heard all of them. "Quick, Lin, drop the genoa. Slow her down or we'll lose the fish. Unclutch the windvane. Pull in the log. Go get something for killing the fish; it's a big one. Grab a bucket of water to soak the deck. Get a dropboard in place so it doesn't jump down the companionway. God, it's a big one!" I did manage to douse the genoa to slow our speed; I got a bucket of water and sloshed the deck so fish blood wouldn't soak into the bare wood; and I got the dropboard in place. When Larry pulled that 3¹/₂-foot-long glowing silver kingfish into the cockpit, I was so excited that I let out a scream. Then I remembered that he needed something for killing the 20-pound fish before it leaped overboard. I took the anchor-winch handle back to the cockpit and then hid behind the dinghy so that I didn't have to watch the murder scene. This was definitely some of the best fish we've ever tasted. We each had a 1-pound fillet, sautéed in butter and garlic, with tartar sauce. The rest was used up within two days.

During the rest of our voyage down the Red Sea, we caught a fish every time we dragged our line. Just before dusk seemed to be the best time, and 5 to 6 knots seemed to be the best speed. Our favorite dish was the kingfish, a fine-nosed, flat-bodied fish. Our least favorite was the large, red-fleshed tuna we caught; they were too dry. The small tuna were delicious when sautéed in olive oil and lemon juice for only a minute on each side. All of the tuna made good cold salads.

A month later, crossing the Indian Ocean, we had a strange fishing adventure. We had been drifting for a week—caught in the intertropical convergence zone where the only wind came in tiny squalls spaced about an hour apart. These squalls would last no more than 10 minutes and the winds in them would swing round the clock. We'd already been at sea for 16 days and had only covered 800 miles, so the miserable 28-mile-a-day averages we were now recording, plus constant sail trimming, were getting more than a bit boring. Then we noticed a large fish using the shade of our hull for shelter. Each time we'd spurt ahead on a squall, *Seraffyn's* bow would scare up a flying fish. The big fish under our transom would take off at unbelievable speed. Then, two or three hours later, we'd see the flicker of his tail under our transom again. This went on for four days. We tried everything we could think of to catch him: lures, casting, etc. Larry even tried shooting at him with the spear gun.

The fourth afternoon, when we were absolutely becalmed, Larry said, "I'll climb down very quietly from the bowsprit, you hand me my spear gun, and I'll try to get that devil." Larry barely had time to take the gun from me before that curious fish swam right at him. The fish was so close to Larry's face mask that Larry had to backpaddle to get a shot with the gun. The spear took that fish right in the center. I was reluctant to take the jerking and bleeding fish, the spear, and the gun from Larry, especially when he had warned me, "You drop that fish or spear gun, you'd better dive in after it." Fortunately, Larry climbed on board quickly to take charge, and when the dust settled, we saw we'd caught a 15- or 18-pound mahimahi (dolphinfish, dorado), one of the sweetest-tasting of all fish. To this day, we know of no one else who has ever caught this deepwater fish on a spear gun.

One problem with trolling for fish at sea is that you usually catch fish that weigh 15 to 20 pounds. This seems to be more fish than the average crew can eat, but there are ways of preserving the flesh so that it can be used for up to two weeks without formal canning. When we catch a large fish, we fillet it, removing all bones by cutting the fillets down the center. Then we take about 3 pounds of the filleted fish for each of us and sauté it lightly in butter or oil and lemon juice. Then I remove from the pan everything except what we plan to eat at that meal, and I finish cooking our dinner. After that, I return the partially cooked fish to the pan, cover the pan, and let it sit until the next day. We usually use another third of the fish for lunch the next day. Reheating the remaining fish for a minute on each side will make it last yet another day, even in the tropics. Larry enjoys two meals of sautéed fillets with a sauce, then a third meal of spiced fishcakes.

If we have more fish than we can use in this way, I sterilize several jars by dipping each jar and its lid in a pot of boiling saltwater for two minutes (peanut butter or jam jars are best because of their wide mouths). After letting the jar cool off under a clean towel, I fill the jar 3/4 full with large chunks of the uncooked, filleted fish. I add three or four garlic cloves, a piece of carrot if it's available, and several peppercorns. Then I fill the jar completely with a mixture of equal parts olive or salad oil and vinegar or lemon juice. I put a sterilized, 1-inch-square block of wood or cork from a wine bottle on top of the fish to keep it below the level of the marinade at all times. We then stand the well-sealed jars in our bilges, where they have lasted for as long as 10 days—even in the Arabian Sea, where we had water temperatures of up to 85 degrees. The marinade "cooks" the fish during this process. When it is time to use it, I drain off the marinade; chop up some onions, tomatoes, and green peppers; and mix everything well to make a lovely salad. Or you can create a main course by adding the fish and a few tablespoons of the marinade to precooked rice and heating thoroughly.

We have never been tempted to try drying the extra fish because during our stay in Costa Rica, we often caught the aroma of the fishing boats hung with drying cod, which was the major cash industry. I know I couldn't live with that smell on board a boat as small as ours. But if you have a larger boat—or a less-keen sense of smell—you could fillet any extra fish, rub it well with coarse salt, and then lay it to dry on sheets of newspaper. At night, cover the fish with something waterproof to keep the dew from settling on it. Turn the fish twice a day for three days. When it is stiff as a bone, store it away in a dry container. Reconstitute the dried fish by soaking it for three hours in freshwater, changing the water at least twice. Fried in olive oil, this is the national dish of Portugal. Good fish jerky can be made by soaking boneless fillets of any white fish in soy sauce for 24 hours, then drying them by hanging the fillets from a line. The Japanese variation of this is to use equal parts soy sauce and sake, plus a pinch of ginger.

We once asked a marine biologist how to decide whether fish we caught were poisonous. His answer was, "If it looks like a fish should look and isn't ugly, eat it. If it is a barracuda and weighs less than 4 pounds, eat it." We've followed this advice and have had no problem, nor have we heard of anyone else getting even an upset stomach from fresh, caught-on-board fish. Deep-sea fish are almost all safe, as most poisonous fish get so by eating reef life.

One of our very favorite fish recipes comes from that voyage down the Red Sea. I had some spaghetti Bolognese sauce left over when we were coming through the Straits of Bab El Mandeb. In fact, I was planning on using that for dinner when we caught an 8-pound kingfish. I sliced an onion and arranged the rings all over the bottom of my deep skillet. I set three large fillets of kingfish on top, added 1/4 cup of freshwater, then covered the pot and steamed the fish for about eight minutes—just until it started to flake apart easily. I poured the Bolognese sauce on top and steamed it for two minutes more. We ate that with our last bottle of Italian sparkling wine—to celebrate clearing the

Red Sea! I don't know if it was as spectacular-tasting as I remember, but with food, it's often the mood of the moment that counts most.

Now in the North Pacific, our luck is back to normal (meaning bad), even though the Japanese fishermen we met presented us with five or six different lures that were absolutely guaranteed to work. But Larry is the sort who will keep on dragging what I call his "optimist line," because there is nothing as good as a freshly caught mahimahi—unless it's a freshly caught kingfish!

Taleisin's Fish Tales

Our fishing luck seems to be slightly better as we voyage on board *Taleisin*. We do best by skin diving while we lie at anchor; Larry has chosen the fish he'll catch by its size. At sea, it seems he always catches huge fish when I'd prefer something in the 5- or 10-pound range. His most horrendous catch was made just after we left Tonga's islands. Fortunately, we were almost becalmed when we hauled in a dorado that was only one inch shorter than I. (I'm just over 4 feet 10 inches, and we actually used a tape measure to check that fish so that neither of us would feel we were exaggerating when we spoke about it later.) We could only use half the fish, even though we put almost 5 kilos of it on ice and another 5 kilos into marinades. But it isn't only the waste that makes me ambivalent about dragging a line at sea. It seems the most common fish we snag is the magnificent dorado, or mahimahi. It comes flashing from the water clothed in glowing royal blue and gold and then fades to dull gray as it dies in front of me. I'm a real softy, I know. The other problem is the mess that a flailing fish can make if it is not subdued quickly. We have been told of five ways to calm a fish while it is either clubbed to death or dies naturally.

1. Pour alcohol of any sort into its gills.
2. Cover its eyes with a towel. If it cannot see, it will stop leaping about.
3. Have a large nail set into a wooden handle and use it to spike the fish just above the eyes. This should hit the brain and kill it instantly.
4. Hold it on its back.
5. Shove it head-first into a canvas bag and hang the sack from the rigging.

We have tried methods two and five with moderate success. The fish did lie still in the bag or under the towel. But then I had the problem of cleaning the bag so I could use it again for shopping when we reached shore.

When Larry is skin diving, we always try to catch fish that are in the 3-pound range. That way, we have no wastage and, more important, it is extremely rare for the poison known as ciguatera to be a problem with fish weighing under 4 pounds. Ciguatera is present on most coral reefs; it tends to accumulate slowly in fish that feed near or on the reef. In very small amounts, it is not problematic to humans. But in the quantities that could be present in fish larger than about 4 pounds, the concentration of ciguatera can make some people extremely ill. If you are concerned, and you plan to do a major portion of your cruising in coral-reef areas, you can purchase a special kit to test the flesh of any fish. We have rarely heard of prudent sailors suffering from ciguatera, and in each case, those who did had speared large fish near tropical shores, or had eaten species that the local people had warned them might be a problem.

If you enjoy fishing (and are successful), do not hesitate to try for some extra fish as you approach any port or island. Fresh fish is a welcome and accepted gift for the people you'll meet when you reach shore. I am always surprised to see how much people who live on islands and depend on the sea for their livelihood still appreciate deep-sea fish as a gift.

. . . .

Day 28

Noon to noon: 143 miles
Miles to date: 2,329
No fog, smoother sea, all sail set to a light southerly

Lunch
dressed-up pork and beans
hot dogs (canned American-style sausages)
sweet pickle chips

Teatime
fresh buttered popcorn

Dinner
country-style French onion soup
squash with honey sauce
Camembert, biscuits
red wine

. . . .

DRESSED-UP PORK AND BEANS

Combine
1 can pork and beans
1 tbs. Dijon mustard
3 tbs. ketchup
1 tbs. sugar

Heat well and serve topped with chopped onions.

. . . .

COUNTRY-STYLE FRENCH ONION SOUP

Sauté in deep saucepan
until onions are transparent

    3 large onions, sliced
    3 tbs. butter

Add

    10 cloves garlic, chopped
    ½ cup red wine
    water to cover onions
    salt to taste
    Bring to boil and simmer 10 minutes.

Combine

    1 package beef gravy mix or 1 tbs. Bisto
    water

> Bake in a hot oven (425 F) 25 to 30 minutes, until cheeses brown lightly and soup forms a dark film. Be sure to let cool 10 minutes before serving.

Add to onion soup until it is as thick as cream.

Pour soup into a casserole (I used a bread tin).

Top with pieces of stale bread, then grated cheese (I used processed cheddar cheese; fresh is better). Sprinkle heavily with Parmesan.

On Catching a Gull

Pandemonium at 0700 today. A gull dove on the fishing lure, got hooked by the wing, and tried to take off, but it only managed to water-ski along, with its wings flapping wildly. Larry heard birds squawking at the same time that the fish alarm went off. He rushed on deck and reeled in the wildly flapping bird. "Lin, get up," he yelled. I opened the companionway cover to see a tangle of fish line; a subdued, bleeding bird; and a white-faced Larry. Fortunately, the hook had not gone into the bird; it had only hooked behind its wing, causing a small flesh wound. While Larry held the bird somewhat quiet, I cut the leader, disentangled the hook, and unwrapped the fishing line from around the frightened bird. Then Larry tossed it into the air. After one indignant cry, the bird spread its wings and flew off. My only thought was, "Thank God we didn't catch the 9-foot-wingspan albatross that has been following us for the past 10 days." Subduing that creature would have been quite a struggle.

Larry put a larger lead sinker on the fish line before resetting it. I hope it stays below the gull's diving range now.

This afternoon, the fog cleared and the decks dried off for the first time in 16 days. We opened up the whole boat, and I was able to take a careful inventory of stores. It seems the only items that are running a bit short are saltine biscuits (crackers) and cooking oil. It seems a shame to use olive oil for frying, but we'll have to do that at some point before the end of the voyage. We also have several cans of butter left. The variety of our can lockers is not as great as when we started, but that's to be expected.

We are past the halfway mark, closer to Canada than to Japan. There is a fair wind and a lovely sea. So thoughts of actually reaching our goal occupy my mind. A big, juicy hamburger; a steak; fresh strawberries and cherries—guess we would never appreciate them so much if we didn't have to do without sometimes.

. . . .

Day 29

Noon to noon: 128 miles
Miles to date: 2,457
Light fog, watery sun shinning through, but it's not warm
Seas regular, moving fast on a close reach with all sail set

Lunch
  clam chowder
  scrambled eggs
  leftover beans

Dinner
  spaghetti Bolognese
  red wine

. . . .

CLAM CHOWDER

3 potatoes, in small chunks
half saltwater, half freshwater to cover potatoes

Boil until potatoes are tender.
Drain half of the water off.

Sauté separately
  1 small onion, in small pieces
  3 tbs. butter

  Add to cooked potatoes.

Add
  1 small can clams (with juice)
  ½ can evaporated milk
  1 tsp. oregano
  1 tsp. garlic, chopped fine

> Heat until milk starts to simmer. Add salt if necessary. If you have bacon or sausages, add small cooked chunks with the onions.

. . . .

Paper Towels

I don't know how Columbus crossed the Atlantic without paper towels. Our boat seems to be fueled by them. We use at least a roll a week. So Larry has installed a paper-towel rack on the underside of the deck—above the sink and a good distance from the stove. Since paper-towel sizes are different in almost every country, a standard holder doesn't work. The simplest solution is two pieces of wood fastened to the underside of the deck 12½ inches apart, with holes drilled for a ½-inch wooden rod to slip through (fig. 36). This has fit every size of paper towel we've encountered.

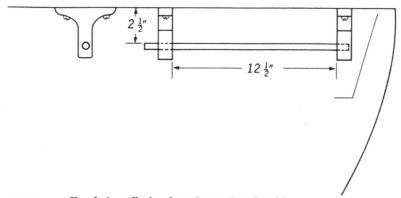

FIGURE 36. *Simple Installation for a Paper-Towel Holder*

Annabelle Yates, on board *Amobel,* found that by cutting each roll of paper towels in half, she saved a tremendous amount. I know I have grabbed a whole paper towel for a job where half would have worked well.

. . . .

Day 30

Noon to noon: 122 miles
Miles to date: 2,579
Foggy-cold, no sun; close-reaching on a fresh breeze
By evening, almost close-hauled

Lunch
fried tuna steaks
tartar sauce
cabbage, raisin, and onion salad

Teatime
hot chocolate
raisins

Dinner
chili and beans
tuna steak bits
bread, butter

....

TARTAR SAUCE

Combine
⅓ cup mayonnaise
2 tbs. sweet pickle relish
1 tsp. lemon juice

....

We caught a fish today! It's the first one since we left the Indian Ocean. I sure was glad, because Larry has been trying so hard, and early this morning something big took half his fishing tackle. He repaired the tackle and reset it. Only minutes later, a 15- or 18-pound tuna grabbed one prong of the plastic squid-covered 3-prong hooks.

DAY 30. *We finally caught a fish today.*

I must admit that I was disappointed to have caught a tuna, because the ones we'd had in the Red Sea were strong-flavored and dry, no matter how we cooked them. But there must be some difference in the type of tuna, or it might have something to do with water temperature (Red Sea: 85 degrees; North Pacific: 60 degrees). This tuna tasted absolutely great. The uncooked flesh was a lot lighter-colored, and the cooked steaks were almost pure white.

We ate an amazing amount of tuna for lunch and were both looking forward to another steak for dinner. It's been a long time since we've had fresh meat of any kind.

Larry filleted off about 10 or 12 pounds of meat. I'm not worried about keeping the portion we didn't eat; it's only about 45 degrees out in the cockpit right now.

On Cooking for a Crew

During our first delivery job together, there was another woman on board—the wife of the owner. We'd been hired because the owner had a heart condition and wanted the insurance of extra crew for the 1,200-mile offshore passage. At the wife's suggestion, we took turns in the galley. One day she did all the work—cooking, serving, and cleaning; the next day was my turn. Never again. Though we didn't have any open disagreements, both of us grew to hate the arrangement. I'd inadvertently used up the exact piece of meat she'd planned for her dinner. She'd used up the leftovers from my previous day's work, so I had to re-plan my next day's menu. I didn't clean up the galley the way she preferred. She moved the can of such-and-such, so I couldn't find it. Just as in a house, two chefs can't use the same kitchen constantly. And on a yacht during a long passage, the problem of keeping track of stores and menu ideas for three weeks ahead makes two cooks even worse.

In Malaysia, we met Peter Thuell, who had retired from his job as manager of a local tin mine, outfitted his 35-foot ketch for a voyage "home" to England, then advertised for three crew to make the voyage with him. Three experienced onshore sailors joined him—two young men and a woman. Peter had never made any passage longer than two or three days, and he asked us how to arrange galley duties. "Put one person completely in charge of the galley. Have that person keep track of stores, water, and making sure the galley stays in order. Have each crewman help the cook all of one day—washing dishes, serving, peeling carrots," I suggested. Larry agreed, and Peter, who was locally well known for his ability to get along with people, felt our suggestions made sense.

A furor erupted that night in the tiny Perak Yacht Club bar. Both of the young men challenged me. "Peter told Janice she's in charge of the galley! That's not fair. What if she gets seasick? What if I don't like the way she cooks? I like to cook, too. Why should we do all the dishes and the dirty work?"

Almost five months later, when we were in Brunei, we read a long letter telling the end of the story. "Food was great on the trip," wrote Bob, one of the young men. "Janice took charge of the galley and turned out great food except for the few days when she was seasick. But that didn't matter because all of us were too seasick to eat anyway. Each of us men took turns making breakfasts so we got to indulge our cooking instincts. Boy, the competition to create the most exciting breakfasts sure got good results. Janice cleaned the breakfast dishes, we guys did the rest. All of us tried our hand quite successfully at bread making; Janice did a great job of keeping track of stores. Only small problem—ran short of nibbles towards the middle of the Red Sea. All of us gained weight too."

This problem of nibbles is most acute when there is a crew of hungry young sailors on board. It's amazing how important snacks become for night watches. Fresh popcorn, individual candy bars, peanuts, sausage slices, dried fruit or trail mix, potato chips, fruit, cheese, cookies, cake, or pie—anything that can be a snack with no cooking or dishes will evaporate. On deliveries or whenever we sail with crew, we've found it best to have a snack box easily available to the man going on watch. I put everything in the box that is available for that particular day without cutting into our stores. But if a snack item is a particularly favorite sweet that can disappear into an unconsciously greedy sailor's stomach, leaving the rest of the crew feeling left out, it's best for the cook to give out rations to each person. I say this because of one incident that occurred when we had two extra crewmen on a long delivery. All of us loved a particular English toffee that I'd come across in Gibraltar. I'd bought an 8-pound sack of it, and it seemed to grow shorter in inches every day. So we decided that six toffees per man per day was a fair amount. Three days later, I handed out rations. Jim was asleep when I did so. I gave Ken his six and also gave him six to be handed to Jim when watches were changed. The next afternoon at cocktail time, Jim asked, "Why didn't we get any toffees yesterday? Run out already?" Seems Ken put all 12 in his pocket and steered happily though the night popping candies, forgetting that only half of them were his. Fortunately, both men had good senses of humor. A court-of-inquiry to punish Ken reached the following verdict: no toffees for one night, double ration for Jim, one extra for the rest of the crew except for the cook, who was personally to hand each crewman his ration in the future. This may sound a trifling matter, but, at sea, trifling matters can create ego-bruising blowups.

The snack box (or fair rationing of snack items) is important because it makes clear to the crew what foods are off-limits. I've had an uninformed crew eat a 1-pound chunk of Cheddar as a snack, thereby ruining prospects for a ham-and-cheese casserole I'd planned for the evening. I was at fault because I hadn't told him to ask first—nor had I explained what foods were off-limits. This was his first long passage, and he was used to rummaging through the refrigerator at home.

The same crewman taught me another important lesson. We'd picked him up during a 3-day stop in Antigua. One of our original crew had asked if he could jump ship because he'd fallen in love. He helped locate the crewman for us the evening before we set sail for the last 2,000 miles of the voyage. Two days out, I discovered that our new crewman didn't like candy, pancakes, waffles, French toast, or doughnuts. He didn't like cakes, either. In fact, he didn't like anything sweet. Providing enough nonsweet breakfasts and snacks for him severely taxed our stores. Since then, I've been careful to find out ahead of time if any potential crew members have special dietary likes, dislikes, or restrictions. Some interesting new ideas have come from these few minutes with the crew before each voyage, and a quick trip to the local market has made for a happier crew situation at sea.

Though it's important to find out generally what particular crewmen do or don't like to eat, I find it best to avoid saying, "I'm going to cook such and such today; does that sound good to you?" Invariably, someone will say, "I don't really feel like . . . ," or "Can't we have such-and-such instead?" And if that doesn't happen, the weather will deteriorate and it will be impossible to cook what was planned, so the crew ends up disappointed. Take it from me: Keep your cooking plans to yourself. Keep the crew in suspense until you put dinner on the table. It's much more fun to be surprised.

One final secret about cooking for a crew was told to me by a well-respected charter cook: "Save the best meals you can for the last four days of the voyage." Crewmen, like everyone else, have short memories. They'll soon forget that fabulous stew and salad with fresh bread and crème caramel you served on day 16 of a 30-day voyage. But serve that the night before you get into port and they'll leave the boat saying, "What a cook; made the whole trip more fun."

As for the expense of feeding extra crew, on deliveries we pay for all expenses and have found that food costs us between 15 and 22 cents per crew per mile (based on average prices for provisioning in the United States, the Caribbean, New Zealand and South Africa 2005). For shorter passages the lower figure seems to apply; for longer ones the costs goes up as more canned and packaged provisions are required. This would be a reasonable amount to charge for food if the crew on your boat were sharing expenses. It would include food, beverages, and basic stores for menus such as those in this book, but it would not include wine, liquor, or beer.

With regard to liquor and crews, we have found that it is best to discuss how you feel about drinking on board before you leave port. In our case, on deliveries we provide two beers a day for warm-weather passages and liquor for one cocktail at night, plus wine for occasional dinners. We keep the liquor supplies separate from other galley provisions and ask that the crew let us bring them out when we wish. The crew is invited to bring along extra if they wish to be able to treat the rest of the crew to a drink. But we ask that they limit the extra drinks to cocktail hour. This may seem dictatorial, but when we are delivering another person's boat, it is an expensive responsibility, and crew alertness is important.

One comment for those who are invited to crew for a generous drinker. Even if the host seems to pour drinks with abandon, always ask permission before pouring yourself a drink or offering others a drink from the host's supplies. It is surprising how often skippers have become angry with crew over this simple matter. "How dare they offer my liquor as if it were their own?" is a comment I have heard more often than you would expect from skippers who were looking for a crew member to replace one who had just been asked to leave.

For those who take crew and share expenses, one other item should be cleared up before taking off for a cruise. What happens in port when the skipper feels like eating ashore? Do crew members pay for their own meals? Is the food bought for days in port part of the general sharing? This can be decided in many different ways. When we are on a delivery, we provide food on board at sea, plus basic provisions for times in port. If our port visit is for more than one day, I continue to provide all meals. But if it is a 1-day stop, we usually give the crew sufficient money for lunch and dinner onshore at an average café and then take a break and eat out by ourselves at the restaurant of our choice.

It is definitely harder to cook for a crew than for a husband-and-wife cruising team. I'd say that one extra crewman adds one hour a day to the cook's workload. Shopping for the extra food adds time before your voyage. Most cooks feel obliged to cook slightly fancier meals when there are extra crewmen on board. I know I would never suggest cook's night off when we are on a delivery. That's one of the reasons couples seem to make the most lasting cruising and voyaging teams.

. . . .

Day 31

Noon to noon: 91 miles
Miles to date: 2,670
Raining, heavy wind
Right down to reefed staysail and double-reefed main,
close-hauled

Lunch
   canned tomato soup
   cheese
   canned pâté
   biscuits

Dinner
   tuna steaks (with tartar sauce or Bolognese sauce)
   mashed potatoes
   canned sweet corn
   white wine

....

Perfect Tuna

A bit too rough for fancy cooking. But the tuna is keeping well, since the temperature outside is about 50 degrees F. Larry feels our tuna was perfectly cooked, and he suggested I tell my secret. I only followed the instructions of an Italian fisherman. I selected pieces from near the belly of the fish, cut them across the grain in 1/2-inch-thick slices, and put them into a pan with 1/8 inch of hot olive oil for 1 1/2 minutes. Then I turned over the slices to cook for one minute—no more—only until the meat was white all the way through.

We had an especially lovely evening. It's been 18 days since this cold, foggy weather set in. Today's progress wasn't great. Every four or five days, we seem to run into a gale. But by dinnertime, the seas were calmer, and we had already unreefed the staysail and shaken one reef out of the main.

Dinner was delicious—nothing like fresh fish eaten at sea with a nice bottle of Liebfraumilch. Then, over our meal, Larry started telling me about some stories he was reading. He retrieved the book from his bunk and asked if I'd like to hear one by Jack London. The chill in our cabin seemed to diminish as the 70-below Yukon winter foiled London's character in his attempts to light a fire. The story drew to its close as we finished the bottle of wine. I turned on our oven to warm us a bit while Larry lit the oil lamps and I did the dishes. One of those special moments drove away the discomfort of a long ocean voyage. Then Larry climbed into the quarter berth and I sat down to my special private hour—pen in hand, heart at home, and peaceful.

. . . .

Day 32

Noon to noon: 100 miles
Miles to date: 2,770
Fog trying to lift
Close-hauled, occasional glimpses of the sun

Lunch
    fresh tuna and egg salad
    sweet corn
    sweet pickle chips

Dinner
    pork stew with onions, potatoes, and red wine

. . . .

 FRESH TUNA AND EGG SALAD

Steam until white
    small chunks of tuna
    Let cool, then break into flakes.

Combine
    1 cup flaked tuna
    2 hard-boiled eggs, chopped
    ¼ cup chopped onions
    ¼ cup mayonnaise
    2 cloves garlic, pressed
    salt, pepper

> Let stand 1 hour before serving.

. . . .

As I was sitting below during our first watch this evening, I began thinking of all the different types of cooking positions on board sailing yachts. I've cooked on delivery trips, voyages, harbor hops. I've even cooked on a shrimp trawler for a month. I've prepared the food for day races and races that lasted three days, but I've never cooked on a charter boat or on a long-distance race.

Charter-boat cooks are often more highly paid than the captains. And well they should be, since most people who are paying US$700 to $1,500 a day expect exceptional cooking. I remember reading through some of the menu plans from *Carina*, the 60-foot schooner skippered by Ian Staniland out of Malta: eggs Benedict for breakfast, sweet rolls (freshly baked) for coffee time, chef's salad, sautéed sanddabs (small, flounder-like fish) for lunch, a fruit platter for teatime, six different hors d'oeuvres for cocktail time, Guinea hen *cordon bleu* with scalloped potatoes and buttered baby carrots for dinner. It's meals like those that help get *Carina* her 65 percent return-business average. With only a day between charters, the cook has a rough time keeping up his or her stores. Some charter cooks I've met were basket cases after a 15-week season. But charter cooks usually have one advantage over offshore cooks: Most charters are planned with stops in various ports, so the cook does have a chance to top up on specialty items along the way.

Race cooks, on the other hand, have the hardest cooking job afloat. When we were on the race committees for the Long Beach-to-La Paz Race and the Los Angeles-to-Acapulco Race, I had a chance to see some of the problems they face.

DAY 32. *Feeding two shifts of eight hungry racing sailors takes a special kind of cook.*

294

Some of the interviews for the section that follows were done in 1980, when I wrote the first edition of this book. As I read them a quarter of a century later, I am surprised at how little life has changed for the cook on a race boat. Yes, today's extreme racers—such as those who singlehand around the world, or people like Ellen MacArthur, currently one of the most successful of yachting's trophy-hunters—do everything possible to save weight, including restricting crew diets to freeze-dried items rehydrated with water made by the watermaker. But for the people who will be reading this book—whether preparing for an eventual cruise or for that first big job as cook for an offshore race—the words of wisdom shared by these cooks are still highly relevant and reflect the thoughts of each racing cook I have asked to review this chapter recently.

Cooking for a Long-Distance Racing Crew

Being a cook on a long-distance racing sailboat must be the hardest job afloat. Since the whole purpose of the voyage is to win—to push the boat and its crew to the limit—the cook is under tremendous pressures. No one considers shortening sail to give the galley crew a break. The cook has to be able to rush out in case there is an all-hands-on-deck emergency. He/she has to feed two shifts three times a day, plus snacks. Galley facilities may be limited. I've never cooked on any race that lasted more than three days, so I interviewed six different long-distance racers and cooks, trying to find the hints that made these sailors a welcome addition on board.

Sandy Mackenzie represents the maxi racers, since he has worked as cook on 73-foot *Windward Passage* during seven Transpac Races. Jim Hollywood, on his ultra-light-displacement Santa Cruz 30 just finished the 1,000-mile race between Long Beach and Cabo San Lucas. He represents the small end of the offshore ocean-racing fleet. In between are four more cooks on boats from 35 to 67 feet; each had suggestions that could help you be more prepared when cooking or provisioning for a long-distance offshore race.

Sandy Mackenzie's full-time hobby is joining maxi race boats for each of the major ocean races. He started when he crewed for Bob Johnson on *Zia*, a 75-foot ketch, back in the late 1950s. Someone on board had to cook a meal; he volunteered. Bob Johnson liked the meal, Sandy enjoyed cooking; the position stuck. Since that time, he has been cook on 73-foot *Ticonderoga*, 73-foot *Windward Passage*, 65-foot *Robon*, and, more recently, 79-foot *Kialoa*. His list of races includes seven Transpacs, Los Angeles to Tahiti six times, SORC seven times, Transatlantic once, Sydney-Hobart twice, Hong Kong to Manila, plus several others. Sandy is blue-eyed, trim, and fortyish. He wouldn't go to sea if he couldn't go to cook. "I like racing, but I don't like being out in the weather when I can be dry and warm next to the galley stove," he says. He takes care of all the provisioning, all the cooking, and usually all the cleanup during races. He stands no watches but says he "could be available in case of emergencies."

On *Windward Passage*, which carries a crew of 15 to 18 men, Sandy had no limit on his food budget, but he figures on US$6,000 to $7,500 (in 2005 values) for the average Transpac. The owner covers this. Although Sandy writes out a general meal plan for various races, these are only to be used as a shopping guide. At sea, it's open the freezer and see what interests the cook. His meal plans, however, keep some basic facts in mind: Racing crews eat more; most of the crew members on *Windward Passage* are 30-year-old businessmen straight from offices who may be prone to seasickness or have a tendency to be overweight; storage space is no problem as far as food supplies go, nor is weight; and finally, the freezer on this boat carries 20 cubic feet of food and will work 90 to 95 percent of the time.

Sandy does almost all of his shopping right at the local supermarket, looking for one that has a good butcher and a specialty section. Occasionally he'll buy a prepared meal from a specialty restaurant, such as the chicken prepared by the Rusty Pelican in Newport Beach, California. This prerace shopping now only takes Sandy about two days in an American port. But when he joins in a place like Hong Kong, he likes to have at least three days to shop and get readjusted before a race.

At least 90 percent of the food eaten on *Windward Passage* and *Kialoa* is prepared right at sea. Sandy is definitely a meat-and-potatoes sort of cook—fancy sauces and elaborate casseroles are reserved for the races that last more than 10 days. His typical menus include:

Breakfast	juice, sausage, cereal, eggs, toast, coffee
Lunch	soup, sandwiches, sometimes grilled sandwiches
Dinner	roast, salad, potatoes (baked or mashed), vegetables, cookies, beverage
Beverages	Tang (the main standby), Coke, 7-Up, Gatorade, lemonade, beer, tea, coffee (no hard liquor on board *Windward Passage* during races)

Sandy says that his menu plans rarely change with the weather. When it's particularly rough, he may substitute scrambled eggs for over-easy eggs. But he did mention one particularly rough Sydney-Hobart Race when hot soup was all anyone wanted.

Frozen, large-size packages of vegetables are a dinner mainstay: broccoli, beans, mixed vegetables. One crate of fresh oranges and apples, and another of lettuce, are stored in the lazarette. As things are used up in the refrigerator, Sandy brings in lettuce from the lazarette to extend its life. English muffins come out far better than toast for a large crew, and almost everyone prefers trail mix to candy bars. It seems that most of the crew hope to lose a few pounds and return home lean, mean, and tanned—with a few scars to prove they've been out ocean racing. A box full of candy tends to be hard for them to resist.

Sandy goes light on desserts, choosing Sara Lee frozen cakes and pastries for long races, strawberry shortcake for short ones. Leftovers are never a problem; they just don't happen.

Sandy had a lot to say about stoves. First and foremost was, "I hate alcohol stoves; bottled gas is the only way to go." Both *Windward Passage* and *Kialoa* have large propane, four-burner stoves with ovens and broilers. But *Kialoa's* stove has two ovens. "It's great," says Sandy. "I can cook two separate 12-pound roasts and feed a hot one to each shift of nine men." Gimbaling a stove as large as this is a problem. Sandy feels that most gimbaled stoves swing too easily: "They need lots of lead on the bottom." But life with gimbaled stoves has proven less than rosy for Sandy. In the 1972 Bermuda race, *Windward Passage's* stove came right out of its gimbals. Later, for the Sydney-Hobart Race, the crew added a 50-pound chunk of lead to the bottom of the stove to slow down its motion. Unfortunately, no one thought to check the stove at its most extreme angles before the race. When they hit the rough stuff, the lead lump caused the stove to land up on a bilge stringer. "I had to watch it every minute. If the stove stuck, everything on top came flying off the next time we surged over a wave!" From that experience and many others, Sandy warned, "Never stand in front of your stove during heavy weather. No matter how good the gimbaling, no matter how high the rails, someone could bump into you, then you bump the stove, a pot tips, and you've got a nasty burn."

Although freezers are a necessity on a race boat with crews as large as *Windward Passage's*, they are no less prone to failure than on smaller boats. Just before the Transatlantic Race, the generator started giving trouble. Mechanics worked through the night trying to find the problem. Just as the boat reached the starting line, the mechanics got off. Fortunately, Sandy had decided to lay in a supply of canned food, just in case. Unfortunately, five days later, when the electricity quit, he found out that the crew hated meat pies. "I tried making casseroles, adding spices, but there's no way around it—the results were awful," Sandy told me, adding, "With the electricity out, nothing worked. Good thing the stove was butane and we found a box of candles on board."

The storage areas of both *Kialoa* and *Windward Passage* are quite open, so Sandy keeps no stores list. But one comparison he makes bears repeating: "*WP* has all the cooking things in holes under the counter. I think that's a lot safer than *Kialoa,* where everything is in racks above the stove." He found two very special pieces of galley equipment on *Kialoa*. First was a 5-foot-long, gimbaled serving shelf right in the galley between the stove and the tables. The shelf is a perfect place to dish out nine bowls of soup or plates full of sandwiches. His second favorite item was a large rectangular griddle with 2-inch-high sides especially fabricated out of 1/4-inch-thick aluminum that completely covers the front half of the stove and two burners. Wooden caps on its ends act as handles. "I can fry up eight or 10 steaks at the same time that way. No worry about hot fat overflowing or steaks sliding off."

For pots and pans, Sandy prefers Farberware or Revere Ware with stainless-steel sides. Solid plastic mixing bowls and Tupperware bowls with covers are on his list, along with disposable foil pans for roasts. One other special item he carries to feed large racing crews is a set of Teflon-lined muffin tins. "I break an egg in each hole, bake them in the oven 24 at a time. They come out just like poached eggs—perfect for eggs Benedict."

On *Windward Passage,* all dishes and cups are good-quality disposable plastic, so there is very little galley cleanup. On *Kialoa,* dishes are heavy-duty plastic, which the crew helps wash. Sandy said he does all the galley work on *WP.* "These guys have sailed together for years. They've never been asked to help in the galley. They probably wouldn't like it. *Kialoa's* crew have always been expected to chip in, so there are no questions, no complaints."

Sandy plans on a half-hour for each meal for each watch: "That's all the time they seem to want." His meal schedule is:

Breakfast	0630	first watch
	0700	second watch
Lunch	1230	first watch
	1300	second watch
Dinner	1830	first watch
	1900	second watch

Seasickness worries Sandy a bit, because if he got sick, it would slow up the team effort. But he says seasickness is rarely a problem on *Windward Passage*—possibly because pierhead jumpers are discouraged. All of the crew are supposed to be on board two days before a race, to get acclimated and to help with last-minute preparations and decisions.

Sandy has tried cooking on cruising boats. He says it's easy. You can eat when you want; the crew pitches in to make their own sandwiches. But there is none of the excitement or thrill of being involved in big-league offshore racing. And that's why Sandy cooks.

Big-boat offshore racing has traditionally been a world closed to women. In the 1965 Transpac, Helen Henrickson was the only woman registered as crew on any boat over 38 feet in length. She only joined the crew of the 67-footer *Nam Sang* when absolutely no one else could be found to cook. I've met some of the men who sailed with Helen on that race, and their comments ranged from "good job" to "great!" But Helen said she'd never again volunteer to cook on a large racer: "It's just too much work, too much responsibility."

During the race, *Nam Sang* carried a crew of 11. Helen planned each day's meals, precooking a large ham, a turkey, and a sirloin roast. Then she stored the precut meat in the refrigerator. *Nam Sang* only had a small freezer, which was used for about 50 pounds of meat. Greens were stored in the hard dinghy, which sat upright amidships. Burlap bags covered the vegetables, and each day the cook wet down the bags to keep things fresh. All other stores were canned or packaged.

Helen definitely feels that today's racing cook has a better selection of canned goods available. She had only bacon, pork sausage, ham, or fish from which to choose. Helen now sails extensively on her own 36-footer and finds modern freeze-dried products a boon she could have used on *Nam Sang*.

One thing Helen told me was especially interesting in light of today's racing rules and concepts of super-fast sailing machines. The 1965 Transpac rules required every boat to carry a minimum of 30 days' stores, including 1/2 gallon of freshwater per man per day. The current racing rules only require 20 days' provisions and 1 quart of water per man per day in tanks separate from watermakers. When I commented that today's races take less time, Helen answered, "We finished on *Nam Sang* in 11 days and two hours; *Morningstar*, who beat us, finished in only nine days." I remember this, as I listened to the results of a recent light-air transpacific race out of Victoria, British Columbia. The boat first to finish, a ULDC, came in after 16 days; others finished after 20 days. Theoretically, under the new rules, their provisions could have run out.

Pat Walker joined 61-foot *Sorcery* as a cook because "that's the only way I could go! If I had my druthers, I'd be a watch keeper or deck hand. The cook has a lot more work, not much more recognition, but it's about the only position available for women on most offshore racing boats today."

Pat is a redheaded, elegant 40-year-old who'd look more at home at a board meeting or cocktail party than on the foredeck of a sailing yacht. In exotic foreign ports, she's often seen bound for a night on the town dressed in a long, slinky evening gown and mink coat she carries as standard equipment, along with her wet-weather gear and sea boots. Pat has spent most of her adult life working on boats ranging from 36 feet overall to ships the size of *Star of the Pacific*, a 3-masted schooner that's 138 feet on deck. The sheer magnitude of the cook's job on the schooner would have daunted any less-determined person. Its electric restaurant-style range had two ovens, each large enough for a 45-pound turkey. Food was stored in a walk-in freezer with a separate icemaker. Baking meant nine pies at a time; lunch called for menus including 60 grilled cheese sandwiches. Yet Pat told me that cooking for 19 people on the *Star of the Pacific* was far easier than taking care of 13 men on board *Sorcery*, even when the boat was between races. The main reason for this was that she had two galley helpers on the schooner and "the best of everything" in the galley. On *Sorcery*, the cook did everything on her own, including washing up, and dinnerware consisted of seven sets of plates, which had to be washed between each change of watches.

Pat joined *Sorcery* in Puerto Vallarta after the Marina del Rey-to-Puerto Vallarta Race. The cook on that race quit and returned home, so Pat took over for the voyage to Hawaii, Hong Kong, and Okinawa. During this time, the boat joined various day races and one long-distance race. After several months, Pat left from Okinawa and *Sorcery* continued on to Japan.

Cooks who join a race boat in a foreign port have special problems. Pat found that the previous cook had supplied many of his own pots, pans, and spices, and of course he had taken them home with him. "Next time I join a boat in a foreign port," Pat said, "I'll bring my own spices, my favorite knife, a decent frying pan, and measuring spoons." She really missed American supermarkets, and such foods as English muffins and prepackaged breads. She shopped at public markets and substituted local foods such as tortillas and chiles. With only four days to provision the boat in Puerto Vallarta, Pat was glad to have the help of some crewmen who ran after last-minute items such as bread and perishable vegetables. The owner put no limit on the budget and supplied liquor until there was a fiasco on the Okinawa Race. The owner had bought 40 cases of beer, and halfway through the 10-day race, the beer ran out. From then on, the owner declared, each man had to bring his own beer.

Pat says she is always pessimistic compared with the skipper when it comes to carrying emergency supplies.: "I add a week to his estimate and buy extra rice, flour, and powdered milk, just in case."

According to Pat, it's a good idea to make a meal plan of the main courses for any race that will last more than a week. It helps avoid repetition and guides the storage plan. In her planning, she tends toward mixed dishes rather than roasts: "Roasts large enough for 13 people take up a lot of space in the freezer and mean leaving the oven on for three or four hours. In hot climates, that's no good." Although Pat asks the owner about his preferences before planning her menus, she says it's a disaster to ask the crew.

Racing crews eat more than cruising crews. They never miss a meal and are burning up more calories; the cruising man might sleep through a few breakfasts or skip a meal to keep his weight down. So Pat buys about 25 percent more food for races.

Before leaving port, Pat tries to cook up at least a large coffeecake and as many main meals as possible. She uses disposable aluminum pans for such items as lasagna and casseroles, and the morning before the races, she makes up a big pile of sandwiches.

Real baking (such as a lemon meringue pie) is rare during a race. Coffeecakes in disposable pans fill the gap. Pat stocks a goody drawer with candy bars, raisins, and fruit for the crew. The stores lockers are off-limits.

Sorcery, like most class-A racers, has good cooking facilities. Stores go under bunks. There is a large pantry, and bread goes in with the sails. The freezer has a list of its contents taped to the top so those items can be found quickly to cut down cold loss. Pat commented that *Sorcery*'s stove had some burners that couldn't be used because of the position of the sea rails. *Sorcery* carries two big Thermos jugs in permanent holders—one for ice water, one for hot water. Pat gave these special mention.

Meal schedules were planned to fit watch changes. On short races, this was quite flexible, but on longer ones, it was up at 0530 for the cook, first breakfast at 0730, second at 0800. Pat found breakfast the worst meal of the day: "You can't let the eggs sit, and no one wants cold toast."

As cook on *Sorcery*, Pat did not stand watches, but she did work 12 hours a day, including occasionally helping to bag sails. On short races, where food could be prepared ahead, she was able to join the crew on deck more often. She did get the only bunk on board (other than the owner's) that didn't have to be shared.

According to Pat, there is no problem finding crew for class-A boats. On most, the sailing master is often the only person who always stays with the boat; cooks can change as often as every race. The attitude of the owner influences not only the life of the cook but also the spirit of the crew. If the owner expects the crew to help the cook, they will. If the owner appreciates his crew, isn't too tightfisted, and provides a good cook, a team is likely to form that stays together through race after race.

Women definitely have a harder time on racing boats. They have to work twice as hard to prove themselves, Pat says. But, she adds, "Any girl who has free time, is a decent cook, and is good-natured, can get a spot quite easily, especially in a foreign port." She warns, "Try to choose a boat with disposable dishes and try a short race first."

One crewman just to handle the cooking may be an ideal way to race, but on boats under 50 feet, it's just not practical. Besides, the cooking facilities on smaller offshore racers are rarely conducive to the type of menus maxi-race crews expect. So for the long-distance offshore races on boats 30 to 50 feet, most of the food preparation usually is done beforehand by wives or crew. Comprehensive menu plans seem to be standard, and often the weight of provisions is a major consideration.

Ed Greeff crewed and skippered in more than 20 Bermuda races. His wife, Betty, took charge of menu planning but rarely joined the crew for a race, as she prefers the cruising that comes afterward. For 30 years, the Greeffs owned and raced 47-foot *Puffin II*, a Sparkman & Stephens yawl.

The galley facilities on *Puffin* are planned with cruising in mind: an alcohol stove with an oven and a refrigeration unit but no freezer. The alcohol stove is a bit of a problem, because the flame can't be regulated easily. It tends to overcook food, especially the portions being kept warm for the second watch. The only solution Betty found is to carry three flame-tamers (asbestos pads that go between the pot and the flame).

Food storage is a problem on long-distance races with *Puffin's* full complement of nine crew. But Betty claims that racing crews tend to eat less than cruising crews because they are more prone to seasickness. This surprised me at first because of what I'd heard from the maxi-racer cooks, but as I spoke to other smaller-class racers, it became clear that seasickness is a problem that plagues class-C and -D races (50 feet and under) and the people who cook on them.

Betty plans her complete menu, then uses it as a guide for her shopping. Since fresh meat can only be kept for three days, canned meats form the main courses for the bulk of any race longer than seven days. *Puffin* has room to store fresh fruit and vegetables for 10 days, and Betty plans on two pieces of fresh fruit per person per day. But no other snacking is allowed during the day; it throws off the menu. Snacks for night watches include peanut butter, jam, crackers, nuts, and candy.

The Greeffs found that their crew prefer concentrated fruit-juice drinks to carbonated beverages. Concentrates also take up less room. One predinner cocktail is standard.

Lack of storage pace is the thread that ran through our whole conversation with the Greeffs. A boat built for cruising with six in comfort just doesn't have the room for elaborate stores for nine racing sailors. But Betty and Ed stressed that during a race, hot, dependable food counts more than fancy cooking. It's the party after the finish line that's the real goal!

Bill Lapworth, designer of Cal boats and an active ocean racer, told me, "Most people racing on 35-to-40-footers get lots of peanut butter and jam." In many cases, this may be true. One Cal 40 crew that was preparing for the Transpac wanted to remove the stove and table in order to save weight. Trail mix and freeze-dried meals were planned to lighten the boat further. This may have been a satisfactory solution, but for team morale and good health, I was far more impressed with the menu plans issued by Doc Holiday on board his Ericson 35 during two successful Long Beach-to-La Paz Races. In 1969, *Aquarius* took first in class. In 1975, she finished first in the Ocean Racing Fleet. Other *Aquarius* wins include the Puerto Vallarta race, Whitney series, and Ensenada Race twice overall.

Betty Holiday takes charge of the provisioning for offshore races but does not join the crew. She explained, "On *Aquarius* we had a total of six crew including the skipper. The crew shared in the food preparation in that I would have the wife of married men prepare one main evening meal, usually a meat dish or casserole. All meals were cooked in advance and put in disposable aluminum pans, wrapped with foil, then frozen. The watches were three men on, three off, so the food packages were servings for three. The single fellows contributed hors d'oeuvres for happy hour or canned meats, which were used the last days of the race when the ice was gone. You must remember that ours was a small boat, and all the crew knew each other very well and all were friends. We tried to have the best food possible with excellent French or domestic wine with each evening meal. The crew were all experienced deepwater sailors, most with boats of their own. They were taking time from their companies and professions to race on *Aquarius* and win. So food-wise, I really tried to keep them happy.

"Liquor was limited to one cocktail of their choice at happy hour, plus wine with dinner. Food was heated in the oven. Everything was precooked, and roasts were presliced, so if there was a malfunction of the stove, the crew could at least eat the food cold. They went strictly by the menu, so no decisions had to be made. They decided among themselves who would cook.

"Dry storage was a problem on the Ericson because she didn't have a bilge. In a knockdown, even a few quarts of water from the bilge would wet the storage lockers as high as the dish racks. So all the under-the-bunk storage compartments would be a little damp.

"Our icebox was very small but efficient. We carried 75 pounds of ice and put the frozen food on top, arranged efficiently according to the menu plan, plainly labeled. Every morning the menu was checked and the frozen evening meal taken out and allowed to thaw, so minimum time was needed for heating.

"Each canned meal was stored with all its ingredients together in a plastic bag labeled with the appropriate day. Alternate days' meal packs were put on opposite sides of the boat so the weight would be distributed evenly as the meals were used up. Any food that was not eaten and could spoil was discarded, as there was no room to store leftovers.

"Paper plates were used for all meals, plastic glasses for cocktails and wine. Each crew had his own labeled ceramic cup, which he kept clean or dirty himself. We used regular silverware because storage for plastic sets for three meals a day for 10 days takes a lot of room. There were a few sets of plasticware on board, so if the weather was rough, everything could be discarded. No Styrofoam was used, for obvious litter reasons.

"We had a sketch of the boat (see fig. 37) showing storage areas, which corresponded to the menu plan so the crew knew where to look for everything they needed. Ice was at a premium and was used only for cocktails. The race rules specified the amount of liquid required for each crew and not a drop more was carried."

The Holidays used the same basic meal plan for every long-distance race. As Betty said, "It works, everyone likes the food, and who cares if two weeks out of every year you get the same menu." The captain is expected to prepare the fanciest meal. Doc chooses Rock Cornish game hens stuffed with cheese and ham, which he freezes and then seals inside a dry-ice-packed Styrofoam chest. This is served at the halfway point of the race. Another crewman always provides a Chinese-style meal, which he spices by putting his own original fortunes inside each cookie.

For night watches, there is the usual goody drawer plus a Thermos of hot water to cut down the use of the stove. Betty has had some serious doubts regarding the use of the gimbaled stove at sea during a race and the tendency toward meals sealed in bags that are heated in boiling water. She feels that a pot of boiling water on top of the stove is extremely dangerous during a race. Betty told me about two recent cases of cooks being badly burned. One woman was boiling corn on top of the stove. She opened the oven to check her casserole and the open door changed the gimbaled stove's center of gravity. The boiling water and corn tipped onto the cook's arm and lower body, causing third-degree burns. In a second case, a crewman bumped the cook and the cook bumped the stove, upsetting a pot of spaghetti and again causing third-degree burns. So on *Aquarius,* all meals are heated in foil-wrapped pans in the oven. Betty also commented that meals in boilable bags have one other disadvantage: If the bag springs a leak while it is boiling, a complete meal can be waterlogged.

On *Aquarius,* cooking may be secondary, since all of the crew is needed to sail the boat. But the highlight of the day comes at cocktail hour and dinnertime.

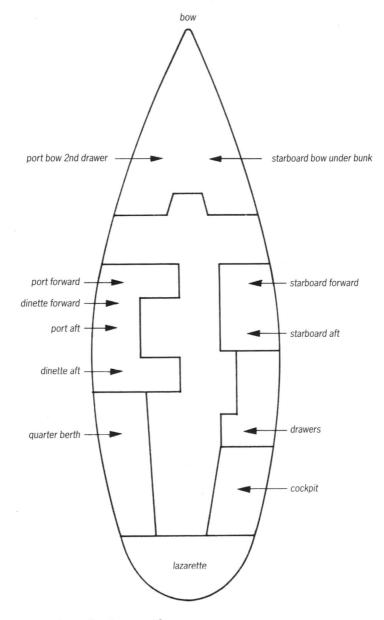

FIGURE 37. **Aquarius** *Storage Plan*

Menu Plan for Aquarius

SATURDAY

Lunch	Bring your own brown-bag lunch	
Supper	pot roast and vegetables	in oven
	sourdough garlic bread	
	lettuce, tomato, and avocado salad	lazarette
	salad dressing and croutons	galley locker
	red wine	
	cake—Hickory Farm, your choice	

SUNDAY

Breakfast	juice	
	scrambled eggs, 1 doz.	quarter berth
	canned mushrooms	
	packaged chopped ham and grated cheese	icebox
	salsa *(put a couple spoonfuls over each serving)*	
	banana bread	port bow
Lunch	poor-boy sandwiches *(heat in oven and add a package of Thousand Island dressing after heating)*	icebox
	carrot and celery sticks *(already cleaned)*	lazarette
	fruit	
	soup *(optional)*	dinette aft
Supper	sweet and sour pork	meat in icebox
	2 cans sweet-sour sauce	
	can mandarin oranges	stbd. aft.
	(heat these together with meat in large pan)	
	rice—follow instructions on box	dinette aft
	lettuce, avocado, and crouton salad	lazarette
	salad dressing	
	French rolls	port bow
	fortune and almond cookies	dinette fwd.
	rosé wine	stbd. aft

MONDAY

Breakfast	juice	port fwd.
	hash brown potatoes	dinette aft
	fried eggs	quarter berth
or	instant hot cereal	dinette aft
or	granola	
	milk for cereal	icebox
	date bread	port bow
Lunch	meatloaf sandwiches *(may be fried)*	icebox
	small loaf white bread	port bow
	pickles, relish, ketchup, etc.	galley
	chips and cookies	dinette fwd.

Supper	prime rib *(put in foil and heat in oven)*	icebox
	cans white potatoes with butter and parsley *(heat in same pan with meat)*	stbd. aft
	whole green beans—marked "Monday supper" *(cold with mayonnaise on top)*	
	sliced tomatoes and avocados	lazarette
	biscuits and honey	stbd. aft
	chocolate pudding	stbd. aft.
	red wine	dinette fwd.

TUESDAY

Breakfast	juice	pt. fwd.
	eggs Benedict	quarter berth
	ham	quarter berth
	English muffins	port bow
Lunch	chili	stbd. fwd.
	crackers	dinette fwd
	carrots and celery	lazarette
	cookies *(your choice)*	dinette
Supper	roast pork *(put in foil pan, add gravy, heat)*	icebox
	2 boxes instant mashed potatoes	stbd. fwd.
	asparagus tips *(cold)*	stbd. fwd.
	sliced tomatoes	lazarette
	mushroom gravy	icebox
	biscuits and honey *(2 packages)*	icebox
	rosé wine	
	date bars	dinette fwd.

WEDNESDAY

Breakfast	juice	
	French toast *(3 eggs and powdered milk)*	pt. fwd.
	2 cans corned beef	
	syrup and jelly	
Lunch	hot dogs	icebox
	buns	port bow
	pickles, relish, peppers	galley
	shoestring potatoes	port aft
	soup *(optional)*	dinette aft
Supper	shrimp cocktail *(serve in plastic glasses with chopped lettuce and avocado)*	icebox
	cocktail sauce	
	6 chicken cordon bleu *(Place chickens in foil pan, keep them wrapped so the cheese sauce won't run out. Heat up a can of chicken gravy if you wish, but I don't think it is necessary.)*	icebox
	rice	

canned peaches		stbd. fwd.
biscuits and honey		icebox
lettuce, artichoke, tomatoes, and avocados		lazarette
dressing		
white wine		
fruitcake		

THURSDAY

Breakfast	juice	
	hotcakes (use 2 eggs)	quarter berth
	Spam	
	eggs (fried)	
	syrup or jelly	galley
Lunch	fried cheese sandwiches	icebox and
	port bow	
	pickles and olives	galley
	fruit or cookies	
Supper	spaghetti and meat sauce	icebox
	(spaghetti and sauce in are together	milk carton
	already; add can tomato sauce)	stbd. fwd
	sourdough garlic bread (use garlic salt	
	from galley with butter)	port bow
	Parmesan cheese	
	lettuce, tomato, and avocado salad	
	salad dressing	lazarette
	red wine	stbd. fwd.
	Hickory Farm cake	stbd. fwd.

FRIDAY

Breakfast	juice	
	scrambled eggs with mushrooms	
	link sausages	
	salsa	
	apricot bread	port bow
Lunch	tuna sandwiches	
	small jar mayonnaise	
	pickles, peppers, chips	stbd. fwd.
Supper	canned corned beef	
	German potato salad	
	onions (heat)	port fwd.
	canned brown bread	
	cabbage salad	lazarette
	dressing	
	butterscotch pudding	
	cookies	
	red wine	

SATURDAY

Breakfast
juice
pancakes *(3 eggs, powdered milk)*
canned ham
fried eggs

Lunch
dried salmon
cheese spread
canned sardines
pickles
Ry-Krisp   stbd. fwd.

Dinner
canned turkey and gravy   pt. aft
cranberry sauce
instant mashed potatoes
green beans
canned brown bread
cabbage salad   lazarette
fruitcake
wine

SUNDAY

Breakfast
Tang
canned hash
eggs
dried orange toast

Lunch
tuna salad sandwiches
bread or crackers

Dinner
canned beef
potato pancakes
cabbage salad   dinette aft
cookies
wine

Emergency Meals Behind Dinette

MONDAY

Breakfast
Tang
cereal

Lunch
soup
open-faced cheese-spread sandwiches
candy
Kool-Aid

Supper   roast beef
          gravy
          potato pancakes
          three-bean salad
          candy

TUESDAY

Breakfast   Tang
             hotcakes
             coffee

Lunch   tuna sandwiches

Supper   Lipton's beef stroganoff
             garlic bread
             candy

WEDNESDAY

Breakfast   Tang
             hash and eggs

Lunch   soup
             crackers

Supper   macaroni topped with canned chili sauce
             canned brown bread

THURSDAY

Breakfast   Tang
             cereal

Lunch   soup
             sardines and crackers

Supper   Lipton's chicken casserole
             three-bean salad

FRIDAY

Breakfast   hotcakes
Lunch   tuna sandwiches
Supper   dried chipped beef
             instant mashed potatoes
             candy

SATURDAY

Breakfast   cereal
Lunch   soup
Supper   Lipton's stroganoff with tuna

Jim Hollywood had raced extensively with the Holidays on board *Aquarius*. So when he took his own Santa Cruz 30 on the 1,000-mile Cabo San Lucas Race, Jim chose to follow a proven example for his food. There was no built-in ice chest on the super-light-displacement *Mas Rapido*, so Jim bought two cheap Styrofoam iceboxes. One he packed with regular ice. The second he used for the meals planned for the last part of the race. These were prefrozen, then placed on top of dry ice. The chest was then sealed with two layers of duct tape and stored under the sail bags. Five days later, when the chest was opened, the meals were still frozen.

Mas Rapido had only a two-burner stove and a Sea Swing, so casseroles had to be heated carefully in their disposable foil pans. The most successful meal of the race—one that had the whole crew raving—was burritos. Jim simply fried up some ground beef and then set out flour tortillas, grated cheese, salsa, and chopped onions. Each person made his own burrito and ate it on top of the napkin without messing up any plates.

Whatever the size of boat on which you are racing, the cook's job is mainly one of organization beforehand. Good food helps the crew work harder. It also improves the morale and creates a team that works together to win races. I'll never forget reports that came from the first Round-the-World Race. Chay Blyth, on 80-foot *Great Britain II*, raved about the toughness of his paratrooper crew. They could race on C-rations and curry eaten with the one spoon carried for each man. But the Mexican entry, *Sayula*, a 65-footer, won the race, and her crew raved about prime-rib dinners, fine wines, and frozen strawberry desserts in the middle of the stormy southern seas.

Changes on the Racing Scene

With the quest for ever-lighter racing boats and the development of the IOR and IMS racing measurement rule, things have changed for cooks and crew on the most competitive maxis and pocket maxis. Galleys have been cut to the minimum, and freeze-dried foods have become the norm. The stove on *Brindabella*, the 65-foot winner of the 1991 Sydney-Hobart Race, had only two burners and a grill. There was no such thing as dining, and the crew depended on Cup-a-Soup, prepackaged meals, and cold snacks. The cook's job was more one of management—keeping track of provisions, making sure lots of hot water was available for soup and hot chocolate, cleaning up the litter.

For round-the-world racing, this quest for lightness has resulted in dependence on watermakers and minimum freshwater tankage. The racing rules now require tankage sufficient to provide only 1 quart of water per day per crew for the estimated length of the voyage if there is a watermaker on board. I feel that this could be dangerous, as engine and/or generator failure is definitely possible during the rough sailing that can be part of ocean racing. Watermakers can and do fail. In the 1991 race, one watermaker broke down a day before its crew reached Auckland. The crew had emptied the reserve water tank a few weeks earlier in an attempt to lighten ship for the drifting winds they'd encountered in the Tasman Sea. After that experience, they left Auckland with a complete complement of spares for the watermaker.

Not all serious racing skippers feel that this lightweight-rations approach pays sufficient dividends. Crew contentment counted for more on both of the French entries in the last Round-the-World race. Though many of their meals were supplemented with freeze-dried foods, wine was served with each main meal, along with an assortment of specially preserved cheeses and pâtés. As the cook on La Poste said, "A crew who has high morale might trim a sail better or steer better and gain us that tiny speed difference we lose by carrying 200 kilos more food on each leg of this race."

In the top echelon of racing, a dietitian will probably be employed to plan menus and may even go along as cook. One such dietitian I met in Auckland said she figured that the crew on the leg past Cape Horn would require 1,500 calories a day more than they did on the leg from England to Punta del Este. The extra calories would be chewed up by the effort their bodies made to keep warm in the extreme temperatures of the "screaming fifties." When I asked about providing heaters to help racing crew warm up between watches, the skipper on the boat said, "Too much weight." The dietitian/cook disagreed, claiming the same weight could have been saved because of needing less warmup food.

Costs are definitely higher if you use lightweight foods for your crew. As one owner noted, not only does the freeze-dried food cost more, the crew hate the rations so much that they insist on a day of the best eating in town before the race, and again as soon as they finish the race. "That costs me a bundle," the owner commented.

On boats under 50 feet and on lower-key large race boats, little has changed for cooks. Galleys may be a bit more sparse on all-out race boats. Microwaves are often used, and people swear by them when they work and swear at them when they don't. Cooks usually try to use the microwave when the generator is on for radio transmissions and battery top-ups, in order to cut down on fuel consumption.

Mary Thornton, who with her husband, Joel, loves both cruising and racing out of Seattle, reviewed this section just before we sent this third edition off to press. I thought you might find her tips interesting. "I have always enjoyed cooking on sailboats—what an ego trip to get so much gratitude for something that would barely get noticed at home," Mary writes. "I cruised the South Pacific for a year with my four sons (ages 2 to 13) and some of my best memories are of the meals we cooked and shared either on passages or in anchorages with friends.

"I have done the cooking for a lot of short Puget Sound races and Swiftsures [an overnight passage race] and a Pacific Cup [includes a race from Puget Sound to Hawaii]. So far I have been lucky in that I haven't had weather so bad that I couldn't manage to cook the meals I had planned. Your chapter is well done, and I can't think of much to add, but some of my tips are:

"1. I don't believe in disposable anything (except paper towels). I always pack the preprepared meals in reusable Tupperware and transfer to my cooking pots (deep ones) for heating. I had a friend who had one of the 'disposable' aluminum pans collapse as she took a hot pan of lasagna out of the oven, which resulted in a bad burn.

"2. If the weather is bad I serve 1-dish meals in deep solid bowls—paper bowls usually end up spilling and so far I have only had to 'bag' the dishes for delayed washing a few times.

"3. Alcohol on racing boats has become a bigger issue in recent years than I remember from the past. Lots of skipper/owners are having 'dry' boats, and I really am sympathetic with their reasoning. With the speed that things happen on racing boats, just a little alcohol can be dangerous, and it always seems that there is one crew who manages to have more than their share. When alcohol is allowed in moderation, I try to make the one drink special—a margarita with enchiladas for Mexican night, or a mai tai with the Hawaii menu for the halfway party. I think it is important that the cook be in charge of the alcohol on the boat. (That said, I love to surprise the night watch with a touch of Bailey's in their coffee or cocoa.)

"4. I love the cookie dough that can be kept in the freezer or fridge and a batch popped in the oven for a special treat. Those are great, and so are the refrigerated dinner rolls and biscuits. Most of the time, I don't think the crew knows that I didn't make them from scratch.

"5. The insulated coffee mugs that everyone carries around in Seattle are great on racing boats. Hardly any spills, and a cup of tea can stay warm for sipping through an entire watch. I try to have one for each crew member.

"6. The first few days of a race, there is bound to be a crew member or two who is seasick, and even the smell of food cooking is torture. I try to make really bland 'comfort food' for the first few days. Foods such as chicken stew with biscuits, mashed potatoes and meatloaf."

. . . .

Day 33

Noon to noon: 73 miles
Miles to date: 2,834
Light ESE winds; foggy, not so cold
Close-hauled; very calm sea in spite of large swell from SW

Lunch
>   potluck soup
>   Camembert, biscuits

Teatime
>   blueberry cream pie

Dinner
>   peas (Surprise brand freeze dried peas)
>   oven-browned potatoes
>   grilled Spam slices

. . . .

POTLUCK SOUP

Combine
>   leftover pork stew (about 1 cup, mostly gravy)
>   2½ cups water
>   1 package dried cream of mushroom soup
>   ½ onion, chopped
>
>   Bring to boil, stirring constantly.
>   Cover and simmer 8 minutes.

Add
>   1 cup cooked tuna chunks
>   ¼ cup red wine
>
>   Simmer 2 minutes more.

. . . .

BLUEBERRY CREAM PIE

Graham cracker crust

21 graham crackers, crumbled finely
¼ cup sugar
¼ cup melted butter
Mix well, then press into pie tin (or small frying pan).

Add

1 can pie filling (blueberry, cherry, whatever)
Bake at 350 degrees 15 minutes, until crust thickens and sets.
Let cool completely.

Combine

1 6-ounce can Nestlé's cream
2 tbs. sugar
1 tbs. rum
Spread over filling and serve.

OVEN-BROWNED POTATOES

Wash and cut potatoes into large chunks (leave skin on). Boil until they are tender but don't fall apart. Drain and place on cookie sheet or in baking pan. Dot liberally with butter, sprinkle with garlic powder, salt, and pepper. Place under grill and cook until browned, turning potatoes occasionally.

On Sinks and Counters

As a birthday treat for me, Larry offered to do all the dishes today and to cook dinner. It is a good chance for him to see how the galley works. Since he is in charge of research and development, he'll possibly have more sympathy for some of my requests. I must admit that my day is slightly emptier without cooking.

The sink drain plugged up today—a sure sign the sea temperature is dropping below 70 degrees F. Seems that any cooking oil or grease from canned meats coagulates at that temperature and forms a clot in the sink drain right at the waterline level. The cure? A pot full of boiling saltwater in the sink, then Larry squeezes on the sink drain hose—it always works. That's one good reason for having clear, flexible drain hoses. You can see the blockage and massage it along its way to the sea. Prevention: Don't pour grease in the sink; pour used coffee grounds down the drain once a day. They seem to absorb any floating grease and flush it away.

Our sink doesn't drain when we are hard on the starboard tack. That is one of the problems on small boats or those with deep keels and moderate freeboard. The way to get around this is to have the sink as near as possible to the centerline of the boat, but even this may not solve the problem.

Even if your sink is above the waterline when the boat is level, it may submerge when you are heeled well over. Therefore, it is imperative that you have a convenient shutoff valve for the drain. Kelly, a friend of ours who was new to cruising boats, had a real catastrophe when he set off on his new 30-foot racing-cruiser. He was hard on a starboard tack enjoying the exhilaration of a fresh breeze in the Solent. Since he was singlehanding, he didn't go below until an hour later, when he wanted a cup of coffee. His boat was filling with saltwater. As he went over each wave, a geyser of saltwater would shoot up through the sink drain. He came about on the other tack and pumped the 40 or 50 gallons of saltwater out of the bilges and cabin. Then he found the shutoff valve. The only problem was that the saltwater had been spraying over his new gas stove. Four days later, all the stove's parts were beginning to rust and corrode, and within six weeks Kelly had to buy a new stove.

If I had the space, I would definitely have double sinks on a boat. They give you that secure spot to put dirty dishes while you wash and rinse the others. One sink available for vegetables you plan to rinse or chop up, one for dishes you are using to cook with means that few things roll off the counter and onto the floor. Fiddles around the edge of the sink counter are never high enough to catch a whole cabbage or a large jar of mayonnaise.

While I am speaking about sinks and counters, I'd like to say that there is really only one material for both that works perfectly and lasts year in, year out. That is stainless steel. If you are fortunate enough to be able to get a fully molded, 1-piece sink and counter unit, you'll find it's easy to keep clean and rotproof. You can cut on it without worrying, and it will polish up beautifully, even 10 years after you install it. I know stainless steel is nowhere near as handsome to look at as our laminated maple drainboard was, but that maple had to be scrubbed and bleached every week. It got scratched if I was the least bit careless with my chopping knife. It rotted near the corner where the water gathered next to the sink, and it delaminated so that two years ago we had to replace it (which took four days' work and cost $145 in materials). We used laminated ash this time; it is more rot-resistant and again looks very handsome and white. But I know that next time I'd like stainless-steel counter tops, with a big, beautiful, but easily replaceable maple cutting board sitting on top.

Formica is a very poor choice for cutting-board or counter surfaces. It marks easily after it is only six months old. Since it is rarely applied with resorcinol glues, the plywood base under it usually starts to rot within a year or two, especially where any water faucets come through.

Fiberglass is slightly better in that it doesn't rot or delaminate, but it nicks quite easily when you are chopping vegetables. After a year, a fiberglass counter will lose its gloss and start to show scratches and stains.

To relieve the starkness of a stainless-steel counter top, I would still use teak fiddles like we have on *Seraffyn's* ash counter. They are 1 1/4 inches high and we leave them bare; to keep the fiddles nice-looking, we need only scrub them once a month with a pot scrubber. Galley fiddles should be at least 1 1/4 inches high in order to catch plates and bowls, but making them any higher creates too much of a barrier for the cook.

Maple cutting boards—or, in fact, any wooden chopping board you use—should have small rubber feet underneath. These feet keep the board from roaming around if there is any dampness on the counter top. They also elevate the board and let air circulate underneath it so that no mold, fungus, or insects start to grow on its bottom. I always remember Larry's story of one voyage he made to Honolulu on an 85-foot schooner. The cook was terrible. He kept the galley somewhat tidy, but his cooking was worse than uninspired. After two weeks at sea, the crew demoted the cook and took turns doing his job. On Larry's day, he decided to do a thorough cleanup of the galley. When he moved the big cutting board from its position on the counter top, he found the whole surface covered with maggots. Small, rubber, screw-in feet would have prevented this by allowing more air circulation.

To keep the wooden cutting board or drainboard on our boat looking good, I scrub once a week with bleach. I use straight bleach, let it sit for five minutes, add some cleansing powder such as Ajax, and scrub with a Golden Fleece or plastic Scotch-Brite pad. If it is sunny outside, I put the cutting board out to dry and further bleach out. Pure lemon juice will work almost as well if you are out of bleach.

One further item on sinks and cleaning: Never carry Brillo pads on board. They will rust almost instantly if exposed to salt air. The little metal strands will break off and create rust spots on any white paint you have. For pot scrubbers, use either Golden Fleece or plastic Scotch-Brite pads, available everywhere. And they are useful far beyond their service in the galley. Scotch-Brite makes a perfect scrubber for cleaning your boat's bottom when you are skin diving. It cleans teak decks and trim beautifully without digging out the soft summer grain, as bristle brushes do. Scotch-Brite can be used as a filter over the end of your bilge-pump hose. It can also be used as an insulating barrier or rattle-quieter when cans, dishes, or pots start rolling in a seaway.

Meanwhile, back to the North Pacific. With Larry's usual luck, it was so calm at dinnertime that he was able to set the table with our pewter wine goblets, a Japanese linen tablecloth, his version of fancy folded napkins, and silverware. It was a lovely treat to sit back and play the guitar while Larry cleaned up after dinner.

Galley Sink Upgrades

It is interesting to look back at my wish to have a stainless-steel sink/ counter combination when I was crossing the North Pacific on *Seraffyn*. The sheer practicality definitely sounded attractive. But when faced with the final decisions of outfitting *Seraffyn*'s big sister, *Taleisin*, we once again chose a stainless-steel sink set into a laminated ash countertop with ash fiddles surrounding it. The reason? Appearance. A solid slab of stainless steel would not have looked as attractive in the classic wooden interior.

Larry added two new ideas on *Taleisin* that have proven invaluable. The first is one that can be adapted for almost every galley. He made the

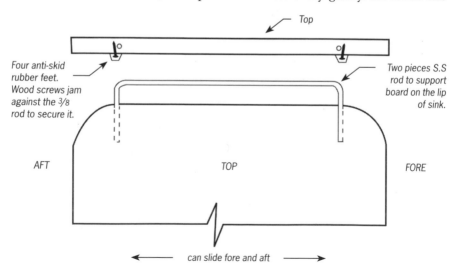

FIGURE 38. *Cutting Board for Galley Sink*

simple cutting board/galley sink cover shown in figure 38. Initially, he used the piece of laminated ash he had cut out to fit the sink—to create a board that matched the counter top. Later, when this became badly worn, friends in Brazil gave us a piece of local hardwood known for its durability and resistance to warping. That cutting board, with its rubber feet, is a daily reminder of our wonderful times around Rio de Janeiro.

For the first 14 years of our voyaging on *Taleisin*, we used the same sink-drain shut-off valve system as we had for *Seraffyn*. Each time we headed out for a sail, I turned the valve handle, which was in the locker directly under the sink. Only if we were on port tack did I open it so water could drain as I did the dishes. On starboard tack, I either bailed the sink into a bucket or washed dishes in a basin in the cockpit. Then, when we were outfitting to leave Rio de Janeiro, Larry reminded me that for the first time we were facing a voyage that was going to require going to windward for thousands of miles. We would be hard on the starboard tack for most of the voyage north to the Azores. That meant 15 or 20 days at a time with the drain closed off, and dishwashing would be a hassle.

I finally agreed to spend the money, adding the complication of more plumbing in the bilge and giving up some storage space. This let him install a two-way valve under the galley sink, plus a second 1 1/2-inch outlet hose that runs through two of my storage lockers and connects to the 10-gallon sump tank we use to catch gray water from our shower. On port tack or in port, the galley sink still drains as it always has, through a seacock in the bilge of the boat. On starboard tack, I swing the valve and the sink drains into the sump tank and it is pumped overboard once every few days. The valve is very easy to access (see fig. 35, page 267). I can readily see whether it is open or closed. The only small drawback is that small bits of food, coffee grounds, and grease from dishes mean we need to clean out the sump tank once yearly. I sure wish I had been more interested when he first suggested the idea 15 years earlier.

. . . .

Day 34

Noon to noon: 87 miles
Miles to date: 2,930
Foggy, close-hauled, fresh breeze

Lunch
onion-and-garlic omelet
fried chopped ham
blueberry pie

Dinner
chicken-tomato casserole

. . . .

CHICKEN-TOMATO CASSEROLE

Into greased bread tin, put
1 layer cooked noodles (linguine or similar style)
1 layer canned tomatoes
1 layer sliced onions
sprinkle of oregano
Repeat layers.

Top with
canned chicken, in chunks (and juice)
Sprinkle with
¼-inch layer of bread crumbs

Add
light layer of grated Parmesan

Bake 35 minutes at
about 375 degrees.

. . . .

Cooking at a tilt is always frustrating, especially with the pitching motion of a small boat going to windward. Today was no exception. That is why I scratched the idea of baking fresh bread when the wind got up a bit. Seems like I made a good choice, because by dinnertime the wind started to back, and now at 2030 we are on a fast beam reach for the first time in two weeks. If this keeps up, tomorrow I'll enjoy a baking spree.

On Lighters and Matches

Nowadays, many stoves have piezo lighters installed to help the sailing cook. No longer do you have to search for a match before you can cook. But it is still important to carry a good lighter or waterproof matches for those times when moisture gets on the piezo ignition, for lighting oil lamps in the evening, or for those barbecues onshore. The flame on these long-snouted lighters can be adjusted so you can reach burners under a hot pot without getting your fingers close to the heat. They work well for burning the ends of lines to seal them (Brion Toss calls this "the infamous butane back splice"), and they have a large-enough fuel chamber to let you heat-seal the edge of a sail patch with only one refilling. It is best to buy these lighters in countries such as the United States, Australia, and South Africa, where barbecuing is a regular pastime. They are almost impossible to find elsewhere. We find that one can of refill butane lasts a year, and we depend on these lighters for the eight oil lamps and the oil heating stove we have on board.

The butane lighter will not work if it gets soaked with saltwater, so for safety, we also carry a few boxes of waterproof matches in a kit of small items near our medicine locker.

. . . .

Day 35

Noon to noon: 131 miles
Miles to date: 3,061
Cold, drizzling; fresh S wind
Beam-reaching over a growing swell

Lunch
leftover casserole (reheated by adding a few tablespoonfuls
of water and covering with aluminum foil, then warming on
top burner)

Dinner
fresh, hot whole-wheat bread
butter, honey
baked salmon loaf and onion sauce
baked potatoes
steamed cabbage

. . . .

By noon, we were screaming along at $5\,3/4$ knots. The barometer fell by
3 millibars in two hours, occasional rainsqualls swept by, and whitecaps
crowned half of the waves. So I decided it would be wise to prepare for a blow.
I set bread to rise and planned a fish loaf so I'd have leftovers for tomorrow
in case it grew real rough. But by dinnertime, the barometer started rising
slowly, the seas grew steadier, and our speed dropped to $5 1/2$ knots, with one
reef in the mainsail and the lapper set.

Dinner was a success. The hot oven warmed up the boat wonderfully
and also dried out Larry's boots so we could patch them.

On Preserving Butter

Canned butter is definitely the easiest way to solve the butter dilemma,
but it is not easy to find in the United States. One brand that you can
often order is Dairygold, which comes in 1-pound cans. According to the

manufacturer, it requires refrigeration, but we have found that it lasts well without refrigeration for up to three months if stored in the lowest part of the boat. This butter is delicious and tastes just like fresh, although it has a bit more salt in it, which we both like. In the Far East, you can often buy canned Australian or New Zealand butter, which is also good.

On the other hand, preserving your own butter isn't difficult, and it's definitely cheaper. In Malta, where excellent butter costs only about 75 cents a pound, we bought 15 pounds of butter in quarter-pound cubes. I sterilized old peanut-butter jars by immersing them completely in boiling water for two minutes, then lifting them out with sterile tongs and placing them on a clean surface to cool under a clean towel. I boiled a quart of freshwater and added about 5 tablespoons of salt, then I let it cool. After putting two cubes of the butter into each jar, I filled the jar to overflowing with the cooked saltwater mixture. Larry screwed on the tops as tightly as he could. We stored these right away with our canned supplies. The butter kept for up to five months, even though we were in places such as the Red Sea, where water temperatures were close to 90 degrees F.

When we opened each jar of butter, we rinsed it once with freshwater. The butter tasted the same as it had the day it had been put up.

Margarine purchased in individual plastic tubs is a good substitute for butter. We've kept the unopened containers for up to four months with no spoilage.

. . . .

Day 36

Noon to noon: 131 miles
Miles to date: 3,192
Force 7 beam reach; intermittent rain, fog

Lunch
salmon loaf sandwiches topped with sweet pickles
tomato soup

Dinner
sloppy sea soup
bread, butter

· ·

 SLOPPY SEA SOUP

Combine in saucepan
1 can whole tomatoes
1 onion, in chunks
1 can kidney beans
1 tsp. oregano
2 tbs. sugar
1 tsp. garlic powder
1 tsp. chili powder

Bring to boil, then simmer 5 minutes.

Add
1 large can (1 lb.) stewing beef or stewing pork

> Heat until boiling.
> Serve with bread
> and butter.

· ·

I don't think this soup is as good as the raves it draws. I just think anything hot and spicy that you serve on a day like today will seem like ambrosia.

Today is one of those times when I remember the gentleman at the yacht-club bar in England who said, "I can't understand you chaps who go out of sight of land for weeks at a time and don't wash and all that rot."

We seem to be leaping from wave top to wave top. It's damp as hell, and we need two sweaters to keep warm in the cabin. The stove is festooned with socks hanging to dry. If you stick your head outside, you are likely to get a faceful of spray. Slicing a piece of bread is almost an acrobatic feat. Thank God I prepared something yesterday when I saw the barometer taking a plunge.

Clothes for Offshore Sailors

A rollicking trade-wind sail; sunshine and sparkling seas; a cold and windy night beam-reaching across a boisterous sea; dinner and dancing to the sound of mariachis at a lovely resort in the far reaches of Baja California; an exhilarating climb to the top of a volcanic peak in the Azores—all are part and parcel of offshore voyaging. The adventure that lies ahead may last six months, a year, or even longer, so your offshore wardrobe must be adaptable enough to carry you through changes of season and changes of lifestyle. But the space limitations on board a cruising boat demand that you be discriminating about what you choose to carry—a tall order for the first-time voyager.

The single most important component of your sailing wardrobe is foul-weather gear. We find it really pays to buy two sets. The first set: relatively inexpensive, lightweight gear (usually called Inshore, Breeze, or Lightweight in the catalogs) for tropical sailing and for those days at sea when it is raining but not too blustery. This gear is less bulky, so it lets you move around more easily, and it dries more quickly below decks. Because it is easier to stuff into a small carry bag, we carry this lightweight gear for sojourns ashore. If it gets lost or damaged, it is far less of a drama (i.e., less expensive to replace). Because we use this lighter gear the majority of the time, it tends to need replacing every two or three years.

The vast range of prices for various brands of heavier foul-weather gear can make this choice very difficult. At times in our sailing career, we have paid for the best-known name brands; at other times, we have chosen the less-expensive generic brands. Our experience has shown that if you get the features you want, and you are not concerned about making a fashion statement, the generic brands are a good choice. We have also found that few cruisers need the extreme-weather gear sold to offshore racers. When we were preparing to sail south from the Atlantic, around Cape Horn to the Pacific, I insisted that we spend the money on the best extreme-weather gear we could find. After intensive comparison shopping, I backed off and chose West Marine's Explorer breathable gear—not their more expensive offshore gear—because it was less bulky yet still offered the features I needed. I'd choose it again.

The sleeves on your foul weather gear should have Velcro-adjustable inner storm cuffs, with outer cuffs that can also be snugged up. The pants cuffs should be easily adjustable to keep rushing water from sneaking up your legs. Suspender attachments should be easy to clip and unclip, even when wearing gloves. Check the zippers on any gear you buy—the bigger the zipper teeth the better. Always choose plastic zippers. Avoid aluminum zipper cars. They tend to fail and need replacing after a year of offshore use.

Do not buy white or dark-blue foul-weather gear. Bright yellow, orange, and red are the best, as any of those colors will be more visible in a man-overboard situation. I remember trying to keep an eye on Larry in our white dinghy when he went to help rescue a launch that had broken its mooring during a storm in Knysna, South Africa. The only thing that stood out in that rainy, windy, whitecapped bay was his red foul-weather jacket.

Gina Salares used a pair of women's bib-style foul-weather pants with a drop seat for her voyage from New Zealand though the Pacific islands. When she reported in after the first six months, she had found them very satisfying. They have a side zipper that lets the seat be opened without removing the bib.

When you are trying on heavy-duty gear, put on three or four layers of clothing, just as you will on very cold nights at sea. Wrap your arms tightly around your body, then stretch as if you were trying to climb up a ladder. If the jacket binds across your shoulders, or if the inner cuffs pull up your arms when you reach above your head, go for a larger size. I like the arms of my jacket to reach to the end of my thumbs when my arms are at rest, and the cuffs of my pants to sit just at my ankle before I tighten the Velcro straps. Put fashion aside as you shop for this gear. Looser is definitely better than close-fitting if you want to be able to move easily and keep the water outside, where it belongs. You'll also find it less fatiguing than clothing that binds each time you try to move. If at all possible, buy your gear in person. If you have to order by mail, be careful to emphasize whether the gear is for a man or woman. We once sent our measurements to one firm that offered to alter gear to fit at no extra cost. The size they supplied to me was "boys' large" (with the legs and arms shortened to fit). Unfortunately, the gear was too narrow around the hips, and I had to have a pleat put in the jacket before I could use it.

Foul-weather gear must be comfortable and as light as possible. It also must be loose enough so you can add an extra layer or two of inner clothing yet still be able to move about quickly. I wore mine almost every day for the three months we sailed near Patagonia, the Beagle Channel, and south around Cape Horn.

Your sea boots should be roomy enough to hold your feet, a pair of cotton socks, and some heavy wool socks and still be loose enough to pull off easily. There may come a day when you end up overboard and have to swim to a life ring or climb up the side of your plunging boat. If you can't get those boots off fast, their waterlogged weight could spell the difference between life and death.[11] We like 16-inch-high, relatively stiff-topped sea boots because, for wet-weather sailing, we can use what we call the "fireman's fast-pants drill." We shove the foul-weather pants down over the top of the boots, step out of the boots, and leave the pants and boots together, ready for the next use. I am slightly reluctant to recommend specific brands, as products often change in quality and availability, but after four years of extreme use, I definitely feel the 16-inch Offshore boots sold by West Marine for less than US$50 are a real bargain. I especially like the small knob on the back of the heel that makes it easy to get the boots off without using your hands.

Waterproof sailing gloves have proven problematic for us. Most are hard to dry when water gets inside. Though we carried brand-name specialized gloves for our Cape Horn adventure, in the end we went back to using our old standby—large fishermen's gloves over heavy cotton gloves. We both had two pair of each, so one pair was always hanging over the stove drying.

Foul-weather-gear storage should be as close to the companionway as possible, with hooks for hanging gear while it drips dry. I am not impressed with enclosed foul-weather drip-off lockers, as I find it is better to have the gear highly visible until it is fully dry before putting it away in any enclosed (read: less-ventilated) spot. On the other hand, we have come to accept the fact that all wet gear, no matter how carefully aired and stored, will eventually develop unsightly but harmless mildew spots. We do try to wash the gear in freshwater two or three times a year while we are cruising. This gets the salt out of the inside so the gear dries more quickly at sea and feels less clammy.

A huge array of sailing shoes is available today: strap-on sandals; thongs; canvas-topped footwear; traditional leather-topped mocs. For daytime sailing, any of these might work. But for offshore voyaging or racing—where you will have to be moving around on deck at night—or for whenever you will be working quickly under the pressure of changing winds, such as during squalls, it is imperative that you buy boat shoes that will offer protection for your toes. Choose either shoes with leather uppers or enclosed cloth shoes with well-padded toe guards. Also, look for boat shoes with a tight pattern on the nonskid sole. Many of the more open-patterned soles pick up rocks and pebbles from shore, which can damage decks and cabin soles.

Even if you plan to cruise only in middle latitudes, cold-weather clothes are a must. Not only will you have occasional cold nights as you reach toward

. . . .

11   Fishermen's sea boots usually have a hole right below the top at the back of the boot leg. They keep a string through here—not just to hang the boots in a storage locker but also for man-overboard emergency situations. If they find themselves in the water, they remove their boots, empty out the water, tie the two together, put one boot under each armpit with the line across their back, and have instant buoyancy.

the tropics, you'll also find areas within the tropical seas—such as near the Galapagos, at the northern end of the Red Sea, in the Sea of Cortez during winter months—where night temperatures drop dramatically, especially if you encounter headwinds (the wind-chill factor). Even before we headed out of the middle latitudes, we found it important to carry two complete sets of cold-weather clothing on board at all times. Our forays north to Norway and then to far southern latitudes taught us the importance of layering—starting first with snug-fitting long johns and T-shirt, then a looser lightweight sweater, then a bulkier sweatshirt.

With the advent of excellent synthetic fabrics, I find I no longer need to feel like a teddy bear to keep warm in near-freezing sailing weather— nor is it necessary to spend a lot of money on this gear. We set off on our Cape Horn expedition outfitted with specialty expedition-quality inner clothes. In Mar del Plata, Argentina, I was taken to a shop that sold clothes for gauchos, the men who work on horseback out on the windswept plains of Patagonia. There we purchased an extra set of inner clothes for a quarter of the price we had paid for the specialty items. We found absolutely no difference in the warmth and wearability of the gear. Tightly woven jeans over long johns work well with wet-weather gear, providing the extra layer for frosty, windy days. A ski toque and soft knitted scarf around your neck will cut out stray gusts for nighttime sailing. With this gear on board, we have not only handled the cooler nights at sea but also been prepared when folks we have met along the way invited us inland for a few days of skiing or a horse journey into the mountains of their homeland.

At the opposite end of the weather scale is the dream picture of sailing, beautiful sunshine, basking nude on deck in the tropical breezes. It sounds grand, and there will be times when it feels grand too—at anchor in a beautiful bay with the sun awning stretched across the boat, or late in the evening when the sun is low on the horizon. The rest of the time, it is important to cover up and protect your skin from the heat and UV rays of the sun. For comfort and convenience, we find that long-sleeved, light-colored cotton men's shirts are excellent. During the heat of the midday sun, they actually made us feel cooler than being completely without clothes. A bonus to wearing lightweight shirts is what Larry calls his "poor man's air-conditioning." We keep a squeeze bottle of freshwater in the cockpit during hot sailing days and wet down our shirts periodically. The cooling caused by the water evaporating feels absolutely grand. These shirts also can be used to protect yourself from sunburn when you swim or snorkel in the tropics.

In spite of the desire to go native when you reach foreign shores, and to reduce your wardrobe to shorts and bikinis, I'd recommend that every cruising person keep some special dress-up clothes on board. Margaret Irvine, a delightful Australian artist we met in Greece, cursed her friends back home who had told her not to take along any fancy dresses on her 2-year cruise. She'd been invited to spend an evening at a local formal dining-and-dancing spot with folks she had met onshore, but her family's cruising budget couldn't stretch to buy some new shoes, a dress, and a sport jacket for her husband. So they missed a grand time. Since you'll be meeting new people in new places each time your dressy clothes are called into use, one or two sets will be sufficient. Larry carries a corduroy blazer jacket, which passes for "jacket and tie" evenings in British yacht clubs or in casinos. I carry the traditional little black dress, plus a slim, long black skirt, velvet shirt, and a bolder wrinkle-resistant dressy outfit that seems to cover all occasions.

For everyday tropical cruising life, try to stick to cotton as much as possible. Although it is slightly harder to care for, it helps prevent rashes—unlike synthetic fabrics, cotton absorbs perspiration and allows your skin to breathe and also is less likely to harbor bacteria. Choose cotton or cotton-lined underpants for tropical use to avoid crotch rashes or, for women, cystitis, both of which can be encouraged by persistent perspiration. (See "Health and the Cook," page 218, for more on this subject.)

Carry some shirts or shifts that can be used for quick coverups when you leave your boat for a row ashore. It is amazing how respect for local dress customs will improve your cruising life. We spent three weeks secured at Marina del Sol, in Rio de Janeiro, only 6 kilometers from the bold and brazen beaches of Copacabana, where thousands of women strolled in bikinis so small they were locally called *fila dentale* ("dental floss"). The café owner at the marina, however, made it clear he would not serve anyone who came to his shoreside table without shoes and a shirt. Though local custom worldwide seems to allow for men to wear Bermuda shorts onshore, I have found I get pinched or nudged less in Italy and North African countries, and also get better service, if I choose a skirt instead of shorts.

An excellent addition to a woman's cruising wardrobe is the pareau worn by many women in the South Pacific and along the rim of the Indian Ocean. This piece of light cotton—2 meters long by 1.2 meters wide—can be wound around your body in a dozen different ways. It can be draped over your shoulders as a sun protector or shawl when cool breezes chill you after a swim; it can be draped from a tree to provide shade. In its most elegant guise, I have worn a hand-painted Tahitian pareau as an evening dress. Look for the finest of these in Papeete, Suva, Mauritius, and Singapore. If you ask the local salespeople, they can show you a dozen ways to tie these lengths to create an endless wardrobe.

Although going barefoot feels wonderful, it is a dangerous pleasure in tropical climates. Not only is there a chance of stepping out of your dinghy onto a stingray or a black sea urchin hidden in the sand, but staph-type infections thrive in the dust of tropical villages. The slightest nick on a toe, or an open blister, and you can pick up infections that will turn into boils that can ruin a month of your cruise. As you fossick alongshore or search for dinner on a nearby coral reef, nylon-strapped sandals, water socks, or tennis shoes are a must. Rubber flip-flops may seem handy, but wear them with caution. A sailing friend lost his wife in Telok Intan, Malaysia, when she was carrying a load of groceries across the deck of another yacht onto her own, which was tied alongside. As she stepped over the lifeline of the first yacht, her damp, sweaty foot slipped off the sole of the rubber flip-flops. She tripped, hit her head on the toerail of her own boat, broke her neck, and died instantly.

A final note on shoes. If you enjoy walks ashore, buy good walking shoes before you set off; in less-developed places, we found the quality and selection to be quite poor. On the other hand, you can find inexpensive beach shoes, handmade leather sandals, and fine everyday shoes as you cruise, so don't carry any extra on board or you'll miss shopping for lovely handcrafted shoes along the way.

Clothes kept on a boat do require extra care. They need airing three or four times a year. If they are in a hanging locker, they must be tied down before each passage, or the motion can cause hangers to wear holes through the shoulders of your favorite jacket. For rarely used items, and for leather goods such as Larry's favorite jacket and our horseback-riding boots, I use heavy-duty plastic bags like the ones used to vacuum-pack meat (if necessary, I buy them from butcher shops). I then squeeze as much air out as possible and use wide packing tape to create a seal.

As I always remind folks who attend our seminars, people all over the world eat. So even if you do not have the perfect array of provisions on board, you will always be able to find food to buy as you cruise. The same holds true for clothes—even wet-weather clothing. Though you may save money by having all the right clothes on board before you set sail, you can buy additions to your cruising wardrobe as you voyage. On the other hand, just as proper food promotes a healthy, happier crew, the right clothes can add to your health, safety, and pleasure as you sail toward new experiences.

. . . .

Day 37

Noon to noon: 100 miles
Miles to date: 3,295
Hove-to, storm winds; in evening, set para-anchor to keep
the bow of the boat riding at about a 50-degree angle to the
wind and waves of the rising storm[12]

Lunch
    leftover soup
    Camembert
    bread, butter

Dinner
    tuna and baked beans
    (eaten from the can and swilled down with rum-and-water)

....

Cook is miserable. WWV Honolulu reports this storm has a gale radius of
600 miles and storm-force winds within a 300-mile radius. We are less than
200 miles from its center. Another storm is forming in the North China Sea;
I hope we can get to Canada before that one hits us, too!

Long-Distance Cheeses

Cocktail nibble, late-night snack, sandwich filler, main-course "extra"—
cheese can be one of the most versatile ingredients in a cruiser's galley.
The addition of tasty chunks of spiced feta can change a boring salad into
a gourmet treat. A hefty spread of toasty, melted mature Cheddar can top a
simple onion soup to turn the grayest day five shades brighter. But buying,
preparing, and keeping a variety of cheeses afloat and edible for long periods
does take planning.

....

12   For more about heaving-to and using a para-anchor, see our book Storm Tactics and/or the
     DVD by the same title—both available at www.landlpardey.com.

If you enjoy the flavor and texture of long-life processed cheese products, such as Kraft Cheddar, you'll have little problem finding them worldwide. I was surprised to see three brands of boxed, processed cheese in the most isolated African villages, clad in the same packaging I'd seen in Aden and in the Tuamotus. These processed cheeses last up to two years with no refrigeration, as long as they are kept in their sealed containers. Cut into half-inch cubes and skewered with pickled onions or green olives, they make a fine cocktail snack for a cruisers' picnic—not wondrous, but definitely edible. Grated, processed cheese adds variety to salads. But this manufactured milk product is no substitute for unprocessed cheese in cooking, as it does not melt and brown, so it can cause some cheese-dependent recipes to fail.

Grated Parmesan cheese also keeps well afloat, with no care other than protection from moisture. I find it is best to avoid cardboard tubes of Parmesan and instead buy sealed plastic pouches. The humidity afloat will cause the cardboard container to soften and the cheese to mildew. If you have been at sea long enough to use up your fresh cheese, a good quick-browning cheese topping for casseroles can be made by making a mixture of equal parts Best Foods (or Hellmann's) mayonnaise and grated Parmesan cheese, plus a few drops of vinegar, and then grilling or baking. This same mix works for cocktail treats. Put a dill pickle slice on a small round of toast, top with a mound of the Parmesan-mayo mix, and grill until browned.

The cheeses we depended on during passages on 24-foot *Seraffyn* were canned Brie and Camembert. We try to buy the Danish brands, which are not stored in the refrigerated section of the market. If we were only able to find cans (usually packed inside small, flat, square cardboard boxes) that were marked "keep refrigerated" or "keep cool," I still bought a dozen for each passage. In our experience, these last up to six months if stored low in the boat, where temperatures are the same as the outside water temperature. In tropical waters, I would only count on two months. These cheeses do age in their cans. Most of them fortunately are marked with a "use by" date. I look for ones near their expiration date, as I found that we like the texture and flavor of more-aged Brie and Camembert.

To enjoy a wider variety of cheese—such as Cheddar, Edam, or feta—you can try several preservation ideas. Sailors with freezers can seal Cheddar in plastic containers in the upper area of the chest. The cheese will be more crumbly when it is defrosted, so it is wise to select younger Cheddars for preservation this way. The flavor will change very little if the cheese is well sealed. Water-packed cheese, such as feta, will freeze well as long as there is more space inside the container to allow for expansion of the liquid. But I have never been satisfied with the flavor or texture of Edam or Colby cheese kept this way.

Simple refrigeration or icebox storage in sealed containers works well for cruises that last less than three weeks (and the majority of passages we make fall within this time limit). If you can get small waxed cheeses and store them so the wax stays intact, they will keep perfectly for up to two months at temperatures below 55 degrees F. Unwaxed cheese should be wiped lightly with vinegar and then wrapped in plastic wrap and stored where it will not be bumped around too much. If any mold forms, cut it off and wipe the cheese with vinegar again. If you prefer using plastic cheese boxes rather than wrapping each cheese separately, be sure to wipe the whole inside of the box with vinegar once a week to discourage mold formation. Since mold does not penetrate more than a fraction of an inch below the surface of a hard cheese, it is most economical to buy one large chunk rather than several smaller ones. About once a week, cut off the cheese you plan to use for the next meals, remove any mold from the main supply, and wipe it down with vinegar. Your loss due to mold will be reduced by up to 50 percent this way. (When I have had room in my ice chest for 2-kilo blocks of Cheddar, such as sold by many ship chandlers, I tend to lose 8 to 10 percent of the cheese to mold during a month's cruise.)

I learned a lot about preserving cheeses by questioning the people who sell their own produce at farmers' markets around the world.

Water-packed feta will last for two months under refrigeration or on ice. But when we were reprovisioning *Taleisin* in Fremantle, Australia, the proprietor of the Mousetrap cheese shop taught me an even better way of preserving and improving the flavor of feta with no refrigeration at all. Simply submerge the feta in pure olive oil in any sealed container. The feta that I put in olive oil (I used the oil straight from its container; I did not preheat it in any way), stored in a clean glass pickle jar, lasted more than a year in the bilge during a cruise through the Indian Ocean, with no apparent change in flavor.

The same cheese specialist taught me a wonderful way to create what can only be called "gourmet feta." I clean a 1-gallon pickle jar and fill it loosely with 2-inch cubes of feta. I then pour 3 tablespoons of green peppercorns on top of the feta and shove about 10 inches of fresh rosemary into the jar. Then I fill it with fresh olive oil—to within one inch of the top. As a substitute, you can use 1 tablespoon of black peppercorns, plus several bay leaves—or green and red sweet-pepper flakes if you do not like things that are spicy hot. After three months, it will be at its prime. You can add fresh feta to the oil at any time, but before you do so, be sure to dry the cheese well by letting the water in which it was stored drain off for at least 10 minutes. Then just pat it dry and shove it in. I do like to wait until I have used enough of the original cheese so I can place the fresh supply below the more-spiced cubes without making a mess with the olive oil.

To serve this oiled feta in salads, I use it as it comes from the jar, and even use some of the spiced oil as a dressing. For hors d'oeuvres, I drain the feta on a paper towel before slicing it onto crackers or toast. The texture of the cheese becomes creamier as it ages. After six months, the feta packed in green or black pepper becomes a bit stronger than I like, so I transfer any that is left to plain olive oil. The plain oil can be reused for up to three years. The spiced oil can be used two or three times, but after 18 months, mine became cloudy and less appetizing-looking, so I discarded it and began with fresh oil.

Hard Cheddar can also be kept this way. I put up five kilos of it in plain olive oil before we left Fremantle, and it didn't change flavor or texture for three months. After that, I detected a slight flavor change that was noticeable if we used the Cheddar as it came from the jar. But when mixed with other ingredients and cooked in any way, the cheese tasted just fine.

Olive oil will try to leak out of everything! So I store my big cheese jars inside a bucket in the bilge; I line the bucket with old newspapers to absorb any leakage. A bit of trouble, yes, but what a treat that spiced cheese becomes when all your other fresh food is a memory.

Dorothy Skeates, who cruised extensively for several years on *Wylo II*, a boat with spartan facilities, and then worked as a charter cook along the Great Barrier Reef, still waxes her own cheeses to keep them for up to six months. She chooses firm cheese and cuts it up to the size she'll use in one week. She then wipes each chunk with vinegar and wraps it in three layers of muslin that has been soaked in a solution of equal parts boiled water and boiled vinegar and then sun-dried. Each cheese is painted with melted candle wax (called paraffin wax in the United States). She coats each cheese three times to be sure it is perfectly sealed. The cheeses are then stored below the waterline, well wrapped in newspaper to prevent the wax from breaking. This method is more labor-intensive than the others listed, but the waxed cheese requires less storage space than jars filled with oil, so waxing is a good choice for non-spiced cheese on small cruising boats. The cheese can last up to six months with this system.

The final cheese preservation method I have learned in our years of exploring is a famous British Yuletide treat—expensive, but wonderful anytime, anywhere. Purchase a 7-pound, relatively young wheel of Stilton or blue cheese. Find an airtight crockery or glass container to fit closely around the cheese (within 1/2 inch on all sides). Scoop a hole—approximately half the size of a teacup—into the top center of the cheese (eat this center scoop with fresh grapes or a slice of apple). Into the depression, pour fine port wine of your preference. Set the cheese in a locker low in the boat, where it will keep relatively cool and the motion will not be too violent, while the wine seeps slowly through the holes and permeates the cheese. Top up with port once a week. Taste the cheese two or three months later. If you get a hint of port at the outer edges of the round, it will last for up to a year. In England, this is called a "drunken Stilton," traditionally eaten by spooning it onto crispy toast as you sip your after-dinner wine in front of a holly-bedecked fireplace. But it is equally good as a reminder of your faraway friends and family when you are finishing a meal of fresh lobster and enjoying a dessert of fine sweet pineapple to celebrate Christmas at anchor beside a coral atoll.

. . . .

Day 38

Noon to noon: 11 miles
Miles to date: 3,306
Lying at sea anchor, but wind is a bit lighter
Caught some glimpses of the sun for the first fix in six days
(That's why we made 11 miles when we weren't moving.)
In late afternoon, set staysail and reefed main
Beam-reaching over a big swell

Lunch
> chicken curry with raisins and onions
> noodles

Dinner
> country-style potato salad
> last cabbage salad
> hot dogs

. . . .

COUNTRY-STYLE POTATO SALAD

Boil until fork-tender
> 4 potatoes, cubed (skins left on)

Mix in gently
> ¼ cup mayonnaise
> 1 tbs. Dijon mustard
> 1 tsp. Worcestershire sauce
> 1 onion, diced
> 1 tsp. sugar
> 1 tsp. garlic powder
> 1 tsp. dill

Add salt and pepper to taste. Let stand at least 1 hour before serving.

. . . .

A hot cup of chocolate seemed to compensate for my absence during the wet, cold job of pulling in the sea anchor. Radio reports state that both large storm systems that have been chasing us seem to be dissipating and heading northeast, away from us. It's good to be underway again, and it's easier to cook, since the boat's motion is more regular than when we were hove-to.

The rattling of pots and pans during the storm has convinced me: The next boat will have individual holes for each pot, lined with felt so that they can't ping against their neighbors. Searching out the pot that is rattling, stuffing rags and potholders around it, then climbing back into the bunk, only to have a new solo start up somewhere—it drives you crazy.

DAY 38. *No matter what type of salt shaker you choose, a few spoonfuls of rice will keep the salt pouring.*

Rattle Suppression

No matter how carefully you arrange the storage lockers on your boat, every new passage will turn up its own supply of rattles, thumps, and bumps to disturb the off-watch.

We carry a bag of soft sponges to stuff between the hull and shifting china, or to stop offending bottles from shifting and adding to the cacophony of sounds made by a boat at sea.

Several cruisers use old socks to wrap every second wine bottle they store in the bilges or in large lockers. This reduces the clinking noise of bottle

338

rubbing against bottle. We carry several lengths of plastic nonskid matting that we use on the galley table. This works as well as socks as a bottle wrap to suppress rattles.

In every case, try to store bottles and cans athwartships. If possible, intersperse plastic containers with glass ones and pack cans just as tightly. When provisions begin to run low, I sometimes consolidate cans and bottles into one section of my storage lockers to cut down on rattles and clanks.

Even if you have worked hard to secure everything before you set sail, make sure the on-watch crew takes a few minutes to listen for, hunt out, and quiet any rattles or thunks that might wake the sleeping crew. I can remember many watches when I was jarred awake half a dozen times because it seemed like too much trouble to climb out of the bunk to find the offending rattle.

Salt

Larry is at it again, pounding the salt shaker on the table, trying to clear out the holes so he can put some salt on his meat. Even with our closing-top Tupperware salt shaker quarter-filled with white rice, we still have problems getting salt to pour, especially if I have used the shaker to flavor something that was steaming away on the stove top. There are several solutions—most of which I try at one time or another—but during the recent bad weather, I've gotten lazy.

First, keep a separate salt shaker for cooking so that the one for table use doesn't get opened as often. Second, when you are filling the shakers from your main salt container, place a thin layer of salt on a flat dish and bake it in the oven for 10 to 12 minutes. Then pour this super-dry salt into the shaker with a fresh supply of rice. This way, the rice only has to absorb moisture let in while the shaker is in use. Third, buy only salt that comes in plastic containers of a half-pound or smaller, and keep the container inside a sealed plastic bag. Fourth, buy a rock-salt grinder for table use.

On *Taleisin*, we have been testing a salt grinder with nylon cutters (made by Maddison in England) for the past three months, and so far I'm absolutely sold. Rain or shine, we get just the right amount of salt on our salads.

. . . .

Day 39

Noon to noon: 100 miles
Miles to date: 3,406
No fog! Cloudy, dead run with 12-to-15-foot seas
Reefed main and staysail on the whisker pole

Lunch
leftover potato salad
hard-boiled eggs
pickled beet salad

Dinner
spaghetti Bolognese
red wine

. . . .

PICKLED BEET SALAD

Combine and mix well

1 can sliced beets, well drained
¼ onion, sliced thinly
3 cloves garlic, sliced thinly
1 tbs. olive oil
2 tbs. vinegar
1 tsp. sugar

> Mix well and let sit 4 or 5 hours before serving.

. . . .

It was under circumstances just like this that I chipped my tailbone in *Seraffyn's* galley. We'd been in a gale—hove-to for a night in the North Sea off England. The winds abated and filled in from astern, so we started running. All seemed great—the motion was much better than it had been. So I was caught off-guard and just wasn't holding on when a cross-sea from the previous day's gale made *Seraffyn* lurch. I flew only three feet before hitting the edge of the ice chest. The damage was painful but not serious. I still have to sit on hard chairs, since tailbones don't heal well. Lesson learned: Wear a galley harness or hold on, even after a storm has gone by!

Vegetarians Afloat

Back in 1980, one of the racing cooks I interviewed for the first edition of this book said, "If you find a vegetarian in the crew, toss him overboard." That is something that has definitely changed in the sailing world. I now expect to find a vegetarian among my guests or crew in a 1-to-20 ratio. In fact, I find our own meals tending toward vegetarian-type lunches, with red meat (which once was an expected part of our menu twice a day) only making up four or five meals a week, even onshore. But once you are voyaging, providing well-balanced, interesting meals for vegetarian crew does become harder.

If you are not a vegetarian and are faced with unexpected non-flesh-eating daysailing crew, you will usually find that your visitor is used to this situation. He or she will be quite satisfied with the same sandwich you eat, minus the meat, and the same dinner you eat, minus the slices of roast beef. But to satisfy your desire to be a good host, to fill each spot on your visitor's plate, you can add a small can of drained mushrooms or asparagus, topped with mayonnaise, to the vegetarian plate. Or for sandwiches, you can slice additional fresh vegetables and add them, or spread a layer of spicy chutney, cheese, onion slices, or pickled beets to perk up the meatless sandwiches.

If you know beforehand that vegetarian crew will be sailing with you, ask if they enjoy fish, cheese, or eggs. Very few have diets that exclude all these items. If they do, ask that they bring along a dish they enjoy, one that can be shared with the crew. Otherwise, plan a meal based on casserole-type foods. Prepare one small casserole exactly the same as the main dish, minus the meat. Substitute eggplant (aubergine), extra onions, leeks, or spinach. I was surprised when I once prepared a large meat lasagna for the majority of my guests at dinner on board and then made a smaller, meatless one for our vegetarian crew member. To spice up the meatless lasagna, I added a layer of spinach and a layer of eggplant, topped with spiced feta cheese. The vegetarian lasagna ended up being just as popular with everyone as the meat dish.[13]

. . . .

13 For casseroles such as lasagna, which are dependent on a precooked sauce, I make the sauce without meat and then sauté the meat and add it to the casserole when I assemble it. The flavor is often better this way.

For longer passages with a vegetarian on board, discuss menus with the crew beforehand, explaining that you cannot prepare two sets of meals—one for meat eaters and one for meat abstainers. Then plan occasional meals created by the vegetarian. This will add variety to your menu and create a feeling that everyone on board has a special place. At all costs, avoid setting up a pattern of bilateral meals. This can lead to a serious drain on provisions and the cook. I found this when I was cook on a shrimp trawler where half of the crew was North American and half Costa Rican. At first, I offered to make meals to suit the desires of both contingents—the highly meat-oriented North Americans and the vegetable-, rice-, beans-, and fish-oriented Costa Ricans. This was easy while provisions were fresh and before we were busy with trawling and trapping. But it became a problem when both groups began enjoying each other's favorite foods and expectations of constant dual menus put a lot of pressure on the cook.

If you are vegetarians who plan to cruise to exotic locations, you'll have some problems with finding replacements for the provisions you brought from home. Fresh fruit and vegetables—on which you depended for adding variety to your diet (and sufficient vitamins)—become difficult to find in small island nations and in the tropics. Tom Linskey, a well-known dinghy-racing sailor, writer, and vegetarian who sailed the South Pacific in his 28-foot cutter *Freelance,* said the most difficult part of that cruise was the lack of fresh foods and the problem of finding interesting nuts, grains, and dried replacements when outside the few bigger centers. On the majority of islands, your choice of fresh produce will be limited to cabbage, tomatoes, onions, and potatoes, plus bananas, coconuts, and occasionally pineapples. Cheeses are difficult to find (see Day 37, "Long-Distance Cheeses"). Fortunately, many French people prefer a vegetarian-based eating style, so excellent grains, beans, and rice varieties are available in Papeete, New Caledonia, and Réunion in the South Pacific and Indian Ocean. The prices are steep, but it is worthwhile overstocking, as these locations may provide your last chances to add variety to your menu. In South America and the Caribbean, again look to French colonies for the best sources of vegetarian staples and treats.

Although many island people depend on fresh fish for the majority of the protein in their diets, the mainstay of their meals is either rice or tubers such as yams. So you never need be without potential provisions, even in the most remote areas of the world. But it will pay to have local people introduce you to the recipes they use for the vegetables and grains found in the local shops; you may find some wonderful new ideas. I came to really enjoy the Costa Rican way of eating beans-and-rice after my stint on the trawler. Boiled pinto beans were spiced with onions and garlic and then mixed in equal parts with cooked white rice to form the local substitute for potatoes. Another cruiser told of leaving Brazil with 30 kilos of a special black bean that tasted "10 times better than any other bean in the world." Beans are a dependable source of protein that can add variety and cut cost for any cruiser, whether vegetarian or meat eater.

In fact, for any cruiser on a budget, I would recommend looking into vegetarian cookbooks and eating styles. These books contain fine fish, casserole, and sandwich recipes, which will help you either cut down on the use of meats or add variety when your only meat supplies have to come from cans. Meat is one of the most expensive food items you will buy, and it is one of the hardest items to keep on board. Without refrigeration, it is almost impossible. Besides, a good vegetarian dish, spiced with the meat you intended for just the two of you, can easily stretch a dinner to include the welcome but unexpected guests who just sailed in and anchored next to you.

. . . .

Day 40

Noon to noon: 111 miles
Miles to date: 3,517
Less than 1,000 miles to go!
Dead run—lumpy sea, drizzle, and gray sky

Lunch
  chili and beans

Teatime
  hot buttered rum
  cheese, biscuits

Dinner
  silver dollar pancakes
  maple syrup
  canned hunters' sausages
  long-life milk

. . . .

Galley Slave or Hero?

The term *galley slave,* used in yachting circles, has the same connotations as the term *mother-in-law* when used by comedians. It is an overworked, generally untrue bad joke.

Sure, cooking on an ocean passage is hard work. But being part of any adventure is hard work. And that's the reason most of us sail small boats across oceans. It still is and always will be an adventure—one fraught with the unseen, the uncontrollable.

Even the best-prepared ocean voyagers can't control the weather. A voyage planned to last about 20 days can take 50 because of unusual calms or unexpected storms. An untimely typhoon can damage the most perfectly built, perfectly prepared vessel.

At times, being cook may seem the hardest job afloat. But it can also be the most important, and it is definitely the most rewarding—especially to an ego-tripper like me. It's a job that requires foresight, planning, and then creativity as you go.

I know of one group of vastly experienced racing sailors—they could almost be called the "elder statesmen" of the fleet—that spent the last three days of a 1,000-mile ocean race completely without freshwater because no one thought to keep track of their consumption. When we were in Antigua in 1976, two young men were towed into harbor on the verge of starvation and too weak to sail their boat any farther. They'd left England with a boat full of food, but they just ate it all up without realizing they might hit light winds. They assumed that since they were making what was called a trade-wind passage, they'd have nothing but trade winds.

But it's not just the near-disasters that count. Larry has often told me of the otherwise-good passage from Honolulu to Newport Beach when he was mate on the 85-foot schooner *Double Eagle*. The cook almost ruined the voyage. He was a paid cook but had a repertoire of only two dishes: teriyaki steak and bacon and eggs.

How often have you heard someone tell the skipper, "Nice job of gybing," or "lovely sail change"? The only compliments the skipper gets may be, "Boat's moving well." The navigator might hear, "Good landfall." Only if all hell breaks loose because some piece of equipment fails and the captain exhibits a feat of seamanship or clever jury-rigging does he really get any appreciation. And even that is tinged with the often-unspoken thought, "Maybe that wouldn't have happened if the skipper had kept things maintained better."

But the cook—the holder of the only creative job on board—can win applause three or four times a day. She or he can hear raves for an unexpected batch of cookies, a cup of hot chocolate served at midnight, or a masterpiece of a casserole. If one meal is a bit of a flop, you have three chances a day for the rest of the voyage to override that memory.

On the other hand, I can understand why many female sailing partners dread the idea of cooking for an extended voyage. I've seen the hassles most sailing wives have when they plan a weekend cruise. Hubby says, "Let's go down to the boat Friday night and sail to the island for the weekend." Before they set off, he throws a few things in the car and maybe he carts the supplies down to the dock when they get to the boat. Meanwhile, the wife has to spend a day planning meals, shopping for food and supplies, and packing pots, pans, towels, and toiletries for the boat. Once on the boat, she has to set up housekeeping and do all the same chores that she does at home without the facilities she's used to. Then, come Sunday evening, she has to pack up the boat and clean it out. On Monday, she has to clean up the things that have come back from the boat. Hubby has the weekend off; wife has double the housework load on Friday and Monday and no time off during the weekend.

If this situation happens in your family, consider investing in a complete set of pots, pans, and cooking utensils for your weekender, plus a good stock of canned and packaged foods so that nothing has to be brought from home except for fresh fruit and vegetables. Convince your wife to plan extra-simple meals or arrange for some meals out. You offer to take care of some of the cooking; or, if you are a hopeless cook, you take care of the cleanup after dinner while your wife sits back with the cocktail you prepared for her.

If you are getting ready to take off on your first ocean passage, remember that you will probably be worn out from all of the stocking-up, shopping, saying good-byes, and storing away. I highly recommend a very short hop as the first leg of any offshore passage. Sail to the next harbor or even just across the bay. Set your anchor, then row ashore for a nice dinner or eat a special one you've brought along. Then use the next morning to put the boat to rights before you sail out to sea.

I know that we couldn't have had nearly as good a cruise if we had set off for Mexico straight from Newport Beach, where we launched *Seraffyn* and put her through three months of sea trials. We said all our good-byes, put everything we thought we needed on board, and sailed 80 miles to San Diego. There we spent a week being tourists, checking over the boat, and arranging the stores properly without the interruptions of friends, family, and friendly onlookers. Even after all our years of voyaging, we like to stop away from the hustle and activity of a town where we've stocked up and rest for the night before we set off to sea. That way, there are no hangovers from farewell parties. You are well rested, and clearing harbor early in the day means a good chance to get a good offing before nightfall.[14]

During the year and a half prior to writing the original edition of this book, we made three times as many long-distance passages as we usually do (14,000 miles in one year and one day!), and I learned that the crew is usually more easily satisfied than the cook is when it comes to food. Just when I am getting tired of the selection of food left on board, Larry will say something like, "That meal sure hit the spot." I guess crew at sea are pleased to have any variety at all. Most people I have met can tell of one voyage in their lives

....

14   For more on ways to make life afloat enjoyable for you and your mate, read "Free the Galley Slave," chapter 7 in our book *The Self-Sufficient Sailor*.

where all they ate was peanut-butter-and-jam sandwiches, or tuna casseroles and cold cereals. If you can provide any variety at all, occasional treats, and lots of hot soup or hot chocolate during a long passage—plus a few fancy meals at both ends of the trip—you'll be doing great.

Planning for a voyage and buying stores gets easier every time you do it. After all our years of voyaging and delivering boats, I can now feel comfortable about stocking up in almost any U.S. port for a voyage of up to 1,500 miles with only 1 1/2-days' warning (unless it's a weekend). Overseas, I am happy if I have three days to shop and prepare.

I am convinced that the galley-slave jokes should be a thing of the past. The days of one-burner stoves and galleys forward of the foremast are gone. Modern galleys can be the most elegant part of a yacht. Good seagoing cookware and proper galley equipment are available. But being cook on a voyage will always be a challenge, and the person who accepts the challenge with a good sense of humor will always be welcome on any boat that heads out to sea.

. . . .

Day 41

Noon to noon: 121 miles
Miles to date: 3,640
Sun!
Running under full canvas—great!

Lunch
   tuna salad
   bean salad
   mashed-potato salad

Dinner
   fresh white bread and honey
   baked potatoes
   sautéed tuna steaks
   tartar sauce
   ½ bottle Liebfraumilch
   Nana Mouskouri sings of love on the tape stereo.

....

Another Fish Story

It must be some kind of coincidence. We've had our fish line overboard for four days, but no go. Then today, just as we were eating lunch—in fact, I'd just served the tuna salad—whammo, the fish alarm rang and Larry pulled in a 15-pound—you guessed it—tuna. But there is no comparison between the texture and flavor of fresh tuna and that of canned tuna.

There were a few moments of comedy pulling that fish on board. Because of the first real sunshine in four weeks, *Seraffyn*'s decks were covered with things drying: the sea anchor, 300 feet of sea-anchor rope, towels, and, of course, 200 feet of fish line, sinkers, and hooks coiling around the cockpit and afterdeck. There wasn't one place to put that fish so Larry could beat it on the head and kill it. "Here, Lin, you put a towel around him and hold him

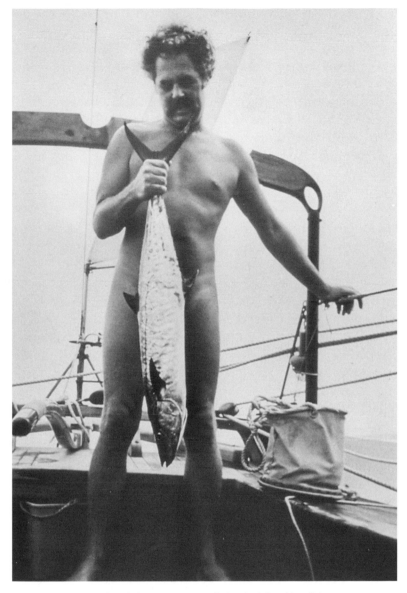

Every time we catch a fish at sea, I recall the Red Sea kingfish story.

over the bucket so his blood doesn't get all over the deck," Larry suggested. He knows I am terrified of touching living, slimy fish; in fact, I hate to touch fish until it is filleted and ready for the pan. This afternoon, he learned that that fish was almost as strong as I am! Within seconds, I was panicked, as that 15-pounder desperately tried to get away. "Larry, Larry, grab him; I can't hold him. He's trying to get loose. I can't stand it. He's dying. I don't want to watch!" I guess I was a ridiculous sight, holding that fish by the tail, rooted in place while its head shook that bucket farther and farther away from me. Larry was roaring with laughter when he grabbed the fish, whipped a spare sail gasket around its tail, and lashed it to the leeward lifelines, so it could bleed into the scuppers. After I got over the convulsive feeling that fish's jerk had sent through my arm, I got the scrub brush and a bucket of saltwater and went after the blood and scales scattered around the side deck. I was wondering if catching fish was worth the trouble. Ten minutes later, when Larry handed me a bowlful of beautiful tuna steaks, I changed my mind.

Sleep

The four men on board their 40-foot aluminum racing cutter had been slogging up the coast of Portugal against the wind and current for 10 days. Their last rest stop on the windswept lee shore had been Cascais, just outside Lisbon, where the Atlantic curls around the point and makes the anchorage less than comfortable. Now, three days after that 1-night stop, they spotted the cliffs that mark the entrance to the welcoming port of Bayonna, Spain.

It was near dusk, so, motorsailing against the almost ceaseless northwest wind and swell, all four men stayed on deck chatting and planning—as voyagers often do when a safe port looms ahead. But current, seas, and underestimation meant the headland was not close at hand until just after midnight. The navigator read off the sequences on the two range lights that keep ships clear of Wolf Rock, a nasty breaking reef that lies almost 1/4 mile north of the entrance point. All four on board were tired—tired of being at sea; tired of being damp and uncomfortable; tired of going to windward; tired simply from lack of sleep. When the first range light came into view and stayed visible and alone for what seemed ages, the crew made a communal decision—the second range light must be out of order. The helmsman headed onshore. For the first time in days, the sheets were eased, and in what seemed like only seconds later, a large sea lifted the hull and smashed it against Wolf Rock. When a second wave washed over the boat, one crewman was swept to his death. The next waves sent the boat clear, and the remaining three men were able to nurse the battered hull into Bayonna, where authorities had a search underway within an hour. We arrived in Bayonna three days later. The aluminum hull had dents almost a foot deep along the starboard side. The dead crewman's body had been recovered. Ship captains, fishermen, and other yachtsmen confirmed that both range lights had been working. The crew on the yacht could only comment, "We were tired and wanted to get into port."

Decisions made by tired crew are a frequent cause of groundings, navigation errors, and gear failures. One of our closest calls came after a bad delivery trip out of Miami, when we had to leave a crewman in the Bahamas with an infected foot. The two of us stood 3-on, 3-off watches, constantly hand-steering a motorsailer with defective rigging for seven days, close-hauled in the boisterous Gulf Stream. In the middle of the seventh night, we mistook an airfield approach light for the main lighthouse at the entrance to San Juan Harbor, Puerto Rico. We, too, altered course, eased sheets, and spotted our error only a mile off a rocky lee shore—when other lights suddenly appeared onshore where the harbor entrance should have been. We then had to tack offshore and make up 5 miles we'd lost because of a decision made when we were exhausted.

Rest is imperative for the sailor. Getting it isn't always easy, but there are important ways to improve your chances.

One rule we've finally learned: Start watches promptly at 2000 hours, even if you are only on a 1-day passage and even if the harbor entrance seems only a short distance away. Time and time again, tides, strong currents, adverse winds, or engine failures have delayed what looked like certain just-at-dusk landfalls. Having one watch below decks getting some sleep is like insurance. You may not need them, but they don't cost you much. Their well-rested judgment could be the deciding factor in a close situation.

On a shorthanded cruising boat, it may pay to heave-to just before making a landfall so that the whole crew gets some extra rest. Every boat heaves-to differently. Test yours in various wind conditions so that when the time comes, you can use this "sailor's safety valve" quickly and easily. Make sure you have sufficient sea room before you heave-to and all go to sleep; a changing wind could set you ashore. If there is any doubt about your position, heave-to and wait for dawn. Keep a watch. The more comfortable motion, and the lack of concern about running full speed onto a reef, will help you get the rest necessary for making proper decisions.

Offshore sailors can win or lose races with their sleep habits. The 1974 Round Britain 2-man, 2,200-mile race proved this to us. Larry was on board 30-foot *Chough*, a Sparkman & Stephens half-ton sloop. His partner was Leslie Dyball. After three days of hard racing, the two decided to make it a rule—man off-watch stayed in his bunk, day or night, unless a spinnaker had to come down. The on-watch crew did everything by himself—navigation, sail changes, steering with the help of the windvane. This decision gained them the handicap prize and brought them in as thirteenth boat over the line out of 16, even though they were number 43 in overall length. They beat three Admiral's Cup racing yachts boat for boat. The other crews were amazed to see 67-year-old Leslie eagerly trotting down the roads of Lerwick in the Shetland Islands bound for a famous salmon-fishing stream only an hour after tying up—after five days of beating around the north end of Ireland, past the Outer Hebrides, and past the northern limits of Scotland.

On racing yachts with a large crew, getting sufficient rest is just as important. Except during all-hands-on-deck emergencies, or at the start and finish lines, the off-watch crew belongs in the bunk. I was planning on joining a Cal 40 in the 1979 Transpac until a broken leg got in the way. As part of our preparations for that race, I spoke with several successful Transpac sailors, including Don Vaughn, who often crewed on 73-foot *Windward Passage*, and Doc Holiday with his successful Ericson 35, *Aquarius*. Both agreed that off-watch crew members belong in their bunks for at least one daytime watch in addition to the night off-watches. Sleep doesn't win races, but good decisions and alert, keen, on-watch crew do. In fact this is one of the problems most often sited for causing mishaps on the current crop of race boats. With carbon fiber or aluminum hulls being driven at speeds in excess of 15 or even 20 knots, the noise is such that sleep becomes extremely difficult. Off-watch crew is encouraged to use earplugs to ensure they get sufficient sleep.

The first two or three days at sea, almost everyone on a small vessel feels tired. The motion, the excitement of a long-planned departure, last-minute preparations, and farewell parties all contribute to this weariness. Tiredness is also the first sign of seasickness, and often the only symptom displayed by those with strong stomachs. Even among voyagers who have only been in port for a week or two, the first few days out create a feeling of lassitude. So plan on arranging for extra napping time or longer off-watches until the crew gets its sea legs.

There is only one problem: It is hard to fall asleep at 2000 hours in a strange bunk with the unusual motion. In far north or south latitudes during summer, it may still be light when it's time to start watches. The cook can generally help in this situation.

First, avoid offering any crewman coffee or tea for four hours before watches start. Plan a leisurely but somewhat heavy meal within an hour of 2000 if the crew isn't prone to seasickness. (Seasick crew will usually fall asleep easily.) Finish the meal with a cup of hot sweetened milk or hot chocolate for the first sleeper, or offer him/her a shot of brandy, port, or sherry as he or she gets ready for the bunk.

On board Taleisin, or any boat we may be delivering, if one of us lies eyes wide open, unable to sleep for more than 30 or 40 minutes, we change places and restart watches. Then, 30 minutes before the sleepless one's next off-watch, one Dramamine or Marezine tablet ensures a sound sleep. We have found that these seasickness tablets are the best possible sleeping pill. They leave no side effects and wear off in two or three hours. I've never felt hungover when I've used them, and if there was a need to get up during my off-watch, I didn't feel drugged.

To help the off-watch sleep, make it the on-watch's job to quiet down or stop every possible rattle or noise on board—or if that's not possible, at least to investigate and explain the noise. A can rolling around in the locker next to your bunk can wake you each time you almost doze off. But climbing out of the bunk and searching out each noise just doesn't seem worthwhile. So have the on-watch do the search as part of his/her duties. On our last delivery job to Mexico, our crew member, Mary Baldwin, didn't mention that the noise from the internal halyards inside the empty aluminum mast next to her bunk was driving her crazy. When she finally told us, four days out, we were able to find ways to tighten the unused halyards and quiet them a bit. But if one of us had thought to stand next to Mary's bunk and listen while she tried to sleep, we could have helped her get a few more hours of sound, deep sleep.

If there is any way for the on-watch to leave the helm—whether by leaving steering to the windvane or by tying the helm for a few moments—it pays to take a stroll through the boat past sleeping crew at least every hour. This seems to subconsciously reassure the sleeper that all is well. The watch-stander can also take this opportunity to check for wayward pots, pans, and rattles.

The captain who doesn't quite trust his crew is rarely going to get enough rest. So take time before each voyage to be sure each person on board knows basic sailing and emergency procedures. Let it be known that calling the captain on deck when something looks amiss is the *right* thing to do. When we delivered a 60-foot ketch across the Atlantic, I just didn't like the look of some dark clouds forming up astern of us. Though Larry had just crawled into the bunk a half-hour earlier, I called him up. His second opinion made us decide to drop all sail except for the jib, even though we only had about 15 knots of wind. Twenty minutes later, the clouds covered us and we roared along in a 30-knot squall, perfectly canvased. The rest of the crew never woke up. Larry returned to his bunk with these last words: "Call me up anytime you have doubts. Sure was easier to shorten down before that one hit." If you can impress on your whole crew the fact that it's easier to handle situations before they're all-hands-on-deck affairs, everyone will sleep better.

After two or three days at sea, watch patterns will become a way of life. We usually stick to the same watches all through a passage. We stand three hours on, three hours off, with Larry taking the first off-watch right after dinner and oil-lamp-lighting time. With a small crew, this works best, since our bodies and minds seem to adjust well to an unchanging schedule. We stand watches at all times at sea, with both of us getting two uninterrupted 3-hour night sleeping periods plus occasional afternoon naps. Three-hour watches seem to work well with a 2-person crew. That gives the sleeper enough time to really rest, yet the watch-keeper doesn't seem to get bored. Each crewman gets two full sleeping periods during the 12-hour night. When we have a crew with us on deliveries, we shorten watches to two hours a person.

Nothing helps the person coming off watch to fall asleep faster than climbing into a dry, warm sleeping bag. Work to keep it that way. If it has been a wet watch, dry yourself off before you climb into the bunk. Wash any saltwater off your hands, face, and feet before you slide between the sheets, or you'll soon have a clammy, salty bunk.

We put our spare bed pillows against the hull as padding when we are sleeping underway.

We've all dreamed of nestling down in the foredeck under a starry sky padded by sail bags, lulled to sleep by the low roar of a bow wake in a trade-wind sea. Only problem with that is that right after you doze off, some crewman will step on your foot when he comes to check the foredeck. Maybe a flying fish will land on top of you, or you'll wake up damp and covered with dew.

So plan from the beginning to create a comfortable below-deck sleeping arrangement. If you can, make sure there is good air circulation into the foot of each bunk that can be increased in tropical conditions. This is an area often forgotten by many designers, builders, and owners. Sliding door type vent at the end of the bunk is one solution. A Dorade-type ventilator is better, because it can be kept open in wet conditions.

To help the off-watch sleep well at sea, we put up this dark cotton curtain.

Lee cloths are nicer to sleep against than lee boards. Carry some extra throw pillows. When you are beating to windward, one or two of these spare cushions placed against the hull in the lee bunk will help crewmen settle in more comfortably.

On board *Taleisin*, we have done more "high latitude" voyaging than we did on *Seraffyn*. With the far longer days, we often have had to start watches well before the sun has actually set and continue sleeping well after daylight arrives. To ensure better sleeping conditions, we added a curtain to enclose the pilot berth. Close-weave, dark green cotton, secured in place with a shock cord, works to create the feeling of dark and also to cut down the noise and changing light patterns made when the on-watch crew moves around in the cabin. We both find that we sleep sounder with the curtain in place.

We've found sleeping bags to be the very best solution on board, because the bag under you keeps you insulated from chilly bunk cushions. We choose single bags that can zip together to form a double-bed-size bag for use in port. We carry two sets—one winter weight and the other summer weight. For intermediate climates, we zip together one bag of each weight in port so we can choose which one we want to use as the top blanket according to that night's temperature. (We store the spare set in zip-up bolster-pillow bags made from the same fabric as our cushions.)

We have made two all-cotton sheets into double sleeping-bag sheets, which we can change every seven days. In the tropics, these sheets take the place of a sleeping bag, with a light blanket available just in case. Cotton is by far the best choice for sheets and pillowcases in very warm or very cold climates. Dacron or nylon may dry faster, but synthetics feel hot and sticky in the tropics, cold and clammy in northern seas.

Washable dacron-filled pillows with cotton ticking are now available. They are a wise choice for sailing. Foam rubber attracts moisture and can contribute to aches such as arthritis or rheumatism. It will also start to pick up odors quickly. Down pillows tend to start leaking after a year of use on board and can't be washed or cleaned easily.

Although fabric-covered bunk cushions are more elegant to look at and nicer to sit on, vinyl-covered ones are easier to keep dry. Since nothing is less conducive to sound sleep than a wet bunk, we have come to a compromise that works well on *Taleisin*. The forward double bunk—which is never used at sea except during the calmest conditions—is fabric-covered. (We used draylon—synthetic velvet backed with cotton—and it has worn like iron. Our current set, the second in 20 years, is now 11 years old and looking only slightly shabby.) Our pilot-berth cushions, on the other hand, are vinyl-covered, with draylon slipcovers. This way, we can easily remove the covers and wipe down the cushions in this more vulnerable part of the boat. The slipcovers are also easy to wash or rinse to keep them free of small traces of salt that are carried in by even the most careful of bunk users. The vinyl-covered pilot-berth cushions can also be used for sleeping out in the cockpit on tropical evenings. On a smaller boat, such as *Seraffyn*, we would still choose vinyl for the cushions in the main cabin, as it is far harder to keep salt spray clear of the sleeping area when the cabin is only 7 feet long. We did make up cotton slipcovers for the settees and bunk cushions to cut down on the sticky feeling of vinyl against slightly sweaty skin.

Sleeping is just as important to the health of the offshore sailing crew as food. By carefully considering your watch schedule and sleeping arrangements, you can ensure an alert, amiable crew when you need it most.

. . . .

Day 42

Noon to noon: 132 miles
Miles to date: 3,772
Running before a 35-to-40-knot wind with
only the staysail set
Cold, drizzle, rough sea; Barometer falling
Afternoon: hove-to, gale winds

Lunch
    tuna steaks
    leftover potato salad
    leftover bean salad

Dinner
    beef stew
    bread, butter
    hot rum

....

Too Rough to Do Much Fancy

Again it's rough, but I did at least steam up the last pieces of tuna that Larry caught yesterday. Now they'll be good for tomorrow.

Larry got soaking wet when he went out to take down the staysail and set the mainsail with two reefs so we'd be hove-to. His boots have been leaking most of the passage, and now he has a hole in his wet-weather pants. During our past few years of voyaging, we've rarely needed the warmth of wet-weather gear that was absolutely watertight. As soon as we get to Canada, we are going to look into some new stuff. Meanwhile, Larry came below shivering and blue-lipped. I got him out of his wet clothes, warmed some freshwater so he could wipe down, and got out his dry clothes. But it wasn't until he had had some hot, solid food that he started to warm up and stop shivering.

....

357

Day 43

Noon to noon: 51 miles
Miles to date: 3,823
Lying a-hull
Seas rougher than previous storm, but wind not as strong
Barometer rising

Lunch
    stew and bread
Dinner
    tuna steak Italian

. . . .

TUNA STEAK ITALIAN

Combine and simmer
    1 can whole tomatoes
    10 cloves garlic, chopped
    1 large onion, chopped
    1 tsp. oregano
    1 tsp. Worcestershire sauce
    1 tbs. sugar
    3 tbs. white wine
    1 tsp. lemon juice

> When onions are soft, pour sauce over precooked fish steaks in a frying pan. Heat 3 minutes more.

. . . .

Don't Count Your Chickens

Only yesterday, we were figuring that if we could continue making 130 miles a day, we could be in within five days. I'd started thinking about what to serve our last night at sea. Shore seems so close. Then the gale that reportedly was dissipating formed up again, right on top of us. So we're hove-to, which proves once again that you can't plan the last day of a voyage until the end of the breakwater is past your beam.

The first time this was really brought home to us was when we were delivering the *Vagrant Gypsy*, a 50-ton ketch, from Palma, Mallorca, to New Orleans—a distance of 5,800 miles. At 1600, Larry and I were discussing our plan of action, since the entrance to the 5-mile-long channel into the port of Gulfport, Mississippi, was only 35 miles ahead of us. We were powering along at almost 6 knots over a flat sea. That morning, it had been at least 70 degrees F on deck, but it was cooler now. "We'll keep up full speed for another four hours," Larry suggested. "Then we'll throttle back to 2 knots so that we don't make the entrance until morning." I agreed wholeheartedly with this idea and decided to splurge with dinner preparations. I made an angel-food cake using 13 of our last 20 eggs. I cooked up ratatouille with the last of our assortment of fresh vegetables from Montego Bay, Jamaica. By midnight, we were hove-to while a blue norther brought 50-knot winds, 18-degree temperatures (Fahrenheit, that is), 20-yard visibility, and water spouts. We lay hove-to for three days before the wind abated enough so we could set sail. Oh, how I wished I'd had those 13 eggs and just one of those extra fresh vegetables.

. . . .

Day 44

Noon to noon: 27 miles
Miles to date: 3,850
Underway again, winds growing lighter
Dead run, foggy

Lunch
scrambled eggs
canned corned-beef hash
canned pears

Dinner
[For some reason, I didn't write down what we had for dinner.]

....

Bad Day for the Cook

I found 12 eggs that were rotten because they had small cracks in them. They were the larger ones in each of the plastic egg holders, so maybe something fell on the egg cartons during one of the storms we had.

Then I made a pudding—you know the kind, just add cold milk and stir. Well, it flopped. I've had the packaged pudding on board since Malta, so that's probably why it went wrong.

A survey of the lockers shows loads of food left; the only things on which I'm cutting it close are butter, cooking oil, coffee, and eggs. But with luck and fair winds, they'll last just until we reach Victoria.

....

Day 45

Noon to noon: 120 miles
Miles to date: 3,970
Foggy—running fast under full sail

Lunch
canned hot dogs
baked beans dressed up with chopped onions
sweet pickle chips

Dinner
chicken-and-ginger casserole
creamed corn
fresh whole-wheat bread, butter

....

CHICKEN-AND-GINGER CASSEROLE

Mix carefully (so chicken doesn't disintegrate)
1½ cups cooked rice
1 can roasted boneless chicken
1 onion, chopped
8 cloves garlic, sliced
2 tbs. shredded fresh ginger
½ cup water
1 tbs. chicken gravy mix

Place in a greased pan. Cover with aluminum foil. Bake 30 minutes at 350 degrees.

....

Cook's Complaint

I must admit that I'm running out of imagination. No matter what you add to a can of baked beans, they are still the same old baked beans you've served four times already on the same voyage. And hot dogs are the same;

the cans of fruit juice all seem to taste the same. Larry says he's not the least bit bored with our diet, and he cites examples of families ashore who eat pork chops every Thursday, lamb on Sundays—month in, month out. But I'm tired of looking at the same stock of food. Favorite items are starting to dwindle. I've never felt quite this way before, but then it's a rare voyage that lasts more than 25 days. Before this, the longest we've ever been at sea is 35 days. Few passages, races, or deliveries cross 4,500 miles of ocean at one go. Having to buy final stores in Japan also meant we have a lot fewer treats hidden away. I couldn't bring myself to pay $3 for a 4-ounce package of dried apricots or 75 cents for a single chocolate bar. We've had about half the number of treats we'd usually carry.

But the real reason for my boredom with cooking is obviously that we are only 500 miles from our goal and I'm getting impatient. Another gale is approaching from the west, but it's 1,200 miles astern of us. With any luck, we could outrun it. I sure hope so.

Entertaining as You Cruise

The evening is abuzz with talk of favorite anchorages, haul-out blues, the next passage, the next destination. To add to the camaraderie, cruising musician Bill "Keys" Kerslake plays rock-and-roll tunes on his well-traveled electric piano.

As unofficial food organizer for two dozen cruisers, I say, "I'll slice this fruit cake. Why don't you uncover those salads?" With the eclectic array of food logically organized on the picnic table, Kyle Hopkins and I have time to chat. She and her husband, Doug, arrived in New Zealand's Bay of Islands after spending two years sailing their 32-foot cutter *Astrala* from Connecticut via Easter Island and Pitcairn Island with two youngsters on board. Now they are upgrading *Astrala* while their children are getting a firsthand taste of Kiwism at the local school.

"I never guessed how social life would be when we set off cruising," Kyle comments. "First new anchorage we sailed into, folks rowed by. I invited them on board, then realized we didn't have spare coffee mugs to offer them." From etiquette to expectations, entertaining afloat was an unexpected part of Kyle's cruising education.

As Kyle found out, work, family, and community commitments no longer dictate how you spend each hour of your cruising day. This leads to the opportunity and need to entertain (and be entertained) far more than many people expect. But ask returned voyagers what they miss, and the vast majority will say, "the easygoing social life."

When casual drop-in visitors like Denise Lindenhall come on board, don't stress out about serving anything fancy—just some fruit and a cold drink will do.

Easygoing is the word to remember. Entertaining afloat does not have the same constraints, expectations, or rules that often leave shore-based hosts nervous or exhausted. On the other hand, the casualness of this new lifestyle may hide some potential pitfalls for unwary hosts and guests alike.

Entertaining afloat tends to be more spontaneous and far more frequent than onshore. You see a familiar-looking boat sail in. It's crewed by folks you met three months earlier in another part of the world. You call out, "Come on over and have dinner with us." Or, a dozen cruisers are congregated at the post office and someone suggests a gathering on the beach that evening—"bring a plate," the New Zealanders call it; "potluck," those from North America say. Every day afloat seems to offer reasons to entertain. This socializing afloat tends to break down into five categories:

Row-by, come aboards
Casual, just happened because someone came by to trade books
Planned invites—for fellow cruisers
Planned invites—for folks from shore
Potlucks

The quiet of morning lures you out into your cockpit for a second cup of coffee. As you absorb the world around you, someone rows by and says,

"I like your boat." A conversation ensues and you learn that cruising social life can be like a throwback to those days when folks used to have the time and confidence in the world around them to sit on the front porch and greet neighbors as they walked by. You also know that each of the people you meet will immediately have something in common with you. Many of our favorite cruising friends have come into our lives this way. Some were fellow voyagers, others were local folks who could not speak more than a few words of English (our first language) or Spanish (a distant second language for us). Each showed a real interest in our boat or lifestyle. A translation dictionary, a pad of paper and pencil for diagrams, and some pictures of our home and family helped break the ice when there was a limited common language. Refreshments for these row-bys are simple: an offer of whatever it is you are having—coffee, a cookie, or a piece of toast. This is not a time for adding pressures to your day by trying to impress someone with the food you offer.

The same is true of what we consider casual, just-happened-to-come-by gatherings. When folks come to trade charts or ask how to fix something, I like to offer a cool or hot drink. Not only to keep our cruising budget in control, but also because many folks do not feel comfortable refusing alcoholic beverages, even when they might prefer something lighter, I offer coffee, tea, lemonade (see "Drink Ideas", page 372), fruit juice, along with wine or beer. Since these get-togethers usually have been a bit more planned than row-bys, I often set out popcorn or fresh fruit, any small thing that lets me avoid the appearance of having spent a lot of time prepping for what is intended to be an easygoing, relaxed situation. This is important, as just like ashore, cruisers can feel the pressures of "keeping up with the Joneses."

In each of these situations, it is also important to consider the space constraints of a cruising boat. Onshore, homes have separate kitchens and separate rooms, so one partner can easily entertain a friend while the other continues with his/her project of the moment. Afloat, especially in cruising boats under 40 feet (which the majority of us sail), this is not the case. So it definitely pays to find ways to help both partners enjoy visitors on board. "Mary loves this full-on social stuff, but I don't get any personal time. My privacy is out the window as soon as we get to port," is one complaint we've heard. "John loves it all; I get all the work while he sits and pontificates," is another.

Over the years, Larry and I have set up some signals and protocols to help keep the balance. Situation: Larry is in the cockpit savoring his morning coffee, I'm below answering some letters. Someone from another boat rows by and says hello. They chat for a while, and then Larry says, "Hold on while I see if Lin is decent." He pokes his head into the boat and I have a chance to say quietly, "Invite him on board." Or, "I'm not dressed yet," or "Not right now—invite him for later."

Once a spur-of-the-moment guest joins us onboard, it is the responsibility of whoever did the inviting to get the coffee or drinks. Since I do the majority of provisioning and cooking, we decided long ago that any spur-of-the-moment invitations to join us for a meal are my decision. If Larry would like visitors to stay longer, we have a prearranged signal system that lets me know his wishes. It is then up to me to invite them to stay or to suggest another time to share a meal with us. (It's Larry's home too, so I do feel obligated to extend an invitation for a more convenient time, and I almost always enjoy the shared dinners that ensue.)

We also have prearranged time-to-end-the-gathering signals. One of these is to ask our guest to sign the guestbook. British sailors recognize this as a farewell timer. But for others, it is up to the inviter to find an opportune moment to say, "It's been fun but I promised to help Lin with a project," or "Let's adjourn to your boat or ashore so Lin can finish her project." Even when get-togethers are the result of a more organized invitation, it is rare for all partiers to sense the end of the evening simultaneously. I know Larry and I often differ on this. It has taken us some time, but when we feel sated and a bit tired, we've each learned to feel comfortable saying something such as, "Larry, I think it is time to go to bed so these nice folks have an excuse to go home."

From my perspective, entertaining fellow cruisers with lunch or dinner is exceptionally easy. They understand the pace and problems of life afloat. If marketing, cooking, or just a need to recoup makes me want to delay a gathering, I feel comfortable asking Larry to row over and tell the invitees to take their time and arrive an hour later than originally planned.

There are a few tricks to make an evening like this flow even better. One I learned when, as an 18-year-old, I worked for a Beverly Hills business hostess. It works for cruising dinners, too: Never tell anyone what you plan to serve. If you aren't locked into a set menu, a shortage of a particular ingredient won't matter; a scorched pan of rice can be tossed and potatoes substituted without your feeling like a failure. Above all, keep your menus simple. This is not a game of impress-the-boss—it's an excuse to have some laughs and share serious thoughts with people of like mind. And since all of us understand the limitations, there is no reason to feel pressured to have the perfect serving dish for each course.

Have some sort of starter or nibbles ready before your guests arrive, but only put out half at first. If there are two or three different starter items, bring them out one at a time at intervals. This lets you extend or shorten the time spent waiting for your dinner to be ready—depending on the mood and cooking times. An important rule of etiquette is, please, don't leave your SSB radio or VHF on and expect guests to converse over the noise. If you are hooked to a radio schedule, extend your invitations for a different time. Finally, once you learn how easy it is to entertain other sailors, beware of getting wrapped up in the potential round of invitations that will ensue, or you won't leave time to meet folks onshore.

In isolated anchorages—or even at anchor in False Creek, in the middle of Vancouver—entertaining afloat is even better with a bit of music. Here, Patsy Thompson and Tony Latimer celebrate with us on board Taleisin *after the Wooden Boat Race.*

One of the nicest ways to get to know, or to thank, folks you meet onshore is by inviting them onboard for a meal. (Even better, offer to take them sailing, anchor at some lovely spot, and serve lunch there.) Land folk will find it an adventure to join you onboard and see your floating home. On 24-foot *Seraffyn,* we entertained people as divergent as two barefoot shark fishermen from the offshore islands of Mexico and the oil-baron owner of a 2,400-acre estate in the south of England. These dinners always turned out well and often had unexpected outcomes. On 29-foot *Taleisin,* we entertained a newlywed Tongan couple. Lisa was enchanted with her first taste of chilled white wine. A year later, she named her first child, Lini, after me, claiming it was the wine that created her. Almost every nonsailing invitee reacts the same way when they first come aboard. They shower us with questions, have a few awkward minutes figuring out how to climb below, then turn from near-strangers to "amigos" in an amazingly short time. For these folks, I always try to make a simple meal that they can identify as North American. A totally simple choice that has proven universally successful is hamburgers. I bake hamburger-style rolls using my standard bread recipe, then I put out a platter with slices of tomatoes, lettuce, cheeses, pickles, and onions, plus condiments such as pickle relish, mustard, and ketchup. While I grill the meat, Larry instructs the guests on how to build their own hamburgers. I have the local butcher grind the meat with about 10 percent fat, but no bread crumbs or additives. (In most countries, hamburger patties are like meatloaf.) With or without potatoes, salad, or side dishes, this always makes a hit.

Shore-based guests may be unfamiliar with the customs of life afloat, and also with getting into and out of the dinghy you used to ferry them from shore. So as soon as dinner is over, I say something such as, "Be sure to let us know as soon as you feel like going ashore. We'll row you there any time you wish." If we feel the wind rising, we have sometimes suggested going ashore to a local café for dessert rather than risk staying until the ride ashore could be bumpy, wet, and potentially scary for people who may already find it a major adventure to cross the bay in an 8-foot dinghy.

One of the most memorable potlucks we've joined was at Horta, in the Azores, after seven days of waiting for a hurricane to fizzle out. The local café owner opened his doors to crews from 15 boats on the condition that we would buy our drinks from him. Sailors provided the music, locals joined in, and the winds died as we sang the night away.

Potluck (share-the-cooking) dinners will be a large part of any cruising life. In fact, most people you invite for meals will offer to bring something in order to share the cooking load. Unless you have a very specific menu planned, accept the offer, then tell your guests candidly what you would like them to bring—whether a salad, a dessert, or a starter. Why not share the load and thus make entertaining—financially and workwise—easier for everyone? As several New Zealand sailors told us when we first arrived here, "Of course, we always potluck. That way, we can afford to have more parties!" The larger dinner parties promoted by sharing the load can sometimes turn quite boisterous, however. To show respect for those anchored nearby, try to move the noise inside after 10 p.m. Or, better yet, if there is going to be music and singing, invite cruisers on nearby boats to come by after dinner.

The crews from 10 local boats at Mar del Plata, Argentina, introduced us to the best of local sparkling wines and tango during many potluck dinners at the marina.

Onshore potlucks—especially with a beach fire to add a sense of romance—form some of the most special memories of our wandering life. We shared a catch of fresh salmon with 80 Canadian sailors after watching the full moon rise in mid-August near Desolation Sound, and we savored a bushel basket full of oysters and mussels with local fishermen on the banks of the Ria de Arosa in northwestern Spain. Sampling the different dishes and trying new foods added spice to the evenings. But since customs differ, we have learned to ask if those who are starting or hosting the potluck are providing plates and cutlery. If we cannot ask, we take along the pair of plastic plates and glasses, plus plastic cutlery, that we keep just for occasions such as this. We also check to see if it is completely potluck or if we are expected bring our own meat as well as a side dish (as is the case at many New Zealand potluck gatherings). If the group is going to be large, I also tape my name to the bottom of the container I bring ashore to be sure I can identify it afterward. It is amazing how many cruisers carry the same kind of cookware. A good rule of thumb is to make enough of your chosen dish to feed about eight people. If you have some very special recipe that always has guests looking for seconds, it's appropriate to double the quantity. Add some kind of meat or fish to any salad that you take, thus letting it double as a main course. (The usual shortfall at potlucks is with meat or fish dishes.)

Presentation, good flavors, generous proportions—those are the goals with any dish you take to a cruisers' potluck.

If you plan a potluck ashore in an anchorage shared by half a dozen yachts, be sure to extend an invitation to every crew. That way, your party will not disturb anyone—nor will anyone feel left out. Invite everyone to bring along any musical instrument they may have on board. Many special memories come from singing along while someone strums a battered guitar and finding that people from every country in the world seem to know the words to "Bobby McGee."

There will be times when you feel that someone within the cruising cohort is not contributing his or her fair share, or who appears to be, as

Americans say, "a freeloader"—turning up empty-handed at potluck dinners or arriving at your boat just as a dinner gathering is getting underway. Rather than worry about hurt feelings, we have found it simpler to say something such as, "Could you row over to your boat and make up a salad?" Or, "We are having a potluck and think it would be good if you brought along that rice dish you make so well." If you are not comfortable doing this, include everyone rather than make a fuss, and remember that you will soon be sailing onward.

A more difficult problem occurs when the weather starts to deteriorate as you are sharing a meal ashore or afloat. Unfortunately, the security of your boat must always come first. We forgot this once as we were voyaging south from Sydney, Australia, bound for Tasmania. We were anchored in Port Eden, just north of the infamous Bass Straits and a perfect place to shelter from strong northerly wind, when we met an interesting couple onshore. Larry invited them to join us on board for breakfast the next day. By the time he rowed them out to *Taleisin,* the wind had shifted to the south. Before he rowed ashore, Larry had said, "I'll row them out, we'll have a nice breakfast, then we can find a safer place after they leave." Unfortunately, the wind kept rising. Our guests were completely unconcerned as the boat began to buck a bit. By the time we felt it was gracious to take them ashore, Larry had a hard time rowing back to the boat. By the time we got the anchor straight up and down, the swell was up to four feet. The jerking on the anchor rode before it broke free was enough to bend the anchor shackle.[15] The bent shackle shook our trust in the chain, which led to the expense of not only replacing the shackle but also having the whole chain tested in Tasmania so we could stop worrying about it. It would have been far wiser and less costly to be candid with our guests by apologizing and canceling the breakfast invite as soon as the wind shifted.

Even with the open schedules of cruising, each of us has times when reality strikes. We need to buy provisions, do maintenance, or, in many cases, handle outside commitments. It may be that you or your partner just feels the need for some downtime. Sooner or later, you'll have to learn that it is fine to just say no, or to regulate the potential for a constant round of casual visitors. We recently planned a rendezvous with Evans Starzinger and Beth Leonard in a quiet anchorage just big enough for our two boats. They were sailing south from the Queen Charlotte Islands of British Columbia and we were sailing south from Desolation Sound, bound for Seattle. Their 47-footer,

. . . .

15   Since that incident, we do not leave the anchor-winch dog in place as we bring up the chain. This way, the cathead can slip on its clutch and prevent shock-loading on the whole system.

Hawk, was at anchor when we sailed in, and Evans same out in his dinghy to greet us as we short-tacked up the bay on the fading wind. "Beth is really seriously into her project," Evans told us. "I suggest we don't disturb her until 1600, then she'll feel good about her day." I was very impressed with his desire to make us feel welcome, and at the same time to encourage Beth. Our 2-day rendezvous was full of laughter, good food, and time for all of us to get our own projects done, too.

Like all of the best things in life, entertaining afloat takes some discipline, some planning, and a sense of adventure. But, as Kyle Hopkins and the band of cruisers who danced the evening away reminded us, it is one of the greatest pleasures of cruising.

Special Stores for Entertainment

With imagination, almost any provisions you carry can be turned into treats for unexpected visitors. But to add to the pleasure of entertaining afloat when I am far from shops, I like to have an extra supply of the following items in my treat locker:

> packaged tortillas, both corn and flour (preferably burrito size)
> canned cheeses
> dried whole eggs
> panko-style bread crumbs (Japanese crispy bread crumbs)
> several cans of reduced cream or UHT (long life) whipping cream
> canned coconut milk
> canned whole mushrooms
> canned baby sweet corn
> small jars of pimientos
> jars of caviar-style fish roe (these keep well in the bilge until opened)
> onion soup mix
> pickled onions
> pickled mixed vegetables
> assorted chutneys
> sweet pickle chips
> assorted olives
> nuts and dried fruits
> popcorn
> *membrillo* (Found in most Latin American countries, this is made from the pulp of guava fruit, which is cooked down and compressed into a bar to be sliced and served with cheese. Excellent. Membrillo lasts up to six months without refrigeration.)

packaged crème caramel (flan) mix

canned lychees

If I had mechanical refrigeration, I would also carry rolls of prepared cookie dough

dinner rolls in cardboard refrigerator rolls (the kind that expand dramatically when you open the container)

puff-pastry sheets

Using Provisions Creatively for Entertaining

Most of the recipes used during *Seraffyn's* passage across the stormy North Pacific could be adapted for company. Below are some additional ideas and recipes that I have tested on visitors over the years. They are based on provisions that I usually have hiding in my lockers even after a month or two away from reprovisioning ports.

NONALCOHOLIC DRINKS

To spruce up lemonade or limeade—made from either freshly squeezed fruit or bottled lemon or lime juice—use dark brown sugar instead of white sugar and add 1/4-teaspoon vanilla extract per cup of water.

Brew up regular or Chinese tea, add a pinch of sage or mint, plus sweetener (sugar, honey, or maple syrup), and serve over ice.

To make fruit juice more refreshing for hot days, add half sparkling water, plus, if available, some fresh mint leaves. Serve over ice.

The mix used for hot chocolate makes a nice cold drink, too; use powdered milk and then add a bit of instant coffee. Serve over ice.

STARTERS/NIBBLES

Any fruit and almost any vegetable can be cut up into bite-size pieces and arranged around a bowl of creamy salad dressing or sour cream-based dip. It will please those who are trying to avoid salty or calorie-laden snacks. If my carrots are getting a bit droopy, I perk them up by peeling and slicing them, then steaming them for three minutes before adding them to the platter. You can make a quick, tasty dip by mixing sour cream with onion soup mix. If you have no sour cream, use canned reduced cream plus 2 tsp. vinegar.

Freshly made vegetable chips can be added to the platter. Rather than deep-fry these the vegetables, I boil them (just until a fork goes in relatively easily), then drain and spread the chips on a foil-covered baking tray. Spray olive oil over them and put them under the grill until one side is browned. Turn them over, spray, and grill again.

Grillable chips can be made from potatoes, yams (any sweet potato or kumara variety), breadfruit, plantains, green bananas, and any hard squash (such as pumpkin or butternut).

CRACKER SUBSTITUTES

I almost always have cheeses put up in oil filling their own special spots in our provision lockers, but crackers or biscuits take up a lot of space, so I sometimes run short and need substitutes. Take stale bread, slice it thinly, then toast it. Or use small pancakes. (In New Zealand, these are called pikelets and are sold in packages to use as snacks.) Now, whenever I make regular pancakes for breakfast, I also make up a few dozen small ones (two inches or 50mm in diameter), to be used later. After those have sat for a day or so, they can be toasted to use as cracker substitutes. Or quick-fry flour or corn tortillas in a Teflon pan, then cut them into bite-size pieces.

FANCY PUFF-PASTRY STARTERS

If you have puff-pastry sheets in your freezer, you can use them to make all sorts of fancy-looking starters (and desserts, for that matter). Simply cut each sheet into six or eight rectangular pieces. Put a spoonful of filling in the center of each piece and wipe the edges of the pastry with water. Fold, squeeze the edges together, and bake in a hot oven (425 degrees) for 10 minutes.

Sample fillings: (1) feta, small pieces of tomato, sprinkle of basil; (2) canned salmon or tuna with capers and a squeeze of lemon; (3) fresh fish (any type) with a dab of mayonnaise and a small piece of pimiento; (4) wedge of canned Brie plus three or four cashews.

For dessert, fill each rectangle with your favorite jam, then fold and squeeze the edges together tightly. Sprinkle lightly with white sugar and bake in a hot oven for 10 minutes. For another filling, drain any canned fruit well, put it into a plastic bag with 3 tbs. flour and 1/4 cup sugar. Toss lightly.

CAVIAR EXTRAVAGANZA

An attractive-looking and unexpectedly tasty snack or starter, this takes some forethought because you need to boil the eggs beforehand, but it really impresses your friends.

> 3 hard-boiled eggs, grated or chopped fine
> ¾ cup sour cream (fresh, or combine 1 can Nestlé's reduced cream with 1½ tsp. lemon plus 1 tsp. vinegar)
> small container of lumpfish caviar (black or red or a combination)

Sprinkle a pinch of salt on the chopped eggs, then shape them into a mound on your favorite serving plate. Use a bread knife to cover the eggs carefully with sour cream. With the caviar, create a pattern across the sour cream. (When I have both red and black caviar, I make alternating lines across the mound.) Serve with crisp crackers or thin slices of toasted bread.

CRUISER'S ANTIPASTO

Next time you go to an Italian *trattoria,* order an antipasto plate to get ideas for your cruising entertainment. You'll notice that the majority of items on the plate can be kept for long periods without refrigeration. A combination I used to entertain crews from two French yachts when we were all enjoying the isolation of Suvarov Atoll included:

> two types of olives
> pickled assorted vegetables
> canned button mushrooms in Caesar-style salad dressing
> canned baby corn
> thinly sliced dry salami
> chunks of spiced feta cheese
> onion rings (fresh)
> cubes of lightly grilled mahimahi (which we had caught the previous day)
> dip made from mayonnaise, ketchup, lemon juice, and a pinch of sugar
> slices of fresh bread

Served with "Chateau de Cardboard" wine as the sun set behind the motu's on the far side of the lagoon, this seemed the perfect dish at the perfect time.

OMELETS

Powdered eggs or whole eggs that have been on board for more than a few weeks will make good omelets. A favorite omelet, which can be made either on the stove top or in the oven, is one we first encountered in the cafés of northern Spain. There it is served cold, cut into small wedges.

. . . .

SPANISH OMELET

Boil until tender
   2 scrubbed potatoes, sliced thinly

In lidded frying pan, sauté
   1 onion, in medium-size pieces
   4 cloves garlic, sliced thinly
   cooked potatoes
   olive oil
   ▼

Reduce heat to medium.

Beat together

6 eggs

2 tsp. cream (or milk powder equivalent and pinch of salt)

Cook

Add eggs to frying pan. Cook 1 minute, then slide spatula under omelet to let uncooked egg mixture flow underneath. Cover and continue cooking slowly until entire egg mixture is firm. Remove from heat and let cool before turning out omelet onto a plate. If desired, garnish with pimento.

If you prefer to make this in the oven (i.e., quiche style), sprinkle 2 tbs. flour on onions and potatoes as you sauté them. Put entire mixture into Teflon baking tin and bake at 350 degrees about 25 minutes, or until firm.

. . . .

MAIN-COURSE IDEAS FOR ISOLATED ANCHORAGES

As I've mentioned throughout this book, I usually cook extra rice or pasta and save it to use the next day. By adding it to chopped leftovers, I can create a fast and tasty lunch. This works wonderfully for guests, too. If we have fresh fish, I cook it and then add chunks of spicy sausage. If I plan to serve this as a heated dish, I slightly undercook the fish before adding it to the rice or pasta. Otherwise, the fish will be overcooked, dry, and crumbly.

Most cruisers learn to bake their own bread, and many make pizza crust from the same dough. Here's another way to use the dough for a special entertainment dish, especially when your provisions might be running low:

. . . .

Make up white-flour bread dough and knead for about three minutes. Let rise once or twice. Remove enough dough to make one loaf of bread and lay it on a floured board. Roll out the dough until it is about 1/4 inch thick. Lightly brush melted butter or cooking oil to within one inch of the edges. Open a can of stewed steak chunks or chicken chunks and drain. Spread meat over the dough. Slice onions thinly over the mixture. Sprinkle lightly with your favorite herb (such as oregano, sage, marjoram). If you have a sharp cheese, such as Cheddar, place pieces across the center of the dough. Then roll the dough into a long cylinder and pinch or fold the ends closed. Bake at 325 degrees, until the dough turns golden brown. Let cool 10 minutes before slicing.

THREE FISH IDEAS

I asked Dean Betts—a professional chef and owner of the Fish Market restaurants in Southern California and elsewhere—what special ingredients he would carry if he needed to spice up freshly caught fish to serve guests at an isolated anchorage. His answer introduced me to my favorite new ingredients, so I'm including his response verbatim. Thanks, Dean!

> I would focus on two or three special meals—e.g., I could imagine one where I wanted a very crispy crumbed fish which had just been caught. I would pack some panko bread crumbs, and the ingredients to make a fresh tartar sauce, and some grapeseed oil for frying. Then, using those, I could imagine an outstanding result.
>
> In addition, I want to make a Thai curry one meal, so I would take along coconut milk or cream, Thai red curry paste, fresh lemongrass, kefir lime leaf, and fresh limes.
>
> Or a special Teriyaki glaze for which I would make up a bottle of soy, garlic, ginger, chiles, and an equal amount of honey. Then, when grilling the fish, paint on this glaze for a sweet, flavorful, spicy taste.
>
> The coconut milk and lemon or lime juice are also prime ingredients for a fine ceviche.

CAPETOWN BEANS

This is the dish I usually bring to potlucks. It sounds deceptively simple and is definitely a good one for the limited-budget cruiser, but it always gets folks coming back for seconds.

Sauté until onions are transparent

- 1 onion, chopped
- 2/3 cup raisins or sultanas
- 2 tsp. mild curry powder
- 1 tbs. cooking oil

Add

- 2 tbs. sugar
- 1 large can inexpensive baked beans

Stir as you bring mixture to a boil.
Reduce heat and cook another 5 minutes, stirring frequently.
Turn off heat and allow mixture to sit at least 2 hours.

> Reheat just before serving. The "sitting time" is important—it lets raisins absorb moisture and curry flavor.

DESSERTS, AFTERS, AND SWEETS

Desserts are not my forte. When I am near markets, I usually serve fresh mixed fruit over banana slices topped with sour cream sprinkled with brown sugar. Or, to be fancy, I make jam-filled puff pastry (as described above). If I have a special bit of chocolate on board, I break it into pieces and put it out with coffee. But the simplest, most elegant after-dinner sweet I remember from my days of cruising came from a dinner with Chinese friends when we were anchored at Lumut, on Malaysia's Dinding River.

The host filled a bowl with ice cubes. He emptied a can of lychees (including juice) into the bowl and let it sit for a few minutes while he poured a bit of the local liqueur into tiny glasses for each of us. Then he placed the bowl in the center of the table and gave us wooden skewers to catch the floating orbs of deliciously icy and sweet fruit.

. . . .

Day 46

Noon to noon: 127 miles
Miles to date: 4,097
Cloudy, must be almost gale-force winds
Running wing-and-wing with triple-reefed main and
staysail set on pole

Lunch
leftover chicken-and-ginger casserole
creamed corn

Dinner
freeze-dried green beans (Surprise brand)
oven-browned potatoes
fried canned-ham slices

....

We picked up U.S. West Coast broadcast stations this afternoon for the first time in 9 1/2 years. So dinner was accompanied by a mélange of country music, football scores, women's-club meeting notices, and hometown news reports. Nostalgia and the thrill of the approaching landfall spiced our dinner as nothing else could have.

Recommended Reading for the Offshore Cook

Although I really enjoy cooking, on *Taleisin* I have only one cookbook—*Joy of Cooking,* by Irma S. Rombauer, Marion Rombauer Becker, and Ethan Becker, available in hardcover, paperback, or spiral binding from Simon and Schuster. I carried this same book on *Seraffyn*. I find the latest edition—completely rewritten in 1997 and updated twice since then—to be even better than its predecessors. There is a wealth of recipes, plus information on nutrition, ingredients, meat cuts, and fish preparation. Unfortunately, the sections on canning and on preserving fruits and jams have been dropped.

The Cruising Chef Cookbook, by Mike Greenwald (Paradise Cay Publications) is one of the best cruising recipe books I've come across. It has good fish recipes and an excellent section on bean sprouting, plus some light stories that evoke the mood of cooking for onshore cruises.

The Captain Is the Cook, by Neil Hollander and Harold Mertes (John Murray, London), has some excellent advice and good English-type recipes.

Stalking the Wild Asparagus and *Stalking the Blue-Eyed Scallop,* by Euell Gibbons (David McKay), are both excellent additions to the cruising sailor's cooking library. They tell about food you can find by scavenging for yourself.

Other than that, I would like to find a book that shows fruits and vegetables around the world, what they look like and what to do with them. I have been told such a book exists, but to this day I can't find it.

None of these books will be much help when you are offshore for 20 or 30 days and looking at a selection of canned tuna, sardines, corned-beef hash, and chicken meat. But few people make more than one or two voyages that last more than 10 days during the same year. So plan your cooking library for your time near shore. Your imagination will take care of the voyages.

....

Day 47

Noon to noon: 132 miles
Miles to date: 4,229
Beam reach
Fresh winds—reefed main and staysail
Scattered rain showers

Lunch
   chopped ham
   rice-and-onion salad
Dinner
   spaghetti Bolognese

. . . .

Cook's Reward

Here we go again, talking about bowls of ice cream topped with fresh strawberries, thick beefsteaks, fresh tomatoes, crisp cucumbers. But now it's almost reality. If all goes well, in 48 to 50 hours, we'll make port. It's so close that Larry's planning what he'd like me to wear for the traditional "cook's night on the town." Every time we make a passage for more than six days, Larry takes me to a dress-up dinner at the best restaurant in town. Some of these past voyage-ending dinners have been memorable. After a 6,000-mile delivery ending in Biloxi, Mississippi, we shared Chateaubriand, lobster tails with drawn butter, salad with blue cheese dressing, baked Idaho potatoes with sour cream, sherry before, wine with. When it came to dessert, we were too full—not only with the delicious food but with the thrill of a job well done.

Another voyage-end dinner we both remember well came when we arrived in the Malaysian island group of Langkawi after an 18-day passage from Sri Lanka that included a sideswipe from a typhoon. The tiny village had no "good restaurants," but the local Indian restaurant served us curried chicken, strange fried bread cakes, and lemonade with loads of ice. As we walked back toward *Seraffyn,* we saw a vendor carrying large live crabs, their claws tied together with pink string and a lassolike carrying strap. For 28 cents, we bought two that must have weighed 1 1/2 pounds each. Dangling them by their little pink ribbon lassos, we strolled the mile back to where *Seraffyn* was anchored and fixed a late-night snack of steamed crab with lemon butter. Since Larry did the cracking and picking, and since we were at anchor in a calm, safe, and beautiful spot, and since I had no night watch to worry about—that, too, was a memorable "cook's night on the town."

DAY 47. *Now that landfall is almost a reality, we spend a lot of time talking about the thick steaks and fresh tomatoes that lie ahead.*

Larry is dreaming of fresh food, I am dreaming of easier shopping. And in the back of my mind is something even better: the chance to forage again for mussels, oysters, and crabs in the sheltered waters of the Gulf Islands.

. . . .

Day 48

Noon to noon: 120 miles
Miles to date: 4,349
Blowing near a gale
Beam reach with triple-reefed main and staysail

Lunch
    leftover spaghetti Bolognese

Dinner
    canned mushroom soup
    pâté sandwiches
    rice salad
    red wine

. . . .

This morning, Larry was talking about heaving-to at midnight if we didn't get some sights to fix our position. It had been six days since we'd last seen enough sun to get more than one Line of Position on the same day. He just didn't want to risk getting within 75 miles of the rocky coast of Vancouver Island without knowing our exact position. The currents out here are not always predictable. We could be off by up to 17 miles a day. But with marvelous luck, and no little amount of skill and patience on Larry's part, we were able to get a position when the clouds broke up for three hours right at 1100 hours. He shot three sights before noon, a noon sight, and three after noon. So we know almost exactly where we are—right on course for the center of the Strait of Juan de Fuca.

This may be our last night at sea. But there's little chance of a captain's dinner. The motion is too rough to make much more than soup and sandwiches possible. So I'll have to save that blueberry pie and clam chowder for tomorrow, when we hope to be making harbor.

The Official Word

You reach into a safe, calm anchorage just before dark, feeling exhilarated by a fast passage. Moments after you remind yourself, "Hurrah, no watches to stand!" sleep overtakes you as you savor the first night in a steady bunk. But morning brings reality. Before you can jump into the new adventures waiting onshore, you have to face officialdom and clear your boat, its cargo, and its crew through customs and immigration. There are visas to arrange, and a health clearance so you can take down your quarantine flag and enjoy this new destination. In a survey published by a major yachting magazine, this was the single most intimidating and annoying aspect of cruising cited by respondents.

This surprises us as, during almost four decades of voyaging to 80 countries and dozens of territories, we have rarely met an official who was difficult to deal with—even though we often had a language barrier. Only once did we have to pay a bribe. In several instances, officials have gone beyond the call of duty to make our visit to their country more enjoyable. But we did start with an advantage. Before we set off voyaging, Larry had worked with top professional delivery and charter skippers. To keep to their schedules, these sailors had become expert at clearing in and out of ports efficiently and getting spare parts through customs without undue delays. Their secrets? Having the right attitudes, the right clothes, the right papers, the right answers, and a few "special weapons."

Whenever officialdom looms, I repeat the following mantra: *They don't like the paperwork I am forcing into their lives any more than I like having to do it. I am adding to their workload.* This reminds me that it is work, something they have to do correctly to hang onto their job. In most societies, this is a respectable, relatively well paid, and secure position with a pension waiting at the end. In less-developed countries, it may be one of the very few cash-paying jobs available. So the men or women holding customs and immigration jobs will be, by nature, conservative. What you see as overbearing officiousness may just be someone's desire to protect his/her good position by crossing every t, dotting every i, and filling in every blank space so no superior officer can doubt their job efficiency.

Maintaining the right attitude may often require acting patient—a hard part to play when all you really want to do is find the nearest café and tuck into lunch and an ice-cold beer. The key is twofold. First, remind yourself that you may have to work with this same official a few months hence when it is time to extend your visa; and second, try to start the paper chase when you are well rested. This is relatively easy if you are entering a country where you can anchor and wait until you are ready to go ashore for clearance. Officials in ports as disparate as Polynesia, Mexico, Hawaii, and smaller towns in Australia and Canada are content to see you the first time you actually row ashore, even if it is 18 or 20 hours after you arrive.[16]

But if you are entering a port where there is a clearly indicated quarantine or customs dock, with officials standing by 24/7, it could pay to heave-to offshore for a few hours of rest before tackling the hustle and bustle of port traffic and clearance procedures. We had been told that clearance into Australia at Sydney would require several hours' worth of paperwork, including intensive questioning by agricultural officials. Our crossing of the Tasman Sea from Nelson, New Zealand, had been a tedious beat through three frontal systems. It was 0200 hours when we finally could make out the headlands protecting this labyrinth of inland waters. Though the harbor was well lighted and our charts were current, we decided to heave-to for six hours so both of us could get three hours of sleep and enter port in daylight. We cleaned up the boat as we short-tacked up the bay. Arriving midmorning, feeling well rested and organized, definitely paid off, as the piles of paperwork were worse than we expected. But the officials—possibly because we were able to remain patient—were supportive and helped us slog through the lot.

Whenever clearance procedures require that we visit offices ashore, I carry along a good book. In Latin countries, we have sometimes had to wait two or three hours for the right official to return from siesta. The most extreme case was at Rio de Janeiro, Brazil, with a 2-hour lineup for immigration, a 2-hour siesta break before the customs department reopened, and another 90 minutes' wait for final papers to be signed by the port captain. A thick, juicy novel saved my patience and surprisingly paid dividends six months later, when we had to overstay our visas by nine days due to airline problems. "I remember you," the immigration official told me. "It looked like you were really enjoying the book, so I went and got a copy. Now, let's figure out the least expensive way to extend your visas."

When we first set off cruising, our destination was Mexico. I had a 200-word high-school Spanish vocabulary, so I volunteered to do the paperwork.

. . . .

16 When in doubt, always anchor out rather than tying up to a dock—unless it is a specially designated customs-clearance dock with locked gates between you and the shore. This is the safest way to assure officials that you are not trying to smuggle anything onto shore or onto another boat. If you cannot contact officials by VHF to receive their instructions, and if they do not send a boat alongside to clear you, send only the captain ashore with the ship's papers and have the crew stay on board until he/she returns. You may not invite anyone on board or visit any other vessel until you have cleared; if you do, you could be subject to heavy fines.

The reception I received convinced Larry that female crew sliced through the official red tape more quickly than males. Now, after a few hundred visits to clearance offices worldwide, I have to agree that officials of both genders tend to prefer women visitors. Maybe women are less intimidating, less macho, more patient, or simply fewer in numbers—therefore a pleasant change of routine. But whatever the reason, though our ship's documentation shows Larry as owner of *Taleisin*, I am the captain. As Larry likes to joke, I am his "secret weapon"—the paper captain in charge of paperwork.

A translation dictionary and—if you can pick one up on the way to the port offices—a local map can both be helpful. In countries such as Mexico, Cape Verde Islands, Brazil, and Argentina, we had to visit three different offices in three different parts of town. The guards at the port entry marked the first destination on our map. The officials at that destination marked the next two and sent us on our way.

Dressing the right way definitely matters. Remember that you are dealing with conservative government employees, and in most cases they are used to working with ships' officers or military personnel—also conservative types. The officials don't really want to be reminded that you are on holiday and they are stuck in a hot office working all week. For the best results, dress to blend in, taking your cue from local businesspeople. Avoid acting like a "cool cat dude" or a "super-casual yachtie" until you are officially cleared.

Having the right papers to make clearance flow smoothly is relatively simple. Proof of ownership of the vessel, current passports for all crew on board, and clearance papers *(zarpe)* from your last port of call will usually suffice. Officials have reacted no differently toward us when we presented them with a bill of sale to identify the boat we were delivering than they did when presented with a state registration certificate or *Taleisin's* formal, clothbound, foldout, royal-crested Canadian Ship Registry documentation form. All they are looking for is a legal document that contains the owner's name, the hull number, and the boat name, to match what they will find if they inspect your boat.

In a few countries, you will need a visa prior to arrival. (We've been able to obtain visas upon arrival in 80 different countries—with the exception of Mexico, Russia, Poland, and Brazil). Information gleaned from websites maintained by or for cruising sailors should serve only as guidelines. Double-check directly with consulates, as visa requirements can change with little notice, especially with the tightening of borders as a result of the 9/11 attacks. Any country whose citizens are required to pay for a visa to enter the United States is likely to impose a similar fee on American visitors to their country. This, however, can change quite quickly. When we arrived in Chile, no one was asked for an entry fee. We left *Taleisin* there and flew to our home in New Zealand for five months. When we returned, all passengers except those holding U.S. passports were sent to a separate line. U.S. passport holders, though requiring no visa in advance, were told they had to pay $200 to enter Chile. Several months later, the U.S. dropped their fees for Chileans and the Chilean government quickly followed suit.

What happens if you look up visa fees and regulations just before you set sail and they change during the two or three months it takes to reach your next destination? For security, we keep with us a copy of the information we obtain from consulate websites, and we have found that officials have been willing to make allowances for our special circumstances. But we have also learned that most countries will not issue visas for more than half the time remaining before your passport expires. Thus, if you would like to stay in Argentina for six months, make sure your passport has at least another year before it runs out.

Occasionally, when we have entered countries that did not require visas prior to arrival, immigration officials have asked for proof of funds to support us during our stay in their country. Our bank savings-account statements for the previous few months have always been sufficient to cover the situation. How much reserve money have officials indicated is sufficient? We have never seen any figure written down by any consulate. However, when I spoke with Chilean officials about this in 2003, I was told that small-boat voyagers who entered Chile were given 3-month, extendable visas if they could show they had a reserve of at least US$10,000, including cash and traveler's checks.

One extra document you should carry—albeit one that will be necessary only occasionally—is a list of the medicines you carry in your ship's medical kit if any of them require a prescription in the country you are visiting. Our doctor in New Zealand provided us with a complete list, including those that did not require prescriptions, indicating the quantity we had on board. It was on his letterhead and carried his signature and seal. It was "trainee day" when we sailed into Victoria, British Columbia, from Hawaii, and our boat was chosen as one of 20 to receive full inspections—under the watchful eye of a senior officer. The large quantities of several medications that are not available over the counter in Canada caused some consternation among the trainees until we produced our list.

Carrying firearms onboard will definitely complicate your contacts with officialdom. In fact, this was the reason we disposed of the shotgun and pistol we carried 37 years ago when we left to cruise on *Seraffyn*. To get an idea of the paperwork that firearms can create—and the highest penalties for entering a country without declaring you have firearms on board—contact any U.S. Customs office and ask for the rules pertaining to firearms on foreign yachts visiting American ports. If you do choose to carry firearms, be prepared to surrender them to customs officials in the majority of countries you visit. No matter how carefully concealed your weapons may be, please do not be tempted to deny you have them. In many countries—including, but not limited to, the United States, the United Kingdom, New Zealand, Australia, and Mauritius—the penalties, if someone steals your undeclared weapon and uses it in a criminal manner, can be confiscation of your vessel and its equipment, plus jail time for the captain. (See "Cruising, Guns, Pirates and Thieves," in our book *The Self-Sufficient Sailor.*)

The right answers at the right time can help make your dealings with officialdom flow more smoothly. I've learned the hard way that the right answers are short, simple, and direct replies only to the question being asked. Friendly chitchat about the really good buys I'd found when provisioning to set sail from Cartagena, Colombia, caused the Jamaican customs officials to ask for a complete list of all the food and stores I carried on board. I've since learned to say, "Only enough for our own consumption," when asked either to fill out a stores list or to make a statement. If, after saying this, an official asks a direct question, such as, "How many bottles of liquor do you wish to declare?" don't try to hide the case or two you bought duty-free at your last port. Instead, state your estimate and ask permission to go back on board to make an exact count if that is required. In most cases, officials will say, "Just give me an estimate." On the other hand, on entering Canadian West Coast ports, you will be required to provide an exact count. If an official decides to do a search, any extra that may be found on board will be confiscated.

Now for the big question: How many times have officials actually come on board and searched our vessels on entry? The answer is three times—once in Poland, again in Mauritius, and finally in Victoria, Canada.

Never offer a bribe to speed the entry process. In some countries, such as Chile, this can lead to immediate imprisonment. If you reach a stalemate, you can try to move things along by asking, "What do you suggest I do now?" or you can ask for a translator to come in and help things along. If there is no language barrier, you have the right to ask that a senior officer (arbitrator) be invited to help all of you solve the problem that has arisen. If, on the other hand, an official asks you to pay him/her a bribe, saying it is a necessary fee for clearance, ask if he/she will provide you with a receipt. If they say yes and produce a receipt book, it is almost always a legitimate fee. When the request is truly for a bribe, this question usually provokes an answer such as, "We'll dispense with the fees just this one time." Which brings me back to my comment above about only once having been faced with paying a customs official a bribe. This was in the Suez Canal, where it was euphemistically called, "a gift." Having been forewarned, we had rolled a US$10 note around several $1 notes, and we handed over this roll of cash.

Officialdom is part and parcel of sailing your home into someone else's homeland. If handled diplomatically, it will be no more of a nuisance than the first big load of laundry you have to sort out after each passage. Occasionally, entry procedures will seem tedious, but those will be balanced by other times when procedures are so casual you may wonder if the local officials actually know of your existence. This was definitely the case in Dingle, Ireland. We had called customs immediately after our arrival from the Azores, only to be told, "Someone will be down. Small town—we'll find ya, go on and enjoy yourself." We called each morning; on the fourth day, we were told, "We know you are here—not to worry." Our actual (and only) contact with Irish customs came three months and many lovely anchorages later, when we were sailing into Cork Harbor. A garda (police) boat came alongside, and we were asked for the exact spelling of our boat's name and its length. Then we were told the port captain had answered all the other questions after he bought us a drink at one of the ancient, music-filled pubs that lined the cobblestoned streets of Dingle.

. . . .

Day 49

Noon to noon: 89 miles
Miles to date: 4,438
Becalmed, cloudy, big swell left over

Lunch
    potato salad
    tuna sandwiches

Dinner
    pork goulash
    canned corn on the cob
    fresh whole-wheat bread and butter
    blueberry pie with double cream
    red wine

· ·

Landfall

Well, we are only 30 miles from our landfall at Cape Flattery, 70 miles from Victoria. Only 20 hours ago, we were worrying about having to heave-to in yet another gale. But in a way, this calm offers a nice chance to clean up the galley before we get into the hectic greeting I'm sure our family will have waiting for us.

Customs and Agriculture Quarantine Clearance

Many voyagers have complained of the harshness of the quarantine restrictions they have encountered when arriving at foreign destinations. To protect local farmers, native flora and fauna, and meat industries from invasions of foreign insects and bacteria, agricultural officers (or the customs officials who act as their agents) will confiscate and destroy some of the foodstuffs you carry as provisions. Pets, such as dogs and cats, will either be confined on board or put into quarantine. In extreme cases, you may be refused entry to some countries if you have pets on board. The rules regarding foodstuffs are easiest to comply with.

In those countries with major farming economies, you may find that fresh produce or fruit will not be allowed entry. Oranges, for instance, and seed products are not allowed into New Zealand or Australia unless they come from one of these two countries. Fresh potatoes cannot be brought into Canada. Since most voyagers on small boats use up the majority of these items during their passages, it will matter little if they are asked on arrival to hand over a dozen almost-shriveled onions or a box of month-old eggs. But we've heard stories of cruisers losing a hundred dollars' worth of cereals or canned meat when they arrived in New Zealand or in Australia. So sailors bound for those destinations should ask for an agriculture quarantine brochure when they apply for visas. The cruisers' grapevine can also give you hints and warnings about the latest regulations, so you can use up your popcorn and trail mix long before you make landfall.

If you arrive to find the officials demanding that you turn over larger amounts of provisions, ask if they have bonding facilities to hold your supplies for you until departure. In Auckland, facilities such as these exist at no charge, as they do at Whangarei and Nelson. But in Opua (Bay of Islands), there is no bonding depot. So if you are carrying very large supplies of fresh produce or grains, it would be wise to call ahead to determine which port is your best bet for entry. If you have only a dozen or so eggs, or a small supply of uncooked meat, ask the officials if you can boil and peel the eggs or cook the meat. The bacteria on the shells are what concern farmers. Once boiled or well cooked, the eggs are no longer a threat. Bacteria in meat are killed at temperatures above 140 degrees F.

It does not pay to deny possession of quarantined items. You risk confiscation of your boat if a search is instigated; you will find further entry procedures are more difficult if the search finds even a few illegal items; and you will also have made the situation more difficult for those who follow. But to ease your mind on this matter, we have never come across agricultural restrictions in any countries other than the United States, New Zealand, Australia, Japan, and Canada.

In each of these countries (and in Bermuda, Malta, England, and South Africa), there is strict control on soil from other countries. So as a courtesy, and to avoid hassles for yourself, wash the tires and chains of any bicycles you carry on board before you pack them for your passage. The same applies if you are a trekker carrying heavy-duty hiking boots or a tent. These items may catch the attention of agriculture officials. If they look well cleaned, they will be passed with no further ado.

Animals on board present a far larger problem. In the quest to prevent the spread of animal-borne diseases such as rabies, many countries restrict pet entry. In the United Kingdom for instance, there are no exceptions; all cats, dogs, monkeys, and birds must be put into six months' quarantine on arrival. This can cost you several thousand dollars. In New Zealand and Australia, you must stay at anchor or on a mooring and pay for weekly inspections to prove the animal is still on board. If you are caught concealing an animal, you will be fined and the animal will be destroyed immediately. The fine for letting a pet onshore illegally in New Zealand is US$8,000.

The countries that have strict animal-importation regulations are the same as those listed above for soil-importation restrictions. Other countries have far less strict rules concerning animals, but a large majority require that you prove your animal has been vaccinated against rabies and distemper. In fact, one friend said she had to present her cat's vaccination card five times more often than her own documents during a circumnavigation. Regulations regarding pets and quarantine change from year to year, so if you wish to carry a pet on board, it pays to check with the visa offices of each country you plan to visit. You may decide to change your itinerary based on your findings.

Note: For more on this, see *Cruising with Your Four-footed Friends,* by Diana Jessie (Seaworthy Publications 2003).

Liquor presents another customs problem. With the low price of duty-free liquor, it is tempting to stock up and hope you can carry a good supply from one country to another. I know we plan to take a good supply of California and Washington State wines with us when we set off across the Pacific toward New Zealand next year. Though most countries limit importation of spirits to 1 liter per person and wines to 2 liters, we have never had our excess confiscated, nor have we been charged duty or import fees. Instead, in countries with restrictive entry procedures, we have asked if our excess liquor could be placed "in bond." If the excess is only half a dozen bottles, the officials have always turned a blind eye. But when there has been more, we have been allowed to wrap the bottles in a sail bag, which was then sealed by the officials (with lead and wire seals) to be stored in the bilge until we left the country. The bag must be available for inspection by any customs official who asks. If you have room on board for a bonded stores locker, one that can be kept sealed for a few months at a time without its being a concern, that is even better. But beware of using a locker containing items you might need during your stay. We once found we needed a particular item that was sealed in with the excess liquor we'd carried into Jamaica. As a result, we had more than a day's worth of hassle and paperwork, plus a $50 fee, to get a customs official to come out to our boat and remove the bonding seals and then replace them. And yes, the officials did come to check the seals when we finally cleared to sail onward.

For your own safety, make a list of the serial numbers of any cameras, easily removable electric and electronic gear, bicycles, and scuba equipment, such as tanks and compressors. Make several copies and use this list to complete customs forms on arrival. Should any of this gear be stolen, you can have replacements brought into the country with no duty.

On the other hand, if you happen to carry a microlight aircraft on board, as a friend of ours did, don't even mention it. Mark sailed from South Africa to the Comoros in his 40-foot catamaran; his microlight was disassembled and stored in one of his hulls. When he mentioned he wanted to bring it ashore to fly it, he was given 12 hours to leave, an order enforced by gunboats. Reason? His yacht was reclassified as an aircraft carrier. Nothing he could say to the officials he visited personally during that long, hot day changed anything. He was escorted from the harbor at gunpoint, in spite of heavy winds and seas. Three weeks later, a coup attempt was in fact instigated in the Comoros. The rebels waded ashore from small boats, two yachts, and a small helicopter. Fortunately, Mark was nowhere near the scene.

. . . .

Day 50

Noon to noon: 40 miles
Miles to date: 4,478
Rain, calms, and variable winds; fog patches

Lunch
    soup (made from cream of mushroom and leftover goulash)
    potato salad
    corned-beef sandwiches with pickle relish and mayonnaise

Teatime
    blueberry pie with sweetened double cream

Dinner
    chicken curry
    Chinese noodles
    red wine

. . . .

Last Day at Sea

Spotted the light on Cape Flattery just after midnight.

Just after noon, we were able to flag down a sportfishing boat bound across the strait for some American port. We threw them a plastic-topped peanut can we'd saved. The note inside said, "Yacht *Seraffyn* of Victoria, 49 days out of Yokohama, Japan; all's well. Please phone Frank and Beryl Pardey, North Pender Island; call collect." I hope they do telephone and catch someone at home; Larry's parents live only 30 miles north of Victoria.

As I write this at 2100 hours, we are in the Strait of Juan de Fuca in calm, flat water for the first time in seven weeks. Victoria is only 40 miles away. Local forecasts are for winds to freshen from the west. So tomorrow we should be tied up—at home after 9 1/2 years. Looking back over the cook's chronicle of this voyage, I wonder if it was such a good one to choose for this book. Not only was it an exceptionally long passage, but the weather was

394

unusual. According to routing charts and other people's experiences, there should have been less than a 2 percent chance of force-7 gales anywhere on our route. Yet we had a least three full gales and one storm. I'm sure if this had been my very first ocean passage, I'd have given up cruising for good.

But, as usual, it's a case of "all's well that ends well." We have lots of food left—probably enough for 20 days more, if necessary. There are more than 35 gallons of water in our tanks, thanks to Larry's raincatching schemes.

Larry greatly enjoys eating in the cockpit once we get into sheltered waters.

We're looking forward to one of the big joys of cruising—tasting the foods of our new land. The ads we hear on the radio make our mouths water. Fresh Okanagan peaches, turkey breasts, ripe juicy strawberries.

The end of every voyage is a unique and deeply satisfying time. The end of this one is extra special, as we have now closed the circle of an eastabout global circumnavigation on *Seraffyn*. The last 4,500 miles of sailing may have been a bit rough, but already we're talking about our voyage southward to join cruising friends in San Francisco. And I'm thinking about how easy it will be on the cook. I'll only have to buy enough stores for a 700-mile voyage. I'll be shopping in stores where all the labels on the cans are in English. I'll find prices that are not going to break the bank, and I'll be able to buy treats I haven't seen in years.

. . . .

Day 51

Noon to noon: 70 miles
Miles to date: 4,548
Cool, broken clouds
Running wing-and-wing with pole set—full sail

Breakfast
pancakes
maple syrup

....

The Finale

The breakwater for Victoria Harbor is less than a mile off. Larry's parents are powering along beside us in the boat they just finished building. My parents have flown up from California and are with the Pardeys. They spotted us just after we rounded Race Rocks at 0800 this morning. As soon as they came alongside, a steady stream of plums, bananas, and apples descended upon us. We've yelled greetings back and forth. As soon as we clear customs, they plan to take us to a wonderful-sounding French restaurant.

We've sailed 4,548 miles in almost exactly 49 days and have hove-to seven different times for total of five days (125 hours)—not a bad passage time. Larry is most satisfied with food we've eaten. I can think of a few items of which I wish I'd bought more. There is a hot shower waiting, there are old friends to meet. And even as this voyage is ending, thoughts of future ones come to mind.

....

The Cook's reward, Sunday Brunch at Victoria's famous waterfront Empress Hotel.

....

Afterword to the Third Edition

I am pleased to say that we have never again had a passage that was as difficult as *Seraffyn's* crossing of the North Pacific in 1979. Though we have suffered through a few that had consistently rougher weather—twice in the Tasman Sea and once in the Indian Ocean—in each case, those voyages lasted 17 days or under. Even during our voyage south from Argentina, life for the cook never grew to be as frustrating. In fact, during the seven days we spent beating against 40-to-60-knot headwinds, through the Strait of Le Maire and then southwest from Isla de los Estados toward Cape Horn, Larry often encouraged me by saying, "Remember *Seraffyn's* North Pacific passage? Not as bad as it was back then."

The end of each passage is still a favorite time, and after a rough voyage it is even more special. I welcome the quiet hours we usually have as we sail gently into a new country—I clean up the galley and interior while Larry tidies up on deck. I look forward eagerly to that first meal ashore, the first fresh tomatoes, the ice cream, and, best of all, the ease of planning meals from the never-empty shelves of the local markets.

Then it happens—a week, a month, or maybe six months of easy shopping, never-ending supplies, and I begin wishing for something different from what the local stores offer, something completely new. Larry seems to feel it, too—the drive of changing seasons, the call of a fresh easterly wind, the itchy feet. I begin to scour the shops for what are no longer "bits to use for dinner" but provisions. And another voyage germinates.

. . . .

Recipe Index

Index

About the Author

Lin Pardey has been caring for crew on boats of various types and sizes since 1965. With Larry, she has accumulated sea miles that equal almost seven circumnavigations. The majority of these miles have been on *Seraffyn* and *Taleisin*, two cruising boats that Lin and Larry built for themselves. As a couple, they have delivered boats and cared for hired crew, raced under sail, and worked on commercial fishing boats.

Since the publication of the second edition of *The Care and Feeding of Sailing Crew*, Lin and Larry have voyaged an additional 35,000 miles, including an east-to-west rounding of Cape Horn. The Ocean Cruising Club, Seven Seas Cruising Association, and the Royal Oceanic Society have all recognized the Pardey's with awards acknowledging their sailing accomplishments and their contributions to the sport. They have also been inducted into the Cruising World Hall of Fame.

At present, the Pardey's are savoring endless summers—cruising the Pacific Northwest aboard *Taleisin* during the northern summer; racing and enjoying New Zealand aboard 111-year-old *Thelma* during the southern summer.

What the Reviewers say

"As well as being the best new reference book on provisioning, *The Care and Feeding of Sailing Crew* is an insightful and entertaining guide to preparing oneself physically and emotionally for passage making and the cruising lifestyle. Filled with invaluable tips, tables, recipes and stories; Lin Pardey's practical, up-beat personality shines throughout the book."

—Barbara Marrett, Contributing Editor, **Cruising World**

. . . .

"A fine, useful, tightly organized manual with a sense of anecdotal immediacy . . . I enjoyed *The Care and Feeding*, all 4,548 miles of it."

—Patience Wales, Editor Emeritus, **Sail magazine**

. . . .

". . . Should be in the library of any sailor planning to set sail and should be referred to regularly while fitting-out the vessel, while planning menus and when on passage."

—Neil Rusch, Editor, **South African Yachting**

. . . .

"A distillation of the best information on that vital subject—eating well at sea."

—**Guernsey Evening Press**, Channel Islands

. . . .

"This meaty book should help any sailor preparing himself and his galley and cabins for sea."

—**Yachting**, USA

. . . .

"Lin and Larry have earned the right to their passionate opinions the hard way: by spending nearly a lifetime at sea aboard small sailing vessels. For first-hand, practical, sea-tested sailing advice, well, you can't do better than the Pardey's."

—Cap'n Fatty Goodlander, Editor-at-large, **Cruising World**

. . . .

Enjoy Lin and Larry's newsletters and cruising tips at **www.landlpardey.com**

. . . .